Philosophy of Language

Also available from Bloomsbury:

Ethics: An Overview, Robin Attfield
Metaphysics: An Introduction, Jonathan Tallant
Phenomenology, Tanja Staehler and Michael Lewis
Philosophical Logic: An Introduction to Advanced Topics, George Englebretsen
   and Charles Sayward
The Philosophy of History, Mark Day
The Philosophy of the Social Sciences, Robert C. Bishop

Philosophy of Language

An Introduction

Chris Daly

BLOOMSBURY

LONDON • NEW DELHI • NEW YORK • SYDNEY

Bloomsbury Academic
An imprint of Bloomsbury Publishing Plc

50 Bedford Square	175 Fifth Avenue
London	New York
WC1B 3DP	NY 10010
UK	USA

www.bloomsbury.com

First published 2013

British Library Cataloguing-in-Publication Data
A catalogue record for this book is available from the British Library.

ISBN: HB: 978-1-4411-7350-8
       PB: 978-1-4411-8051-3

Library of Congress Cataloging-in-Publication Data
Daly, Chris.
Philosophy of language : an introduction/Chris Daly.
p. cm.
Includes bibliographical references and index.
ISBN 978-1-4411-7350-8 (hardcover) – ISBN 978-1-4411-8051-3 (pbk.)
1. Language and languages–Philosophy. I. Title.

P106.D248 2012
121'.68–dc23   2012012760

Typeset by Deanta Global Publishing Servicing, Chennai, India
Printed and bound in India

Contents

viii Contents

Preface

This book was commissioned by Sarah Campbell, then commissioning editor for philosophy at Bloomsbury books. I am indebted to two anonymous referees for very helpful comments on my book proposal.

I am very grateful to Eve Garrard and Harry Lesser who each read a draft of the entire manuscript and provided a wealth of invaluable comments and advice. My thanks also go to Rina Arya, Paul Audi, Simon Langford, Daniel Nolan, and Kelly Trogdon for their extremely helpful comments on various chapters.

This book is dedicated to the memory of Clare Daly (1926–75).

Introduction

A helpful first step in the study of the philosophy of language is to consider some of the central questions which it is concerned with. Different fields in philosophy are characterized by their interest in different kinds of questions. For example, epistemology is concerned with such central questions as 'What is knowledge?' and 'How much do we know?' Again, philosophy of mind is concerned with such central questions as 'What is a mental state?' and 'What is the connection between mental and physical states?' Philosophy of language also has its central questions. What follows is a list of ten key questions. The list is not in order of importance; nor is it supposed to be exhaustive. It does, however, give an indication of the issues to be dealt with in the book. (For similar lists, see Moravcsik 1974, pp. 3–6; Cummins 1979, p. 357; Block 1986, pp. 616–27.)

(Q1) *What is the difference between marks and sounds that have meaning and those that do not?*

The marks on the page in front of you have meaning; the scuff marks on your shoes do not. Your conversations have meaning; your sneezes do not. What underlies this difference? It is not a basic inexplicable fact (a 'brute fact') about the world that some noises or marks have meaning whereas others do not. Some explanation is then needed of this difference. What is it?

Hilary Putnam gives a vivid illustration of this issue (Putnam 1981, chapter 1). Here is a variant of it. Imagine that an ant falls into a pot of ink. It crawls out and leaves a trail of ink behind it. The trail looks as follows:

Winston Churchill . . .

The ant has produced marks that are qualitatively identical to marks that, let us say, a history teacher has just now put on a white board. Nevertheless, while the marks which the teacher has made are about Winston Churchill, those which the ant has made are not. Indeed, they are not about anything at all; they lack meaning.

It is tempting to say that the explanation of why the ant's marks do not mean anything is that the ant is not thinking about Churchill and, in particular, it does not intend its marks to be about Churchill. The teacher, by contrast, is thinking about Churchill when she puts those marks on the board, and she is intending her marks to be about him.

Linking meaning in this way to psychology, and especially to a language-user's intentions, is an interesting idea. Notice, however, that it assumes that certain psychological states have meaning. The reply takes it that certain marks have a particular meaning only if those marks are produced by someone who intends those marks to have that meaning. The teacher intends that the marks represent Churchill whereas the ant has no such intention. The teacher's psychological state, her intention, itself has a meaning – it is *about* Winston Churchill. The ant has no psychological states involving Winston Churchill – if it even has any psychological states at all. The reply seeks to explain the difference between marks with meaning and marks without meaning in terms of marks produced by intentions and marks not produced by intentions. Let's grant, at least for the sake of argument, that this explanation succeeds. But the explanation raises a question closely related to our original one. Our original question was: What is the difference between marks and sounds that have meaning and those that do not? The new question is: What is the difference between those mental states that have meaning and those that do not? The teacher has mental states that are about Winston Churchill. It is not an inexplicable brute fact that she has such states. What makes it the case that she has such states? The ant has no mental states that are about Winston Churchill. Perhaps ants are biologically too simple to have any mental states. Yet the example need not be about an ant. Suppose instead that a baby overturned the paint pot and its footprints happened to leave a pattern of ink tracing out Churchill's name. The same problem arises: the teacher's marks have meaning, the footprints none, despite the fact that the baby has many psychological states.

In sum, appealing to someone's psychological states pushes the problem back a stage. There is a problem about what makes the difference between those marks and sounds which have meaning and those which do not. There is a still more general problem about what makes the difference between those states which have meaning and those which do not. The teacher's marks are about Churchill and she has a mental state which makes it the case that the marks are intended to be about Churchill. What gives her marks meaning? What gives her mental state meaning? This more generally stated problem is called 'the problem of intentionality'. It is the problem of how anything can mean or be about anything else (Searle 1983, chapter 1).

A constraint which various philosophers place on a solution to the above problem is that the solution needs to show that meaning is a natural phenomenon. Taking the natural world to be the world which the natural sciences investigate and describe, these philosophers think that truths about the natural world determine truths about what words and sentences mean (Fodor 1990, p. 32).

The approach to the problem which we have just explored has been to look at the psychology of any would-be language user. Another approach would be to look outside of any would-be language user and, in particular, to see whether it is part of a wider linguistic community. This approach would claim that language is a social phenomenon: that words and sentences have shared meanings and interpretations and are used in a rule-governed way by a linguistic community so that its members can communicate with one another effectively. On this approach the reason why the ant in the example does not mean anything by its scribbles is because it is not a member of a linguistic community that uses the marks it made to communicate information about Winston Churchill.

Like the appeal to psychology, this appeal to a linguistic community helps itself to various intentional phenomena. To see this, consider what it takes for a group of things to form a linguistic community. Imagine that an entire colony of ants clambers in and out of the ink pot and that each ant leaves one or other of the following marks:

Winston Churchill
Charles de Gaulle
Franklin D. Roosevelt

Notwithstanding the fact that the ants have left marks that are qualitatively identical to ones that are used in rule-governed ways in English-speaking communities to talk about various statesmen, the ants do not form a linguistic community and the ants' marks do not have meaning: their marks are not about anything. Furthermore, what is a linguistic rule? And since it is so hard to specify the rules that supposedly govern even languages that we are familiar with – just try it – what reason is there for thinking that there are such rules? Similarly, saying that the difference between the ant's marks and the history teacher's marks lies in a difference in the context in which they are produced may be true, but it is not very helpful unless more can be said about what a context is. If a context is a stretch of conversation, then what makes the sounds or marks produced meaningful sentences in a conversation rather than mere sounds or marks which are not part of a conversation? Perhaps a context can also involve non-linguistic factors, such as a would-be language user's actions. But, for something to be an action, it needs to be produced by an agent with certain intentions, and this returns us to the issues facing the appeal to a would-be speaker's psychology.

Some philosophers doubt whether there is a solution to the problem about how words and sentences have meanings. They think that the natural world fails to determine what words and sentences mean. Consequently, they doubt whether there are truths about what words and sentences mean (Quine 1960, chapter 2; Kripke 1982, chapter 2). These doubts are radical and far-reaching. They challenge the widely held and natural assumption that there are truths about what our words and sentences mean. We assume, for example, that the English word 'squirrel' means *squirrel* and not anything else, and that the English sentence 'There's whisky in the jar' means that *there's whisky in the jar* and not that *there's a doctor in the house*. The above doubts threaten to expose these assumptions as illusory.

(Q2)   *What gives words and sentences their particular meanings?*

Words and sentences do not merely have meaning; they have *particular* meanings. For example, the English word 'cat' means *cat*. It does not mean *dog*. 'Winston Churchill' is a name of Winston Churchill. It is not a name of Charles de Gaulle. The English sentence 'There is a squirrel on the lawn' means that *there is a squirrel on the lawn*. It does not mean that *France is a republic*. It is not a brute fact that 'cat', 'Winston Churchill' and 'There is a squirrel on the lawn' mean what they do. Some explanation is needed of this and similar facts. What is it?

Here is another way to see the problem. If a given word or sentence means one thing rather than another thing, there is a question about whether it means the same as some other word or sentence. For instance, both the English word 'cat' and the French word 'chat' have meaning, but do they have the same meaning? Presumably we do not answer these questions in a haphazard or arbitrary way. But then what criteria are there for establishing whether they have the same meaning or not? What does it take for words or sentences to have the same meaning? Some philosophers query whether these questions can be answered informatively. This reinforces their scepticism about whether there are truths about what words and sentences mean (Quine 1951).

(Q3) *How do we understand words and sentences?*

The fact that words and sentences have meanings is only half the story. It is also a fact that people understand what many words and sentences mean and that very often people can understand what words and sentences mean instantaneously and without conscious effort. For example, when you read a newspaper you come across many types of sentences that you have never seen before, and yet you understand those sentences as readily as you read them. Your understanding can then influence your behaviour. If you understand what you have read and also believe it, then you may appropriately act on that information. It is because you understand the message 'Meet me under the clock in Grand Central Station at noon', that you see to it that you arrive at that location by noon. But what is involved in our understanding a word or sentence? What does the difference consist in between someone who understands a sentence and someone who fails to understand it?

(Q4) *What is the relationship between understanding an expression, learning it and using it?*

There seem to be some obvious connections between each of those things. To learn an expression is to learn what it means, and that involves understanding the expression. To learn an expression also apparently involves being able to use the expression correctly. But perhaps these statements are over-simplifications. For example, what is it to be able to use an expression correctly? Suppose that understanding a word like 'ant' involves being able to apply it correctly, that is, being able to apply it to all and only ants. Yet if some of us cannot distinguish ants from (say) termites, it would follow that we do not all understand what 'ant' means and that we never learnt what it meant. Furthermore, how we use an expression such as 'ant' partly depends on our beliefs about ants. Suppose that someone has some eccentric beliefs about ants because they have been misinformed. Suppose that this person believes that no ants fly. When that person says that no ants fly, they are speaking falsely, but are they misusing the word 'ant'? If they are, then does it follow that they do not understand what the word means? If it does follow, then there are serious ramifications. Since everyone has false beliefs about many things, it would follow that everyone misunderstands much of their own language.

To avoid this consequence, it might be suggested that only some beliefs are important in understanding what 'ant' means, where those beliefs are widely held and are known to be widely held. Provided that a given person has those beliefs, then that person understands the word 'ant'. One problem with this suggestion is to say what distinguishes the beliefs in question from any other beliefs about ants. The privileged beliefs in question might be beliefs about what is obviously implied by the assumption that something is an ant. Yet the person we just considered mistakenly thinks that, from the assumption that something is an ant, it obviously follows that it does not fly. Since people differ about what they take to be the obvious implications of something being an ant, and since whether an implication is an *obvious* implication depends on whether people find it obvious, there remains the problem of specifying what distinguishes the beliefs or the implications that supposedly fix the meaning of 'ant' from those beliefs or implications that do not (Fodor and LePore 1991).

(Q5) *What is the relation between meaning and truth?*

Sentences have meaning. They can also be true or false. What, if anything, is the connection between these two facts? Moreover, expressions shorter than complete sentences (sub-sentential expressions, as they are called) have meaning. They are also components of sentences that are true or false. What, if anything, is the connection between these two facts?

   One suggestion is that the connection is very close. The sentence 'Someone is talking' is true under exactly one condition: it is the condition that someone is talking. Call the condition under which a sentence is true its 'truth condition'. The suggestion is then that sentence meaning is at least the sentence's truth condition and that to understand a sentence's meaning is to know what the truth condition of the sentence is (Davidson 1967). Is that suggestion correct? Or, if it is false, is it false because of matters of detail or because the suggestion is entirely wrong-headed?

(Q6) *What is the relation between the meaning of sentences and the content of thoughts?*

This question concerns the link between the meaning of sentences and the meaning of psychological states. If a teacher intends that the marks she puts on the board are about Winston Churchill, she has a psychological state that has a certain meaning. The meaning of a psychological state is what is known as its content. The content of a psychological state is commonly reported by means of a that-clause. For example, the teacher has a psychological state with the content that *these marks are about Churchill*.

Here is an important difference between words or sentences, on the one hand, and psychological states, on the other. You have to read or hear words or sentences in order to understand them. But you do not have to visualize or hear thoughts in your head in order to understand them. According to John Searle, what underlies this difference is a difference between the *derivative meaning* of words and sentences and the *intrinsic meaning* of thoughts (Searle 1980). To claim that words and sentences have a derivative meaning is to claim that they get their meaning by being interpreted by someone. Thoughts are unlike that. They do not get their meaning by being interpreted by someone, and, more generally, they do not get their meaning from anything else. But are there such different kinds of meaning and, if there are, how are they related? Is one kind of meaning more fundamental than the other, and, if so, which one? Some theories take the content of thoughts to be more fundamental than the meaning of sentences in public languages and seek to explain the latter in terms of the former (Grice 1957). Other theories take the meaning of sentences in public languages to be more fundamental than the content of thoughts and seek to explain the latter in terms of the former (Dummett 2010, chapter 13). Which approach is correct?

(Q7) *How can a theory of the compositional nature of sentence meaning be given?*

In discussing (Q3) it was mentioned that people can readily understand sentences which they have never encountered before. How do people do this? Moreover, people can readily produce sentences which they have not encountered before. How do they do this? These two facts might have a common source. The source, it might be suggested, is that language has a compositional structure. The meaning of a sentence is a function of the meanings of the expressions in it, plus the grammatical structure (or syntax, as it is known) of the sentence. In this sense, the meaning of a sentence is composed from the meanings of its component expressions (Szabó 2000). So, if you understand the component expressions of a sentence, and if you understand the syntax of the sentence, then you understand the sentence. You can then understand a sentence which you have not previously encountered because, although you were not previously familiar with the sentence, you were familiar with both what its component expressions mean and with the syntax of the sentence.

It seems that a theory of meaning should specify the compositional nature of languages. This would involve specifying compositional mechanisms that determine the meaning of more complex expressions given the meanings of less complex expressions. (Some philosophers, however, question whether language has a compositional nature: see Margalit 1978; Schiffer 1987, p.140; Pelletier 1994.)

We can distinguish 'bottom-up' from 'top-down' theories of meaning. A bottom-up theory proceeds by giving an explanation of the meaning of less complex expressions (typically, words) and then gives an explanation of the meaning of more complex expressions (including sentences) in terms of it. Such a theory readily accommodates the above claim about the compositional character of language. A quite different direction of explanation is taken by a top-down theory of meaning. Such a theory begins with an explanation of the meaning of the more complex expressions. This explanation might be in terms of the obvious implications involving them. An explanation of this type was canvassed in discussion of (Q4). For example, some obvious implications of the sentence 'a is an ant' are the sentences 'a is an insect' and 'a eats things'. The theory then proceeds to give an explanation of less complex expressions, such as 'ant', 'insect' and 'eats', in terms of the role which they play in the more complex expressions. A major issue in the philosophy of language concerns which, if either, of these two kinds of theory (bottom-up or top-down) we should favour.

(Q8) *How do different features of meaning determine the reference of an expression?*

The reference of an expression is what that expression is about. Suppose that, unknown to me, I am the winner of a lottery. Then 'the winner of the lottery' and 'I' (as uttered by me) refer to the same person. My thinking that *the winner of the lottery will be rich* may have little effect on my behaviour – it may cause only passing envy on my part. By contrast, my thinking that *I will be rich* may have an appreciable effect on my behaviour – it may cause me to collect my winnings and spend like crazy. So there is a striking difference between how those thoughts would affect my behaviour. Those two thoughts have different contents and sentences expressing them have different meanings. Nevertheless, both thoughts are about me since I am the winner of the lottery, and both thoughts take me to be rich in the imminent future. Understood in that way, the thoughts have the same content and sentences expressing those thoughts have the same meaning. The difference here is a difference in how we classify thoughts or sentences. We may classify them 'widely' so that if two sentences are attributing the same thing to the same individuals, then those sentences are classified as being of the same type. Or we may classify them 'narrowly' so that only if two sentences are referring to the same individual in the same way and are describing that individual in the same way do the sentences belong to the same type. These two ways of classifying sentences can be taken as specifying different aspects of meaning (Frege 1892; Perry 1977).

(Q9) *What is the role of pragmatics in language?*

The role of context in determining the meaning of utterances is part of what is called 'pragmatics'. When an expression is uttered, contextual factors co-operate with the meaning of the expression to determine the meaning of the utterance. For example, if someone says 'This is flat', what they mean, and whether what they mean is true, depends on the context in at least two ways. First, what the word 'this' is being used to refer to depends on the context. In different contexts occurrences of 'this' may refer to different things. Second, what counts as flat depends on the standard the speaker is employing in the context, and what that standard is may vary from context to context. If what is being evaluated is whether something is flat enough to be a bowling green, one standard of what counts as flat is being used. If what is being evaluated is whether something is flat enough to be an airfield, a different standard of what counts as flat is in play. Given the role that context has in determining the meaning of expressions, what can be said in more detail about how it fulfils this role? (Grice 1975)

(Q10) *Can there even be a systematic philosophical study of natural language?*

We can distinguish between so-called natural languages, such as English and Turkish, and artificial languages, such as the language of set theory or the languages used in computer programming. Natural languages are complex. Many of their terms are ambiguous. Almost all of their terms are vague. Does this entail that the rigorous and precise techniques of logic cannot be applied to the study of natural languages? Some philosophers answer in the positive: they think that the sentences of natural languages cannot be studied by using formal notions and techniques. Attempts to study them in these ways lead to grave distortion and counterintuitive results (Strawson 1950). Other philosophers also answer in the positive but take artificial languages to provide more precise and unambiguous vehicles of expression than natural languages do, at least for scientific purposes (Frege 1879, pp. 194–5; Russell 1944, pp. 693–4; Carnap 1937, p. 2; Beth 1963; Sainsbury 1979, chapter V; Rein 1985; and Makin 2000, chapter 7). Still other philosophers answer in the negative: They take formal techniques and artificial languages to illuminate the actual workings of natural languages (Montague 1974, p. 188). Which of these approaches is correct and how can we tell?

These ten questions convey many of the important issues in the philosophy of language. The scope of the questions addresses the overlapping concerns of philosophers who work in this field, many of which will be considered in this book. The broadness of the questions means that it would be artificial and unsatisfactory to do a point-by-point mapping of each question onto a separate chapter. Instead, each chapter in the book concentrates on a particular topic that is raised by considering the work of a leading figure in the field and by the cluster of issues that preoccupied that philosopher. The figures – Frege, Russell, Grice, Davidson, Quine and Lewis – each identified a problem or series of problems in the philosophy of language, and then offered theories designed, among other things, to solve those problems. Each chapter proceeds by stating the problems, setting out the theory offered as their solution and then considering how effective the theory is in solving those problems. We will then consider what problems the theory itself generates and whether they can be overcome. Various rival theories that arise from these difficulties will also be discussed. In the course of reading the book, the reader should keep in mind the issues raised in the introduction by the above ten questions. In each chapter's conclusion, these questions will be referred back to when evaluating what has been accomplished in the chapter.

Although the above ten questions are key ones in the philosophy of language, they are not exhaustive in their range. Some other important issues include conditionals, vagueness, idioms and metaphor, adverbs, mass terms, count nouns, quantifiers and pronouns. Important theories which will not be discussed in the book include conceptual role semantics, game-theoretic semantics and translational semantics. The work of Wittgenstein has also been excluded. This is partly because there is already a wealth of books and papers which seek to interpret and evaluate Wittgenstein's gnomic remarks.

Furthermore, the interpretation of Wittgenstein is a fraught and much contested matter. This is compounded by Wittgenstein's tendency not to give explicit arguments for his claims. This book concentrates on a selection of issues where we can get reasonably clear on what the problems at hand are, what some leading proposed solutions are, and what the case for these proposed solutions consists in.

The philosophy of language is connected to other sub-disciplines in philosophy. The philosophy of language is concerned with such notions as meaning, reference and truth and with fathoming the relations between them. But its work adjoins issues in the philosophy of mind concerning representation and content. Developments in either of these sub-disciplines have beneficial consequences for the other. The philosophy of language also abuts issues in metaphysics concerning what there is and what is more fundamental than what. We have seen that there is a question about the relation of putative truths about what words and sentences mean to truths about the natural world. That is a special case of a more general question about the relation of putative truths about things that are apparently not natural (things such as minds, values or sentence meanings) to truths about the natural world (Jackson 1998). Lastly, issues about knowledge of meaning raise general epistemological issues about what it takes to have knowledge and what we can have knowledge of. In the book's conclusion we will consider the relation of the philosophy of language to other sub-disciplines of philosophy, and, in particular, the issue of whether the philosophy of language should have a unique foundational role in philosophy (Dummett 1981, chapter 15).

Some fields outside of philosophy also have a bearing on the philosophy of language. Theoretical linguistics, and especially studies in formal grammar or syntax, are notable examples. Just as different fields in philosophy have their own characteristic concerns and questions, so too does linguistics. Despite their shared interest in the nature of language, linguistics and philosophy of language do not have exactly the same set of concerns and questions. Considerations of space require that we cannot follow up on the leading theories and findings of linguists. We should note, though, that any complete evaluation of many issues in the philosophy of language should take into account the data and theories of linguistics. (For expositions of theoretical linguistics, see Martin 1987, chapter 1; Bach 1974; Fromkin et al. 1978.) We will return to the issue of the relation between linguistics and philosophy of language in the book's conclusion.

Further reading

(Full bibliographical details for the material listed here, and at the end of each chapter, are given in the bibliography).

Blackburn, Simon (1984) *Spreading the Word* chapter 1.
Davies, Martin (2006) 'Foundational Issues in the Philosophy of Language'.
Lycan, William G. (2008) *Philosophy of Language: A Contemporary Introduction* chapter 1.
Weiss, Bernhard (2010) *How To Understand Language: A Philosophical Inquiry* chapter 1.

1

Frege on Names

1. Introduction

In the first four chapters of this book we will be considering central aspects of Gottlob Frege's philosophy of language. Frege's philosophy of language is developed from his research in philosophy of mathematics. Frege seeks to show how we can have mathematical knowledge. In order to show this, he advances a programme known as logicism. This programme attempts to reduce mathematics to logic. As part of this programme, Frege devises a system which would perspicuously represent chains of inference in mathematics (Frege 1879). Devising such a system requires, among other things, devising a language which clearly expresses the logical notions introduced by the system and which makes transparent the logical structure of sentences formulated in that language. For these reasons Frege is led into developing a philosophy of language. (For further discussion of the background of Frege's thought, see Currie 1982, chapters 1 and 2.)

In this first chapter, we will consider Frege's views about the meaning of names. The philosophical issues concerning the meaning of names are as follows. Is there anything more to the meaning of a name than whatever it refers to? For example, does the meaning of your name consist solely in its referring to you? Does the meaning of 'Barack Obama' consist solely in its referring to Barack Obama? Or does that name not only refer to Obama but also tell us something about him?

[margin note: Is there more to a name than it's referent?]

Frege argues that there is more to the meaning of a name than what it refers to because of an important puzzle: the puzzle of informative identity sentences. To solve the puzzle, Frege distinguishes between two aspects of the meaning of a name: its sense and its reference. Frege subsequently extends this distinction from names to predicates and sentences. (See Chapters 2 and 3, respectively.) Before we discuss the difference between sense and reference, however, we need first to consider a different distinction, that between names and descriptions.

2. Names and descriptions

On the face of it, there is a distinction between two kinds of linguistic expression: proper names and descriptions. Consider descriptions. Some descriptions do not purport to pick out any particular thing. These are called 'indefinite descriptions'. An indefinite description applies to anything which fits the description, and there may be more than one thing that fits it. Examples of indefinite descriptions include 'a reader', 'a President of the United States', 'some capital city' and 'some planet'. Other descriptions purport to pick out exactly one particular thing. These are called 'definite descriptions'. They include 'the author of this book', 'the 35th President of the United States', 'the capital of France' and 'the largest planet in the Solar System'. Now consider proper names. Proper names include 'John F. Kennedy', 'Paris' and 'Jupiter'. Unlike indefinite descriptions, proper names attempt to pick out a particular thing. Yet proper names also seem to differ from definite descriptions as well. A proper name purports to pick something out apparently without describing that thing, or at least some philosophers, such as John Stuart Mill, think so. Mill writes:

[margin note: 'a' vs. 'the']

> Proper names . . . denote the individuals who are called by them, but they do not indicate or imply any attributes as applying to those individuals.

When we name a child by the name ['Paul'], or a dog by the name ['Caesar'], these names are simply marks used to enable those individuals to be made subjects of discourse. (Mill 1843, book I, chapter II, §5, p. 33)

In Mill's view, using a proper name to pick something out does not provide any information about whatever has been picked out. It does not 'indicate or imply' that the thing picked out has any features. Using the name 'Jupiter' to talk about something, for example, does not indicate or imply anything about what the thing you are talking about is like. Names, according to Mill's view, are 'simply marks'. Contrast this with the case of the description 'the largest planet in the Solar System'. By using this description to talk about something, you would be indicating that it is not only a planet and that it is in the Solar System, but that it is the largest planet in the Solar System. (For further discussion of Mill's theory of names, see Cargile 1979, chapter 2.)

3. The puzzle of informative identity sentences

Frege poses the following problem for Mill's theory of names. It is the problem of how there can be informative identity sentences. Suppose that, as Mill claims, the meaning of a name consists solely in whatever unique object it picks out. It follows that two names that pick out the same object will have the same meaning. So if 'a' and 'b' are names of the same object, then 'a' will have the same meaning as 'b'. Now if 'a' and 'b' have the same meaning, then any sentence involving one of these names will have the same meaning as any sentence that differs only by containing the other name instead. So, for instance, 'a is F' and 'b is F' will have the same meaning, for any one-place predicate 'F'. Moreover, if these sentences have the same meaning, then they will convey the same information to anyone who understands them. But this generates the following puzzle. The identity sentence 'a = b' can be more informative than the identity sentence 'a = a'. 'a = a' is obvious and trivially true, whereas 'a = b' need not be obvious and trivially true – it can tell us something which we did not already know. Since 'a = b' can be more informative than 'a = a', these identity sentences do not have the same meaning. But the only difference between the sentences is that the first sentence contains the name 'b', whereas the second sentence contains the name 'a' instead. The difference in meaning of the two sentences then traces back to the difference in meaning between 'a' and 'b'. Yet if a is identical to *b*, then '*a*' and '*b*' refer to the same thing. And, according to Mill, names that refer to the same thing have the same meaning.

We can appreciate this puzzle further with an example. Radovan Karadžić was the President of Serbia following the break-up of Yugoslavia in the early 1990s. As a public figure, it was widely known that:

(1) Radovan Karadžić is Radovan Karadžić.

From the late-1990s, Dragan Dabić was a practitioner in alternative medicine in Belgrade. Many of the same people who knew (1) also knew that:

(2) Dragan Dabić is Dragan Dabić.

In fact, as a fugitive from international law, Karadžić had been living under an alias, and in 2008 it was revealed that:

(3) Radovan Karadžić is Dragan Dabić

Many people who had known both that (1) and (2) had not known that (3). Those people found both (1) and (2) obvious, even trivial. Yet they found (3) far from trivial and very informative.

The problem for Mill's theory of names is how (1) and (2) are obvious but (3) is not. Equivalently, the problem is how (1) and (2) are uninformative whereas (3) is highly informative. As Frege would put it, (3) differs from both (1) and (2) in 'cognitive value'. Now, in Mill's view, when a name picks out something, it does not provide any information about what it picks out. The names 'Radovan Karadžić' and 'Dragan Dabić' pick out the same person. Mill's view entails that sentences (1–3) convey the same information: each of those sentences are saying merely a certain person is identical with himself. But that consequence seems mistaken.

The same kind of puzzle is generated by other examples. Consider sentences (4) and (5):

(4) $6 \div 3 = 6 \div 3$.
(5) $6 \div 3 = \sqrt{4}$.

Like sentences (1–3), sentences (4) and (5) are identity sentences. The expressions '$6 \div 3$' and '$\sqrt{4}$' refer to the same number, that is, the number 2. But whereas what (4) says is trivial and uninformative, what (5) says is more informative. But if the linguistic role of expressions such as '$6 \div 3$' and '$\sqrt{4}$'

consists solely in referring to a certain number – in fact, the same number – then it is difficult to see how sentences (4) and (5) could differ in informativeness.

Frege has a subsidiary argument in the case of examples such as the Karadžić/Dabić one. It is an argument that turns on differences in the ways in which we can know certain identity sentences to be true. We can know *a priori* that:

(1)   Radovan Karadžić is Radovan Karadžić

and also that:

(2)   Dragan Dabić is Dragan Dabić.

Yet we cannot know *a priori* that:

(3)   Radovan Karadžić is Dragan Dabić.

But if the meanings of 'Radovan Karadžić' and 'Dragan Dabić' consist solely in what they refer to, and they refer to the same person, then it is hard to see how (1) and (2) can be knowable *a priori* but (3) cannot.

4. Frege on names

Frege calls the expressions flanking the identity signs 'proper names' (*Eigennamen*). He would regard expressions such as 'Radovan Karadžić' and 'Dragan Dabić' as names, but also expressions such as '6 ÷ 3' and '$\sqrt{4}$'. Frege takes a proper name to be any expression that refers to a single object. A consequence of this is that Frege would also regard definite descriptions as proper names.

By 'object' Frege does not mean *perceivable object*. He uses the term 'proper name' to apply also to places, instants, periods of time and numbers. This is reflected in the range of examples of identity sentences that Frege presents. He introduces objects as the referents of proper names rather than introducing proper names as those expressions which refer to objects. His thinking is that we can identify which expressions are proper names before having to consider what those expressions are names of. An object can then be understood as whatever can be referred to by a proper name. Frege's methodology – of taking the notion of a proper name to be explanatorily prior to the notion of an object – has been adopted by various other philosophers. Some of them propose what they call 'the syntactic priority thesis'. According to this thesis, our understanding of ontological categories, such as the notion of an object, is determined by our understanding of syntactic categories, such as the notion of a proper name. For example, Crispin Wright says that:

> If . . . certain expressions in a branch of our language function as singular terms, and descriptive and identity contexts containing them are true by ordinary criteria, there is no room for any ulterior failure of 'fit' between those contexts and the structure of the states of affairs which make them true. So there can be no philosophical science of ontology, no well-founded attempt to see past our categories of expression and glimpse the way in which the world is truly furnished. (Wright 1983, p. 52)

> The lynch-pin of Frege's platonism, according to our interpretation, is the syntactic priority thesis: the category of objects . . . is to be explained as comprising everything which might be referred to by a singular term [a proper name, in Frege's sense], where it is understood that possession of reference is imposed on a singular term by its occurrence in true statements of an appropriate type. (Wright 1983, p. 53)

(We will return to this issue in this book's conclusion. For further discussion, see also Wright 1983, pp. 13, 129 and 153; Dummett 1981a, chapter 4; Reck 1987. For a query about this interpretation of Frege, see Currie 1982, chapter 6 §b; Milne 1986).

If names are to have such a central theoretical role, we need more than an intuitive understanding of what names are. In particular, we need something more than the ability to provide examples and foils (i.e. contrast cases). Frege does not undertake this task: 'he was content to allow the whole distinction between proper names and expressions of other kinds to depend upon intuitive recognition, guided only by the most rough and ready of tests' (Dummett 1981a, p. 54. But see also Diller 1993, p. 346). We need a criterion for identifying proper names, but it is far from easy to provide one. For example, a name need not occur in the subject-place of a sentence (as 'Caesar' does not in 'Brutus killed Caesar'). Furthermore, an expression that occurs in the subject-place of a sentence need not be a name (as in 'Nobody won the election'). We might think that if '*a*' is a genuine name, then '*a* is F' entails 'something is F'. But presumably 'Pegasus' is a name and yet 'Pegasus does not exist' does not entail 'Something does not exist'. Ingenious efforts have been made to provide the needed criterion (Dummett 1973, chapter 4; Hale 1987, chapter 2). Unfortunately, those efforts have been thought to be unsatisfactory (Williamson 1988, pp. 487–8; Künne 1989, pp. 90–2; Wetzel 1990).

5. Frege's distinction between sense and reference

Frege seeks to solve the puzzle of informative identity sentences by drawing a distinction between what he calls an expression's 'sense' (*Sinn*) and what he calls its 'reference' (*Bedeutung*). A name such as 'Radovan Karadžić' has both a sense and a reference. Its reference is to a certain object, the man Radovan Karadžić. Karadžić is then what the name refers to. Similar considerations apply to the name 'Dragan Dabić'. These names have the same reference: they refer to the same object. But they have different senses because they differ in cognitive value. That is to say, they differ in what information they convey.

Frege makes five key claims about the sense of a name. These five claims specify different roles which the senses of names play in his philosophy of language.

1. First, the sense of a name is what is grasped (in Frege's phrase) by anyone who understands that name. Understanding a name is then a matter of having a certain kind of access to the sense associated with that name.

2. Second, the sense of a name determines what the name's reference is. The sense of the name 'Radovan Karadžić' determines that the name refers to a particular object, the man Radovan Karadžić, rather than to any other object.

3. Third, the sense of the name is a certain 'mode of presentation' (in Frege's phrase) of its referent. The sense of the name 'Radovan Karadžić' presents a certain person in a certain way. The sense of the name 'Dragan Dabić' presents the same person in another way. In other words, 'Radovan Karadžić' and 'Dragan Dabić' have different senses: those names involve different modes of presentation of the same person. This third point shows that names can have the same reference but have different senses. An analogy to a mode of presentation of a referent is that of a perspective on an object. When you look at a table, you look at the table from a certain perspective. As you walk around the table, you look at the same table from different perspectives. These are different visual representations of the same object. Senses are themselves abstract representations. Different senses can represent the same object in different ways. By expressing different senses which represent the same object, different names can represent the same object.

4. Fourth, if the names '*a*' and '*b*' differ in sense, then the sentences '*a* is F' and '*b* is F' will differ in cognitive value. As mentioned above in §3, Frege points out that sentences can differ in the information that they convey, their cognitive

what about what my name is to me?

value (Frege 1892a, p. 32). What underlies this difference in cognitive value is a difference in the senses of the names contained in these sentences.

⑤ Fifth, the sense of a name consists in its contribution to the truth conditions of the sentences which it occurs in. First of all, we need to understand what a truth condition is. The sentence 'Barack Obama is a president' is true on the following condition: the condition that Barack Obama is a president. That condition is the truth condition of the sentence 'Barack Obama is a president'. The name 'Barack Obama' occurs in that sentence, and it has a certain sense. It is partly because that name has that sense that the sentence has the truth condition that it does. If we were to replace 'Barack Obama' in the sentence 'Barack Obama is a president' with a name with a different sense, say, the name 'Bill Clinton', we would have a sentence with a different truth condition. It would be a sentence that is true on the condition that Bill Clinton is a president. So the sense of the name 'Barack Obama' partly determines what the truth condition of 'Barack Obama is a president' is. That name occurs in infinitely many other sentences and its sense partly determines what the truth conditions of each of those other sentences are. More generally, the sense of a name 'a' contributes to the truth conditions of every sentence in which 'a' occurs.

Frege now has the materials in place to solve the puzzle of informative identity sentences. In particular, he claims that names can have the same reference but different senses, and that sentences containing names with different senses will differ in cognitive value. Let's go back to our earlier example. 'Radovan Karadžić' and 'Dragan Dabić' have the same reference but different senses. Sentence (1) was:

(1)   Radovan Karadžić is Radovan Karadžić.

That sentence is relatively uninformative because one object is picked out on the left-hand side of the identity sign by using a name with a certain sense and the same object is picked out on the right-hand side of the identity sign by using a name with the same sense. Sentence (2) was:

(2)   Dragan Dabić is Dragan Dabić.

(2) is relatively uninformative for the same reason as (1) is. But contrast these cases with sentence (3):

(3)   Radovan Karadžić is Dragan Dabić.

That sentence is informative because, although it purports to pick out the same object, that object is picked out on the left-hand side of the identity sign by using a name with a certain sense (the sense of the name 'Radovan Karadžić') while that object is picked out on the right-hand side of the identity sign by using a name with a *different* sense (the sense of the name 'Dragan Dabić'). Since the names 'Radovan Karadžić' and 'Dragan Dabić' have different senses, (1) differs in sense from (3). It is this difference in sense between these names that explains the difference in cognitive value, in relative informativeness, between (1) and (3). The same account can be given to explain the difference in cognitive value between (2) and (3).

The reason why (1) and (2) are knowable *a priori* but (3) is not is that, although 'Radovan Karadžić' and 'Dragan Dabić' have the same reference, they differ in sense. Consequently, (1–3) have different senses. Whether we can know something *a priori* at least partly depends on what its sense is. So even if (1) and (2) are knowable *a priori*, it does not follow that (3) is knowable *a priori*.

Frege's solution in terms of *different sense but same reference* applies to our other example:

(4) $6 \div 3 = 6 \div 3.$
(5) $6 \div 3 = \sqrt{4}.$

'$6 \div 3$' refers to the same number as '$\sqrt{4}$' does, but these names differ in sense. They present the same number in different ways. One way is as the division of 6 by 3. The other way is as the square root of 4. It is this difference of sense between these names that explains why (4) and (5) differ in cognitive value.

Lastly, note that although Frege frames his puzzle in terms of identity sentences, the puzzle is not confined to cases involving such sentences. Consider the following two examples:

(6) Superman is a superhero.
(7) Clark Kent is a superhero.

Anyone who understands (6) will find it obvious. But people can understand (7) without finding it obvious. Clark Kent is the secret identity of Superman and it is precisely because it is secret that people can understand (7) without finding it obvious. But if the meanings of 'Superman' and 'Clark Kent' consist solely in what they refer to, and these names refer to the same person, then it is a puzzle how (6) is obvious whereas (7) need not be. Unlike our earlier examples, (6) and (7) are not identity sentences. They are not of the form

'$a = a$' or '$a = b$'. Instead, they are of the form 'a is F'. Each of these sentences contains a name of an individual and predicates the same thing of that individual. The point of this example is to show that the puzzle Frege raises is not due to any supposed oddity of identity sentences; the puzzle is a pervasive one.

We can summarize the key points in this section as follows:

The sense and reference of names

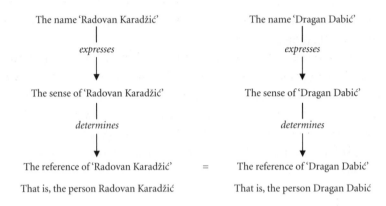

6. What is the sense of a name?

In §5, we saw how Frege draws a distinction between two aspects of the meaning of a name: its sense and its reference. We gave an initial characterization of the sense of a name in terms of the roles it plays in Frege's theory of language. These roles were as follows: The sense of a name is what is grasped by anyone who understands that name. The sense of a name determines what the name's reference is. The sense of the name is a certain 'mode of presentation' of its referent. Differences in the senses of names underlie differences in cognitive value. And, finally, the sense of a name consists in the contribution that it makes to the truth conditions of the sentences it occurs in.

But if those are the roles that the sense of a name plays, is there anything that can be said about what it is that occupies those roles? Frege takes it to be central to sense that it can be communicated. He says this about the senses of sentences:

> One can hardly deny that mankind has a common store of thoughts [i.e. the senses of sentences] which is transmitted from one generation to another.

What Frege overlooks is that people might effectively communicate with each
other not by grasping the very same senses but by grasping sufficiently similar
senses. Since similarity is not transitive, the same sentences can be used by
generations to transmit information to their successors, even though, across
time, the same information is not transmitted (Harman 1967, pp. 148–50;
Feldman 1986, pp. 705–6).

Frege takes his thesis about the communicability of senses to have a negative
consequence and a positive consequence. The negative consequence is that the
senses of names (and indeed of any linguistic expression) are not mental
entities. Frege assumes that mental entities are private entities which cannot be
shared between different people. Senses, however, can be communicated and
so can be shared. It follows that no mental entities are senses. (Even before
Frege distinguished between sense and reference, he argued that the
communicability of meaning shows that word-meanings are not ideas in the
mind: see Frege 1884, p. vi.)

senses are not mental entities.

Frege has independent reason to reject the view that meanings are mental
entities, or 'psychologism', as he calls it. He criticizes the view that word-
meanings are ideas or mental images. He points out that different people may
associate different ideas with a certain word, even though they associate the
word with the same sense. For example, people may associate different mental
images with the name 'Joseph Stalin'. Ardent Communists might associate
images of a jovial father figure with it; other people might associate images of
a gulag with it. Similarly, a person might associate different ideas with a certain
word at different times of their life, depending on their life experiences, and
yet all along associate the same sense with that word. It follows that a sense
cannot be identified with any mental image.

The positive consequence that Frege draws from the communicability of
senses is that they are objective and abstract entities. Given that senses can be
communicated by people and that different people can grasp the same sense,
senses are objective entities which exist independently of minds. For the same
reason, Frege takes senses to be abstract entities. You and Aristotle grasp the
same sense when each of you think that friendship is reciprocal good will. But
there seems to be no physical thing that you are each entertaining. Senses,
then, are not physical entities, entities in time and space.

senses must be objective.

In addition, senses are objects. Recall that, for Frege, an object is anything
that can be referred to by a name. It is possible to give names to senses. For
example, 'the sense of the name "Joseph Stalin" ' is a name of a certain sense
(namely, the sense of the name 'Joseph Stalin'). Yet if senses are objects, how

should we count senses? How do we tell whether two names express the same or different senses? This issue is especially pressing given the widely-held view that we should posit entities of a certain sort only if we have a way of counting or identifying entities of that kind. This is called a 'criterion of identity'. Quine sums this up in the requirement 'no entity without identity' (Quine 1969, p. 23).

[handwritten margin note: senses as measured by their contribution to sentences]

To address this challenge, it might be suggested that two names have the same sense if and only if they contribute equal information to any sentences which they figure in (Frege 1892a, p. 32). The rationale behind this is as follows. Frege introduces the notion of sense in terms of informativeness. '$a = a$' is uninformative whereas '$a = b$' is informative. What underlies this difference in informativeness is a difference in sense between 'a' and 'b'. One consequence of a difference in informativeness between sentences is that someone can understand both sentences while believing one of the sentences but not the other. For instance, it is possible to believe both (1) and (2) without believing (3):

(1) Radovan Karadžić is Radovan Karadžić.
(2) Dragan Dabić is Dragan Dabić.
(3) Radovan Karadžić is Dragan Dabić.

This suggests the following criterion: Names 'a' and 'b' differ in sense if there is a sentence '. . . a . . .' and a sentence '. . . b . . .' such that it is possible for someone to understand both sentences but, at the same time, quite rationally believe one sentence but not the other. (The sentences '. . . a . . .' and '. . . b . . .' are any two sentences that differ in just one respect: the first sentence contains an occurrence of 'a' where the second sentence contains an occurrence of 'b'.)

Gareth Evans formulates a related criterion for the identity of the senses of sentences:

> [The sense] associated with one sentence S as its sense must be different from the [sense] associated with another sentence S' as *its* sense, if it is possible for someone to understand both sentences at a given time while coherently taking different attitudes towards them, i.e. accepting (rejecting) one while rejecting (accepting) the other. (Evans 1982, pp.18–9)

A sentence is informative if it is coherent that you understand it without believing it. Two sentences differ in informativeness if it is coherent that you understand them without believing both of them. The qualifier 'it is coherent that' is important. It is supposed to restrict a person's attitudes to those that the person can rationally hold at the same time.

Here are three comments on the suggested criterion for the distinctness of the senses of sentences. (These comments have a straightforward application to the criterion for the distinctness of the senses of names.) First, the criterion offers a sufficient condition for sentences to have distinct senses. Here is a counter-example. Consider a pair of sentences that are obviously true such as '2 + 2 = 4' and '2 + 1 = 3'. It is impossible to understand those sentences while taking different attitudes to them – say, by believing one but not the other. Nevertheless, those sentences presumably do not have the same sense. Moreover, this point cannot be overcome by extending the criterion from beliefs to include other attitudes (Broackes 1987, p. 96).

Justin Broackes' own solution is to require in addition that sentences have distinct senses if entertaining them involves different conceptual abilities (Broackes 1987, pp. 97–8). He claims that if you understand sentences such as (8) and (9)

(8) The direction of line a = the direction of line b
(9) The direction of line a is not a steamroller

the same ability is involved. That same ability, however, is not involved in your understanding sentence (10):

(10) Line a is parallel to line b.

Broackes concludes that sentences (8) and (10) differ in sense. Yet it is hard to see how to generalize from this example and how to make precise the intended criterion that sentences have different senses if understanding them involves different conceptual abilities. Understanding sentences (8) and (9) involves a conceptual ability that operates on the sense of the expression 'the direction of line a' whereas understanding sentence (10) does not. Senses are distinct if they involve different conceptual abilities. But this appeal to conceptual abilities requires that we have some independent principle for counting conceptual abilities – some principle that is independent of how senses are counted. No such principle seems forthcoming.

Second, to return to Evans' principle, an issue of circularity arises when we consider the nature of rational belief. What does it take for your beliefs to be rational? To put it another way, what is the criterion for establishing that someone's beliefs are rational? Given that you understand sentences S and S^*, it is rational to believe S but not believe S^* only if S and S^* differ in sense. For example, given that you understand the sentences 'There's a doctor in the house' and 'There's whisky in the jar', you are rational in believing the first sentence but not the second sentence only if they differ in sense. By contrast, given that you understand the sentences 'The boy was premature' and 'The male child was premature', you would be irrational in believing the first sentence but not the second since those sentences (presumably) have the same sense. So a necessary condition of your beliefs being rational is that you do not take different attitudes to sentences which you understand to have the same sense. But if that is a criterion for rational belief, then we need an independent criterion for sameness of sense – a criterion that is independent of issues to do with rational belief. (There is a question as to whether this kind of circularity is bad. See Horsten 2008.)

Here is another way to put the last two points. There are cases for which we need guidance as to whether certain sentences have the same sense. Those cases are also ones for which we need guidance as to whether it would be rational to take different attitudes to those sentences if we understand them, or as to whether understanding those sentences involves different conceptual abilities. Appealing to rationality or to conceptual abilities does not help settle whether a given case involves sentences with the same or different senses.

Here is a further problem with trying to define sameness of sense in terms of what a person would rationally believe, given the appropriate knowledge. The problem is that the same point applies to sameness of reference, when the sense is different. For example, (11) and (12) have different senses:

(11) The author of *The Mill on The Floss* was Mary Anne Evans.
(12) The author of *The Mill on The Floss* was George Eliot.

Yet if a person knew that Mary Anne Evans was George Eliot ('George Eliot' being a pseudonym of Mary Ann Evans), it would be irrational for that person to believe one of those sentences but not the other.

Third, contrary to Evans' principle, it seems possible for someone to understand a pair of sentences but, quite rationally, to take different attitudes to those sentences, *even though those sentences have the same sense*. Consider a pair of terms with the same sense such as, let us suppose, 'wager' and 'bet'. Someone, call him 'Laird', could understand those terms but rationally doubt whether they have the same sense. Laird could have learnt each of these terms normally but separately. Laird could even believe that, for any act, that act is a wager if and only if it is a bet. Nevertheless, Laird could rationally doubt that 'wager' and 'bet' have the same sense. Perhaps Laird has had a track record of taking pairs of terms to have the same sense, only later to find out that the terms differ in sense. Laird's awareness of this bad track record makes him doubt whether 'wager' and 'bet' have the same sense. (Perhaps it even causes him to believe that the two terms differ in sense.) Despite this doubt, Laird's use of 'wager' and 'bet' is otherwise as competent as anyone else's use. Laird has no doubt that 'wager' has the same sense as 'wager' and that 'bet' has the same sense as 'bet'. In this situation, then, Laird quite rationally takes different attitudes to the following sentences:

(13) To wager is to wager.
(14) To wager is to bet.

[handwritten annotations in margin: "I'm rational in believing both, so do they have the same sense?" and "Is 14 rational if we doubt. If we know what the words mean."]

Laird has no doubt that (13) is true but rationally doubts whether (14) is true. Nevertheless, (13) and (14) have the same sense (Rieber 1992. See also Baldwin 1975, pp. 81–2; Salmon 1989, pp. 265–6; Soames 2003a, pp. 46–7).

Here is a related example. Suppose there is someone who is very knowledgeable about what the senses of various words are. Call this person 'the Sage of Senses'. Someone else, call her 'Barbara', knows that the Sage is reliable and takes into account what the Sage has to say about which pairs of words do (or do not) have the same sense. Suppose that, in the case of 'wager' and 'bet' the Sage happens to get it wrong and misinforms Barbara that 'wager' and 'bet' differ in sense. (Alternatively, suppose that the Sage in fact says that 'wager' and 'wet' differ in sense but Barbara mishears her as saying that 'wager' and 'bet' differ in sense.) Given Barbara's knowledge of the impressive track record of the Sage, Barbara is rational in doubting that 'wager' and 'bet' have the same sense, although she would otherwise have no such doubts given her experience of how those words are commonly used. In this circumstance, Barbara does not doubt that (13) is true but rationally doubts whether (14) is true, even though in fact (13) and (14) have the same sense and she understands those sentences.

Our search for a principle for counting the senses of names has been unsuccessful. Various options face us. We might continue our search. Or we might take our failure to support the scepticism about meaning espoused by Goodman and Quine (Goodman 1949, 1953; Quine 1951). Or we might reject the claim that we should posit senses (or any other kind of entity) only if we have a principle for counting them (Anderson 1987, p. 156; Jubien 1996; Priest

2005, p. 111). (For further discussion on the topic of counting senses, see van Heijenoort 1977; Weitzman 1997; Klement 2003.)

7. The puzzle of empty names

Frege thinks that there is a further puzzle facing Mill's theory of names. Recall that in Mill's view the meaning of a name consists of the object that it refers to. But some names are 'empty': they do not refer to anything. Consider names in myths (such as 'Atlantis' and 'Excalibur') or names in defunct scientific theories (such as 'Vulcan'). We can understand sentences containing these names ('They are looking for Atlantis', 'Le Verrier believed that Vulcan affected Mercury's orbit'). Since we can understand those sentences, they have meaning. They have meaning only if the names contained in them have meaning. It follows that the names that occur in them have meaning.

One straightforward account of empty names suggests itself. This is that, on the supposition that there are such things as senses, empty names are names that have sense but no reference, and that a sentence containing an empty name has sense but no reference – it has no truth value. (But see Frege 1892a, p. 41 footnote where Frege suggests that when a name lacks a reference, we may give it an arbitrary one, such as taking it to refer to the number zero.) On the face of it, this seems a pleasingly simple account that follows on naturally from Frege's introduction of the distinction between sense and reference in order to solve the puzzle of informative identity sentences. Nevertheless, the account may mask a difficulty. Frege tells us that the sense of a name is a mode of presentation of the referent. But an empty name has no referent. So the would-be sense of an empty name is not presenting anything. There is nothing for it to present. It is then hard to see how an empty name can have a sense (Evans 1982, p. 22).

Empty proper names pose the following dilemma for Frege. Either a sentence containing an empty name has a sense or it does not. If it does, the sense of the sentence will be neither true nor false. For, as we will see in Chapter 3 §3, according to Frege, a sentence is true or false only if all referring terms in the sentence have reference. But according to the Law of Excluded Middle, a law of classical logic which Frege accepts, every sentence is either true or false. Alternatively, suppose that a sentence containing an empty name lacks a sense. It follows that any sentence containing the name within the scope of a propositional verb will also lack a sense. For example, if 'Frodo was a hobbit with many friends' lacks sense, then (say) 'Jemima hopes that Frodo was a hobbit with many friends' will also lack sense. Yet Jemima might have just that hope, in which case the sentence, far from lacking sense, will be true (Rein 1985, p. 519).

There are various options to choose between here. One is to admit that an empty name lacks sense but to claim that it has something else: a mock sense. Similarly, according to this option, a sentence containing an empty name does not have a sense (does not express a thought) but has a mock sense (expresses a mock thought) (Evans 1982, p. 30). The analogy here is with other mock things. When a film crew builds the façade of a Tudor house, they have not built a Tudor house. They have built something else: a mock Tudor house. Similarly, when you understand a name that has no referent, such as 'Atlantis', you do not grasp the sense of 'Atlantis'. It does not have a sense. What you grasp is something else: the mock sense of 'Atlantis'. According to Evans, 'Atlantis' is not a genuine name either. It is a mock name.

Although Frege has been read as taking this option, there is a question whether it is a plausible reading of his work (Bell 1990). That aside, there is also a question of how satisfactory a solution this is to the puzzle of empty names. Three comments can be made.

First, the distinction between sense and reference was introduced in order to solve the puzzle of identity sentences. If that same distinction can be used to solve the puzzle of empty names, then the case for that distinction would be strengthened. But now a yet further distinction has been made – the distinction between sense and mock sense – to solve the latter puzzle. Since a new distinction has been made, it is in effect being conceded that the sense/reference distinction alone does not suffice to solve the puzzle of empty names. In that case, introducing the sense/reference distinction to solve the puzzle of informative identity sentences seems *ad hoc*: the distinction has been introduced only in order to solve that one puzzle. (Fortunately, as we will see in Chapter 3 §4, Frege shows that the distinction has further benefits.)

Second, the distinction between sense and mock sense also seems *ad hoc*. The distinction is introduced only in order to solve the puzzle of empty names and that seems to be the only puzzle that it addresses. In the absence of independent reason for drawing the distinction, there seems something contrived and unconvincing about the distinction.

Third, a related point is that talk of mock sense is obscure. We understand the distinction between (say) Tudor houses and mock Tudor houses because we know what a Tudor house is and we know what a mock Tudor house is. A mock Tudor house is a house resembling a Tudor house in architectural design (and this can be further specified) but which the Tudors did not build. In the case of a mock sense, however, there seems nothing informative to say about mock senses other than that they are not senses but might be mistaken for senses. But if we are unable to say anything more about what a mock sense is, it is unclear what the distinction between sense and mock sense amounts to, and the distinction cannot be put to work in solving the puzzle of empty names. A similar criticism applies to talk of mock names.

Instead of appealing to mock senses, a different option is to claim that an empty name does have sense. This claim entails that a sense can be the mode of presentation of a referent even if there is no referent. That consequence might not be as paradoxical as it initially seems to be. First of all, we should not think of the sense of a name as *generating* or *bringing about* what the name refers to. The sense does not determine the name's reference in that respect. Instead, the sense determines the name's reference in the following respect: If anything is referred to by the name, that sense specifies what it refers to. The sense of 'Excalibur' specifies what the name refers to, if it refers to anything at all (Bell 1990, p. 275). (For further discussion of whether any names can have sense but lack reference, see McDowell 1977; Dummett 1981b, pp. 129–38; Salmon 1990, pp. 235–46.)

8. Do names have senses?

We have seen that Frege makes the following claims. The meaning of a name consists in more than what (if anything) it refers to. One reason for this is that it can be informative to discover that one and the same entity is referred to by more than one name. In order to account for this informativeness, we have to distinguish between what the name refers to (the name's reference) and how it refers to it (the name's sense). Another reason for claiming that the meaning of a name consists in more than what (if anything) it refers to is that there are empty names: names that do not refer to anything. Since we can understand sentences containing such names, those names have sense (or perhaps mock sense) even if they lack reference. The sense of a name is then something which determines what, if anything, that name refers to; it is what needs to be grasped in order to understand the name; and it is what explains how there can be informative identity sentences involving names.

Saul Kripke presented a series of very important arguments against the view that names have senses, where a sense is construed as something that determines the reference of a name (Kripke 1972, lectures I and II). Kripke assumes that the sense of a name would be specified by some definite description or set of definite descriptions, expressions of the form 'the F'. He then proceeds to argue that names lack senses, given the above construal. (The following classification draws on Soames 2002, pp. 18–19.)

The first kind of argument Kripke offers is semantic: it denies that the meaning of a name is determined by any definite description or set of definite descriptions. Here is an example of this kind of argument, though not one of Kripke's. The University of Manchester has two physicists who won the Nobel Prize for co-discovering graphene, the world's thinnest material. They are Andre Geim and Konstantin Novoselov. Some people who competently use these names cannot provide descriptions which distinguish between these physicists. What they know about Andre Geim – that he is a physicist at the University of Manchester who won the Nobel Prize for co-discovering grapheme and was knighted for his research – is the same as what they know about Konstantin Novoselov. Nevertheless, these users of the names know that they are referring to different people when they use one of the names rather than the other. They use 'Andre Geim' as a proper name of Andre Geim, and 'Konstantin Novoselov' as a proper name of Konstantin Novoselov. (Cf. Kripke's example of Feynman and Gell-Mann: Kripke 1972, pp. 91–2.)

The second kind of argument that Kripke offers is epistemic: it denies that what a speaker refers to by his or her use of a name is determined by what definite description the speaker believes the bearer of that name satisfies. Kripke offers the following example. What is the sense of the name 'Kurt Gödel'? What definite description do you associate with the bearer of that name? You might associate it with the description 'the man who proved the incompleteness of arithmetic'. Yet suppose that Gödel did not himself prove the incompleteness of arithmetic and that someone else did, someone called 'Schmidt'. What happened, we will suppose, was that Gödel stole Schmidt's proof and passed his pioneering work off as his own. Given this situation, who does the description 'the man who discovered the incompleteness of arithmetic' pick out? It would pick out Schmidt, not Gödel. But, even in this situation, the name 'Gödel' still refers to Gödel. It is a situation in which Gödel did not discover the incompleteness of arithmetic (Kripke 1972, pp. 84–91).

The third kind of argument that Kripke offers is modal: it denies that it is a necessary truth that what a name means is determined by what the definite description (or descriptions) associated with the name picks out. What is the sense of the name 'Elvis Presley'? What definite descriptions are associated with that name? Perhaps there is a number of them, including the king of rock and roll, the original singer of 'Heartbreak Hotel', and the owner of the Graceland mansion. Yet consider how Elvis's life could have turned out. He might never have been a singer. On leaving high school, he might have been conscripted into the U.S. Army and died in the Korean War. It seems contingent that Elvis went on to do any of the things that he became widely known for. It follows that it is not a necessary truth that Elvis satisfies any of the above listed definite descriptions. (Cf. Kripke's example of Aristotle: Kripke 1972, p. 62.)

Kripke offers what he calls 'a better picture' of how we use names to refer to things. Suppose you chose to name something 'Jo'. In effect, you 'baptise' that object with the name 'Jo'. You then talk about Jo to other people. You pass on your use of the name to others. They use the name to talk to still further people about the same object. Like links on a chain, other people's use of the name refers to the same object because you introduced the name 'Jo' to refer to a certain object and subsequent users of the name intend to refer to the same object as the one that you were referring to. This causal link between your introduction of the name and these other people's use of the name is what is responsible for you and them referring to the same object by the use of the name 'Jo'. There need be no description commonly associated with that name in order for it to have a settled reference. Kripke writes:

> A rough statement of a theory might be the following: An initial 'baptism' takes place. Here the object may be named by ostension, or the reference of the name may be fixed by a description. When the name is 'passed from link to link', the receiver of the name must, I think, intend when he learns it to use it with the same reference as the man from whom he heard it. (Kripke 1972, p. 96)

Kripke also distinguishes between giving the meaning of a name and fixing the name's reference. For example, 'π' is introduced by the description 'the ratio of the circumference of a circle to its diameter'. Kripke thinks that 'π' is not being used as shorthand for that description. The description is used to introduce the name but not to give it its meaning (Kripke 1972, p. 62). That is to say, 'π' does not refer to the number 3.1459 . . . *because* it satisfies the description. By being a name of that number, it directly refers to it. A name does not refer to an object because of any description associated with that name. (For further discussion of Kripke's arguments, see Soames 2002, chapters 2 and 3; Ahmed 2007, chapter 2; Miller 2007, chapter 2 §2.5; Lycan 2008, pp. 39–43.)

9. Conclusion

This chapter began by distinguishing between names and descriptions, and specifically between names and definite descriptions – expressions that, in English, are of the form 'the F'. This distinction is intuitive but it is a substantive philosophical task to develop and defend it. Perhaps the root of the distinction lies in the idea that names refer whereas descriptions describe. The task then is to say what it is for an expression to refer. Mill explains this in terms of an expression's merely labelling an object. Such an expression, a name, refers to a particular object, but this is its only contribution to the meaning of any sentences in which it occurs.

By contrast with Mill's view, Frege thinks that there is more to the meaning of a name than to what it refers. One of his principal arguments for this is his argument from informative identity sentences. The premise of his argument is uncontroversial. The conclusion he draws is philosophically interesting but controversial. The premise is that there can be pairs of names which refer to the same object but which differ in the information that they supply. Suppose that 'a' and 'b' refer to the same object. Nevertheless 'a' and 'b' may differ in the information that they convey. 'a = a' and 'b = b' each convey little information, whereas 'a = b' may convey more information. As Frege puts it, these sentences differ in their cognitive value. The conclusion that he draws is that there is more to the meaning of 'a' and of 'b' than what objects they refer to. These names each also have a sense. Moreover, the senses of these names determine that these names refer to the same object. So, unlike Mill, Frege thinks that a name refers to a given object *because* that name is associated with a certain sense. The reference of a name is then mediated by the sense that name has.

In the introduction, (Q1) asked what the difference is between those marks or noises that have meaning and those which lack it. Frege's work suggests an answer: it is the distinction between marks or noises that express senses and those which do not.

Frege has little to tell us, however, about how any marks or noises get to express senses or how particular marks or noises which they express have the particular senses that they do. He also says no more about what is involved in understanding an expression or sentence than that it involves grasping the sense involved. This metaphor remains undeveloped and unexplained. So (Q2), a question of why a given expression has the meaning that it does rather than another meaning, and (Q3), a question about what it is to understand an expression, are not answered. Similarly, (Q4), a question about the relation between the meaning, use and understanding of expressions, goes unanswered. Kripke's objections to Frege's views about the senses of names focus on this relation. If knowing the sense of a name is a matter of knowing some identifying information about the bearer of the name, then Kripke claims that a person can understand and competently use a name without knowing any such sense.

Questions for discussion

Question 1

Frege's claim that '6 ÷ 3' and '√4' have different senses has some initial plausibility because we use different means (different mathematical calculations) to work out what each of them refers to. This seems to be connected to the fact that these mathematical expressions are semantically complex: they contain parts that themselves have meaning. For instance, '6 ÷ 3' contains the parts '6', '÷' and '3' and each of those parts have meaning. But how plausible does this view seem in the case of names such as 'Aristotle' or 'Ovid'? Those names are not semantically complex in the way that the above mathematical expressions are.

Question 2

Which of the following sentences have the same sense? Which principles should guide our thinking?

    (A) Bill hit the window with the ball.
    (B) The window was hit by Bill with the ball.
    (C) The window had the property of being hit by Bill with the ball.
    (D) It is not the case that it is not that case that Bill hit the window with the ball.

Question 3

'Shakespeare's plays were not written by him but by a different person with the same name'. Does the preceding sentence make sense? Is there even a sense in which it could have been true? What would (a) Frege and (b) Kripke say about these issues?

Question 4

In 'On Sense and Reference', Frege claims that the sense associated with a name may vary from one person to another (Frege 1892a, p. 58 footnote). If so, the sense of sentences using that name may vary from one person to another.

Yet in the same paper Frege also claims that 'one can hardly deny that mankind has a common store of thoughts which is transmitted from one generation to another'. Are Frege's claims compatible?

Further reading

Dummett, Michael (1981a) *Frege: Philosophy of Language* chapters 4–6.

Frege, Gottlob (1892a) 'On Sense and Reference'.

Kripke, Saul (1980) *Naming and Necessity* lectures I and II.

—(2008) 'Frege's Theory of Sense and Reference: Some Exegetical Notes'.

Linsky, Leonard (1983) *Oblique Contexts* chapter 1.

Mendelsohn, Richard L. (2005) *The Philosophy of Gottlob Frege* chapter 3.

Miller, Alexander (2007) *Philosophy of Language* chapter 1.

Noonan, Harold (2001) *Frege: A Critical Introduction* chapter 5.

Soames, Scott (2010) *Philosophy of Language* chapter 1 §1.1.

Taylor, Kenneth (1998) *Truth and Meaning: An Introduction to the Philosophy of Language* chapter I §§1–3.

Weiner, Joan (2004) *Frege Explained* chapter 6.

Wiggins, David (1976) 'Frege's Problem of the Morning Star and the Evening Star'.

2

Frege on Predication

---

1. Introduction

In Chapter 1, we discussed Frege's views of the meaning of names. Frege argues that if all that there is to the meaning of a name is the object that the name refers to, then there is a problem about how there can be informative identity sentences. For example, in 1990 the Central Intelligence Agency realized that there was a traitor in its ranks. They called this unknown person 'Nightmover'. In 1993, they identified this person as one of their analysts, Aldrich Ames. Now, if all there is to the meaning of a name is what it refers to, then sentences such as 'Nightmover is Nightmover' and 'Nightmover is Aldrich Ames' would have the same meaning, given that Nightmover is Aldrich Ames. In 1990, the CIA would have found what the first sentence said to be obvious, whereas they would have found what the second sentence said to be far from obvious. This seems to imply that the two sentences differ in meaning. It further follows that there is more to the meaning of a name than what it refers to. To account for this, Frege distinguished between the sense of a name and its reference. In terms of our example, 'Nightmover' and 'Aldrich Ames' have the same reference but differ in sense. It is because of this difference in sense that 'Nightmover is Nightmover' and 'Nightmover is Aldrich Ames' differ in informativeness, even though they are both about the same person.

In this chapter, we will assess Frege's views on another class of linguistic expressions, namely predicates. A traditional distinction in grammar distinguishes two main parts of a sentence or clause: the subject and the predicate. The subject is what the sentence is about, whereas the predicate says something about what the subject picks out. So in the sentence 'Ned snores', 'Ned' is the subject whereas 'snores' is the predicate. Different grammatical rules of combination govern subjects and predicates. Predicates include single-place (or monadic) predicates such as '. . . snores' and many-place (or polyadic) predicates such as '. . . is between . . . and . . .' But what exactly is a predicate? And what are predicates for? Are there any important ways in which predicates are similar to names? We have already considered Frege's views on the sense and reference of names. In this chapter, we will see how he extends this distinction to the case of predicates. There are important issues to do with why Frege extends the distinction to predicates and what the consequences are.

2. The sense and reference of predicates

Frege has two reasons for extending the distinction between sense and reference from names to predicates. Both reasons arise from his view that sentences themselves have sense and reference. We will consider that view in detail in Chapter 3. For now we will see why it leads Frege to think that predicates also have sense and reference.

First, we cannot form a sentence simply by juxtaposing proper names. If we were to do that, all that we would get is a list such as 'Socrates, Plato, Archimedes'. Although each of the names in the list has a sense, such a list does not form a sentence. But if we introduce a three-place predicate we can form a sentence such as 'Socrates outrank both Plato and Archimedes'. So, it seems that a predicate has to have a sense in order for a sentence to have a sense.

Second, Frege claims that the sense of a sentence is determined by the senses of its component expressions and that the reference of a sentence is determined by the references of its component expressions. Now consider the following pair of sentences:

(1) Plato was a philosopher.
(2) Plato smoked cigars.

The name 'Plato' occurs in both (1) and (2) with the same sense. But (1) and (2) have different senses. It follows the senses of (1) and (2) cannot be determined solely by the sense of the name 'Plato'. The predicative parts of those sentences must also have senses. Moreover, they must have different senses to account for the difference in senses between (1) and (2).

We can think of the predicate in (1) as consisting of what remains when the name 'Plato' is removed from the sentence. (More generally, an *n*-place predicate is the result of deleting *n* occurrences of or names in a sentence.) Since what is left has a 'gap' where the name was, Frege indicates this by using Greek letters as gap signs. So he would write the predicates in (1) and (2) as 'ξ was a philosopher' and 'ξ smoked cigars'.

Since 'Plato' has the same sense in (1) and (2), it has the same reference in each sentence. According to Frege, however, (1) and (2) have different references because they have different truth values. (1) is true, whereas (2) is false. It follows that the references of (1) and (2) cannot be solely determined by the reference of 'Plato'. The predicative parts of those sentences must also have references. That is, 'ξ was a philosopher' and 'ξ smoked cigars' must each have a reference. These references must differ in order to account for the difference in reference between (1) and (2).

Frege calls the reference of a predicate a 'concept'. He uses this term in a technical sense. (Throughout this chapter we will follow this usage.) Concepts can be characterized in the following five respects.

First, as Frege uses the term, a concept is not a mental entity. It is an abstract entity: it is neither mental nor physical. Moreover, a concept is a mind-independent entity. There may be concepts that no one ever thinks of just as there may be objects that no one ever thinks of.

Second, just as an object is whatever is referred to by a name, so too a concept is whatever is referred to by a predicate. So, for example, the concept ξ *is a philosopher* is the reference of the predicate 'ξ was a philosopher', the concept ξ *is a planet* is the reference of the predicate 'ξ is a planet' and so on.

Third, Frege talks of an object 'falling under' a given concept if the corresponding predicate applies to that object. Socrates falls under the concept *being a philosopher* if the predicate 'ξ is a philosopher' applies to him, and Neptune falls under the concept *planet* if the predicate 'ξ is a planet' applies to it. This relation of *falling under* is asymmetric: Socrates falls under that concept; the concept does not fall under him.

Fourth, until now we have talked of Frege's taking predicates to refer to concepts. This is an oversimplification. He takes one-place (or monadic) predicates to refer to concepts and many-place (or polyadic) predicates to refer to relations. For example, 'ξ is larger than ζ' refers to the dyadic relation of *being larger than*. Since relations will not raise any special problems of their own, it will suffice for our purposes to understand all subsequent talk of concepts to apply to both concepts and relations.

Fifth, the distinction between objects and concepts is exclusive (nothing is both an object and a concept) and exhaustive (everything is either an object or a concept). (For more on the metaphysics of concepts, see Currie 1984.)

We can illustrate Frege's theory of the sense and reference of predicates, and see how it compares with his theory of the sense and reference of names, in the following way:

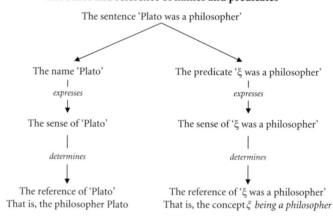

The sense and reference of names and predicates

The sentence 'Plato was a philosopher'

The name 'Plato' — The predicate 'ξ was a philosopher'
expresses — *expresses*
The sense of 'Plato' — The sense of 'ξ was a philosopher'
determines — *determines*
The reference of 'Plato' — The reference of 'ξ was a philosopher'
That is, the philosopher Plato — That is, the concept ξ *being a philosopher*

Frege thinks that the notions of concept, object, function and judgement are indefinable because they are logically simple and not further analysable. Still, he says that they can be informally elucidated:

> One cannot require that everything shall be defined, any more than one can require that a chemist shall decompose every substance. What is

simple cannot be decomposed, and what is logically simple cannot have a
proper definition. . . ; there is nothing for it but to lead the reader or
hearer, by means of hints, to understand the words as is intended. (Frege
1892b, p. 193)

What is it for concepts to be identical? Frege thought that there is a relation
between concepts that is distinct from, but analogous to, the relation of
identity between objects (Frege 1894, p. 320). Let's call this relation 'quasi-
identity'. Concepts are quasi-identical if and only if the predicates that refer to
them have the same extension. That is, concepts are quasi-identical if and only
if whatever the one predicate applies to, the other predicate applies to, and vice
versa. For example, since the predicates 'ξ is a member of the Beatles' and 'ξ is a
member of the largest selling pop group of the 1960s' apply to exactly the same
things, these predicates refer to quasi-identical concepts.

There are two things to note about this. First, just as names with different
senses can refer to the same object, predicates with different senses can refer to
the same concept. Second, the predicates in question can be substituted for
one another in a sentence without change of truth value. For example,
substituting 'ξ is a member of the Beatles' for 'ξ is a member of the largest
selling pop group of the 1960s' in (3) yields (4):

(3) Anyone who is a member of the largest selling pop group of the 1960s
     has a hefty tax bill.
(4) Anyone who is a member of the Beatles has a hefty tax bill.

(3) and (4) do not differ in truth value.

Frege thinks that even self-contradictory predicates, such as 'ξ is both round
and not round' or 'ξ is tall if and only if ξ is not tall', refer to a concept. Predicates
with the same extension refer to the quasi-same concept. It is vacuously true
that predicates with an empty extension have the same extension as each other.
Consequently, self-contradictory predicates refer to the quasi-same concept.

Frege's theory faces the following puzzle. On the face of it, a name
cannot constitute the whole of a predicate, but it can form part of one, as in
'Aristotle was a pupil of Plato'. But consider the following apparent counter-
examples, (5–7):

(5) The U.S. President is Barack Obama.
(6) The square root of 16 is 4.
(7) The morning star is the planet Venus.

In each of (5–7), it seems as if a proper name constitutes the whole of the predicate. Moreover, each of these sentences is reversible. For example, (5) could be written as (5*) without changing its sense:

(5*)   Barack Obama is the U.S. President.

Frege's response to this puzzle is to distinguish between the 'is' of identity and the 'is' of predication (Frege 1892b, pp. 193–5). Each of (5–7) involve the 'is' of identity, whereas (8) and (9) involve the 'is' of predication:

(8)   A ripe tomato is red.
(9)   The toast is burning.

Where the word 'is' in a sentence is functioning as the 'is' of identity, then it can be replaced in the sentence by the phrase 'is identical to'. By contrast, where the word 'is' in a sentence is functioning as the 'is' of predication, then this replacement cannot be made.

Another indicator of the distinction between these two meanings of the word 'is' is that (8) and (9) are not reversible whereas (5–7) are. (5–7) might be more fully written as:

(5a)   The U.S. President *is identical to Barack Obama.*
(6a)   The square root of 16 *is identical to 4.*
(7a)   The morning star *is identical to the planet Venus.*

The italicized part of each of the above sentences is the predicative part of the sentence. So, for example, (5a) involves the predicate 'ξ is identical to Barack Obama'. In this way, then, Frege can show that (5–7) are not counter-examples to the claim that a name cannot constitute the whole of a predicate.

3. Functions

In §2, we saw that Frege characterizes concepts in several ways. In this section, we will consider a further key way in which he characterizes them. This is by his generalizing from the notion of a mathematical function.

A function is a pattern of correlation between inputs and outputs. Take the arithmetical function that squares numbers. If the number 2 is inputted, this function outputs the number 4. If the number 3 is inputted, the function outputs the number 9. Mathematicians use different terminology to express this idea. Instead of inputs they talk of *arguments*. Instead of outputs they talk of *values*. Take, for example, 4^2. Here the function is the square function. The argument is the number 4. The value of the argument for that function is the number 16. Take 5^2 as another example. Here we have the same function. The argument is the number 5, and the value of the argument for that function is the number 25. Take 6^2 as another example. We have the same function, only the argument is the number 6, and the value of the argument for that function is the number 36. More generally, a function is a pattern of correlation between an argument (or arguments) and a value.

The following table summarizes these results:

Some arguments and values of the function *square of*		
	4^2	5^2	6^2
Function	ξ^2	ξ^2	ξ^2
Argument	4	5	6
Value	16	25	36

The expression '4^2' refers to the number 16, and the expression '5^2' refers to the number 25. (For an example where we have more than one argument, consider $7 + 4 = 11$. Here the function is the plus function. Given 7 and 4 as arguments, that function gives 11 as the value.) A function can be singled out only by patterns displayed in complex expressions. The examples in the table have a common structure with the arguments 4, 5 and 6, respectively. It is the common structure to these examples that is the function. (See Kneale and Kneale 1962, chapter VIII §2; Noonan 2001, pp. 136–8.)

Frege says that a concept is 'a function whose value is always a truth value' (Frege 1891, p. 15). Take the concept ξ *is a philosopher*. Suppose we take Plato as its argument. Then the value of that concept for that argument is the truth value True. Take the same concept but now suppose we take John Wayne as its argument. Then the value of that concept for that argument is the False. In short, the concept ξ *is a philosopher* maps Plato onto the True and John Wayne onto the False. (As we will see in chapter 3 §3, Frege takes truth values to be objects whose names are 'the True' and 'the False'.)

The following table summarizes these results:

Concepts, arguments and values		
Concept	ξ *is a philosopher*	ξ *is a philosopher*
Argument	Plato	John Wayne
Value	the True	the False

The value of the concept ξ *is a philosopher* with Plato as its argument is identical to what Frege says the sentence 'Plato is a philosopher' refers to, namely, the True. (Frege's view that sentences refer to truth values, the True or the False, is explained and evaluated in Chapter 3 §3. For now we will go along with his view.)

Frege takes there to be a hierarchy of concepts. For example, there are first-level concepts, such as the concept ξ *is red* or the concept ξ *is a metal.* A first-level concept is a function which maps every object to a truth value. So every first-level concept is defined for any object. This is Frege's 'principle of completude' (van Heijenoort 1986, p. 32). There are also second-level concepts. A second-level concept differs from a first-level concept in what it takes as arguments. We have seen that a first-level concept takes objects as its arguments and maps every object to a truth value. A second-level concept takes concepts as arguments and maps every concept to a truth value. The existential quantifier denotes one such second-level concept. That quantifier maps every non-empty first-level concept to the True and every empty first-level concept to the False.

In order to have a value, a function has to be supplied with an argument or arguments. Frege thinks of functions as being 'incomplete' or 'unsaturated'. They require objects, things which are complete or saturated, to complete them. In addition, he thinks that expressions that refer to functions ('function signs' or 'functors', as they are called) are also incomplete. Functors characteristically have gap signs (or, equivalently, free variables such as 'x', 'y', 'z' or other place-holders). Frege admits that:

> 'Complete' and 'unsaturated' are of course only figures of speech; but all that I wish or am able to do here is to give hints. (Frege 1892b, p. 205)

And that:

> I must confine myself to hinting at what I have in mind by means of a metaphorical expression, and here I rely on my reader's agreeing to meet me half-way. (Frege 1904, p. 115)

It is questionable, however, how helpful these figures of speech and hints are (see Marshall 1953; Black 1954).

There are, then, three levels of incompleteness to consider (Diller 1993b):

(A) There is incompleteness at the level of predicates (or concept words): these are linguistic expressions that refer to concepts.
(B) There is incompleteness at the level of senses of predicates.
(C) There is incompleteness at the level of concepts: the referents of predicates.

Let's consider each level in turn.

(A) A predicate, such as 'ξ is a philosopher', is incomplete. It also seems to be a function which maps the name 'Plato' (say) to the sentence 'Plato is a philosopher'. Now Frege does not explicitly say that predicates and function signs generally are themselves functions, although he seems to be committed to saying it. He does, however, explicitly acknowledge the incompleteness of function signs:

> The expression of a function *needs completion* and *is unsaturated*. The letter 'x' only serves to keep places open for a numerical sign to be put in and complete the expression; and thus it enables us to recognize the special kind of need for completion that constitutes the peculiar nature of the function . . . . (Frege 1893, §1. See also Geach 1963, pp. 143–4)

(B) The sense of a predicate is also incomplete and it also seems to be a function. Take the predicate 'ξ is a philosopher' again. Its sense seems to be a function from the sense of (say) the name 'Plato' to the sense of the sentence 'Plato is a philosopher'. Frege says this about the incompleteness of the sense of predicates:

> Not all parts of a thought can be complete; at least one must be 'unsaturated', or predicative; otherwise they would not hold together. For example, the sense of the phrase 'the number 2' does not hold together with that of the expression 'the concept *prime number*' without a link. We supply such a link in the sentence 'the number 2 falls under the concept

> *prime number*; it is contained in the words 'falls under', which need to be completed in two ways – by a subject and an accusative; and only because their senses are thus 'unsaturated' are they capable of serving as a link. (Frege 1892b, p. 54)

(C) The referent of a predicate is also incomplete and it is a further function (namely, a concept). Frege says this about the incompleteness of functions:

> The argument does not belong with the function, but goes together with the function to make up a complete whole; for the function by itself must be called incomplete, in need of supplementation, or 'unsaturated'. And in this respect functions differ fundamentally from numbers. (Frege 1891, p. 6)

On Frege's account of predicates, then, there seem to be three different kinds of functions. Predicates themselves – that is, linguistic expressions – seem to be functions. The senses of predicates seem to be functions. And the referents of predicates – that is, concepts – are functions.

Frege replaces the traditional subject-predicate analysis of sentences with a function-argument account. Consider a sentence such as (10):

(10) Someone is loved by everyone.

Sentence (10) involves multiple generality: It involves more than one expression of generality. Notice that (10) entails (11):

(11) Someone is loved by at least one person.

How can that entailment be accounted for? One of the breakthroughs achieved by Frege's replacement of the subject-predicate analysis with the function-argument analysis was that it enables him to give an account of the validity of arguments featuring sentences involving multiple generality. Frege treats expressions of generality as quantifier expressions. These are expressions which, like names, combine with one-place predicates to form sentences. The entities that these expressions refer to are second-level functions. They are functions from concepts (the references of one-place predicates) to truth values. For example, the reference of the existential quantifier is the following second-level function: the function which (a) has the truth value True when it takes as argument a concept which has the truth value True for at least one object, and (b) has the truth value False when it takes as argument any other function from objects to truth values.

Sentence (10) would be represented as (10*):

(10*) $\exists x \, \forall y \, (y \text{ loves } x)$

Sentence (10*) is formed by taking the two-place predicate 'ξ loves ζ' and combining it with the universal quantifier to form the predicate '$\forall y \, (y$ loves $\zeta)$'. That predicate is true of something if and only if everything loves it. Combining this predicate with the existential predicate yields (10*). (10*) is true if and only if there is something which everyone loves.

　　Sentence (11) would be represented as (11*):

(11*) $\exists x \, \exists y \, (x \text{ loves } y)$

Sentence (11*) is true if and only if someone loves something or other. Given these ways of representing (10) and (11), plus the rules of inference for $\exists$ and $\forall$, it can be proved that (10) entails (11). The result is that Frege's account of generality, which is delivered by his function-argument analysis of sentences, solves a general problem which the subject-predicate analysis did not (Dummett 1981a, chapter 2).

　　In addition to this, Frege's claim that predicates and their senses are incomplete entities offers some explanation of the unity of sentences. A sentence is not a mere list of names. A sequence of expressions forms a sentence only if at least one of those expressions is predicative and so is incomplete. A thought is not a mere series of senses. A sequence of senses forms a thought only if at least one of those senses is incomplete. The part-whole structure of thoughts is also what makes it possible for us to have novel thoughts and to understand sentences that we have never heard before. (For further arguments for Frege's theory of predication, see Green 2006.)

　　These considerations in favour of Frege's account of predication have to be balanced against a number of difficulties. Perhaps the most powerful of these is a paradox that faces Frege's theory of concepts. We will address this paradox in the next section.

4. The paradox of the concept *horse*

If there is anything to the claim that a predicate, such as the predicate 'ξ is a horse', is a referring expression, then we should be able to specify what it refers to. We will see in this section that this reasonable point leads Frege's theory of predication into paradox.

Frege takes the distinction between objects and concepts to be 'a distinction of the highest importance' (Frege 1879, p. 54). The distinction is between two fundamental types of entities. It is exhaustive (everything is one or the other) and exclusive (nothing is both). Names refer to objects; predicates refer to concepts. Now take an example drawn from Kerry, a contemporary critic of Frege. Consider (12):

(12) The concept *horse* is a concept.

Assuming that there are concepts, (12) seems to be true. Just as the city of Berlin is a city and the planet Venus is a planet, so too the concept *horse* is a concept.

Now (12) contains the noun phrase 'the concept *horse*'. But, on Frege's own view, a noun phrase governed by the definite article ('the') counts as a name, and a name refers to an object (Frege 1884, §51. See also §57 and the footnotes to §§66 and 67). It follows that 'the concept *horse*' refers to an object. On the principle that if 'a' refers, it refers to *a*, then if 'the concept *horse*' refers, it refers to the concept *horse*. It follows that the concept *horse* is an object. According to Frege, whatever is an object is not a concept. Frege draws the paradoxical conclusion that the concept *horse* is not a concept.

The paradox arises with respect to many of the claims that Frege wants to make about concepts. For example, he says that concepts are unsaturated. But the predicate 'ξ is a concept' is a first-level predicate. That means that it applies only to objects. Yet an object is saturated, not unsaturated. To take another example, Frege says that a concept is a function whose value is always a truth value. Yet 'ξ is a concept' is only satisfied by objects, and objects are not functions.

It should also be noted that the paradox is not confined to concepts. As Frege realized, it also applies to relations and functions generally. For example, the expression 'the relation of an object to the concept it falls under' will refer to an object, and so *the relation of an object to the concept it falls under* is an object, not a relation.

In addition to this paradox, Frege's theory of concepts faces a further objection (Marshall 1955, p. 359; Searle 1969, p. 97). If it refers to anything, we would expect 'ξ is a horse' to refer to the concept *horse*. Presumably 'the concept horse' also refers to the concept *horse*. Given this, we should be able to substitute 'the concept *horse*' for 'ξ is a horse' in (13) without change of truth value:

(13) Silver Blaze is a horse.

But if we make the substitution, the result does not make sense, let alone preserve truth value:

(14) Silver Blaze the concept *horse*.

The objection concludes that what has gone wrong is that we have assumed that 'the concept *horse*' refers to a concept. Frege is fully aware of this line of argument and comments that:

> the behaviour of the concept is essentially predicative, even where something is being asserted about it; consequently it can be replaced there only by another concept, never by an object. (Frege 1891, p. 50)

What this means is that, because 'ξ is a horse' and 'the concept horse' cannot be substituted for one another in sentences without change of truth value, Frege himself claims that 'the references of the two expressions are essentially different' (Frege 1891, p. 50).

We will not assess this line of argument here. We will encounter another line of argument in Chapter 3 §3 which relies on the assumption that co-referring expressions can be substituted for each other in sentences without change of truth value, and we will address that assumption there. (Wiggins 1984; MacBride 2011 address the line of argument concerning predicates such as 'ξ is a horse' and noun phrases such as 'the concept *horse*'.) Here we will concentrate on some responses to the paradox of the concept *horse*.

The paradox is significant because Frege wants to say various things about concepts (such as that they are incomplete, that they are referred to by predicates and so on) and yet he cannot do so on pain of paradox. In 'On Concept and Object', he tries to resolve matters:

> It must indeed be recognized that here we are confronted by an awkwardness of language, which I admit cannot be avoided, if we say that the concept *horse* is not a concept, [footnote omitted] whereas, *e.g.,* the city of Berlin is a city and the volcano Vesuvius is a volcano. Language is here in a predicament that justifies the departure from custom. The peculiarity of our case is indicated by Kerry himself, by means of the quotation-marks around 'horse'; I use italics to the same end. There was no reason to mark out the words 'Berlin' and 'Vesuvius' in a similar way. In logical discussions one quite often needs to assert something about a concept, and to express this in the form usual for such assertions, *viz.*, to make what is asserted of the concept into the content of the grammatical predicate. Consequently, one would expect that the reference of the grammatical subject would be the concept; but the concept

> as such cannot play this part, in view of its predicative nature; it must first be converted into an object, [footnote omitted] or, speaking more precisely, represented by an object. We designate this object by prefixing the words 'the concept'; e.g.
> 'The concept *man* is not empty'
> Here the first three words are to be regarded as a proper name, [footnote omitted] which can no more be used predicatively than 'Berlin' or 'Vesuvius'. (Frege 1892b, pp. 196–7)

Frege blames the failure of language (an 'awkwardness' of it) for generating the paradox. It is not, however, an awkwardness peculiar to natural languages because the same failing would seem to afflict any artificial language with sufficient expressive power (sufficient to form noun phrases that refer to concepts). For Frege, only saturated things (names) can refer to saturated things (objects), and only unsaturated things (predicates and functors) can refer to unsaturated things (concepts, relations and functions). Frege makes a plea for understanding:

> By a kind of necessity of language, my expressions, taken literally, sometimes miss my thought; I mention an object, when what I intend is a concept. I fully realize that in such cases I was relying upon a reader who would be ready to meet me half-way – who does not begrudge a pinch of salt. (Frege 1892b, p. 204)

Frege's suggested solution is that the expression 'the concept *horse*' refers to an object and that that object represents what is referred to by the predicate 'ξ is a horse'. This representation relation enables us to appear to be talking about concepts, whereas in fact we are talking about objects. Frege's solution, however, seems obscure and unsatisfactory. For one thing the paradox resurfaces. The solution requires claiming that, for example, a certain object represents the concept *horse*. Yet the expression 'the concept *horse*' occurs in that very claim where it is supposed to refer to a concept, not an object – and so the paradox returns.

Here is a further difficulty. Frege says that concepts are incomplete. He also says that 'what is asserted about a concept can never be asserted about an object' (Frege 1892b, p. 200) and that 'the assertion that is made about a concept does not suit an object' (Frege 1892b, p. 201). But this prevents him from saying of any object that supposedly represents a concept that *it* is incomplete. Now perhaps when we say of such an object that it is incomplete, the predicate has a different sense to the one when we say that concepts are incomplete. The problem with this suggestion, however, is that we are then at a loss to say what this different sense is (Black 1954, pp. 248–9. For further problems, see Parsons 1986, §VI).

In his paper 'Comments on Sense and Reference', Frege provides another solution to the paradox. He suggests that we can refer to a concept with a 'what' clause. We can use the clause 'what "ξ is a horse" refers to', whereas before we ineptly used the expression 'the concept *horse*'. What-clauses can also be used predicatively. We can use the clause to form the sentence 'Red Rum is "what 'ξ is a horse' refers to"', that is to say that Red Rum is a horse. Here is what Frege says:

> . . . the relation of equality between objects cannot be conceived as holding between concepts too, but there is a corresponding relation for concepts. It follows that the word 'the same' that is used to designate the former relation between objects cannot properly be used to designate the latter as well. If we try to use it to do this, the only recourse we really have is to say, 'The concept Ø is the same as the concept X' and in saying this we have of course named a relation between objects, [Footnote: these objects have the names 'the concept Ø' and 'the concept X'] where what is intended is a relation between concepts. We have the same case if we say, 'The meaning of the concept-word *A* is the same as that of the concept-word *B*'. Indeed we should really outlaw the expression 'the meaning of the concept-word *A*' because the definite article before 'meaning' points to an object and belies the predicative nature of a concept. It would be better to confine ourselves to 'what the concept-word *A* means', for this at any rate is to be used predicatively: 'Jesus is, what the concept-word "man" means' is the sense of 'Jesus is a man'. (Frege 1892–1895, pp. 121–2)

Peter Geach and Michael Dummett have independently offered similar interpretations of Frege's argument in the above passage. Their thinking is as follows. The sentence 'The concept *horse* is not a concept' is the negation of the sentence 'The concept *horse* is a concept'. The latter sentence seems to be constructed out of the name 'the concept *horse*' and the predicate 'ξ is a concept'. It is this putative construction which generates the paradox. According to Geach and Dummett, however, the sentence is not in fact constructed in that way (Geach 1972, pp. 56–7; Dummett 1981a, pp. 211–22). First, they claim that it is false that 'the concept *horse*' is a name. Second, they claim that it is false that 'ξ is a concept' is a genuine predicate. Take these claims in turn.

It is natural to think that 'the concept *horse*' is a name. Geach argues against that line of thought. To begin with, he argues that any referring expression 'Φ' is equivalent to the expression 'Φ is what "Φ" refers to'. So, for example, 'Socrates' is equivalent to the expression 'Socrates is what "Socrates" refers to'. To take another example, a predicate such as 'ξ is a fish' is equivalent to 'ξ is what "ξ is a fish" refers to'. Applying this treatment to the expression 'the concept *horse*' yields the predicate 'ξ is what "the concept *horse*" refers to'. Geach infers from this result that 'the concept *horse*' is not a name, but a predicate.

It is natural to think that 'ξ is a concept' is a predicate. Consider first 'ξ is an object'. That is a genuine predicate. If any non-empty name is put in its argument-place, the result will be a true sentence. If that is how things are with 'ξ is an object', it is natural to think that something similar is to be said about 'ξ is a concept'. We might think that it is a genuine predicate so that if any expression referring to a concept is put in its argument-place, the result will be a true sentence. (And if a name is put in its argument-place, the result will be a false sentence.)

Dummett, however, sees this line of thought as leading to the paradox of the concept *horse*. He suggests that 'ξ is a concept' is not a genuine predicate. Mutually incompatible requirements are being made about this supposed predicate. On the one hand, it is required to apply to concepts. On the other hand, like other first-level predicates, it is required to apply to objects. In its place, Dummett offers the predicate 'Φ is something which everything either is or is not' (Dummett 1981a, pp. 216–17). This predicate can also be expressed as:

(15) $(\forall x)\,(\Phi x \lor \neg\Phi x)$

The predicate Dummett devises is a second-level predicate. It is a predicate such that, if any expression referring to a concept is put in its argument-place, the result will be a true sentence.

What Geach and Dummett have claimed so far, then, is that 'the concept *horse*' is not a name, but a predicate, and that 'ξ is a concept' is not a genuine predicate and is to be replaced by 'Φ is something which everything either is or is not'. Those claims together entail that such apparent sentences as 'The concept *horse* is a concept' or 'What "ξ is a horse" refers to is a concept' are not genuine sentences. What we might have taken those apparent sentences to be conveying is instead conveyed by the (true) sentences 'A horse is something that everything either is or is not' and 'What "ξ is a horse" refers to is something that everything either is or is not', respectively (Dummett

1981a, pp. 216–17). Supposedly the paradox of the concept *horse* does not then arise.

One weakness in Dummett's solution is that it makes it impossible to formulate generic claims about functions. For example, a sentence such as 'Everything which is not an object is a function' makes essential use of the generic predicate 'is a function'. So too does 'Every first-level function is a function and so is every second-level function'. Although Dummett seeks to ban expressions such as 'ξ is a function', there is no other means to convey what those sentences seek to express (Diller 1993a, pp. 348–50). Again, consider the sentence 'Every concept is unsaturated'. According to Dummett's proposal, that would be construed as:

(16) $(\forall \Phi) \, [(\forall x) \, (\Phi x \lor \neg \Phi x) \rightarrow \Phi$ is unsaturated$]$

The problem here is that the predicate 'ξ is unsaturated' is a first-level predicate: It applies only to objects. And so both the original sentence and (16) turn out to be meaningless, despite the fact that the original sentence belongs to Frege's theory (Priest 1995, p. 201).

A further weakness is that Dummett's proposal contravenes Frege's requirement that any expression belongs to no more than one syntactic category. For example, Frege says that names refer to objects. It follows that the two-place predicate 'ξ refers to ζ' is a first-order predicate: it takes names and objects as its arguments. But, Frege also wants to say that concept-words refer to concepts:

> To every concept-word, or proper name, there corresponds as a rule a sense and a *Bedeutung* [reference], as I use these words. (Frege 1892–5, p. 118)

The problem that emerges is that Frege is unable to make generalizations about concepts and objects – even to say that they are different (Diller 1993a, pp. 356–8; Priest 1995, pp. 201–2).

Lastly, Frege claimed that a what-clause should be understood as a predicate. Now the what-clauses in such sentences as 'what "ξ is a horse" refers to is one of Frege's examples of a concept' or 'what "ξ is a horse" refers to is not an object' cannot be understood as predicates. It follows that those apparently true sentences turn out to be meaningless. That is an implausible consequence (Priest 1995, p. 201).

What should we make of the paradox of the concept *horse*? A number of issues face us. First, there is the issue of whether the paradox is the product of some deficiency of the language in which we are describing Frege's system. We have seen that Frege himself in one place suggested that it was. Now suppose that the paradox does not arise by some defect of language, but is generated by Frege's own system namely, by the fact that Frege needs to talk about concepts to state his theory, but his own theory says that he cannot do so. A second issue is then whether this paradox is a trifling one produced by some quirk of Frege's system, or whether it reveals a deep and important problem that faces any attempt to describe the workings of language. This is an issue concerning what can or cannot be expressed in language and whether any theory can coherently state such limits (cf. Priest 1995, p. 245). A third issue will then be whether this problem is solvable and, if it is, how much of Frege's original system can remain in place. (For further discussion of the paradox of the concept *horse*, see Searle 1969 chapter 5 §5.1; Dudman 1972, 1976; Furth 1968; MacBride 2006, 2011; Parsons 1986; Wright 2001.)

5. Vagueness and the sorites paradox

The paradox of the concept *horse* is a problem that arises within Frege's theory of concepts and predication given certain assumptions that his theory makes. A theory of predication which does not make all of those assumptions would not generate that problem. In this section, we will consider a problem that faces any theory of predication. This is the problem posed by vague predicates.

Frege thinks that a first-level function, a function from objects to other objects, is well-defined only if it has a value for every argument (Frege 1893, §56). He denies that there are any functions ('partial functions', as they are known) which fail to map every object onto something. The function ξ *is a philosopher* is, on the face of it, a first-level function. According to Frege, this function will map every object to certain objects, namely to the True or to the False. It will map not only John Wayne, but also, for example, the number 9 and Mount Everest, to the False. As Frege put it, all concepts have sharp boundaries: For every first-level concept, every object either falls under that concept or it does not (Frege 1903, p. 159). The corresponding predicate 'ξ is a philosopher' will map the name 'Plato' to the true sentence 'Plato is philosopher', and it will map each of the names 'John Wayne', '9' and 'Mount Everest' to the corresponding false sentences.

The predicate 'ξ is a philosopher' is vague. It clearly applies to some people. It clearly does not apply to others. But the predicate does not clearly apply to certain other people. And it does not clearly not apply to those people. For example, are Chomsky, Dostoevsky, Alberti or Tenzin Gyatso (the current Dalai Lama) philosophers? For the most part, we hesitate to say one way or the other. To use some terminology, we experience semantic indecision in cases of semantic indeterminacy. That is, there are cases where it is not clear whether 'ξ is a philosopher' maps any of the above names to true sentences or whether it maps them to false sentences. Accordingly, it is not clear whether the function ξ *is a philosopher* does in fact map every object to the True or to the False. Given that a first-level function is well-defined only if it has a value for every argument, there is then reason to deny that there is such a function as ξ *is a philosopher*. Moreover, this point seems to generalize to every predicate that applies to any empirical object, including scientific predicates. That would not be a welcome consequence to Frege. He seeks a 'logically perfect language', a language free of semantic indeterminacy and reference-failure. One of his goals is to express all of science by means of a language based on the language of his *Begriffsschrift*, a language that is to replace natural language in order to express perspicuously valid inferences (Frege 1879, pp. 105ff).

A mathematical expression is incompletely defined if it is not stipulated whether it applies in certain cases. A vague term can be construed as incompletely defined because it is stipulated neither to apply nor not to apply in borderline cases (Williamson 1994, p. 38). Frege thinks that if a term is incompletely defined, it fails to refer to anything. He concludes that vague predicates do not refer (Frege 1903, p. 168).

Here is why vague predicates pose a serious problem for Frege's theory of predication. Suppose that 'ξ is F' is a vague predicate. Then there is a sentence which is neither determinately true nor is determinately false – which, in short, does not have a determinate truth value. Let 'Fa' be that sentence. As we will see in Chapter 3 §3, Frege thinks that if a sentence lacks a determinate truth value, then one or more of its component referring terms lack reference. Now, in our example, we may assume that 'a' refers because it figures as a component in other sentences that have determinate truth values, 'Ga', 'Ha' and so on. It follows that Frege was committed to saying that the reason why 'Fa' lacks a determinate truth value is that its predicate lacks reference. It further follows that any other sentence containing that predicate will lack a determinate truth value. But there will be many sentences containing that predicate which have determinate truth values. Perhaps there are names of other objects, 'b' and 'c', such that 'Fb' is determinately true and 'Fc' is determinately false. Frege is then without a coherent account of vague predicates. In trying to account for them, Frege would flout his own principles concerning what determines the truth values of sentences (Rein 1985, p. 523).

Frege entertained the idea that vague terms are like fictional names in that they have sense but lack reference (Frege 1979, p. 122). We can understand a fictional name, such as 'Othello', or a vague term, such as 'ξ is grey' or 'ξ is painful', because it has a sense, and, although it lacks a reference, we can use it as though it refers. This idea, though, returns us to the controversial issue of whether there can be expressions with sense but no reference (see Chapter 1, §7). It was also an idea of Frege's which remained embryonic. He was later to advocate the view that sentences containing vague terms lack both sense and reference (i.e. truth value) (Frege 1903, p. 159).

Vague predicates are also subject to the following paradox, known as the sorites paradox. The paradox is often illustrated with terms such as 'ξ is red' or 'ξ is rich' or 'ξ is tall'. Let's consider an illustration that uses a predicate of central scientific use. Take the predicate 'ξ is 5 kg-in-mass' and consider any object that we agree is 5 kg-in-mass. Given that paradigm object, we can formulate the following principle:

> (Paradigm) An object that is exactly one microgram more massive than the paradigm object is also 5 kg-in-mass.

(Paradigm) finds support in the idea that some differences in mass between objects are too small to make the difference between one object being 5 kg-in-mass and the other not. There is a sequence of objects, starting with our paradigm object, in which each object is a microgram greater than its immediate predecessor. It is hard to believe that there is some object o in this sequence such that every object before o in the sequence is 5 kg-in-mass, whereas every object after o in the sequence is not 5 kg-in-mass. This idea is captured in the following inductive principle:

> (Inductive principle) If an object o in the sequence is 5 kg-in-mass, then so is o's immediate successor.

Repeated application of this principle will take us along the sequence, and we will then be saying, of each object in the sequence, that it is 5 kg-in-mass just because we have said of its immediate predecessor that it is 5 kg-in-mass. Yet, this clashes with the following fact:

(Fact) It is not the case that a 50 kg-in-mass object is 5 kg-in-mass.

Our acceptance of (Paradigm), (Inductive principle) and (Fact) lands us in contradiction. That is the sorites paradox.

Frege regarded the sorites paradox as a yet further indication of the defectiveness of vague predicates and of the adverse consequences of admitting such predicates into the language of science (Frege 1980, p. 114). Frege was not alone in taking this to be a powerful reason to ban vague terms from science (e.g. Carnap 1950, chapter 1). But this very proposal itself uses a vague term, namely the term 'vague'. (Sorensen 1985 argues that 'vague' is vague.) So the proposal cannot be stated in the idealized language. For a similar reason the proposal cannot be stated as being that all vocabulary in the idealized language is precise. 'Precise' is the complement of 'vague': A term is precise if and only if it is not vague. And the complement of a vague term is itself vague (Sorensen 1996, p. 211).

We can state this problem in more general terms. For Frege, a coherent account of a vague language has to be given in a logically perfect language and so in a perfectly precise language. If the vagueness of a term has to be described in terms that are themselves vague, then the original term has *second-order vagueness*. If the latter terms have second-order vagueness, then the original term has *third-order vagueness*. In general, there is a potential hierarchy of *higher-order vagueness*. Because of this phenomenon, there cannot be a coherent account of vagueness which incorporates Frege's views about the reference of predicates and sentences. Consider some vague term t in the language being theorized about. Then if the corresponding term (or terms) t^* in the language used to theorize about that language is synonymous with t, then t^* will also be vague (Williamson 1994, p. 44). According to Frege, vague terms fail to refer and have no place in a logically perfect language. But disregarding vague terms is no substitute for understanding how they function and how we can reason with them. (For further discussion of Frege's views on vagueness, see van Heijenoort 1985; Burge 1990; Williamson 1994, chapter 2, §2.2.)

6. Conclusion

Frege's ontology – his catalogue of what exists – divides every non-linguistic entity into types. Everything is either an object or a function, but not both. Objects include concrete objects (such as cats and mountains) and abstract objects (such as numbers and truth values). Functions include mathematical functions and also concepts and relations. Frege further thinks that language divides into types. There are complete expressions and there are incomplete expressions. Complete expressions include ordinary proper names, definite descriptions and sentences. Incomplete expressions consist of functors (i.e. expressions whose semantic role is to refer to functions). Predicates are those functors whose semantic role is to refer to concepts. Frege also thinks that the ontological types and the linguistic types are perfectly aligned. What an expression refers to must be of the same logical category as the expression in question. Complete expressions refer to objects (if they refer to anything at all). So a proper name refers to its bearer, a definite description refers to what it describes, and a sentence refers to a truth value. Incomplete expressions, by contrast, refer to functions (if they refer to anything at all). A one-place predicate refers to a first-level concept, whereas the universal and existential quantifiers refer to second-level concepts.

Frege recognizes that naming something and predicating something involve quite different semantic roles. In the light of this difference, Frege takes names and predicates to refer to different types of entity. One of the questions in the introduction to the book, (Q7), asked how to give an account of the compositionality of sentences. Frege's account of predication supplies part of his answer to this question. For any sentence, some part of that sentence is complete and another part (the predicative part) is incomplete. Frege claims that these different parts of the sentence refer to entities of different kinds. The complete part of the sentence refers to something complete: an object. The incomplete part of the sentence refers to something incomplete: a concept or relation.

If we were to reject Frege's view that predicates refer to concepts, several options are available. One is to take the view that predicates refer although not to concepts. We might say that the predicate 'ξ is a politician', for example, has *divided reference*: it refers to all and only politicians (Quine 1960, §19). We then need not posit concepts. What a predicate refers to is not a concept but each object which falls in its extension. Another option would be to take predicates to stand in a *sui generis* relation to concepts – call it the relation of 'ascription'. Whereas names refer to objects, we then say that predicates ascribe concepts. Crispin Wright takes this option:

> For a predicate to stand in the relation of ascription to a property or concept is just this: for its sense so to relate it to that property/concept that it may be used in concatenation with an appropriate singular term to say of the

bearer of that term that it has the property, or falls under the concept in question. (Wright 2001, p. 88)

A still further option would be to abandon both the claim that predicates refer and the claim that there are concepts. According to this view, names refer to objects and objects satisfy predicates. A predicate does not refer to or ascribe anything. Its sole semantic function is to describe objects (Davidson 1967a). What this option requires, though, is a satisfactory semantics for the term 'satisfies': an account of what it is for a given predicate to apply to a given object. (For further discussion of these options, see MacBride 2006.)

Questions for discussion

Question 1

Frege says that a linguistic expression is incomplete if and only if it contains a gap. He then claims that predicates and function signs are incomplete expressions whereas names are not. But we never come across language which contains gaps; we come across sentences. And, if there are gaps in certain expressions, those gaps are filled by other parts of the sentence. Moreover, Frege says that a given sentence can have more than one correct analysis. In one analysis one part of the sentence fills a gap, and in another analysis that same part of the sentence supplies a gap. So how should we tell which parts of a sentence have gaps and which parts fill those gaps?

Question 2

Assess the following argument that predicates are referring expressions. A predicate such as 'ξ is red' can be nominalized to form the expression 'redness'. The expression 'redness' can occur as the subject of a sentence, such as 'Redness is her favourite colour'. Such a sentence is true only if the subject term 'redness' refers to something. Considerations of uniformity then tell us that the predicate 'ξ is red', from which the nominalized expression was formed, is also a referring expression and that it refers to the same thing.

Question 3

Assess the following argument that if predicates are referring expressions, they refer to concepts. Consider what is involved in understanding a predicate, such as 'ξ is red'. It cannot be that you know all of the objects to which that predicate applies, because there are indefinitely many red objects, many of which you will never have knowledge of. So, the predicate 'ξ is red' does not refer to each and every red object. Now, to understand a name is to know the identity of the bearer of that name. By parity, then, to understand a predicate is to know which concept is expressed by that predicate. Moreover, this view does not face the above epistemological problem because you can know which concept is expressed by 'ξ is red' even if you do not know all of the objects to which that predicate applies.

Question 4

Frege says that predicates and what they refer to (namely, concepts) are incomplete, whereas names and what they refer to (namely, objects) are complete. But a name can be part of a predicate (e.g. the name 'Eric' is part of 'ξ is a brother of Eric') or part of a function sign (e.g. '3' is part of '$x + 3$'). So, is there as good a case for saying that a name is an incomplete function sign as there is for saying that a function sign is an incomplete name? Is there as good a case for saying that a name is what remains when a sentence has a part missing as there is for saying that a function sign is what remains when a sentence has a part missing? (Cf. Ramsey 1925).

Question 5

Something which underlies the paradox of the concept *horse* is the assumption that only incomplete expressions (i.e. predicates) refer to incomplete entities (i.e. concepts or relations). Would it be viable to abandon that assumption? How much of Frege's theory of predication could be preserved without that assumption?

Question 6

Suppose that every predicate refers to a concept. Frege's theory talks of an object *a* falling under a concept ξ *is F*. But what is it for an object to fall under a concept? It seems to be a matter of the object standing in a certain relation, ξ *falls under* ζ, to the concept. But then we can equally ask: what is it for a relation to hold between an object and a concept? If we say that it is for a further relation to hold between object *a*, concept ξ *is F*, and relation ξ *falls under* ζ, we seem to be launched on a regress of relations. (This is known as Bradley's regress: Bradley 1897, p. 27f.) Does Frege's theory of concepts provide a way to avoid this regress? (Cf. Currie 1984.)

Further reading

Carruthers, Peter (1983) 'On Concept and Object'.

Currie, Gregory (1982) *Frege: An Introduction To His Philosophy* chapter 4 §(a).

Dudman, V. H. (1972) 'The Concept Horse', (1976) '*Bedeutung* for Predicates'.

Dummett, Michael (1981a) *Frege: Philosophy of Language* chapters 7 and 8.

Frege, Gottlob (1891) 'Function and Object', (1892b) 'On Concept and Object' and (1904) 'What is a Function?'.

McGinn, Colin (2000) *Logical Properties* chapter 3.

Mendelsohn, Richard L. (2005) *The Philosophy of Gottlob Frege* chapters 2 and 5.

Noonan, Harold (2001) *Frege: A Critical Introduction* chapter 4.

—(2006) 'The Concept Horse'.

Oliver, Alex (2010) 'What Is A Predicate?'.

Weiner, Joan (2004) *Frege Explained* chapter 5 and pp. 103–14.

Wiggins, David (1984) 'The Sense and Reference of Predicates: A Running Repair to Frege's Doctrine and a Plea for the Copula'.

Wright, Crispin (2001) 'Why Frege Does Not Deserve His Grain of Salt'.

3

Frege on Sentences

Chapter Outline

1. Introduction

This chapter is concerned with two issues. The first issue is whether sentences as well as ordinary proper names have sense and reference. And, if they do, what is the sense of a sentence and what does a sentence refer to? The second issue concerns a logical puzzle. Here is an instance of it: if Lois Lane believes that Superman flies, and if Superman is Clark Kent, does it follow that Lois Lane believes that Clark Kent flies? If not, why not?

As we will see, Frege extends the distinction between sense and reference from names and predicates to sentences themselves. He takes the sense of a sentence to be determined by the senses of its component names and predicate (plus the syntactic structure of the sentence). He also takes the reference of a sentence to be determined by the references of its component names and predicate. According to Frege, the reference of a sentence is a truth value.

At this juncture, it is helpful to introduce a distinction between two kinds of theory of meaning: *a foundational theory of meaning* and *a structural theory of meaning*. A foundational theory of meaning is a kind of theory of meaning that primarily seeks to answer the question 'Why does a certain sentence have the meaning that it does (for a particular speaker or group of speakers)?' This kind of theory seeks to say what it is about the speaker or speakers that give the sentences they use the meanings that they have. A structural theory of meaning primarily seeks to answer the question 'What is the meaning of a certain sentence (for a particular speaker or group of speakers)?' This kind of theory seeks to specify the meanings of the sentences of a language as used by some speaker or speakers but without seeking to say why those sentences have those meanings. (In some places this kind of theory is called a 'semantic theory of meaning'. That label is apt to mislead because both kinds of theory of meaning are concerned with semantics: the interpretation of words and sentences.)

Here is an analogy taken from chemistry. One kind of theory of chemistry might list the various chemical elements and their properties and specify which ones form which compounds. This kind of theory is analogous to a structural theory of meaning, a theory which lists the meanings that different expressions in a given language have. A different kind of theory of chemistry seeks to explain the properties of the chemical elements and thereby to explain why they form the compounds that they do. It is seeking to explain why the chemical elements have the features they do and why they combine in the ways that they do. This kind of theory is analogous to a foundational theory of meaning, a theory which seeks to explain why our words and sentences mean one thing rather than another.

The expression 'theory of meaning' is not used uniformly in philosophy. Some philosophers use the expression where their concern is with foundational theories of meaning. Other philosophers use it where their concern is with structural theories of meaning. (For a related discussion, see Heal 1978.) A key point for our purposes is that Frege's theory of the senses of sentences is a structural theory of meaning.

2. The senses of sentences

Frege extends the distinction between sense and reference from names to sentences. Let's first consider the sense of a sentence. As a first approximation, Frege's key principle is that:

> The sense of a sentence is determined by the senses of its component expressions.

So, for example, the sense of the following sentence:

(1) The kitten is asleep.

is determined by the senses of 'the kitten' and 'is asleep'. One consequence is that if we substitute any of the expressions in (1) with another expression with the same sense, then we preserve the sense of the original sentence. For example, assuming that 'the kitten' and 'the young cat' have the same sense, then substituting 'the young cat' for 'the kitten' in (1) yields:

(2) The young cat is asleep.

Given the above principle about how the sense of a sentence is determined, (1) and (2) have the same sense.

Frege calls the sense of a sentence 'a thought'. He is not talking about thoughts construed in a psychological way. He is using 'thought' in a special technical way. For Frege, a thought is the sense expressed by a sentence. The thought is itself composed of senses. These are the senses of the various expressions that make up the sentence that expresses the thought.

The above principle about how a sentence's sense is determined needs to be amended. There are pairs of sentences that differ in sense although they are composed of expressions with the same senses. (3) and (4) provide one such pair:

(3) Brutus killed Caesar.
(4) Caesar killed Brutus.

There are also pairs of sentences that differ in sense because they are punctuated differently, although they are composed of expressions with the same senses. (5) and (6) is one such pair:

(5) Oswald killed Kennedy, and Tippett and the crowd looked on.
(6) Oswald killed Kennedy and Tippett, and the crowd looked on.

Here is another such pair:

(7) That is a good way of criticizing Russell.
(8) That is a good way of criticizing, Russell.

Sentence (7) states that a certain way of criticizing is a good way of criticizing Russell. Sentence (8) commends Russell for giving a good way of criticizing something.

Lastly, there are sentences that are ambiguous but whose ambiguity does not lie in any ambiguity in their component expressions. (9) and (10) are examples of such sentences:

(9) Visiting relatives can be annoying.
(10) The policemen stopped drinking at midnight.

During the 1950s, some linguists sought to account for the ambiguity of sentences such as (9) or (10) by claiming that sentences with similar surface forms can have different underlying levels of representation or *depth structures* (Chomsky 1957).

For these reasons our initial statement of the principle about the determination of sentence sense needs to be amended. In each of the above examples, a crucial factor in determining the sentence's sense is how the expressions in the sentence are combined: how the words are arranged in the sentence, how the sentence is punctuated and so on. It is for philosophers or linguists to detail the different kinds of structure which sentences can have and how they bear on the senses of those sentences. Taking this into account, the full statement of Frege's principle is then as follows:

> A sentence's sense is determined by the senses of its component expressions and the mode of combination of those expressions in the sentence.

3. The references of sentences

Frege thinks that many sentences have both sense and reference. (We will see the exceptions shortly.) Frege's key principle here is a counterpart of his principle governing the determination of a sentence's sense. It is the following:

> The reference of a sentence is determined by the references of its component expressions and the mode of combination of those expressions in the sentence.

One consequence of this principle is that if we substitute any of the expressions in a sentence with an expression with the same reference, then we preserve the reference of the sentence. For example, consider sentence (1) again:

(1) The kitten is asleep.

Suppose that 'the kitten' and 'the smallest animal in the house' co-refer. Then substituting 'the smallest animal in the house' for 'the kitten' in (1) yields:

(11) The smallest animal in the house is asleep.

Given Frege's principle about how the reference of a sentence is determined, (1) and (11) have the same reference. Note, however, that (1) and (11) do not have the same sense.

What does Frege take to be the reference of a sentence? His view is that a sentence refers to a truth value. There are two truth values: the True and the False. A sentence that is true refers to the True. A sentence that is false refers to the False. It follows that every true sentence refers to the True and that every false sentence refers to the False. Consider sentences (1) and (3) again:

(1) The kitten is asleep.
(3) Brutus killed Caesar.

Suppose that both those sentences are true. Then they have the same reference: they both refer to the True. The sentences, however, differ in sense. Their senses are different modes of presentation of the same reference.

An empty name is a name that has sense but lacks reference. According to Frege, a sentence containing an empty name also has sense but lacks reference. That is, it lacks a truth value.

In the case of the principle of the compositionality of sense, Frege talks of the sense of a sentence being composed of the senses of its component expressions. The corresponding claim in the case of the principle of the compositionality of reference is that the reference of a sentence is composed of the references of its component expressions. Frege writes that:

> I have in fact transferred the relation between the parts and the whole of the sentence to its reference, by calling the reference of a word part of the reference of the sentence, if the word itself is part of the sentence. (Frege 1892a, pp. 35–6)

Frege was later to retract this claim. He seems correct to have done so. Otherwise he would be committed to claiming that (say) the reference of 'Rome' is part of the reference of the sentence 'Rome is in Italy'. It would be mistaken to claim that Rome (the reference of the name 'Rome') was part of the True (the reference of the sentence 'Rome is in Italy').

Instead of talking of the *compositionality* of sense or reference, we should appeal to another idea of Frege's – his analysis of sentences in terms of the function-argument structure. In Chapter 2 §3, we saw the case for taking the sense of a predicate to be a function from the sense of a name to the sense of a sentence. We also saw that Frege takes the reference of a predicate (i.e. a concept) to be a function from the reference of a name (i.e. an object) to the reference of a sentence (i.e. a truth value). Given an argument, a function determines what the value of that argument is. On these grounds, we can talk of the sense of a sentence as being determined by the senses of its component expressions and of the reference of a sentence as being determined by the references of its component expressions.

This approach also addresses a puzzle that apparently arises from Frege's views. The reference of the sentence 'Paris is in France' is determined by the references of its component expressions. Those references do not coincide with the references of the component expressions of the sentence 'Cows produce milk'. Nevertheless, both sentences refer to the True. There is no puzzle if we think of the issue in terms of the function-argument approach. The reference of '7 + 5' is determined by the references of its component expressions. Those references do not coincide with the references of the component expressions of '3 × 4'. Nevertheless, both complex expressions refer to the number 12. Likewise, different concepts can be functions from different objects to the same truth value.

Frege has three reasons for claiming that the reference of a sentence is a truth value. His first reason raises the question as to why it matters to us that a name in a sentence has a reference (Frege 1892a, p. 33). In some case it does matter to us (as when we assert the sentence). In other cases it does not (such as when the sentence occurs in works of fiction).

> But now why do we want every proper name to have not only a sense, but also a reference? Why is the thought not enough for us? Because, and to the extent that, we are concerned with its truth value. . . . It is striving for the truth that drives us always to advance from the sense to the reference. (Frege 1892a, p. 33)

On this basis, Frege concludes that a sentence refers to a truth value.

The last step of Frege's argument is questionable. Suppose that it matters to us that a name in a sentence refers because it matters to us what the truth value of the sentence is. It is difficult to see why this should show that a sentence refers to a truth value. That further claim does not seem to be part of the explanation of why it matters to us that names refer and it does not seem to be implied by that explanation.

Some philosophers think that, even if sentences refer, Frege's above argument does not show that sentences refer to truth values rather than to states of affairs (Morris 2007, p. 33). A state of affairs is a complex entity that consists of an object having a property or of objects standing in a relation. Whereas Frege would take the sentence 'Barack Obama is the U.S. President' to refer to the True, these other philosophers would take that sentence to refer to the state of affairs consisting of Barack Obama having the property *being the U.S. President*. Frege's first reason for taking sentences to refer to truth values does not show what is wrong with this alternative proposal. But, as we will now see, his second and third reasons for taking sentences to refer to truth values do exclude this and other proposals.

Frege's second reason is as follows (Frege 1892a, p. 35). The reference of a sentence is determined by the reference of its component expressions (and by the sentence's structure). Now it is possible to generate a sequence of sentences in which the component expressions are systematically replaced by other expressions with the same reference (though not the same sense). It follows that every sentence in the sequence has the same reference. Here is one such sequence of sentences (adapted from Church 1956, pp. 24–5):

(12) The United States is the country with the world's leading economy.
(13) The United States is the nation comprised of 50 states.
(14) The number of states that comprise the United States is 50.
(15) 50 is the atomic number of tin (Sn).

Sentence (13) follows from (12) by replacing one expression in (12) with a co-referring expression. Sentence (14) is supposed to be a paraphrase, and so a consequence, of (13). If a paraphrase preserves the sense of a sentence, it will also preserve the reference of that sentence. Sentence (15) follows from (14) by replacing one expression in (14) with a co-referring expression.

Supposing that sentences refer, what do these sentences refer to? Even supposing that there are such things as states of affairs, those sentences do not refer to the same state of affairs since presumably the state of affairs described by (12) differs from the state of affairs described by (15). Since each sentence is true, Frege would claim that they all refer to the True. More generally, he claims that all true sentences refer to the True. A similar sequence of false sentences could also be constructed to show that false sentences refer to the False.

Frege's third reason for taking sentences to be names of truth values draws on his function-argument analysis of sentences. (We saw this analysis in Chapter 2 §3.) A sentence is formed when the gap sign in a function sign is filled by the name of an argument. A sentence formed when the name of an argument fills a function sign is a name of the value of that function for that argument. The value of a concept or relation (the kinds of function associated with predicates) is a truth value. So, a sentence is a name of a truth value. Moreover, when a sentence is formed by the name of an argument filling a function sign, what is formed is something complete. What is complete is an object. So, a sentence names an object. It follows that a truth value is an object. (This is a line of reasoning in Frege reconstructed by Dudman 1970; Geach 1976a, pp. 438–9.)

The claim that sentences refer to truth values strikes some philosophers as odd. In the case of some of these philosophers, it seems to be the claim that sentences refer that is the trouble (Bell 1979, p. 28). For other philosophers, it seems to be Frege's 'treating the True and the False as things' that is the source of their concern rather than the claim that sentences refer (Morris 2007, p. 31).

This scepticism invites a number of responses. First, the claim that sentences refer to truth values may be odd in the sense that it is unfamiliar (at least until we have read Frege). It does not follow that it is odd in the sense of being implausible. Yet, of the two charges, it is only the charge of implausibility that would be damaging. Second, science has made interesting discoveries that confound received opinion. For example, it discovered that white light is composed of light of different colours and that plants get their food from sunlight, not from the soil. One option, then, is to say that Frege made the remarkable discovery that sentences refer to truth values. Third, striking scientific claims should be assessed as part of the overall theory that they belong to. We weigh up the overall evidence for and against the theory and it is on that wider basis that we accept or reject its striking claims. Similarly, in philosophy we should assess an apparently odd claim by its place in the theory it belongs to and in terms of the overall merits and demerits of that theory. How many puzzles does that theory explain and how well does it do so? Does it do this better than any rival theory? Having reached a comparative assessment on this basis, we can then pass judgement on the original claim (Linsky 1983, pp. xxx–xxxi, though see also Anderson 1987, p. 154).

Another criticism of Frege's claim that sentences refer to truth values is that it entails that any true sentence and the expression 'the True' co-refer, and that this generates nonsense (Black 1954, pp. 235–6). Take, for example, the following true compound sentence:

(16) If Barack Obama is the 44th U.S. President, then Obama succeeded the 43rd U.S. President.

The antecedent of (16) is a true sentence. So, in Frege's view, it refers to the True. Now presumably the expression 'the True' refers to the True. 'Barack Obama is the 44th U.S. President' and 'the True' then co-refer. So, it should be possible to substitute 'the True' for 'Barack Obama is the 44th U.S. President' in (16) without changing what (16) refers to (i.e. without changing its truth value). If we make this substitution, we derive:

(17) If the True, then Obama succeeded the 43rd U.S. President.

But, instead of preserving the reference of (16), (17) is not intelligible. Assuming that we can substitute co-referring expressions in a sentence without changing the sentence's truth value, and without violating the rules of grammar, there seems to be a case for rejecting the claim that both 'Barack Obama is the 44th U.S. President' and 'the True' are referring expressions. Since 'the True' seems to be a referring expression of the form *definite article/noun*, there seems to be a reason to reject the claim that 'Barack Obama is the 44th U.S. President' is a referring expression. Since that was an arbitrarily chosen sentence, the lesson we have drawn about that sentence should be drawn about any sentence in general. Consequently, the claim that sentences refer should be rejected. (We saw a variant of this argument in Chapter 2 §4 directed against the claim that predicates refer to concepts.)

The above argument rests on the assumption that co-referring expressions can be substituted in a sentence without violating rules of grammar. Some philosophers have rejected the assumption on the ground that such violations may be no more than a 'linguistic accident' (Marshall 1953, p. 382). At any rate, the assumption faces apparent counter-examples (Wolterstorff 1970, pp. 70–1; Swoyer 1998, p. 308; Oliver 2005, pp. 182–4; MacBride 2006, pp. 468–70). Here are two of them. Barack Obama's use of 'I' refers to him. Suppose too that a token of 'him' is used to refer to Barack Obama. But substituting the second of these expressions for the first in (18):

(18) I am the 44th U.S. President

yields the ungrammatical (19):

(19) Him am the 44th U.S. President.

Again, 'Barack Obama' and 'the referent of "Barack Obama"' co-refer. But if we substitute the second of these expressions for the first in (20):

(20) The 46 year old Barack Obama outwitted the opposition

we derive the ungrammatical (21):

(21) The 46 year old the referent of 'Barack Obama' outwitted the opposition.

These counter-examples exploit the fact that expressions such as 'him' or 'the referent of "Barack Obama"' are not simply referring expressions; they are not mere labels. They also convey information about what they refer to, and some contexts are sensitive to that information, whereas others are not. Depending on which of these contexts such an expression occurs in, the resulting string of words may make sense and have a truth value or may not make sense and lack a truth value. For this reason such expressions are not always substitutable with expressions whose function is only to refer. By the same token, if, as Frege claims, sentences refer to truth values, they also convey information about what they refer to. (For discussion about how to block these counter-examples and defend the assumption, see Dolby 2009. For further discussion of Frege's view that sentences are names of truth values, see Geach 1972, pp. 61–2 and 1976a, pp. 439–40; Sullivan 1994.)

So far, then, we have seen that Frege extends the distinction between sense and reference from proper names and predicates to sentences. The sense of a sentence is determined by the senses of its component expressions and by the syntactic structure of the sentence. The reference of a sentence is determined by the references of its component expressions and by the syntactic structure of the sentence. The reference of a sentence is a truth value. We can summarize these views of Frege as follows:

The sense and reference of sentences

The sentence 'Barack Obama is the 44th U.S. President'

|

expresses

↓

The sense of 'Barack Obama is the 44th U.S. President'

|

determines

↓

The reference of 'Barack Obama is the 44th U.S. President'
that is, the True

4. Frege's theory of indirect sense and indirect reference

Frege considers an apparent counter-example to his principle that the reference of a sentence is determined by the references of its component expressions and the structure of the sentence. He says that

> Exceptions are to be expected when the whole sentence or a part of it is in direct or indirect quotation; for in such cases . . . the words do not have their customary reference. In direct quotation a sentence designates another sentence, and in indirect quotation a thought. (Frege 1892a, p. 36)

To see what kinds of exceptions Frege has in mind, we can distinguish between the following three contexts in which a sentence can be used:

(A) Direct contexts
(B) Indirect contexts and
(C) Quotational contexts.

In a direct context we say, for example, 'The Earth moves'. Here we use the sentence in order to talk about the Earth and ascribe something to it.

Indirect contexts (or intensional contexts, as they are often known) include the following two kinds of case:

(B*)   Propositional attitude reports and
(B**) Indirect speech reports

A propositional attitude report says that someone has a certain attitude to a proposition. For example, we might say 'Galileo believed that the Earth moves'. Here we are reporting that someone (Galileo) has a certain attitude (an attitude of belief) to a certain proposition (the proposition that the Earth moves). Similarly, we might report Galileo as fearing that the Inquisition will torture him, hoping that he will not be imprisoned, and so on.

An indirect speech report recounts what someone said. The report need not use the very words that that person used. For example, we might say 'Galileo said that the Earth moved'. Here we are translating into English what Galileo said in Italian.

A quotational context report tells us what the very words used by someone were. For example, we might report Galileo as saying 'La Terra si muove'. By quoting him, we quote the sentence he uttered.

Sentences in indirect or quotational contexts generate a problem for Frege's principle that the reference of a sentence is determined by the reference of its component expressions plus the sentence's structure. The problem can be illustrated with the following case in which some sentences occur in propositional attitude contexts:

(22) The Earth moves.
(23) John F. Kennedy was assassinated.
(24) Galileo believed that the Earth moves.
(25) Galileo believed that John F. Kennedy was assassinated.

Both (22) and (23) are true. (22) is embedded in (24). Given that the reference of a sentence is determined by the reference of its component expressions and its structure, substituting (23) for (22) as it occurs in (24) should preserve truth value. The result is (25). Yet (24) is true and (25) is false, and so the substitution has not preserved truth value.

Frege's solution to this puzzle is to claim that sentences in indirect contexts and in quotational contexts undergo a shift both in sense and reference. Let's consider in turn his treatment of sentences in (A) direct contexts, (B) indirect contexts and (C) quotational contexts.

(A) In direct contexts, a sentence has its ordinary (or customary) sense and reference. Take the following sentence:

(22) The Earth moves.

In (22), 'The Earth moves' is not embedded in a more complex sentence. The sentence has its ordinary sense, the thought *that the Earth moves*. It also refers to a truth value, the True. The sentence is true if and only if the ordinary sense of 'The Earth moves' refers to the True.

(B) In indirect contexts, a sentence lacks its ordinary sense and ordinary reference. Instead it has an indirect sense and an indirect reference. What is a sentence's indirect reference? When a sentence is in an indirect context, it does not refer to a truth value. There is a shift in what it refers to. Since the sentence's reference has shifted, this new reference is called the sentence's 'indirect reference'. According to Frege, in an indirect context a sentence refers to the sense that the sentence has in direct contexts (its ordinary sense). Frege's reason for claiming that the sentence refers to its ordinary sense is that referring expressions with the same sense can be substituted for one another in indirect contexts without affecting truth value. For example, assuming 'The Earth moves' and 'Terra is in a state of motion' have the same sense, the latter sentence can be substituted for the former in (24) without change of truth value.

Frege further claims that when a sentence is in an indirect context, it does not have its ordinary sense. There is a shift in its sense. It has a different sense in that context and this different sense refers to the sentence's indirect reference. Call this different sense the sentence's 'indirect sense'.

Consider the following sentence:

(26) Galileo said that the Earth moves.

In (26), 'The Earth moves' has indirect sense and indirect reference. Its indirect reference is its ordinary sense, that is, the sense which 'The Earth moves' has in a direct context. Its indirect sense is a mode of presentation of its (indirect) reference. (26) is true if and only if the sense referred to by 'The Earth moves' in that sentence is identical to the sense of the sentence that Galileo used to talk about the Earth. Now the sentence Galileo used to talk about the Earth was 'La Terra si muove'. The sense of that sentence is identical to the ordinary sense of 'The Earth moves'. And the ordinary sense of 'The Earth moves' is what is referred to by 'The Earth moves' in (26). So (26) is true.

We can construct more complex examples such as the following:

(27) Linsky believes that Galileo said that The Earth moves.

In (27), 'The Earth moves' has doubly indirect sense and doubly indirect reference. Its doubly indirect reference is the sense which it has in (26). That is, its doubly indirect reference is the indirect sense it has in 'Galileo believed that the Earth moves'. The doubly indirect sense of 'The Earth moves' in (27) is a mode of presentation of its doubly indirect reference. (27) is true if and only if Linsky believes the sense of the sentence expressed by (26).

(C) In quotational contexts, a sentence does not have its ordinary sense or its ordinary reference. Nor does it have the indirect sense or indirect reference that it has in indirect contexts. It has a yet further sense and reference. Take the following sentence:

(28) Galileo said, 'La Terra si muove'.

In (28), 'La Terra si muove' refers to the Italian sentence 'La Terra si muove'. Its sense in (28) is a mode of presentation of that sentence. Notice, then, that in a quotational context a sentence refers to itself. (28) is true if and only if the sentence referred to by 'La Terra si muove' in (27) is identical to the sentence that Galileo used to talk about the Earth. Since the sentence that Galileo used to talk about the Earth was 'La Terra si muove', it follows that (28) is true. (For an objection to Frege's account of quotational contexts, see Geach 1976a, p. 443.)

Frege now has in place an account that can solve the puzzle posed by sentences (22–25). Recall that these were the sentences:

(22) The Earth moves.
(23) John F. Kennedy was assassinated.
(24) Galileo believed that the Earth moves.
(25) Galileo believed that John F. Kennedy was assassinated.

The puzzle was as follows. The reference of a sentence, a truth value, is determined by the references of its component expressions. Now, since (22) and (23) both refer to the True, then substituting (23) for (22) as it occurs in (24) should preserve the truth value of the resulting sentence. Yet (22) is true, whereas (25) is false.

Frege's solution is to claim that the sentence 'The Earth moves' does not have the same sense and reference in (22) as it does in (24). In (22), 'The Earth moves' occurs in a direct context. In (24), it occurs in an indirect context. In (22), 'The Earth moves' has its ordinary sense and reference. In (24), however, it does not. Its sense and reference shift. In (24), it has indirect reference: it refers to its ordinary sense. In (24), it also has indirect sense.

Similarly, 'John F. Kennedy was assassinated' does not have the same sense and reference in (23) as it does in (25). In (23), 'John F. Kennedy was assassinated' occurs in a direct context. In (25), it occurs in an indirect context. In (23), 'John F. Kennedy was assassinated' has its ordinary sense and reference. In (25), however, its sense and reference shift. In (25), it has indirect reference: it refers to its ordinary sense. In (25), it also has indirect sense.

Now the ordinary sense of 'The Earth moves' is distinct from the ordinary sense of 'John F. Kennedy was assassinated'. It follows that, although 'The Earth moves' as it occurs in (22) co-refers with 'John F. Kennedy was assassinated' as it occurs in (23), 'The Earth moves' as it occurs in (24) does not co-refer with either of those sentences. So 'John F. Kennedy was assassinated' cannot be substituted for 'The Earth moves' in (24) while necessarily preserving truth value.

What this shows is that it is possible to solve the puzzle posed by sentences occurring in indirect contexts in a way that is consistent with the principle that the reference of a sentence is determined by the references of its component expressions and its structure.

Frege also thinks that this reveals an advantage of his theory of names over a view such as Mill's. In Chapter 1 §2, we saw that Mill takes names to be 'tags' that refer to objects but which have no other meaning. One problem is then generated by pairs of sentences such as:

(29) Lois Lane believes that Superman flies.
(30) Lois Lane believes that Clark Kent flies.

These sentences differ in truth value. What is responsible for this difference? The only other difference between them is in the names they contain. Yet the names in question are co-referential. So, Mill would seem to be at a loss to explain the difference in truth value between (29) and (30). (We will return to this problem at the end of §5.)

5. Problems with Frege's theory

Frege's solution faces a number of objections, some stronger than others. An objection made by Donald Davidson is that Frege's solution has the absurd consequence that it would be impossible to learn a natural language such as English or Italian. Not only do these languages have the resources to form sentences occurring in indirect contexts, but there is no limit to the complexity of the sentences that can be formed in these languages. The reason for this is that there is no limit to the number of clauses in which a sentence like 'The Earth moves' can be embedded. According to Frege's solution, 'The Earth moves' has different senses as it occurs in (22), (24) and (27). It would have still other senses as it occurs in progressively more complex sentences. Notice that understanding one of these senses would not enable you to understand any of the others. Understanding 'The Earth moves' when it occurs in a direct context does not enable you to understand it when it occurs in, for example, 'Galileo believed that The Earth moves'. Each of these senses would have to be learnt separately and independently of the others. These senses are *semantic primitives*. There are infinitely many such senses since infinitely many sentences of increasing complexity can be formed. But since it would take a finite amount of time for us to learn each such semantically primitive expression, it follows that we cannot learn a language containing them (Davidson 1965).

Davidson's objection can be queried on several counts (Haack 1978; Leeds 1979; Matthews 1986). At the very least, we currently know too little about how languages are learnt to be confident that the number of semantic primitives anyone can learn has to be finite. That aside, the most that the objection can show is that, under Frege's account, it is impossible to understand every sentence of a natural language such as English. It does not follow that, under Frege's account, it is impossible to understand enough of the sentences of such a language to serve all our purposes. 'After all, human beings, with their limited time and memories, rarely produce or need sentences in which [operators introducing indirect contexts] are iterated more than a few times' (Linsky 1983, p. 66).

Dummett offers a modification of Frege's account (Dummett 1981a, chapter 9. See also Geach 1980, pp. 95–6). He suggests that we regard the sense of a word or sentence as remaining constant in all contexts (direct, singly indirect, doubly indirect and so on) but as determining different references according to the context. He writes that

> . . . while a word or expression *by itself* has a sense, it does not by itself have a reference at all: only a particular occurrence of a word or expression in a sentence has a reference, and this reference is determined jointly by the sense of the word and the kind of context in which it occurs. (Dummett 1981a, p. 268)

For instance, since 'The Earth moves' is embedded in 'Galileo believed that The Earth moves', the reference determined by that context differs from the reference it has when it is in a direct context. The sense of 'The Earth moves', however, remains the same throughout. Dummett further claims that there is no need to say that 'The Earth moves' has a different sense or reference in singly indirect contexts than it does it doubly indirect contexts (Dummett 1981a, pp. 268–9).

Dummett's modification seems to have two advantages. First, Dummett, like some others, thinks that indirect senses are obscure entities (Dummet 1981a, p. 267; Carnap 1947, p. 129; Mendelsohn 2005, p. 140). His modification does not posit indirect senses and so obviates this concern. Second, and as a consequence, it avoids commitment to a hierarchy of infinitely many indirect senses.

In reply, it might be contended that indirect senses are no more (though no less) obscure than ordinary senses. Suppose the name 'Aristotle' has a sense. Call that sense S_1. If 'Aristotle' has a sense, then so too does the expression 'the sense of "Aristotle"'. That expression is a name of sense S_1. That name itself has a sense. Call it S_2. S_2 is a mode of presentation of S_1. It is a sense of a sense. We have introduced an indirect sense: a sense that refers to another sense. Provided we understand what an ordinary sense is, there seem to be no additional difficulties in understanding what an indirect sense is. (See also Beaney 1996, pp. 181–3). Moreover, any case for supposing that a reference-shift occurs from direct to indirect contexts is equally a case for supposing that a reference-shift occurs from singly indirect to doubly indirect contexts. Lastly, it is not clear whether Dummett avoids the postulation of a hierarchy of infinitely many senses. 'What [Dummett] calls "the sense" of a name is just the infinite hierarchy of Frege's indirect senses collected together' (Linsky 1983, p. 52). (For additional criticisms of Dummett's account of indirect sense and reference, see Heidelberger 1975, pp. 37–43. For further discussion of the issue of the hierarchy of indirect senses, see Carnap 1947, pp. 129–31; Baldwin 1975; Holland 1978; Burge 1979c; Parsons 1981; Boisvert and Lubbers 2003.)

Another objection to Frege's account of indirect contexts concerns sentences such as the following:

(31) George W. Bush mistakenly believed that there were weapons of mass destruction in Iraq.

(31) entails both that George W. Bush believed that there were weapons of mass destruction in Iraq and that there were no weapons of mass destruction in Iraq. But how can it be shown to have these entailments on Frege's account? The sentence 'There were weapons of mass destruction in Iraq' is embedded in an indirect context. It then seems that it has indirect sense. If so, how does (31) entail that there were no weapons of mass destruction in Iraq since the sentence it entails is not embedded in an indirect context?

Frege's response to this kind of case is to say that:

> This shows that the subordinate clause in our original complex sentence is to be taken twice, with different reference, standing once for a thought, once for a truth value. (Frege 1892a, p. 48)

What this means is that Frege would analyse (31) as (32):

(32) George W. Bush believed that there are weapons of mass destruction in Iraq and there were no weapons of mass destruction in Iraq.

Note that (31) does not apparently have the form of a conjunction whereas (32) does. Presumably the analysis provided by (32) is more revealing than (31) is of what kind of sense (i.e. what kind of thought) (31) and (32) express. If so, (31) and (32) each express a conjunctive thought. So, although (31) does not have the syntactic structure of a conjunction, it expresses a conjunctive thought. Yet this seems at odds with a view that Frege elsewhere expresses, the view that the structure of a sentence reflects the structure of the thought that it expresses:

> Thoughts are constructed out of building-blocks. And these building-blocks correspond to groups of sounds out of which the sentence which expresses the thought is built, so that the construction of the sentence out of its parts corresponds to the construction of the thought out of its parts. (Frege 1979, p. 225)

Frege's remarks seem best suited as remarks about the sentences of only a logically perspicuous language.

A related objection to Frege's account is that an expression in an indirect context will not be able to pick up the reference of the same expression in a direct context. This objection is best illustrated with an example:

(33) Saddam Hussein was captured alive although few people believed that he would be captured alive.

In (33), 'Saddam Hussein' refers to the dictator and 'he' refers to the same person. 'He' is a so-called pronoun of laziness: it saves us from writing out 'Saddam Hussein' again. But now consider what Frege's analysis would say about (33). On that analysis, 'Saddam Hussein' would refer to the dictator. The sentence 'he would be captured alive' falls within an indirect context, however, and so has an indirect sense. The expression 'he' that is part of that sentence will have an indirect sense too. It will not refer to Saddam Hussein, but to the sense of 'Saddam Hussein'. That seems a mistaken result.

Presumably, this objection would be treated by Frege as a variant of the preceding one and as amenable to the same kind of solution. (33) would then to be construed as (34):

(34) Saddam Hussein was captured alive and few people believed that Saddam Hussein would be captured alive.

The first occurrence of 'Saddam Hussein' is then taken to refer to a person, and the second occurrence to the sense of the name 'Saddam Hussein'.

Some philosophers find such a solution unsatisfactory. It seems evident to them that both occurrences of 'Saddam Hussein' have the same reference. More generally, they think that expressions are *semantically innocent* in that they have the same reference in different contexts (whether direct or indirect) (Davidson 1968, pp. 144–5). The role of 'Saddam Hussein' and of 'he' in (33) are supposed to support this claim. But it is not obvious that Frege should concede this thesis of semantic innocence. First of all, it is not clear that any appeal to intuitions here will be decisive. Second, even if intuition tells against Frege in this case, the strengths of his entire theory may more than compensate for these counter-intuitive results. (For further discussion of semantic innocence, see Oppy 1992.)

It has also been suggested that Frege's account seems incompatible with a certain aspect of the use of indexical expressions (such as 'I', 'me' and 'now') and demonstratives (such as 'this' and 'that'). We can see this with an example. Suppose Jenny utters (35):

(35) Laird hopes that I will win the lottery.

Jenny's utterance of 'I' in (35) does not tell us anything about how Laird is thinking of her. It does not involve anything to do with the sense of Jenny's utterance of 'I'. Also notice that Laird's propositional attitude does not consist in him standing in the relation of hoping to the thought that he would express with the sentence 'I will win the lottery'. That is what it is for Laird to hope that he himself will win the lottery. Yet that is not what (35) says that he is hoping. It seems that only the referent of Jenny's use of 'I' (namely, Jenny), not the sense of Jenny's use of 'I', matters in explaining what (35) says.

The problem is that the perspective involved in a use of an indexical in a propositional attitude report is not typically intended to match the perspective of the target of the report. When Jenny tells us that Laird hopes she will win the lottery, Jenny need not expect the perspective in her use of the indexical 'I' to match any of Laird's perspectives on her. (For further discussion of this issue, see Perry 1977, 1979; Burge 1979; Kaplan 1989, pp. 529–36. See Evans 1985; McDowell 1984; Heck 2002 for replies. For other criticisms of Frege's theory of indirect speech, see Platts 1979, pp. 114–17.)

Lastly, recall that Frege takes his theory of names to have an advantage over Mill's view of names. Mill takes names to be 'tags' and that names have no meaning other than what they refer to. Frege thinks that Mill's view faces a problem with pairs of sentences such as:

(29) Lois Lane believes that Superman flies.
(30) Lois Lane believes that Clark Kent flies.

The problem for Mill is supposed to be that these sentences differ in truth value although 'Superman' and 'Clark Kent' co-refer.

Saul Kripke argues that Frege was mistaken in thinking that he can solve this problem whereas Mill cannot (Kripke 1979). Kripke does not attempt to solve the problem which faces Mill. Instead, he offers several examples to show that, even if we draw Frege's distinction between sense and reference, the problem that Frege raises remains. We will pick two of his examples.

Here is a version of Kripke's first example: his puzzling Pierre example. Pierre is a monoglot French speaker born and bred in pre-war France. By looking through French travel guides he learns about a city called 'Londres' – the city that English speakers would call 'London'. Influenced by the guides' descriptions and photographs, he forms the belief that it is pretty.

War occurs and Pierre becomes a refugee. He ends up in London, by now ruined by bombing and wartime conditions. Pierre learns English by picking it up from native speakers, and not by translation into French. He does not realize that the city he lives in is the same city he calls 'Londres'. He believes that the city he lives in, the city he calls 'London', is not pretty.

Kripke endorses the following principles:

> *Disquotation*: If a normal speaker of English, upon reflection, sincerely assents to 'p', then he believes that *p*.

> *Translation*: If a sentence expresses a truth in one language, then a correct translation of it into any other language also expresses a truth (in that other language).

Given the pre-war part of the story, Pierre knows of the city which he calls 'Londres', and sincerely assents to 'Londres est jolie'. Given his sincere assent, the following seems true: Pierre croit que Londres est Jolie. Given *Translation*, it follows that Pierre believes that London is pretty.

Given the wartime part of the story, Pierre sincerely assents to 'London is not pretty'. Given *Disquotation*, Pierre believes that London is not pretty.

Hence, Pierre believes that London is pretty and also that London is not pretty. This is a surprising result, since, irrespective of whatever his skill at reasoning, Pierre will not be able to reason to the conclusion that he holds contradictory beliefs. So, Pierre is not inconsistent; he only lacks information.

What does this puzzle show? Here is one moral that Kripke draws. Mill's theory says that the meaning of a proper name consists in what it refers to (Mill 1843, book I chapter II). Frege objects that Mill's theory has the consequence that names of the same object can be substituted for each other in any sentence without changing its truth value. Frege believes that that consequence is false because substituting different names of the same object in sentences reporting people's beliefs can change the truth values of those sentences. Kripke's Pierre example is designed to show that the principles which govern our ascriptions of beliefs and other propositional attitudes to people – the principles which justify the claim that Pierre believes that London is pretty and the claim that Pierre believes that London is not pretty – are *alone* sufficient to show that substituting different names of the same object in sentences reporting people's beliefs can change the truth values of those sentences. There is then no basis for specifically impugning Mill's theory of names. (For further discussion, see, e.g. Lewis 1981; Owens 1995; Sosa 1996.)

Here is Kripke's second example: the Paderewski example. Suppose that Peter learns that the name 'Paderewski' is the name of a famous pianist. He comes to believe that Paderewski has musical talent. For this reason, it seems that the following sentence is true:

(36) Peter believes that Paderewski has musical talent.

Now suppose further that Peter also learns that the name 'Paderewski' is the name of a certain politician. Peter takes 'Paderewski' to be a name that two different people happen to share, a musician and a politician. He does not come to believe anything about the musical ability of that politician. For this reason, it seems that the following sentence is true:

(37) Peter does not believe that Paderewski has musical talent.

In fact, although Peter does not realize it, Paderewski the musician is Paderewski the politician. The problem is that, on the face of it, both (36) and (37) are true although they are contradictory. Now there is no reason to suppose that 'Paderewski has musical talent' differs in sense between (36) and (37). So, Frege cannot account for the problem on the grounds that (36) reports Peter as believing one proposition and that (37) reports Peter as not believing some other proposition. The point of the problem is that, even if Frege introduces the distinction between sense and reference, he cannot provide a satisfactory account of propositional attitude reports involving names. In this respect, Frege's view has no advantage over views of reference, such as Mill's or Kripke's, that eschew the distinction between sense and reference. All of these views need to solve the problem of propositional attitude reports, but Kripke takes his examples to indicate that the solution is not achieved simply by distinguishing between the sense and reference of names. He leaves open what the correct solution is, but, as the solution remains open, it may be that the problem can be solved without drawing Frege's sense/reference distinction.

6. Conclusion

Systematic theories of meaning are few and far between. Much work in the philosophy of language proceeds in a piecemeal fashion with different techniques being used to tackle different issues to do with language. Frege's theory of sense and reference is an example of a systematic theory. Frege appeals to senses (the senses of names, predicates or sentences) to explain a wealth of semantic phenomena, including the relation of names to their referents, the relation of predicates to their referents, and the relation of sentences to their truth values. In addition, he takes his theory of sense and reference to illuminate the information content of sentences (their 'cognitive value'), ambiguity (where the same sentence is associated with different senses), sameness of meaning (where different sentences are associated with the same sense) and our understanding of language.

We will conclude by considering how Frege's theory addresses some of the questions raised in the introduction to this book.

(Q2) asked how we can understand novel sentences. Frege offers a pioneering answer in terms of the compositional nature of sentence senses. We can understand the sense of a novel sentence (i.e. a type of sentence that we have not already encountered) provided that we understand the senses of its component names and predicates and the way in which they are combined. Our prior understanding of these things enables us to understand the senses of sentences constructed out of them.

(Q5) asked what the relation is between meaning and truth. Frege offers a detailed answer to this question. He claims that the sense of a sentence determines the sentence's reference and that the reference of a sentence is its truth value. He further claims that the sense of a sentence determines the sentence's truth conditions, the conditions under which it is true. This additional claim bears on his answers to some of our other questions.

(Q7) asked what a theory of the compositional nature of sentences should be like. It might seem that Frege offers a 'bottom-up' strategy in which we start with the senses of expressions and then take them and the structure of the sentence to determine the sentence's sense. But we should notice that Frege's claim that the sense of a sentence determines its truth condition suggests a different direction of explanation. According to this, the sense of a sentence determines the sentence's truth condition, and the senses of the component expressions consist in their contribution to fixing the truth conditions of the sentences in which they figure (Frege 1893, paragraph 32).

Lastly, (Q10) asked whether there can be a systematic philosophical study of natural language. Frege regarded natural language as defective because it contains expressions that are ambiguous or that are vague, as well as empty names and sentences that lack truth value. For the purposes of mathematics and science, Frege advocated replacing flawed natural languages with an artificial language free of those deficiencies and which makes more evident the logical relations between Fregean thoughts.

Questions for discussion

Question 1
Fregeans claim that the primary bearer of meaning is the sentence. They take this to be a lesson of Frege's context principle: the principle that words have meaning only in the context of a sentence (Frege 1884, p. x). Fregeans also claim that the sense of a sentence is determined by the senses of its constituent expressions (plus the sentence's syntax). Are those claims compatible?

Question 2
Fregeans claim that the sense of a sentence is determined by the senses of its constituent expressions (plus the sentence's syntax). They further claim that the sense of every such expression is determined by its contribution to the senses of the sentences in which it figures. Are those claims compatible?

Question 3
If someone claimed that all true sentences refer to the same state of affairs, would their view differ substantially from Frege's view that all true sentences refer to the True? Or would their claim be using different terminology to say the same thing as Frege?

Question 4
Some philosophers, such as Dummett, find Frege's talk of indirect sense obscure. It has been replied that such talk is no more obscure than talk of

ordinary sense. It is further replied that talk of ordinary sense is not obscure by appeal to arguments such as the following:

> Is there some form of words that will spell out for us what *is* a given sense of a given name? I do not think there is: but senses do not thus become mysterious and unidentifiable. Most of us can identify, reidentify and discriminate human voices: but we could not put into words wherein the individuality of a given voice consists. It is the same way with the senses of names. (Geach 1980, p. 87)

Are these replies good ones?

Question 5

Is the following argument valid?

> Smith said that an ophthalmologist is an eye-doctor.
> 'Ophthalmologist' and 'eye-doctor' have the same sense.
> So: Smith said that an ophthalmologist is an ophthalmologist.

Does Frege's theory of indirect sense and reference entail that the argument is valid? (cf. Platts 1979, p. 116; Boër 1980, pp. 147–8).

Further reading

Dummett, Michael (1981a) *Frege: Philosophy of Language* chapters 9, 11 and 12.

Linsky, Leonard (1983) *Oblique Contexts* chapter 3.

Mendelsohn, Richard L. (2005) *The Philosophy of Gottlob Frege* chapter 9.

Taylor, Kenneth (1998) *Truth and Meaning: An Introduction to the Philosophy of Language* chapter I §§4–7.

Wiggins, David (1992) 'Meaning, Truth Conditions, Proposition: Frege's Doctrine of Sense Retrieved, Resumed and Redeployed in the Light of Certain Recent Criticisms'.

tone / color
sense / force

4

Frege on Force and Tone

1. Introduction

As part of his attempt to characterize meaning, Frege introduced a distinction between sense and reference. But are these two aspects of the meaning of a sentence or expression exhaustive? Do they capture all the aspects of meaning that there are? In this chapter, we will see that Frege distinguishes a further aspect of meaning. This is called the 'tone' or 'colour' of an expression: the connotations which certain words or phrases carry. We will also see that Frege draws a further distinction at the level of sentences. This is a distinction between the sense and force of a sentence. A sentence has a certain sense, but, in addition, it may have different forces on different occasions when it is uttered. That is, it may be used in different ways in different utterances. For example, on one occasion it may be used to make an assertion, whereas on another occasion it may be used without making an assertion.

What do the above distinctions come to? They might have an initial intuitive appeal, but we still need to establish what their basis is. Are these distinctions genuine and illuminating ones or not? Can a systematic theory be developed of the different forces with which a sentence can be uttered? More generally, what is the connection between how we use sentences and what those sentences mean?

2. The distinction between sense and tone

We have seen that Frege distinguishes between two different aspects of the meaning of sentences and their component expressions: their sense and their reference. In this section, we will consider a further distinction. This is the distinction between sense and tone.

Consider, first, the sense of a sentence. Take as an example the sentence 'Barack Obama is a politician'. The senses of the expressions occurring in that sentence, and the way which they are put together, determines that that sentence is true under the condition that Barack Obama is a politician. That is the truth condition of the sentence. The sense of a sentence is then that aspect of its meaning that determines its truth condition. The sense of a component expression is that aspect of the meaning of the expression that contributes to the truth conditions of every sentence in which it figures (Frege 1893, §32).

Note, however, that two expressions can differ in their meaning even though they make the same contribution to the truth conditions of sentences. For example, take the expressions 'mother' and 'mum'. These apply to the same thing. They also have the same sense. So 'Mark's mother is at work' and 'Mark's mum is at work' have the same truth conditions. But 'mother' is a relatively neutral term whereas 'mum' has warm and friendly connotations. Introducing someone as 'my mother' would be more formal than introducing the same person as 'my mum'. Again, take the expressions 'the dog' and 'the cur'. These apply to the same thing. They also have the same sense. So 'The dog is asleep' and 'The cur is asleep' have the same truth conditions. But, as applied to an animal, 'dog' is a neutral term, whereas 'cur' has derogatory connotations. If someone who liked dogs said 'The cur was asleep', and the dog was asleep, what that person said would be true but misleading. It would be true because the sentence that she used is true under the condition that the dog is asleep, and that condition obtains. It would be misleading because the form of words she chose implied that she disliked dogs. Moreover, unless her listeners drew that implication from what she had said, they would have missed something that is part of the literal meaning of 'cur' (Dummett 1981a, p. 84).

Another example is provided by the case of euphemisms, such as 'being economical with the truth' as a euphemism for 'being evasive', or 'has passed away' as a euphemism for 'being dead'. These are further pairs of expressions with the same sense but which differ in some further aspect of their meaning. It is this aspect of meaning that Frege calls their tone, colouring or illumination.

What does this phrase mean?

Frege himself offers a third kind of example, one of particular philosophical interest. The conjunctive phrases 'and', 'but', 'although' and 'yet' have the same sense. Given uniform substitutions for '*p*' and '*q*', sentences of the form '*p* and *q*', '*p* but *q*', '*p* although *q*' and '*p* yet *q*' do not differ in their truth conditions. Frege tells us that these different conjunctions illuminate the sense of the clause 'in a peculiar fashion' (Frege 1892a, p. 45). 'But', 'although' and 'yet' each indicate a certain contrast between the first conjunct and the second. The sentence 'She was jet-lagged but slept little' implies that there is some kind of contrast between being jet-lagged and having slept little – perhaps with the implication that if she was jet-lagged, you would not expect her to have slept only a little. If there were no such contrast, uttering that sentence (rather than 'She was jet-lagged and slept little') would be odd or misleading, but what was uttered would not be false.

Frege's notion of tone also applies to pairs of expressions or sentences which are only stylistic variants of one another. These stylistic differences are associated with different ideas by different listeners, and this is something that guides poets and novelists in their choice of words (Frege 1892a, p. 38). Differences in tone may capture different nuances. For example, one nineteenth-century novel began 'It was a dark and stormy night; the rain fell in torrents . . .' This could be written more prosaically as 'One night there was a storm and it rained heavily'. The paraphrase preserves the sense of the original sentence though not its dramatic tone. (For further discussion of tone, see Dummett 1981a chapter 1 and pp. 83–9; Hornsby 2001; Hom 2008, 2010.)

3. The distinction between sense and force

The distinction between sense and tone is a distinction between two aspects of the meaning of an expression or sentence. Frege also draws a distinction between sense and force. This is a distinction drawn at the level of the utterance of sentences. As we will see, a sentence can have the same sense in different utterances while having different forces in those utterances.

In his 1879 work *Begriffsshrift*, Frege anticipates the distinction between sense and force for indicative sentences. There he distinguishes between judgement and content. To judge that a sentence's content is true is to do more than to entertain the content of that sentence. To assert the content of a sentence involves more than just considering it. Someone who asserts a content at least purports to say something true. For example, consider the sentence 'Wind direction determines the gender of unborn babies'. You might consider that sentence's content without judging its content to be true. According to book IV of his *On the Generation of Animals*, Aristotle, by contrast, not only entertains that content but judges it to be true.

Early in his research in the philosophy of language, then, Frege distinguishes the content of a sentence from the assertion of that content. His reason was that, although a sentence's content might be asserted on one occasion, the same sentence with the same content might not be asserted on another occasion. Frege preserves this insight after he went on to distinguish between sense and reference in his 1892 paper 'On Sense and Reference'. He preserves the insight by distinguishing between the sense and the force of a sentence. As we have seen, sense is an aspect of the meaning of a sentence. Force is the type of speech act made when the sentence is uttered on a given occasion. A sentence may be uttered on one occasion with assertoric force – with the force of an assertion. On another occasion the same sentence may be uttered without that force.

Frege has two arguments for claiming that the fact that a sentence is uttered as an assertion is not a fact about the sense of the sentence uttered. His first argument is that a declarative sentence can occur now asserted, now unasserted, without change of sense. Here is an illustrative example. Consider the following argument:

(A) *There is civil war in Syria.*

(B) If *there is civil war in Syria*, the oil price will rise.

(C) So: the oil price will rise.

There are two points to note about the argument (A–C). First, the argument is valid only if the italicized sentence in (A) has the same sense as the italicized one in (B). Otherwise the argument would involve equivocation and would be invalid. (It would be like arguing: he ate a bass for dinner; a bass is a stringed instrument; so he ate a stringed instrument.) Assuming that there is no equivocation in the argument, the argument belongs to the valid argument form of *modus ponens*: $p, p \supset q$, so q.

The second thing to note is that if anyone asserts sentence (A), that person asserts the italicized sentence, but if anyone asserts sentence (B), that person does *not* assert the italicized sentence in it. Instead, they assert the conditional sentence. To use the terminology of forces, the italicized sentence has assertoric force in (A) but not in (B).

These two points tell us that, if the argument (A–C) is valid, the sentence 'There is civil war in Syria' has the same sense in (A) and (B) although it occurs with different forces in them.

Here is another illustration of Frege's distinction between sense and force. Suppose that two people are having an argument. One of them asserts the sentence 'Churchill was prime minister at the start of the Second World War'. The other denies that sentence. For these people to be contradicting each other, the sentence that one of them is asserting has to have the same sense as the sentence that the other person is denying. Otherwise they are not disagreeing with one another: they would be talking past each other. What this tells us is that the sense of a sentence does not differ just because one person asserts the sentence whereas the other person rejects it.

Frege's second argument appeals to the use of indicative sentences in fiction. When Franz Kafka wrote the line 'As Gregor Samsa awoke one morning from uneasy dreams he found himself transformed in his bed into a gigantic insect' in his novel *Metamorphosis*, he was not asserting that sentence. Likewise, when an actor utters his lines, he is not asserting them. The novelist and the actor are mock-asserting, or pretending to assert, various sentences. The same sentences could occur off-stage ('The theatre is on fire') with the same sense but with the force of an assertion. Frege concludes that the same sentence can occur with the same sense now asserted, now unasserted.

We can think of the utterance of a sentence in terms of a pair of elements. First, there is the sense of the sentence and, second, there is a certain force operating on that sentence. Different pairs can be generated by keeping fixed the sense in question and changing the force involved, or, alternatively, by keeping fixed the force but altering the sense.

Frege did not extend the sense/force distinction beyond declarative sentences until near to the end of his life. In his 1918 paper 'The Thought: A Logical Inquiry' he extends the distinction to questions. A question ('Is the chef fired?') and an assertion ('The chef is fired') can express the same sense, but they will have different forces. Frege does not, however, extend the distinction further. He does not, for example, extend it to imperatives. Yet the same consideration applies, for example, to imperatives. If that question and that assertion express the same sense but involve different forces, then, by parity of argument, it seems that an imperative ('Fire the chef!') can express the same sense but will involve a yet further force.

Frege resists this step. He allows that questions express thoughts, but explicitly denied that imperative sentences do:

> One does not want to deny sense to an imperative sentence, but this sense is not such that the question of truth could arise for it. Therefore I shall not call the sense of an imperative sentence a thought. (Frege 1918, p. 21)

Many philosophers share Frege's intuition (e.g. McGinn 1977a), but not all do. David Lewis, for instance, makes the following suggestion. We can paraphrase non-indicative sentences in terms of indicative sentences (Lewis 1970, §VIII). We can see how the paraphrases work by means of some illustrative examples.

(1) Close the door

is paraphrased as:

(1*) I order that the door is closed.

And

(2) Can I have a coffee?

is paraphrased as:

(2*) I request that I have a coffee.

The paraphrasing sentences, (1*) and (2*), have truth conditions. 'I order that the door is closed' is true if and only if I order that the door is closed. 'I request that I have a coffee' is true if and only if I request that I have a coffee. Since the paraphrasing sentences have truth conditions, there is then some reason to think that the sentences that they paraphrase, (1) and (2), have truth conditions as well.

Here is what Lewis says about the meanings of certain sentences:

> Such meanings can be represented by *performative sentences* such as these. [Lewis cites Austin 1962 in a footnote. The notion of a performative sentence will be explained in §4 below.]

> I command you to be late.
>
> I ask you whether you are late.
>
> Such meanings might also be represented, after a more elaborate transformational derivation by non-declaratives.
>
> Be late!
>
> Are you late?
>
> I propose that these non-declaratives ought to be treated as paraphrases of the corresponding performatives, having the same base structure, meaning, intension and truth-value at an index or on an occasion. And I propose that there is no difference in kind between the meanings of these performatives and non-declaratives and the meanings of the ordinary declarative sentences considered previously. (Lewis 1970, p. 222)

Another suggestion is made by William G. Lycan. He straightforwardly suggests that imperatives, questions and requests (and non-indicative sentences generally) *do* have truth values. Lycan dispenses with Lewis's manoeuvre through paraphrase. The suggestion runs as follows. A declarative sentence has a truth condition: the condition under which the sentence is true. What about imperatives, requests or questions? An imperative has fulfilment conditions: conditions under which the command is obeyed. For example, 'Close the door' is fulfilled if and only if the command is obeyed. Similarly, a request has fulfilment conditions. And a question has conditions in which it is correctly answered. A question is correctly answered if and only if the correct answer is given, otherwise it is not correctly answered. Now depending on whether these semantic conditions are met, an imperative, a request or a question will have a certain truth-like semantic value. But then, as Lycan puts it, 'for semantic purposes we may as well treat those semantic values as truth values' (Lycan 2008, p. 118). His thinking appears to be this. Indicative sentences have semantic values, namely truth values. Imperatives and other non-indicative sentences also have semantic values. We do not need to posit new kinds of entity to be the semantic values of non-indicative sentences. We already admit truth values. In the interest of theoretical economy, we can identify the semantic values of non-indicative sentences with truth values. To achieve this economy, we can broaden the application of the term 'truth value' so that it applies to these other semantic values as well as to truth values more narrowly conceived of. It can be acknowledged that pre-theoretically we do not think of commands or questions as being true or false. Lycan is proposing that we would make a theoretical advance by identifying the semantic values of non-indicative sentences with truth values.

Moreover, it is natural to treat the compliance conditions of non-indicative sentences as forming a sub-class of truth conditions. For example, the sentence 'Close the window' is complied with if and only if 'The door is closed' is true. This provides an independent way of understanding compliance conditions, but it also supports the case for identifying them with truth conditions.

We saw that Frege takes both indicative sentences and questions to express thoughts but denies that the senses expressed by imperatives are thoughts. This introduces an inelegant dichotomy between sentences. We have now seen two accounts which each provide a uniform semantics for indicative and non-indicative sentences. These accounts may have surprising consequences, but they have the appreciable merit of avoiding the complications of Frege's view and of giving a uniform account of the meaning of indicative and non-indicative sentences alike. (For criticisms of this line of argument, see Holdcroft 1978, pp. 100–2. But see also Coady 1981, pp. 581–2 for replies.)

4. Austin on speech acts

In this section, we will consider the work of J. L. Austin on a theory of language which is known as 'speech act theory'. At any early stage of the development of this theory, Austin draws a distinction which substantially resembles Frege's distinction between sense and force. Austin's work goes beyond this, however, and provides an especially rich and fruitful approach to understanding language and the uses to which it is put. Speech act theory offers an explanation and classification of the extensive range of forces which sentences can possess.

In what Austin calls a performative utterance of a declarative sentence, a speaker performs a conventional social act. This act is known as a 'speech act'. Here are some examples:

(3) I accuse you of treason.
(4) I apologize for my treachery.
(5) I sentence you to five years imprisonment.
(6) I declare Jim the winner.
(7) I name this ship the *Plankton*.

Each of these sentences has a declarative form. Yet when a speaker utters (3), she is accusing you of treason. When a speaker utters (4), she is apologizing for her treachery. And when a speaker utters (6) in the appropriate context (say, as a judge at a race), she is declaring Jim to be the winner. In each case, the speaker is performing a speech act. To utter a sentence of this sort is to utter what Austin called a 'performative sentence'.

Is there a way of drawing a distinction between performative sentences and ordinary declarative sentences, or 'constative' sentences, as Austin calls them? Austin takes the distinction to be marked by the so-called hereby criterion. According to this criterion, a sentence of English is a performative if the word hereby can be aptly added before the main verb in the sentence. For instance, in (6) the speaker said, 'I declare Jim the winner', but the speaker could equally well have said, 'I hereby declare Jim the winner'. So (6) counts as a performative sentence. Similar reasoning shows that each of the other sentences in (3–7) are also performative sentences. In contrast, if a speaker says, 'Jamine is asleep in the porch', the speaker could not have aptly said, 'Jamine is hereby asleep in the porch'. That is garbled or false: Jamine is not asleep in the porch because the speaker says that he is.

The hereby criterion seems correctly to draw the distinction between performative and constative sentences. Yet there are also utterances which do not seem to be utterances of constative sentences, but which do not meet the 'hereby' criterion. For example, by saying 'I do' in a marriage ceremony, a speaker performs a marriage oath. But it seems ungrammatical to say, 'I hereby do'. Perhaps, however, 'I do' is an abbreviated way of saying 'I do wed this person', and that sentence does meet the 'hereby' criterion.

A deeper problem for the distinction between performative and constative sentences is generated by sentences such as:

(8)   I state that I have not handled stolen goods.

Austin realized that (8) meets the 'hereby' criterion ('I hereby state that . . .). Whenever a person utters (8), the speech act performed is one of stating something. In stating something, a speaker is saying something which is true or false. So in uttering (8), a speaker says something true or false. Two consequences follow. If a sentence is not a constative if it meets the 'hereby' criterion, then (8) is not constative. And if a sentence is not performative if it declares something, then (8) is not performative.

Here are some other examples:

(9)   I surmise that you are Professor Moriarty.
(10) I note that you are holding a gun.
(11) I warn you that the gun may go off.
(12) I recommend that you turn yourself in.

everything
is
everything

Cases such as these lead Austin to think that every utterance of a sentence involves a performative aspect, and that almost every utterance has a constative (i.e. descriptive) aspect as well. Whenever someone uses a sentence to describe something, that person states or asserts that something is the case – that the world is one way rather than another. The speaker is performing a speech act; they are asserting the sentence.

More recently, some philosophers have characterized performative sentences and utterances of them by reference to the following two features. First, due to its meaning a performative utterance expresses the speaker's intention to make it the case that he or she performs the named action (such as an act of promising). Second, the action is of a type such that expressing the intention to perform it is sufficient to perform it (Recanati 1987, pp. 169–75; Searle 1989, pp. 550–5).

Austin draws a distinction with significant parallels to Frege's distinction between sense and force (Austin 1962, lecture 1). According to Austin, a declarative sentence can be uttered with different *illocutionary forces*. A sentence with one and the same propositional content (or *locutionary content*, as Austin calls it) can be used on different occasions to (say) recommend or to note or to warn. Depending on the context, a declarative sentence can be uttered with different illocutionary forces.

Despite these points of similarity with Frege's distinction between sense and force, there are three important points of contrast. First, Austin does not elaborate on what he takes locutionary content to be. Unlike Frege's construal of sense, Austin seems not to treat it as a theoretical entity. Although he introduces it by mentioning Frege's distinction between sense and reference, he seems to do this only as a way of alluding to what locutionary content is.

Second, Austin goes beyond Frege by listing a wealth of different illocutionary forces and their distinguishing factors, including admonishing, congratulating, pleading, permitting, inquiring, insisting and conceding.

Third, Austin distinguishes a further feature of utterances besides locutionary content and illocutionary force. This is an utterance's *perlocutionary effect*. This concerns the characteristic effects utterances of a given speech act have on an audience's mental states. For example, by uttering the sentence 'I suggest that you look at your credit card bill right away', you are instructing or recommending something to your listener. You may also be intending to frighten your listener into thinking that they have run up a large debt. If that is your intention, and you succeed in frightening your listener that they have run up a large credit card debt, then your utterance has had the desired perlocutionary effect.

Notice that, by contrast, to frighten someone that their credit card is running up a debt, a speaker typically cannot simply say:

(13) I frighten you that your credit card is running up a debt.

Again, a speaker cannot fool someone into thinking that their wallet has been stolen by saying:

(14) I fool you that your wallet is stolen..

These examples contrast with performative sentences such as (3–7). Although uttering sentences such as (13) or (14) indicate that certain acts have been performed – an act of frightening or an act of fooling, as the case may be – they do not meet the 'hereby' criterion. By saying 'I hereby fool Ned into thinking that his wallet is stolen', I will not fool Ned into thinking that his wallet is stolen. Saying 'I hereby frighten you that your credit card is running up a bill', will not, of itself, frighten the listener into thinking that their credit card is running up a bill. Nevertheless, fooling someone or frightening someone is a kind of social effect which can be brought about by words. When this does occur, we then have an example of a perlocutionary effect of a certain speech act.

Speech acts are social and conventional acts. Like many other such acts, they are governed by various rules. John Searle takes there to be two kinds of rules which govern speech acts: constitutive rules and regulative rules. Regulative rules 'regulate antecedently or independently existing forms of behaviour'. Constitutive rules 'create or define new forms of behaviour' (Searle 1969, p. 33). The distinction between these two types of rule is a distinction between activities which occur independently of the rules ('Don't eat peas with your knife', 'Signal before turning') and activities which are defined by the rules (such as the rules governing different sports). If a speaker utters a sentence intending to perform a certain type of speech act, and does not violate any constitutive rule governing speech acts of that type, the speaker performs the speech act. If the speaker violates a regulative rule which governs speech acts of that type, the speech act has been performed 'infelicitously', as Austin puts it. For example, a constitutive rule governing the speech act involved in uttering the sentence 'I sentence the accused to five years imprisonment', is that the speaker is the presiding judge at a trial. A regulative rule is that the accused is guilty of the crime. Suppose that, unknown to the court, the accused is innocent. Then the judge has still passed sentence on the accused, although his or her judgement was infelicitous (i.e. the sentence was defective because it sentenced someone innocent of the crime). This is just one example of how a speech act can be infelicitous; there are many others beside. In the example just given, what was defective was a false assumption that the speaker made. But Austin complained about what he called philosophers' 'true-false fetish': the mistaken presumption that the truth value of a sentence is the only thing that matters in speech (Austin 1962, p. 150). This mistake is, in his view, compounded by a further one: the tendency to take any kind of infelicity in a speech act to indicate that the sentence uttered is false. A speech act can, however, be defective without involving the utterance of a false sentence. It may be defective, for example, because it is true but misleading. As we will see in Chapter 7, this is a major theme of H. P. Grice's work on conversational implicature. (For discussion of Austin's general theory of illocutionary force, see Black 1963; Holdcroft 1978; Bach and Harnish 1979; Bird 1981.)

5. Challenges to the distinction between sense and force

The distinction between sense and force faces a series of challenges. In this section, we will consider a number of them.

The challenge of how to classify forces

If a sentence with a fixed sense can be uttered with different forces, what distinguishes these different forces? How should we count them? Suppose we seek to provide a systematic theory of meaning in which we characterize the senses of sentences in terms of the senses of their components and in which we explain how different forces can operate on the same sense. This requires having a theory of sense and a theory of force. But without some way of counting forces, some way of classifying them, we do not have a theory of force (Cohen 1974, pp. 191–2). It would be as if we were seeking to provide a theory of mechanics but did not have any way of classifying what kinds of factor influence the behaviour of mechanical systems.

To address this objection, here is a classification of forces drawn from John Searle 1975 and François Recanati 1987. First of all, the following distinction is drawn within the class of illocutionary acts (i.e. of speech acts):

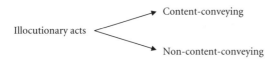

Illocutionary acts — Content-conveying / Non-content-conveying

Content-conveying illocutionary acts have propositional content relating to states of affairs in the world. In Frege's terminology, these illocutionary acts express senses. Non-content-conveying illocutionary acts lack propositional content.

Content-conveying illocutionary acts can themselves be sub-divided:

Content-conveying illocutionary acts — Performatives / Constatives

Both performatives and constatives have propositional content relating to states of affairs in the world. Performative acts are made in order to change the world. More specifically, a performative act such as the uttering of a threat or a promise brings about the state of affairs that the utterance describes. Constatives, by contrast, do not aim to change the world. In a constative act, the utterance made only describes the state of affairs represented by the utterance's propositional content. Performatives and constatives can be classified as follows:

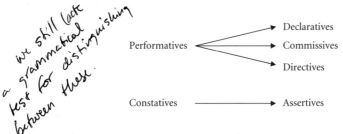

we still lack a grammatical test for distinguishing between these.

Performatives — Declaratives / Commissives / Directives

Constatives — Assertives

An example of a declarative would be to utter 'I name this ship the *U.S.S. Moula*'. An example of a commissive would be to utter 'I promise to not be grumpy in future'. In general, commissive acts commit the speaker to a certain course of action. An example of a directive would be 'Listen up, everyone'.

In general, in a directive utterance, a speaker directs her audience to perform some specified action.

Returning to non-content-conveying illocutionary acts, these consist of expressives:

Non-content-conveying   ⟶   Expressives
illocutionary acts

Expressives include such speech acts as thanking, congratulating, condoling, apologizing and so on. These speech acts do not have a propositional content, hence they are 'non-content conveying'.

This overall classification faces queries. For instance, there is a puzzle about why expressives are classified as non-content-conveying illocutionary acts. Typically, when someone is thanked or congratulated, there is something which the person is being thanked or congratulated for. (Compare the criticisms by Cohen 1964, p. 121; Searle 1968, p. 407 of Austin's distinction between locutionary and illocutionary acts. See Bird 1981, pp. 350–7 for a reply.)

What unifies utterances as utterances of the same speech act?

A theory of forces also requires that each type of force marks more than just a superficial feature of a speech act. For instance, questions in English are often recognizable because of their grammatical *wh*-form ('What is for dinner?' 'Where are my keys?') or by a rising intonation when they are uttered. But not all questions have that form or that intonation. Imagine utterances of 'Is that the best you can do?' or simply 'And?' uttered in a flat sarcastic tone. These examples indicate that features such as *wh*-form or rising intonation are not necessary features of any question that is expressed in English. If interrogative force is to be of interest, it must be a more significant aspect of meaning.

Furthermore, variations in the context of utterance can be enough to change what kind of speech act a sentence is used to make. This is so, even if the sentence is not embedded in a more complex sentence. Suppose the king feels cold and one of his courtiers says to him 'Close the door'. Here the courtier is only advising that the king has the door closed; the courtier is not requesting or ordering the king to close the door. That would be getting above his station. Yet if the king utters the same sentence to his courtier, he thereby issues an order. A difference in context is then enough to generate a difference in speech act. This consideration raises the concern that 'there is no real unity to these similar speech acts; rather, there is a range of acts that superficially resemble one another' (Weiss 2010, p. 85. See also Cohen 1974, p. 196).

The question of the truth conditions of performative sentences

There is a problem facing sentences such as (9–12). Recall (10):

(10) I note that you are holding a gun.

The problem arises when we attempt to say what the truth condition of (10) is. That is, under what condition is (10) true? At first sight, the truth condition of (10) is given by what follows the performative phrase 'I note that', that is, it is given by the sentence 'You are holding a gun'. This might seem plausible because, when a speaker utters (10), the speaker is noting that the person being addressed is holding a gun. The locutionary content of (10) is then that you (the person being addressed) are holding a gun. The role of 'I note that' seems to be just to make explicit the force with which that locutionary content is being put forward. Moreover, the locutionary content of (10) seems to be no more than the locutionary content of the sentence 'You are holding a gun' as uttered by the same speaker and directed at the same audience. It is just that (10) is a more long-winded way of saying things.

L. J. Cohen raised the following problem for the foregoing view. Suppose that Watson witnesses Holmes saying to Moriarty:

(15) I warn you that the gun may go off.

Watson later reports Holmes' words by saying:

(15*) Holmes warned Moriarty that the gun may go off.

Compare what Watson says in (15*) with what Holmes says in (15). Watson refers to the same person that Holmes refers to. He also ascribes the same relation to them that Holmes ascribes to them (namely, that of x's warning y that the gun may go off). The word 'warn' differs in tense between (15) and (15*), but otherwise it has the same meaning. Its meaning does not change between a performative sentence, (15), and a constative sentence, (15*). So, 'warn' in (15) has its standard meaning. Yet, if that is so, this tells against the idea that the phrase 'I warn you that' is a mere force-indicator, and that it can be set aside when giving the truth condition of (15).

Phrases such as 'I warn you that' or 'I surmise that' are known as 'performative prefaces' – they can be used to preface declarative sentences to generate performative sentences. A further consideration of the idea that performative prefaces are mere force-indicators is the fact that they have grammatical structure. This structure can be built upon by the addition of adverbial modifiers. Holmes might say, 'I warn you in no uncertain terms that the gun is loaded' or 'I unreservedly recommend that you turn yourself in', or 'Because of your menacing air and rounded shoulders, I surmise that you are Professor Moriarty'. In this last example, the performative preface contains an entire clause which the speaker *states*, albeit in passing.

Given these considerations, we might abandon the view that the truth condition of a sentence such as (15) is given by what follows the performative preface. We might instead take the entire sentence, that is, the sentence including the performative preface, as providing the truth condition of (15). This suggestion, however, raises a problem of its own. It entails that sentences such as (3–7) are true, provided only that they are uttered and that no constitutive rule is thereby violated. We will consider the case for thinking that that consequence is acceptable in §5 below. (For other responses to Cohen's objection, see Cresswell 1973, chapter 14; Lycan 1984, chapter 6.)

How can the distinction between sense and force apply to performatives?

If there is a distinction between sense and force, then, for every sense, if a given sentence expresses that sense with a certain force in one context, then there should be another sentence which expresses the same sense but with a different force in another context. Yet consider the sense of a sentence which is an explicit performative – a sentence that has a performative preface such as 'I promise' or 'I warn'. When someone makes a promise they utter a sentence with commissive force, that is, they commit themselves to doing what they promise to do. What is the sense of a sentence such as 'I promise to repay the loan' distinct from its commissive force? If a speaker were to utter the sentence in question, what locutionary act would he or she perform? Take another example. If a speaker were to utter the sentence 'Is it raining?', what would be the meaning of the locutionary act performed other than to ask whether it is raining? (Cohen 1964, p. 427). If we were to make the performative preface in the question explicit, we would have the sentence 'I ask whether it is raining', and, in that case, we have made the meaning of the sentence explicit.

The point of the objection is that it is unclear what the distinction between sense and force amounts to in cases where the meaning of the performative preface entirely circumscribes the sense of the sentence uttered. (For further criticism of the distinction between sense and force, see Cohen 1973; Barker 2007.)

6. Illocutionary theories of meaning

An illocutionary theory of meaning seeks to account for the meaning of certain sentences (and perhaps even of all sentences) in terms of the kinds of speech act which are made in uttering those sentences. That is to say, such a theory seeks to account for the meaning of those sentences in terms of the illocutionary forces which utterances of those sentences convey. (Alston 1963 and 2000 each offer an illocutionary theory of meaning intended to apply to the meaning of all sentences of a natural language.)

An influential claim of Austin's provided some of the motivation for theories of this kind. Austin claims that philosophers easily, but fallaciously, fall into thinking that, because a given sentence has the grammatical form of an indicative sentence, the sentence has a descriptive function. Austin labelled this 'the descriptive fallacy' (Austin 1946, p. 174). For example, the sentence 'I know that there is snow on the hills' has the grammatical form of an indicative sentence. It is then tempting to think that the sentence has a descriptive function: namely, describing a relation (the knowledge relation) that holds between the speaker and the proposition *that there is snow on the hills*. Austin claimed that this was a mistake. The sentence may have the grammatical form of an indicative sentence, but (he claimed) its function is not to describe, but to commit the speaker to something. To say 'I know that there is snow on the hills' is more like saying 'I promise to repay the loan'. In saying 'I promise to repay the loan', the speaker thereby makes a promise. Moreover, Austin thinks that in making a promise, a speaker is not describing anything. Uttering 'I promise to repay the loan' is not to be understood as reporting a relation (the promising relation) between a speaker and something else (the proposition *that the loan is repaid*). You cannot sensibly deny what the speaker said. You cannot sensibly say 'What you said is false; you do not promise to repay the loan'. Austin claims that, similarly, in saying 'I know that there is snow on the hills', the speaker makes a promise. The speaker is promising that he or she can be relied upon about there being snow on the hills. The speaker is giving their word on this matter. As Austin puts it:

> . . . saying "I know" is taking a new plunge. But it is *not* saying "I have performed a specially striking feat of cognition, superior, in the same scale as believing and being sure, even to being merely quite sure": for there *is* nothing in that scale superior to being quite sure. Just as promising is not something superior, in the same scale as hoping and intending, even to merely fully intending: for there is nothing in that scale superior to fully intending. When I say "I know", I *give others my word: I give others my authority for saying "S is P"*. (Austin 1946, p. 171)

What Austin has to say about sentences with the performative preface 'I know' has encouraged other philosophers to seek out other examples supposedly of this sort. P. F. Strawson claims that to say '"There is snow on the hills" is true' is not to describe the sentence 'There is snow on the hills', or to attribute the property of truth to it, or even to make any statement at all. Instead, he claims that it is to endorse or to emphasize the sentence 'There is snow on the hills' (Strawson 1949). Again, R. M. Hare claims that to say 'Stealing is wrong' is not to describe stealing in any way, and, in particular, it is not to attribute the property of *wrongness* to stealing. He claims that to utter the sentence is not to say something that is true or false. Instead, uttering the sentence serves to express the speaker's condemnation of people stealing. Similarly, he claims that uttering 'Charity is good' is to commend people's being charitable. More generally, Hare says that 'the primary function of the word "good" is to commend' (Hare 1952, p. 127).

We might criticize one or another of these speech act theories on their individual merits. (See, e.g. Harrison 1962 for a criticism of Austin's speech act theory of first-person knowledge avowals.) A more ambitious strategy would be to try to show that all of these speech act theories involve common failings. The theories in question advance two claims. First, they claim that, for a certain class of sentences, those sentences' having a non-descriptive function excludes their having a descriptive function. Given that an utterance of a sentence is true or false only if it has a descriptive function, it was perhaps for this reason that Austin takes utterances of performative sentences to be neither true nor false (Austin 1962, p. 6). Second, the theories claim that the meanings of the sentences in question can be fully explained in terms of their non-descriptive function. Both claims can be contested. We will conclude this section with an objection to the first claim. In §7, we will consider an important objection to the second claim.

The first claim commits what Roderick Chisholm called *the performative fallacy*: the fallacy of supposing that if a sentence performs a non-descriptive function, it cannot simultaneously perform a descriptive function (Chisholm 1964, p. 10). When I say 'I want a coffee', I can consistently be reporting something about myself – about what mental state I am in vis-à-vis the proposition that I have a coffee – while instructing you to get me a coffee. Likewise when I say 'I know that there's snow on the hills', I can consistently be reporting something about myself – about what mental state I have vis-à-vis the proposition that there is snow on the hills – while guaranteeing to you that there is snow on the hills.

Furthermore, there is a case for saying that, in uttering a performative sentence, a speaker not only performs the speech act in question but also states that he or she has performed that act. So, for example, when a speaker says 'I apologize for spilling the coffee', the speaker apologizes, but, in addition, states that he or she apologizes. Given this, the speaker has uttered a sentence with a truth value. For another example, consider the sentence 'I hereby utter a sentence of English'. In uttering that sentence, one performs a certain speech act and states that one is doing so. (See also Houston 1970; Cresswell 1973, chapter 14; Bach 1975; Ginet 1979. Lemmon 1962 suggested that a performative sentence is a declarative sentence that is verifiable in certain circumstances by its own utterance.)

The second claim which the speech act theories make is that the meaning of the sentences they single out can be fully explained in terms of their non-descriptive function. We will assess this claim in §7. There we will consider Peter Geach's use of the distinction between sense and force in an important objection to Hare's speech act theory of the meaning of moral sentences.

7. Geach's use of the Frege point

Geach believes that speech act theories of the meaning of sentences can be refuted by what he calls 'the Frege point' (Geach 1965). By this he means that they fail to observe the distinction between what a sentence means (its sense) and what speech acts it is frequently used in (its force). These speech act theories fail because they mistakenly seek to characterize the first feature of a sentence, its meaning, solely in terms of the second – its use in a certain type of speech act. As a representative case, we see how Geach uses the Frege point against Hare's theory of the function of moral language. First of all, we need to know a little more about Hare's theory and its background.

There are conflicting theories about the function of moral language. One such theory is cognitivism. Cognitivism claims that the function of a moral sentence is descriptive. For example, according to cognitivism, the function of *can't it also have different senses?*

the sentence 'Gambling is wrong' is descriptive: the sentence describes gambling as being (morally) wrong. Such a sentence can be true or false. It is also a sentence which can be an object of belief: someone can believe that the sentence is true or that it is false, as the case may be. A rival theory about the function of moral language is non-cognitivism. Non-cognitivism denies that the function of moral sentences is descriptive. According to non-cognitivism, a sentence such as 'Gambling is wrong' does not have a descriptive function. That sentence does not describe gambling in any way. Consequently, that sentence is not true or false. Nor does the sentence express something which can be believed or disbelieved. According to non-cognitivism, the function of a moral sentence is instead to express some non-cognitive attitude of the utterer of the sentence. For example, someone sincerely uttering 'Gambling is wrong' would thereby be expressing some attitude that they have against gambling. This might be an attitude of disapproval. Or they might be expressing a more complex set of attitudes, such as disapproval of gambling and a desire that others share their disapproval of it. Hare himself defended a non-cognitivist theory of moral language. A sincere utterance of a sentence such as 'Gambling is wrong' expresses the speaker's disapprobation of gambling and also an instruction that people desist from gambling. A sincere utterance of a sentence such as 'Charity is right' expresses the speaker's approbation of charity and also an instruction that people be charitable (Hare 1952).

Geach objects that a non-cognitivist theory of moral language, such as Hare's, overlooks the fact that moral sentences can be uttered in contexts in which they do not express any attitude on the part of the speaker, whether pro or con. To show this, he invited us to consider an argument such as the following:

Sure, but this requires we accept (D)

(D) *Gambling is wrong.*

(E) If *gambling is wrong*, then getting your brother to gamble is wrong.

(F) So: getting your brother to gamble is wrong.

The same considerations that apply to the argument (A–C) in §3 apply here also. The argument is an instance of *modus ponens*, a valid form of argument. The argument (D–F) is valid only if the italicized sentence has the same meaning in both (D) and (E). And, even if sincerely uttering (D) involves uttering the italicized sentence with disapprobatory force, sincerely uttering (E) does not involve uttering the italicized sentence embedded in it with disapprobatory force. In uttering the conditional, a speaker does not express any attitude pro or con gambling. The problem for Hare is that these facts seem to be inconsistent with his claim that the meaning of any utterance of 'Gambling is wrong' consists in its expressing the speaker's condemnation of gambling.

The Frege point is not confined to the use of moral sentences in the antecedents or consequents of conditionals. A moral sentence can also occur as a disjunct in a disjunction ('Either bear-baiting is wrong, or we can be just as cruel to bears as we please'). It can also be prefaced by a negation ('It is not the case that charity is good'). All of these sentences can figure as premises in arguments.

What options does Hare have? Denying that (D–F) is a good piece of reasoning is not a promising option. People use *modus ponens* and other valid principles of inference in their moral thinking. In using such reasoning, people will often use sentences containing moral terms such as 'right' and 'wrong' without expressing any pro- or con-attitude. Since Hare is seeking to account for ordinary moral talk and practices, it is incumbent upon him to account for the reliability of such patterns of reasoning. For the same reason, denying that the italicized sentences in (D) and (E) have the same meaning is not a promising option. If those sentences differ in meaning, then the argument (D–F) is invalid. Yet it is a valid argument, and we use the kind of reasoning it displays very frequently in our everyday lives.

The only option open to Hare seems to be that of accounting for the meaning of the italicized sentences in the same way. Geach thinks that Hare's non-cognitivism has to be rejected, and, for example, that condemning something by calling it 'wrong' has to be explained in terms of the general notion of predicating 'wrong' of something, and not *vice versa*.

In contrast, given his non-cognitivist account of 'Gambling is wrong' as it occurs in (D), and given that that sentence has the same meaning in (E), Hare has to give a non-cognitivist account of its meaning in both (D) and (E). Hare undertakes that task in a paper replying to Geach (Hare 1970. See also Schroeder 2008, pp. 706–7). We will close this section by considering Hare's strategy in that paper.

Set aside non-cognitivism for the moment. There is a general question about what fixes the meaning of complex *descriptive* sentences. The sentences 'The tomato is red' and 'If the tomato is red, then it is ripe' differ in their truth conditions. Nevertheless, 'red' has the same meaning in each sentence. Hare thinks that the situation facing non-cognitivism is no different. Granted there is a question facing non-cognitivism about what fixes the meaning of complex *evaluative* sentences. Utterances of 'Gambling is wrong' and 'If gambling is wrong, then getting your brother to gamble is wrong' perform different speech acts – the first sentence expresses the speaker's condemnation of gambling whereas the second does not. Nevertheless, Hare adds, that does not commit non-cognitivists to holding that 'Gambling is wrong' has different meanings as it occurs in each sentence.

In the case of a complex descriptive sentence, such as 'If the tomato is red, it is ripe', its truth condition is a function of 'The tomato is red' and 'The tomato is ripe'. The function is given by the meaning of the connective 'if-then'. So 'The tomato is red' has the same meaning whether it occurs unembedded or embedded in a complex sentence. In either case, it makes the same contribution to the truth conditions of 'If the tomato is red, then it is ripe'. So, the sentence 'The tomato is red' has the same meaning whether it occurs unembedded or embedded in a complex sentence.

Let's now turn to consider how this can be used to illuminate the non-cognitivist view of evaluative sentences. Hare thinks that a similar, but non-cognitivist, account can be given for complex evaluative sentences. What kind of speech act is performed by an utterance of 'If gambling is wrong, then getting your brother to gamble is wrong' is a function of what kind of speech act is performed by utterances of 'Gambling is wrong' and 'Getting your brother to gamble is wrong'. This function is given by the meaning of the connective 'if-then'. 'Gambling is wrong' has the same meaning whether it occurs embedded or unembedded in a complex sentence. In either case, it makes the same contribution to the speech act made by any utterance of 'If gambling is wrong, then getting your brother to gamble is wrong'. So, Hare concludes, 'Gambling is wrong' has the same (non-cognitivist) meaning whether it occurs unembedded or embedded in a complex sentence.

Hare's account is promising but programmatic. It is controversial how the details are to be supplied and whether any resulting account is successful. What the non-cognitivist needs to do is to provide an account that systematically says, for each sentence, what speech act it is apt to make. And since, for non-cognitivists, utterances of moral sentences express affective mental states (such as desires), the non-cognitivist also needs to provide an account, for each sentence, of just which mental states utterances of that sentence are apt to express. (For accounts along these lines, see Blackburn 1984, chapter 6 §2 and 1988; Gibbard 1990, chapter 5. For assessment of these efforts, see Cohen 1974, pp. 205–6; Hale 1986, pp. 71–6, 1993, and 2002; Miller 2003, chapters 3–5.)

If Geach is right about the Frege point, a swathe of speech act theories of the meanings of various sentences turn out to be mistaken. We might want a general diagnosis of where those theories go wrong. John Searle's diagnosis is that they commit what he calls 'the speech act fallacy'. This is the fallacy of inferring from what semantic function a word *w* has in simple present tense indicative sentences to what semantic function *w* has in *every* sentence in which it figures. To illustrate the fallacy, here is why Searle thinks that Hare commits it. Simple present tense indicative sentences featuring 'good' are sentences that call something good. Suppose that to call something good is characteristically to approve or commend it. The fallacy is then to infer from this that the meaning of 'good' is given by saying that it is used to commend (Searle 1969, p. 139).

What Searle calls the speech act fallacy seems to be a special case of the so-called fallacy of hasty generalization. This is the fallacy of inferring from only a selection of all known case of a certain kind to all cases of that kind. It involves ignoring evidence already available while making general claims about cases that include that evidence. That is bad inductive practice. Whether Hare and other speech act theorists are guilty of this fallacy turns on the issue we have just reviewed, namely, whether they can give a uniform account of the terms at issue. (For further discussion of the speech act theories of Strawson and Hare, see Soames 2003b, chapters 5 and 6. Schroeder 2010 is a recent book length treatment of non-cognitivism and the Frege point.)

8. Conclusion

Frege distinguishes between the sense and reference of a sentence, where the sense is the propositional content of the sentence, something which can be true or false, and the reference is the truth value of the sentence. Yet not all sentences seem to express senses, propositional contents which can be true or false. How can Frege account for this fact? To do so, Frege introduces a further distinction, the distinction between sense and force. It seems that the sense expressed by the question 'Has the chef been fired?' and by the assertion 'The chef has been fired' is the same. This sense can be specified by a that-clause: that the chef has been fired. The difference between the sentences – what makes one a question and the other an assertion – lies in the different forces with which the sentences are uttered. In Austin's terminology, in uttering those sentences speakers perform different speech acts.

Introducing the distinction between sense and force in this way also marks one traditional way of drawing the distinction between semantics and pragmatics. Semantics concerns all aspects of language which can be described by a truth conditional semantics for a language: a semantics which characterizes the meaning of sentences in terms of the conditions in which they are true. Pragmatics

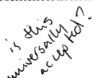
is this universally accepted?

concerns all other aspects of language, such as the kinds of speech act with which sentences are uttered, the use of non-literal language and so forth.

Turning to the questions raised in the introduction to this book, (Q2) asked what gives words and sentences their particular meanings. Our discussion of sense and force introduced different accounts. Frege's account identifies the sense of a sentence with that aspect of the sentence's meaning that determines its truth condition. He then allows that sentences with the same sense can differ in tone: in how they can differ in the reactions they produce in an audience. He further distinguishes between the sense of a sentence and the type of force with which it is uttered on a particular occasion. This is a matter of which speech act the sentence is used to perform on that occasion.

This account also bears on (Q3), the question of how we understand words and sentences. Our understanding of words enables us to select between words with the same sense but different tones so that the words we choose do not mislead our audiences. Furthermore, our understanding of a sentence requires that we can identify that sentence as having the same sense even if it occurs now asserted, now unasserted.

(Q9) asked what the role of pragmatics is in language. We have seen that what speech act a speaker makes, and so what the speaker has said, can depend on the context of utterance. One and the same utterance can be an assertion or an order depending on the context in which it is uttered – who is speaking, whom they are speaking to and what the non-linguistic circumstances are in which the speech act is made. Is force a pragmatic phenomenon or a semantic one? There are rival answers to this question. One answer is that the force of a sentence uttered on a particular occasion is determined by pragmatic factors, such as a speaker's intentions in uttering the sentence. A rival answer is that the force of the utterance of a sentence is determined by semantic properties of the sentence. In particular, the force of a sentence is determined by the meaning of some underlying element of the sentence, or by some associated force-indicating device, such as 'I apologize for . . .' or 'I promise that . . .' (For further discussion of this issue, see Stampe 1975).

Questions for discussion

Question 1

Frege thinks that the tone of an expression is part of its literal meaning and is something objective. But he also says that the tone of a pair of expressions differ if they are associated with different ideas by people. Is Frege consistent? (Cf. Dummett 1981a, pp. 87–8.)

Question 2

Which of the following speech acts involve distinctive forces and which do not? Asserting, joking, pretending to assert, mocking, boasting and teasing. Do difficulties in answering that question support the sceptical claim that there is no way of classifying forces?

Question 3

Can imperatives figure in arguments? For example, do the following sentences constitute an argument?

The Aardvark café is the best cafe in town.
Go to the best café in town!
So: go to the Aardvark café!

Since the would-be conclusion and one of the would-be premises are imperatives, and if imperatives cannot have truth values, in what sense can the above sequence be a *valid* argument? (See Williams and Geach 1963.)

Question 4

There seem to be indefinitely many ways of requesting someone to open the window. Only a few of them are direct ways (such as 'Please open the window'). The many indirect ways vary syntactically and semantically: 'Would you be so kind as to open the window?', 'Are you able to open the window?', 'It'd be a great idea to open the window', 'Now, what should people do when the room's stuffy?' (Levinson 1983, pp. 246ff.) How is it that many of these utterances have the syntactic and semantic properties of assertions or questions and yet they can all be requests?

Question 5

Austin claimed that performative verbs characteristically occur in the first person singular present indicative active form, as in 'I warn you', 'I promise you' and so on. Yet there are also verbs that seem to be performative although they do not have that form, such as 'brag', 'insinuate', 'goad', 'incite' and 'flatter'. For example, no one is likely to say 'I hereby flatter you'. Why is this?

Question 6

When we utter a sentence we can emphasize some particular word or phrase rather than another. The following three sentences provide an illustration:

(A) Why did *Adam* eat the apple?
(B) Why did Adam *eat* the apple?
(C) Why did Adam eat the *apple*?

(A) asks why Adam (rather than someone else) ate the apple. (B) asks why Adam ate the apple (rather than do something else with it). (C) asks why Adam ate the apple (rather than eat something else). Do (A–C) differ in sense (i.e. their truth conditions)? Do they differ in any other aspect of meaning? (See Dretske 1972 or Boër 1979.)

Now consider the following three sentences:

(D) It was unfortunate that *Adam* ate the apple.
(E) It was unfortunate that Adam *ate* the apple.
(F) It was unfortunate that Adam ate the *apple*.

Again, these sentences differ in their *foci*. Do they differ in sense? Do they differ in any other aspect of meaning?

Further reading

Austin, J. L. (1962) *How To Do Things With Words*.
Dummett, Michael (1981a) *Frege: Philosophy of Language* chapter 10.
Frege, Gottlob (1918) 'The Thought: A Logical Inquiry'.
Geach, P. T. (1965) 'Assertion'.
Hare, R. M. (1970) 'Meaning and Speech Acts'.
Hornsby, Jennifer (2006) 'Speech Acts and Performatives'.
Lycan, William G. (2008) *Philosophy of Language: a Contemporary Introduction* chapter 12.
Miller, Alexander (2007) *Philosophy of Language* chapter 2 §2.7.
Schroeder, Mark (2008) 'What is the Frege-Geach Problem?'.
Stainton, Robert J. (1996) *Philosophical Perspectives on Language* chapter 5 §2.
Stenius, Erik (1967) 'Mood and Language-Game'.
Taylor, Kenneth (1998) *Truth and Meaning: An Introduction to the Philosophy of Language* chapter VI §3.

5

Russell on Definite Descriptions

1. Introduction

In Chapter 1 §2, we considered the distinction between names ('Barack Obama', 'Mount Everest') and definite descriptions ('the 44th President of the United States', 'the tallest mountain'). We introduced the distinction by means of examples, and noted that, whereas a name purports to pick out something without apparently describing it, a definite description purports to pick out something by describing it. But what more can be said about definite descriptions? What function do they serve in language? In this chapter, we will consider Bertrand Russell's theory of definite descriptions, the puzzles it is designed to overcome, and some of the major criticisms it faces.

Russell shares many of Frege's philosophical interests. Both of them seek to show how we could have knowledge of mathematical claims. To that end, they each seek to reduce mathematics to logic. This shared programme in the philosophy of mathematics (logicism) greatly influences the development of their philosophies of language. They each devise formal languages ('a logically perfect language', in Russell's phrase) designed to eliminate ambiguity and unclarity, and which are governed by explicit rules of inference in order to facilitate reasoning and to solve theoretical problems (see Sainsbury 1979, chapter V). Russell's theory of descriptions is part of this project. As we will see, Russell formulates it order to solve various logical problems which sentences containing definite descriptions give rise to.

2. Frege and Russell on definite descriptions

In 1905, Russell published a pioneering paper 'On Denoting' that, among other things, presents a novel theory of definite descriptions. To understand his theory, it is useful to draw some distinctions between different kinds of description and then to contrast Russell's approach to the topic of definite descriptions with Frege's.

Here are three cross-cutting distinctions between different kinds of description. First, definite descriptions contrast with indefinite descriptions. In English, indefinite descriptions are of the form 'an F', 'some Fs' or 'a G'. In definite descriptions, a particular individual is picked out. So, in sentences such as 'Tony visited the court house' or 'The lake is polluted', particular individuals – the court house, the lake – are picked out. This does not happen in the case of indefinite descriptions. Sentences such as 'A thief stole my wallet' or 'Some days are better than others', even when they are true, do not pick out any particular individual thief or any particular days.

Second, there is a distinction between singular and plural descriptions. We have already seen examples of singular definite descriptions. Examples of plural definite descriptions include 'the cowboys' and 'the winners'. Russell's theory of singular definite descriptions has received a great deal of critical attention, and it is the theory that we will focus on here. We should note, though, that he also has a separate theory which applies to plural definite descriptions (Russell 1919, chapter 17. For assessment of that theory, see Oliver and Smiley 2005, §1).

Third, there is a distinction between proper and improper definite descriptions. This is an analogue to the distinction between names that succeed in referring and names that do not (so-called empty names such as 'Excalibur' or 'Atlantis'). Confining ourselves to singular definite descriptions, some of these descriptions pick out objects ('the 44th President of the United States', 'the most precious metal') whereas others fail to do so ('the retirement of John F. Kennedy', 'the perpetual motion machine'). Russell's theory of (singular) definite descriptions applies to both proper and improper singular definite descriptions.

Russell's approach to the topic of definite descriptions contrasts with Frege's in two key respects (Morris 2007, pp. 49–50). Frege holds that both proper names and definite descriptions have senses. He also holds that ordinary proper names and definite descriptions belong to the same fundamental category of expressions, the category of names. Russell rejects both claims. Russell rejects Frege's postulation of senses. He thinks that those puzzles that Frege posits senses in order to solve can be solved without positing senses. If senses are redundant, then there is no need to posit them. (For assessment of whether Russell avoided Fregean senses, see Carney and Fitch 1979.) On some interpretations, Russell also has independent but obscure arguments against Frege's senses (Searle 1958; Blackburn and Code 1978; Noonan 1996). Furthermore, Russell also claims that names and definite descriptions form two fundamentally different categories of expressions. The two kinds of expressions, he believes, function in semantically different ways. Sentences in which they each figure have what he called different 'logical forms'. As we will see, Russell also thinks that ordinary proper names are not genuine names, but are in fact definite descriptions.

The notion of logical form which Russell introduces in 'On Denoting' plays an important role in his arguments. Yet it is not entirely clear how he thinks of logical form, and various philosophers have subsequently offered rival interpretations of his thinking. One interpretation, the non-linguistic view of logical form, draws a sharp distinction between the logical form and the grammatical form of a sentence (see, e.g. Soames 2003a, p. 99). The grammatical form of a sentence is a matter of its apparent syntactic structure. The logical form of a sentence is the type of proposition which the sentence expresses. Sentences may have similar grammatical forms but different logical forms.

A rival interpretation, the linguistic view of logical form, takes Russell to distinguish between grammatical form and logical form but does not take him to distinguish between two kinds of entities, sentences and propositions. Instead, it takes the distinction to occur entirely at the linguistic level (see, e.g.

Stevens 2005). On this view, talk of logical form is talk of a special kind of linguistic representation that enables us to utter truths while avoiding falling into any of the absurdities incurred by the original grammatical form. One such absurdity, for example, would be to take 'No one was the winner of the race' to be an identity sentence holding between the winner of the race and an elusive individual known as 'No one'. According to this view, 'the logical form of a sentence is the grammatical form the sentence should have' (Kalish 1952, p. 60. See also Quine 1960, chapters 5 and 7). Having noted these rival interpretations of Russell, however, we can set them aside because each of them is compatible with the material which follows.

Russell thinks that grammatical form is a poor guide to the logical form of a sentence and that it frequently misleads us. In particular, many philosophical problems arise because the grammatical form of various sentences misleads us as to their logical form:

> Some of the notions that have been thought absolutely fundamental in philosophy have arisen, I think, entirely due to mistakes in symbolism. (Russell 1918, pp. 185–6)
> . . . practically all metaphysics is filled with mistakes due to bad grammar. (Russell 1918, p. 269. See also Russell 1919, p. 168)

The fact that the grammatical structure of a sentence and its logical form may differ does not itself warrant the claim that grammar is a bad guide to logical form. It depends how often and how severely the grammatical forms of sentences differ from their logical forms. Until we establish how these matters stand, we would be in danger of over-reacting. We would be over-reacting in the manner of Descartes who, at the start of his *Meditations*, set aside all his perceptual beliefs on the ground that perception sometimes misleads us. That methodological policy deprives us of a valuable source of information about the world. Similarly, Russell's injunction threatens to deprive us of a potentially valuable source of information about the logical form of sentences. In this respect, Frege presents more nuanced views about the powers of natural language. He compares natural and artificial languages to the eye and microscope, respectively. The eye is more versatile than the microscope but 'as soon as scientific purposes place strong requirements upon sharpness of resolution, the eye proves to be inadequate. On the other hand, the microscope is perfectly suited for just such purposes' (Frege 1879, p. 105. See also Rein 1985).

3. Five puzzles for a theory of descriptions

Theories are accepted because of their puzzle-solving abilities. We will see in §4 that Russell's case for his theory of descriptions is that it can solve various logical puzzles (Russell 1905, p. 484). Moreover, he claims that it can do so without positing either Fregean senses or non-existent objects. Before we look at Russell's theory itself, let us first consider the puzzles which his theory seeks to solve. The first three of these puzzles are taken from Frege (Frege 1892). We saw these puzzles in Chapter 1 §3 and §7 and Chapter 3 §4. The fourth and fifth puzzles are presented by Russell in 'On Denoting'. Here are the five puzzles:

Puzzle 1: The puzzle of informative identity sentences

How can '$a = a$' and '$a = b$' differ in informativeness if $a = b$?

Puzzle 2: The puzzle of empty names

How can a name have meaning if it does not name anything?

Puzzle 3: The puzzle of indirect contexts

If $a = b$, then why cannot 'a' and 'b' always be substituted without change of truth value in any sentence that contains one of them?

Puzzle 4: The puzzle of apparent reference to non-existents

How can any sentence of the form 'The F does not exist' be true?

Puzzle 5: The puzzle of the implications of the Law of Excluded Middle

Either 'The Loch Ness Monster has fins' is true or 'The Loch Ness Monster does not have fins' is true; either way the Loch Ness Monster exists.

Since puzzles 1–3 are by now familiar to us, we will not review them again in this section. Let us consider puzzle 4. This is a special case of puzzle 2. Consider the following sentence:

(1) The Loch Ness Monster does not exist.

If (1) is true, then the Loch Ness Monster does not exist. But in that case it seems that the sentence is not about anything. Yet if that is so, it is difficult to see what the sentence could mean, and so it is difficult to see how the sentence could be true. So, puzzle 4 comes to this: how can a true sentence say of something that it does not exist?

Puzzle 5 concerns the implications of a certain law of logic. As Russell understands it, the Law of Excluded Middle (LEM) says that, for every indicative sentence, either that sentence or its negation is true. Consequently, either (2) is true or (3) is true:

(2) The Loch Ness Monster has fins.
(3) The Loch Ness Monster does not have fins.

If (2) is true, there exists something referred to by 'the Loch Ness Monster' and it has fins. It follows that the Loch Ness Monster exists. If (3) is true, there exists something referred to by 'the Loch Ness Monster', and it lacks fins. It follows that the Loch Ness Monster exists. On either alternative, then, the Loch Ness Monster exists.

Positing senses does not solve puzzles 4 and 5. Consider puzzle 4. Even if 'the Loch Ness Monster' has a sense, it does not have a reference. According to Frege, a sentence containing an empty name lacks reference, that is, is neither true nor false. In that case, 'The Loch Ness Monster does not exist' would not be true but truth valueless. Yet that sentence is surely true. Consider puzzle 5. The same considerations show that, for Frege, neither 'The Loch Ness Monster has fins' nor 'The Loch Ness Monster does not have fins' is true, and that result violates the Law of Excluded Middle.

Russell rejects the option of taking empty names to refer to non-existents. At an earlier stage of his philosophical career, he was more receptive to this option:

> Whatever may be an object of thought, or can occur in a true proposition, or can be counted as a one, I call a term. . . Every term has being, i.e., is in some sense. (Russell 1903, p. 43)
>   . . . to mention anything is to show that it is. Existence, on the contrary, is the prerogative of some only amongst beings. To exist is to have a specific relationship to existence . . . . (Russell 1903, p. 449)

Even at that stage of his career, however, Russell does not consistently endorse that option (e.g. Russell 1903, §73 implies a contrary view). In any case, he came to reject thoroughly any view according to which there are entities that exist and there are also entities that do not exist. Among other things, such a view exhibits what Russell describes as 'a failure of that feeling for reality which ought to be preserved even in the most abstract studies' (Russell 1919, p. 169). (Russell's denial that there are any entities that do not exist was endorsed by Quine 1948. Replies to Quine are made by Routley 1982; Priest 2005, pp. 108–15.)

The significance of this issue for our purposes is that Russell takes it to be a constraint on an adequate solution to the above puzzles that it does not posit non-existent entities.

4. Russell's theory of descriptions

Now let us look at Russell's theory of descriptions itself. His theory is supposed to give the logical form of sentences containing singular definite descriptions. A sentence such as:

(4) The 11th World Chess Champion was American.

is, on the face of it, grammatically like the following sentence:

(5) Bobby Fischer was American.

As a matter of fact, these similarities may not extend very far (see Oliver 1999). But, in any case, Russell takes the superficial grammatical similarity between them to mask important logical differences between these sentences. According to Russell, although a sentence of the form 'The F is G' has the same grammatical form as a subject/predicate sentence, it has the following logical form: quantifier/ singular noun phrase/predicate. A quantifier (such as 'all', 'every', 'some' or 'a') is a linguistic device that specifies some quantity of a given group. It answers the question 'How many?' A singular noun phrase 'F' specifies what the group is. In combination with the quantifier it answers the question 'How many F's?' Lastly, a predicate specifies some condition which things meet. In combination with the quantifier and the noun phrase, it answers the question 'How many F's are G?'

Russell's theory analyses sentences of the form of (6):

(6) The F is G

in terms of sentences of the form of (7):

(7) There is exactly one object which is F and everything that is F is G.

Russell also takes (7) to be equivalent to the following conjunction, (8a–c) (Russell 1919, p. 177):

(8a) There is at least one object which is F, and
(8b) There is at most one object which is F, and

(8c)   Whatever is F is G.

In predicate logic:

$$(\exists x)[Fx \wedge (\forall y) (Fy \rightarrow (y = x)) \wedge Gx]$$

Russell takes (7) to reveal the logical form of (6). Despite differences of interpretation about what Russell takes this to involve, it is generally agreed that Russell takes sentences of the form of (7) to specify the truth conditions of sentences of the form of (6).

There are several things to note about this analysis. First, Russell does not seek to analyse the expression 'the F' 'in isolation', in his phrase. His theory provides an analysis of sentences in which expressions of the form 'the F' occur. By analysing a description sentence (as we might call it), he thereby provides an analysis of its component expression 'the F'. Russell is giving a contextual definition of that expression: he explains what it means in the context of any sentence in which it occurs.

Second, no expression equivalent to 'the F' occurs in (7) or in (8a–c). The expression 'the F' has 'disappeared under analysis'. As we will see in §5, this is important to Russell's solutions to the puzzle of empty names and the puzzle of apparent reference to non-existing things.

Third, because no expression equivalent to 'the F' occurs in (7), Russell takes his theory to show that expressions of the form 'the F' are not genuine names and that they do not purport to refer to anything. They are revealed to be quantifying phrases which purport (in Russell's phrase) to denote things. 'The F' denotes object o if and only if only o is F.

With Russell's theory in place, we are now in position to consider how he takes it to solve each of the puzzles.

5. Russell's solutions to the puzzles

Let us consider Russell's solutions to each of the five puzzles in turn.

Solution to puzzle 1: the puzzle of informative identity sentences

Suppose that there is exactly one man who is shifty-eyed. Suppose also that there is exactly one jewel thief. Consider the following identity sentence:

(9)   The shifty-eyed man is the jewel thief.

Russell's theory would analyse (9) as (10a–c):

(10a) There is exactly one object which is a shifty-eyed man, and

(10b) There is exactly one object which is a jewel thief, and

(10c) Whatever is a shifty-eyed man is a jewel thief, and vice versa.

Russell's analysis seeks to explain why (9) is informative in the following way. Two predicates occur in this analysis: 'x is a shifty-eyed man' and 'x is a jewel thief'. (10a) says that the first predicate applies to exactly one object. (10b) says that the second predicate applies to exactly one object. (10c) says that these predicates are equivalent: that they apply to exactly the same object (or objects). According to Russell's theory of predication, predicates designate properties or relations. The two predicates mentioned above designate different properties: the properties of *being a shifty-eyed man* and *being a jewel thief*, respectively. It is then informative to be told that these predicates apply to the same object.

Solution to puzzle 2: the puzzle of empty names

This is the puzzle of how a name can have meaning although it does not refer to anything. Let's consider, first, the case of improper definite descriptions (i.e. definite descriptions that do not apply to anything), and, second, the case of empty names.

Sentence (11) contains an improper definite description:

(11) The Czar of Russia plays chess.

Russell's theory would analyse (11) in terms of (12):

(12) There is exactly one object which is a Czar of Russia and whatever is a Czar of Russia plays chess.

There is no expression in (12) that refers to any object, and, in particular, to any erstwhile Czar of Russia. (There is a predicate, 'x is a Czar of Russia', in (12), but that predicate designates the property of *being a Czar of Russia*.)

Sentence (11) concerns an improper definite description, but what about a case involving an empty proper name such as (13)?

(13) King Arthur wore armour.

Russell's response is to claim that ordinary proper names, such as 'King Arthur' or 'Berlin', are not genuine names but abbreviated definite descriptions:

> Common words, even proper names, are usually really descriptions. That is to say, the thought in the mind of a person using a proper name correctly can generally only be expressed explicitly if we replace the proper name by a description. Moreover, the description required to express the thought will vary for different people, or for the same person at different times. The only thing constant (so long as the name is rightly used) is the object to which the name applies. But so long as this remains constant, the particular description involved usually makes no difference to the truth or falsehood of the proposition in which the name appears. (Russell 1912, p. 51. See also Russell 1918, p. 243)

In the case of 'King Arthur', then, we have something which apparently is a proper name but which is in fact a definite description. What the content of this description is will vary to some degree between people, but it might run along the lines of 'the king who had a round table and who . . .', where further information from the Arthurian legend is used to fill in the gap. In this way (13) will be analysed as (14):

(14) The king who had a round table and who [did such-and-such deeds as the Arthurian legend recounts] wore armour.

Russell's theory of descriptions can be applied to the analysis of (14) just as it was to (11).

Two issues emerge from the analysis of (14). One issue concerns sentences from fiction. The other concerns the relation between ordinary proper names and descriptions. Take these issues in turn.

One might wonder what Russell would take sentences from fiction to be about and what truth value he would take them to have. Russell's theory of descriptions provides the following truth conditions for a sentence of the form 'the F is G': 'the F is G' is true if and only if there exists exactly one F and everything that is F is G. Accordingly, a sentence such as 'The dragon searched for a hobbit' is true if and only if there exists exactly one dragon and every dragon searched for a hobbit. Given that dragons do not exist, the sentence is false. Yet a reader of Tolkien might want to say that the sentence is true. There are various options open to Russell which are consistent with his theory of descriptions. For example, we might introduce the operator 'it is true in the fiction that'. We might then say that it is true in a fiction F that p if and only if: if the story told in *F* were told as known fact, instead of as fiction, then *p* would be true. Although the sentence 'The dragon searched for a hobbit' is false, the sentence 'In Tolkien's fiction, the dragon searched for a hobbit' is true. The reason why it is true is that, if the tale told by Tolkien were told as known fact, instead of as fiction, the tale would state that the dragon searched for a hobbit. David Lewis takes the view that what is true in a given fiction is what is true in the most similar possible worlds to the actual world in which the story is told as known fact, instead of as fiction (Lewis 1978). The point of introducing this account is that a defender of Russell's theory of descriptions can, consistently with that theory, give some account of fictional sentences that distinguishes between true and false fictional sentences (namely, those sentences which are true in the fiction and those which are not).

This is just one account of fictional sentences which is compatible with Russell's theory, and there are others that could be appealed to instead (e.g. Searle 1975a or Walton 1990, Part 1). Furthermore, these accounts of fictional sentences may need to be supplemented by accounts of what fictional objects are. Lewis takes fictional objects to be objects at possible worlds. He further takes possible worlds and their inhabitants to be things of the same kind as the actual world and its inhabitants (Lewis 1986a, chapter 1). Since Lewis takes merely possible objects and worlds to exist, he does not take them to be non-existent objects. In that respect, his view would not contravene Russell's 'sense of reality'. But, as Lewis himself admits, taking these worlds and their inhabitants to exist does conflict with common sense (Lewis 1986a, p. 134). Presumably, then, in this respect Lewis's view would contravene Russell's precept. It is then incumbent on the Russellian who favours Lewis's theory of fictional sentences but rejects his account of fictional objects to find some alternative account of the latter (Brock 2002).

Russell's claim that ordinary proper names are abbreviated definite descriptions (call it his 'Name Claim') faces the same objections that we saw in Chapter 1 §8 face Frege's claim that names have senses. Instead of canvassing those objections again, let's consider a pair of fresh objections. One objection is that Russell's claim faces a difficulty in the case where it is not clear which, if any, definite description is being abbreviated by a name. Perhaps it is obscure what information is associated with a certain person (such as St. Expeditus) and so there is a dearth of descriptions associated with their proper name. Another objection is that if, as Russell says, different people (or the same person at different times) may associate different descriptions with the same proper name, then people would be talking past one another far more often than seems to be the case (Lycan 2008, pp. 37–8). This matters because it is a desideratum for a theory that it identifies as disagreements what we standardly regard as disagreements – or more generally, that it preserves our pre-theoretical judgements about the nature of our disputes. Here is an example to illustrate the objection. Suppose Mimi thinks that Smudge is male, whereas Buttons thinks that Smudge is female. It seems that Mimi and Buttons are disagreeing. But suppose that Buttons associates the description 'the cat that lives at number 16' with the name 'Smudge', whereas Mimi associates the description 'the tabby tortoiseshell that often visits us' with that name. Then Mimi believes that:

(15) There is exactly one object that is a cat that lives at number 16 and every cat that lives at number 16 is male.

and Buttons believes that:

(16) There is exactly one object that is a tabby tortoiseshell that often visits us and every tabby tortoiseshell that often visits us is female.

(15) and (16) are logically compatible claims. According to the objection, it follows that Mimi and Buttons are not disagreeing; they are talking past one another.

There might be a single way of addressing both objections. Take the first objection: what description is associated with 'St. Expeditus'? W. V. O. Quine offered the following tactic; call it 'Quine's expedient' (Quine 1948, p. 27, 1950, pp. 218–24, and 1960 §38). We devise the verb 'is-St. Expeditus' or 'stexpedituses'. This verb designates the unanalysable property of *being St. Expeditus*. 'St Expeditus' is then taken to be an abbreviation for the description 'the object that is-St. Expeditus' or 'the object that stexpedituses'. The theory of descriptions can then be applied to these descriptions.

The second objection was that there is variation in which descriptions are associated with putative proper names. Two questions arise: Is this situation irremediable? And, in the meantime, what are the implications for Russell's Name Claim? Take these questions in turn. Quine's expedient enables us to use a single unambiguous description for each name. For any name 'N', we can co-ordinate which description we will associate with 'N' by following the strategy of devising the verb 'is-N' and then framing the description 'the object which is-N'. We can thereby reach consensus. In lieu of such a co-ordinated policy, it has to be conceded that the likes of Mimi and Buttons are making logically compatible claims simply given the fact that they assert (15) and (16), respectively. But note that (15), (16), and the following factual claim (17) are logically incompatible:

(17) Whatever is a cat that lives at number 16 is whatever is a tabby tortoiseshell that often visits us, and vice versa.

Given this extra information, Mimi and Buttons are not talking past one another: they disagree. This point is not confined to description sentences. Suppose that Moula says that Hesperus is visible in the evening sky and Jim says that Phosphorus is not visible in the evening sky. Their claims are logically compatible. Yet their claims are not compatible with the fact that Hesperus is Phosphorus. So, given that further fact, Moula and Jim are making claims that cannot both be true. It is just that they will realize this only if they realize that Hesperus is Phosphorus. More generally, irrespective of the degree to which the descriptions that people associate with ordinary proper names vary, it does not follow that people are failing to have genuine disagreements. What follows is that they will often fail to realize that they are in genuine disagreement with one another.

Saul Kripke has suggested that all of his objections to Russell's Name Claim apply to Quine's expedient tactic. He suggests that that tactic only shifts one problem back a stage. Kripke writes:

> in particular, the question, 'How is the reference of "Socrates" determined?' yields to the question, 'How is the extension of "Socratizes" determined?' (Kripke 1972, p. 29, note 5)

Even if Russell were not to use Quine's expedient, he faces the general question of how the extensions of predicates are determined. Now Russell has an answer to that question. He thinks that the extension of a predicate 'is F' is determined by which entities have the property that 'is F' designates. The answer to Kripke's second question falls out of this. The extension of the predicate 'Socratizes' is determined by which objects have the property which that predicate designates, that is, which objects have the property *being Socrates*. (There is exactly one such object, namely, Socrates.)

To sum up this sub-section: Russell's theory of descriptions offers an analysis of sentences containing improper descriptions. In conjunction with his claim that ordinary proper names are disguised definite descriptions (his Name Claim), his theory can also analyse sentences containing empty names as well as sentences containing improper descriptions. Russell's theory thereby shows how those sentences can have meaning despite the fact that they contain improper descriptions or empty names.

Solution to puzzle 3: the puzzle of indirect contexts

The puzzle here was that if $a = b$, then why cannot 'a' and 'b' always be substituted without change of truth value in any sentence? Here is an example to illustrate the point. *Goodfellas* and *The Age of Innocence* are very different films. Jim has seen them both and wonders whether the person who directed the first film directed the second. Unbeknown to Jim, the same person *did* direct both films. Yet Jim does not wonder whether the person who directed *Goodfellas* is the person who directed *Goodfellas*. He already knows that. So, the following is an invalid argument:

(18) Jim wonders whether the director of the *Goodfellas* is the director of *The Age of Innocence*.
(19) The director of the *Goodfellas* is the director of *The Age of Innocence*.
(20) Jim wonders whether the director of *Goodfellas* is the director of *Goodfellas*.

The puzzle is then to explain why the argument is invalid.

The first step of Russell's solution is to apply his theory of descriptions to (18) and (20). (18) is analysed as (18*):

(18*) Jim wonders whether: there is exactly one object which is a director of *Goodfellas*, and there is exactly one object which is a director of *The Age of Innocence*, and whatever is a director of *Goodfellas* is a director of *The Age of Innocence*, and vice versa.

(20) is analysed as (20*):

(20*) Jim wonders whether: there is exactly one object which is a director of *Goodfellas*, and whatever is a director of *Goodfellas* is a director of *Goodfellas*.

Russell offers two answers to the puzzle of indirect contexts. The first answer is weak, the second more promising. The first answer is that the puzzle makes the following assumption. It assumes that definite descriptions are referring expressions that have their own meaning, and so definite descriptions that designate the same thing can be substituted for one another in sentences without change of truth value. But, the answer continues, the theory of descriptions rejects that assumption. Definite descriptions are not referring expressions and they lack meanings of their own. So no such substitutions can be made (Russell 1905, pp. 488–9).

That is an unsatisfactory answer. Suppose that definite descriptions are not referring expressions and that they lack 'meaning in isolation', as Russell puts it. Russell thinks that that is sufficient to show that the inference from (18) and (19) to (20) is invalid. That is questionable. For by the same measure it would also be sufficient to show that the following pattern of inference is invalid: the F is G; the F is the H; so the H is G. But that is a *valid* pattern of inference. So, something more needs to be done to show that the inference from (18) and (19) to (20) is invalid.

A more promising answer is that Russell's analyses show that what Jim is wondering about in (18) differs from what he is wondering about in (20). The content of what Jim is wondering about in (18) is shown by (18*) to involve the property of *being a director of the Age of Innocence*. The content of what Jim is wondering about in (20) is shown by (20*) not to involve that property. It follows that the content of what he is wondering about in each case differs: what Jim is wondering about in (18) is not what he is wondering about in (20). That is the reason why the inference from (18) and (19) to (20) is not valid.

Russell further observes that there are two ways of reading a sentence such as 'Jim wonders whether the F is G':

(21) Jim wonders whether: *there is exactly one object which is F* and whatever is F is G.

(22) *There is exactly one object which is F* such that Jim wonders whether whatever is F is G.

(21) and (22) involve differences in scope. In (21), the italicized sentence falls within the scope of the verb 'wonders'. In (22) it does not. In (21) the italicized sentence has *narrow scope* relative to the verb 'wonders', whereas in (22) it has *wide scope* relative to that verb. Russell uses different terminology to make the same point. He would say that in (21) the italicized sentence has *secondary occurrence,* whereas in (22) it has *primary occurrence* (Russell 1905, pp. 489–90, 1919, p. 179).

These differences in scope mark differences in what (21) and (22) each entail. (21) does not entail that there is exactly one object which is F. Perhaps

Jim wonders whether exactly one object is F and whatever is F is G. Nevertheless, perhaps nothing is F. For example, although the Yeti does not exist, perhaps Jim wonders whether exactly one object is a Yeti and whatever is a Yeti is friendly. (22), however, says that there is exactly one object which is F and says something concerning it – namely, that Jim wonders whether whatever is F is G. So, (22) entails that there is exactly one object which is F.

Another difference between (21) and (22) lies in what substitutions they permit. Suppose that the F is the G. Even so, (21) does not guarantee that the italicized sentence in it can be substituted without change of truth value with the sentence 'There is exactly one object which is G'. For example, the morning star (the brightest star in the morning sky) is the evening star (the brightest star in the evening sky). Perhaps, Jim wonders whether there is exactly one object which is a morning star and that everything that is a morning star is visible in the evening sky. Although whatever is a morning star is whatever is an evening star and vice versa, it does not follow that Jim wonders whether there is exactly one object which is an evening star and that everything which is an evening star is visible in the evening sky. He may not wonder about that; it may seem too obvious to him to be something to wonder about.

By contrast, if the F is the G, (22) guarantees that the italicized sentence in it can be substituted without change of truth value with the sentence 'There is exactly one object which is G'. If (22) is true, the italicized sentence denotes a certain object. Concerning that object, Jim wonders whether it is G. Notice that it does not matter how that object is denoted. Whichever way it is denoted, Jim wonders whether *it* is G.

We have examined Russell's suggestion that a sentence can be read in different ways if a description that occurs in it can take different scopes. These differences in scope yield sentences that may differ in truth value. As we will see, this suggestion is deployed in Russell's solution to puzzle 5 below.

Solution to puzzle 4: the puzzle of apparent reference to non-existents

The puzzle here is: How can any sentence of the form 'The F does not exist' be true? For example, (23) is true:

(23) The Loch Ness Monster does not exist.

Sentence (23) is what is known as a 'negative existential sentence'. An existential sentence says that some object exists. (It may also specify what that object is like.) A negative existential sentence is the negation of a sentence stating that some (specified) object exists. So, (23) is equivalent to (24):

(24) It is not the case that the Loch Ness Monster exists.

Sentence (24) is the negation of the sentence that the Loch Ness Monster exists. So, we can analyse (24) in two stages. First, we analyse the sentence 'The Loch Ness Monster exists'. Second, we negate the result of that analysis.

Russell's theory of descriptions analyses:

(25) The Loch Ness Monster exists.

as:

(26) There is exactly one object which is a Loch Ness Monster.

The negation of (26) is:

(27) It is not the case that there is exactly one object which is a Loch Ness Monster.

Russell's analysis of (24), and so of (23), is then provided by (27). There are two things to note about Russell's analysis. First, the expression 'the Loch Ness Monster' has 'disappeared under analysis', as Russell puts it. That expression does not occur in (27). Second, (27) is true. Since (27) provides the analysis of (23), (23) is also true. These two results together provide a solution to the original puzzle.

Russell's theory also applies to sentences such as 'The retirement of John F. Kennedy never took place' or 'The 1940 Olympic Games did not occur'. These sentences are also negative existential sentences. They use phrases cognate to 'does not exist' such as 'never took place' or 'did not occur' in order to say something of the form: *it is not the case that the F exists.*

The example of the Loch Ness Monster concerns an improper description. The case of a sentence that contains an empty name, such as 'Excalibur does not exist' is straightforward. Russell's Name Claim (his claim that ordinary proper names are in fact definite descriptions) can be deployed to analyse any sentence of the form '*a* does not exist' as a description sentence of the form

'The object which is-*a* does not exist'. Russell's theory of descriptions is then applied to the description sentence.

Solution to puzzle 5: the puzzle of the implications of the Law of Excluded Middle

The puzzle here is that the Law of Excluded Middle says that, for every indicative sentence, either it or its negation is true. But if 'The Loch Ness Monster has fins' is true, it follows that the Loch Ness Monster exists; and if 'The Loch Ness Monster does not have fins' is true, it again follows that the Loch Ness Monster exists.

Here is the pair of sentences in question:

(28) The Loch Ness Monster has fins.
(29) The Loch Ness Monster does not have fins.

Russell's theory of descriptions would analyse (28) as (28*):

(28*) There is exactly one object which is a Loch Ness Monster and everything which is a Loch Ness Monster has fins.

Using 'L' for 'is a Loch Ness Monster', and 'F' for 'has fins', (28*) can be symbolized as:

$$(\exists x)[Lx \land (\forall y)\,(Ly \to (y = x)) \land Fx]$$

Sentence (28*) is false since there is no Loch Ness Monster.

In the case of (29), however, Russell thinks that there is an ambiguity in the scope of the definite description. This ambiguity provides two ways of analysing (29). These are given by (29*) and (29**), respectively:

(29*) There is exactly one object which is a Loch Ness Monster and everything which is a Loch Ness Monster does not have fins.

In symbols: $(\exists x)[Lx \land (\forall y)\,(Ly \to (y = x)) \land \neg Fx]$

(29**) It is not the case that there is exactly one object which is a Loch Ness Monster and everything which is a Loch Ness Monster has fins.

In symbols: $\neg[(\exists x)(Lx \land (\forall y)\,(Ly \to (y = x)) \land Fx)]$

In (29*), the quantifiers in the description 'there is exactly one object which is a Loch Ness Monster' have wide scope relative to the negation operator.

The negation operator falls within their scope. (29*) is false since it entails that there is a Loch Ness Monster.

In (29**), the quantifiers in the same description have narrow scope relative to the negation operator. They fall within the scope of that operator. Unlike (29*), however, (29**) is true.

The puzzle is that the Law of Excluded Middle requires that either (28) or (29) is true. Russell's analysis shows that (28) is false, but also that there is a reading of (29) that is true. The puzzle is thereby solved.

This completes our survey of Russell's solutions to the five puzzles. His case for his theory turns on how effectively it solves them. In addition to providing those solutions, the theory has other strengths besides. Here are two of them. First, it explains how someone can understand a description sentence although that person has not perceived the object that it is about. The theory's explanation is given by its solution to puzzle three: the puzzle of empty names. You can understand a sentence of the form 'The F is G' even if you have not observed the F (perhaps because it does not exist). You can understand it by understanding the sentence 'There is exactly one F and everything which is F is G'. Understanding that quantified sentence does not require that there is anything in the domain of the quantifier which is uniquely F. It follows that understanding that sentence does not require that you have observed anything which is uniquely F.

Second, we have seen that differences in the scope of quantifiers affect the truth value of description sentences. This also applies to modal sentences, sentences about what is possibly true or what is not possibly true. For example, Russell's theory can explain two readings of the following modal sentence:

(30) The U.S. President in 2012 might have been a child of Hugh Rodham and Dorothy Howell.

One reading says, of the person who is the U.S. President in 2012, that that person might have been a child of Hilary Clinton's parents:

(31) There is exactly one object which is a U.S. President in 2012 and everything that is a U.S. President in 2012 might have been a child of Hugh Rodham and Dorothy Howell.

Sentence (31) is false assuming, first, that the biological parents of the U.S. President in 2012 are not Hugh Rodham and Dorothy Howell, and, second, that it is impossible for someone to have originated from a different sperm and egg than the ones that he or she actually originated from (Kripke 1972, p. 113).

The other reading of (30) is:

(32) It is possible that: there is exactly one U.S. President in 2012 and everything that is a U.S. President in 2012 is a child of Hugh Rodham and Dorothy Howell.

Sentence (32) is true since the history of the world could have been different so that Hilary Clinton, a child of Hugh Rodham and Dorothy Howell, won the presidential election in 2008, and was U.S. President in 2012.

There are two lines of criticism which might be taken against Russell's theory. One line would be to question the effectiveness of his solutions. We have seen, for example, that his solutions to the puzzle of empty names and to the puzzle of apparent reference to non-existents require supplementing his theory with the Name Claim: the claim that ordinary proper names are disguised definite descriptions. Any weaknesses in the Name Claim will carry over to his solutions to those puzzles. Another line of criticism would be to set aside Russell's solutions to the five puzzles, and to criticize his theory on other grounds. This is the approach taken by P. F. Strawson and by Keith Donnellan. We will assess their criticisms in the next two sections.

6. Strawson's criticisms of Russell

We have seen that Russell claims that definite descriptions are not referring terms but quantifier phrases, and that sentences involving improper definite descriptions are false. P. F. Strawson offers both a series of important criticisms of Russell's theory of descriptions and an account of how definite descriptions are often used to refer (Strawson 1950; Geach 1950 independently makes similar claims).

Strawson distinguishes between:

(A) Expressions and sentences,
(B) Utterances of expressions and sentences, and
(C) Uses of those expressions and sentences (Strawson 1950, §II).

An expression or a sentence is here to be understood as an expression-type or a sentence-type. For instance, if you twice say the sentence 'I am hungry', you have made two utterances of the same sentence. You have uttered two tokens of the same sentence-type. An utterance of an expression or sentence, by contrast, is a token of that expression or sentence. It is an event which happens at a particular time and place and which cannot recur.

An expression or a sentence can be used in different ways. For example, consider the expression 'I'. When you utter it, you use it to refer to yourself. When your best friend utters it, that person uses it to refer to themselves. Each of these utterances of 'I' refer, and to whom a given utterance of it refers depends upon who uttered it. There is, however, no answer to the question 'Who does the expression "I" refer to?' The most that we can say is that, when you utter it, your utterance of it refers to you; when your best friend utters it, their utterance of it refers to them; and so on.

Similar considerations apply to sentences. Take the sentence 'I am hungry'. Suppose that you are hungry but your best friend is not. Then, if you utter the sentence, you are referring to yourself and you are saying something true. If your best friend utters the sentence, that person is referring to themself and is saying something false. Each of these utterances contains an expression which is used to refer to someone, and each of the utterances says something which has a truth value. There is no answer to the question 'Is the sentence "I am hungry" true?' The most that we can say is that, when you use it, and you are hungry, you use it to say something true; when your best friend uses it, and that person is not hungry, they use it to say something false; and so on.

Now consider definite descriptions and sentences containing them. If today we uttered the expression 'the Czar of Russia', our utterance does not denote or refer to anything existing now. Yet, when uttered in 1916, it did denote or refer to someone, namely, Nicholas II. One of these utterances of the definite description refers to someone, whereas the other utterance does not. There is no answer to the question 'Does "the Czar of Russia" refer?' As in the case of 'I', the most that we can say is that, when uttered today, it does not refer; when uttered in 1916, it does refer; and so on.

Finally, consider a descriptive sentence such as 'The U.S. President is a Democrat'. If that sentence is uttered in 2012, its use of 'the U.S. President' refers to Barack Obama, and the sentence is used to say something true. If the same sentence were uttered in 2001, its use of 'the U.S. President' would refer to George W. Bush and the sentence would be used to say something false. There is no answer to the question 'Is the U.S. President a Democrat?' There are answers only to the questions: 'If the sentence "The U.S. President is a Democrat"' were uttered in 2012, would it be used to say something true?', 'If the sentence "The U.S. President is a Democrat" were uttered in 2001, would it be used to say something true?' and so on.

The lessons that Strawson draws from these observations are as follows. Strawson claims that various semantic terms apply to uses of expressions and sentences, not to expressions and sentences. Here is what he says about expressions and their uses:

> 'Referring' is not something an expression does; it is something that someone can use an expression to do. Mentioning, or referring to, something is a characteristic of a *use* of an expression, just as 'being about' something and truth-or-falsity, are characteristic of a *use* of a sentence. (Strawson 1950, p. 80)

Expressions and sentences have meaning. But no expression refers or fails to refer, and no sentence is true or false. It is only uses of expressions that refer or fail to refer, and it is only uses of sentences that are true or false.

These lessons provide the basis for Strawson's first criticism of Russell's theory of descriptions. Russell notes that a sentence such as 'The Czar of Russia plays chess' is meaningful. He then assumes that if a sentence is meaningful, then it is either true or false. But that, Strawson claims, is a mistaken assumption. A sentence is meaningful but it is neither true nor false. It is only uses of that sentence, and specifically assertions of that sentence, that can be true or false.

This criticism is not damaging to Russell's theory. Suppose that we grant all of Strawson's claims about what semantic terms such as 'true', 'false' and 'refers' correctly apply to. These are such claims as that names do not refer, that it is only utterances of names that refer, that sentences are not true or false, and that only utterances of sentences which make statements are true or false. Nevertheless, Strawson's criticism fails to engage with the subject matter of Russell's theory. Russell's theory is not concerned with uses and assertions of description sentences. It is concerned with description sentences and their meanings – the propositions that they express (Grice 1981; Neale 1992, pp. 538–9; Bach 1994b, pp. 96–8). And even if sentences can be neither true nor false, propositions can. (See Lycan 1974 for a survey of some common objections to propositions as well as some rebuttals of them.)

Strawson distinguishes sentences, utterances of sentences and statements. Yet, Russell's theory can be consistently combined with this distinction (Mates 1973, p. 413). The combined view would say that a statement made by using a sentence containing a definite description is logically equivalent to the statement that would be made by using a sentence formulated in accord with the original part of Russell's theory. (That is the part that equates sentences of the form 'The F is G' with sentences of the form 'There is exactly one F and it is G'.)

Strawson's claims about the correct application of certain semantic terms are themselves disputable. For example, Strawson argues that names do not refer, only utterances of names do. A similar line of argument is beloved of many pro-gun campaigners. They argue that guns do not kill, only people do. A natural response is to say that *both* people and guns kill: people kill by using guns to kill. Likewise, Strawson's argument invites the response that names and utterances of names both refer: utterances of names refer by using names which also refer. It is true that different utterances of an equiform name can refer to different objects. (Think of how many people are called by the name 'John Smith'.) That shows that there is a series of equiform names which have different references. If we distinguish each of these names by what it refers to, however, each name has exactly one reference. We can follow a similar procedure when dealing with ambiguous sentences. Once a sentence has been fully disambiguated, we can establish what the truth values of the different disambiguations are. A sentence such as 'The U.S. President is a Democrat' is not ambiguous, but there is a question as to what its subject-term refers to. There is a series of equiform definite descriptions, each of which denotes a different president. Once these different definite descriptions are distinguished, we can then establish the truth values of the sentences formed by appending the predicate 'is a Democrat' to each of them.

Strawson's next criticism involves providing an example that he thinks elicits an intuition that is incompatible with Russell's theory. Strawson then presents a theory of his own which accommodates the intuition. Here is the example. Suppose that someone today were to utter the following sentence in the course of a conversation:

(33)   The King of France is wise.

What would be your reaction? In particular, would you say that what they said was false? Or would you say something else? Strawson intuits that you would *not* say 'That's untrue' (Strawson 1950, p. 330). And if you were asked by the speaker whether you agreed or disagreed with what he said, what would you say? Strawson reports that

> you would be inclined, with some hesitation, to say that you didn't do either; that the question of whether his statement was true or false simply didn't arise, because there was no such person as the king of France. (Strawson 1950, p. 330)

Strawson's alternative account consists of two principal claims. First, it claims that 'the F' is a form of expression which (among other things) can be used to refer to an F. Second, an utterance of the form 'The F is G' is not used to *assert* that there is exactly one object which is an F. Instead, such an utterance *presupposes* it. For any sentences S and S*, an utterance of S presupposes that S* if and only if S makes a statement (something that can be true or false) only if S* is true (Strawson 1954). In uttering (33), the speaker does not assert that there is exactly one object that is a King of France; he or she presupposes that there is such a unique object. What he or she says is true or false only if there is exactly one object that is a King of France. Since there is no such object, what he or she says is meaningful but is neither true nor false.

Strawson's second criticism invites a number of responses. First, it is not clear what philosophical significance such an appeal to intuition has. The rationale behind this appeal seems to be this. You know that there is no King of France. You are also a competent user of English. So, not only do you understand the person's question, but you understand what terms such as 'true', 'untrue', 'agree', 'disagree' and the like mean. Your epistemic situation then makes your intuition a reasonably authoritative response to the person's question.

Even if we do take intuitions about semantic situations to be reliable, it is not clear that all of our intuitions tell against Russell's theory. It helps to consider some other examples such as the following:

(34) My mother is the King of France.
(35) My father had breakfast with the King of France.
(36) The Czar of Russia is the oldest living royal.
(37) The Czar of Russia exists.
(38) Strawson believes that the King of France is wise.
(39) The exhibition was visited yesterday by the King of France.

Whereas it is controversial what we do, and should, say about Strawson's example of (33), (34–39) each seem to be false. Or, at any rate, they each seem to be something very like false. (For further problem cases, see Mates 1973, pp. 413–15.)

In the case of still other examples, people's intuitions may be more divided. Consider the following examples:

(40) The Loch Ness Monster is a monster.
(41) The Loch Ness Monster is the Loch Ness Monster.
(42) The U.S. air force today has more aircraft than the city of Atlantis ever did.

Russell's theory says that each of (40–42) is false. Strawson says that each of (40–42) is truth valueless. Some people, however, are inclined to say that they are true. Moreover, not only do different people have conflicting intuitions about these particular cases, some people may have no intuition either way.

Other cases where this pattern of conflicting or 'missing' intuitions recurs are ones where there is more than one F. Suppose that Oswald was only one of several gunmen who assassinated President Kennedy. Is the sentence 'Oswald was the assassin of President Kennedy' true, false or truth valueless?

One option is to say these cases are 'spoils to the victor': What we should say about them will turn on which theory we should adopt on the basis of the less puzzling cases. (In Quine's phrase, these cases are 'don't cares': Quine 1960, p. 182.)

As to (33), the sentence 'The King of France is wise', when asked whether we would agree or disagree with the speaker, we are not obliged to reply with a one-liner. There is much that could be said in reply to him. We might say, 'If you think that, then you've a lot to learn. What you've said shows that you think that there is a King of France. You've been badly misinformed. There is no such person. So, no, I don't agree with you that the King of France is wise'. Yet such a reply is consistent with Russell's theory.

The pragmatics of conversation are also relevant here. There are cases in which speakers would mislead an audience if they uttered sentences that are true – consider cases where speakers are deliberately underinformative. So, there can be good reasons for criticizing an utterance even if it is true. The relevance of this for our purposes is as follows. Strawson needs to show that, even if we are reluctant to say that the sentence 'The King of France is wise' is false, our reluctance is due to the fact that the sentence is neither true nor false. He needs to show that there is not some other reason why a speaker would be criticized for asserting the sentence.

If, in the course of a conversation, someone says 'The King of France is wise', presumably we have reached a stage where talk of the King of France has already been introduced and the speaker is saying something further about him, namely, that he is wise. Now if, at this stage, you merely say to the speaker that what he said was untrue, you would seem to be complying with his earlier introduction of talk of the King of France and to be disputing only whether the King is wise. For the issue the speaker has put on the table is not whether there is a King of France but whether he is wise. Your disagreement, however, is not about whether the King is wise; it is about whether there is a King of France. And you cannot signal the focus of your disagreement merely by saying 'That's untrue' (Grice 1981; Sainsbury 1979, pp. 120–1).

Finally, recall the response made to Strawson's first criticism. Russell is concerned with sentences and the propositions which they express, not assertions of those sentences. It is open to Russell to grant that someone who *asserts* (33) asserts a sentence that presupposes, but does not say, that there is exactly one object that is a King of France. That is, it is open to Russell to grant, perhaps for the sake of argument, that Strawson gives the correct account of the semantics of the *assertion* of description sentences. That, however, is not the topic of Russell's theory. In the case of (33), his theory is concerned with whether the proposition expressed by (33) entails that there is exactly one object which is a King of France. Strawson's criticism has no bearing on that issue (Bach 1994b, p. 98).

Strawson's third and last criticism is that Russell's theory has false entailments. For example, suppose that someone utters (43) in a situation in which there are several tables but only one table with a cup on it:

(43) The table has a cup on it.

Given the circumstances in which (43) was uttered, the speaker says something true. According to Strawson, the Russellian analysis of (43) is (44):

(44) There is exactly one object which is a table and whatever is a table has a cup on it.

The claim made by (44), however, is false since there exists more than one table.

Cases such as (43) concern what are known as incomplete definite descriptions – cases in which an object is picked out by a description even though the description apparently underspecifies it. Russell can respond that (43) involves some contextually indicated domain (e.g. that of tables visually salient to the speaker and the audience) and that this is the domain of the quantifier phrase in (44). So understood, (44) is true provided that there is exactly one object in the relevant domain that is a table and that it has a cup on it. An invocation of a contextually indicated domain is often made in connection with quantified sentences. Utterances of such sentences as 'There's no milk', 'Everyone was at the party' or 'All stand for the national anthem' often have domains fixed by conversational context. The utterances are concerned with such domains as (say) what is in the fridge, your friends or all the people at the political rally. So, these sentences are to be understood as saying: concerning what is in the fridge, there is no milk; concerning your friends, everyone of them was at the party, and concerning the people at the rally, everyone was requested to stand for the national anthem. There seems nothing amiss with appealing to the same device in connection with (43). (43) might be analysed as saying: concerning tables which are visually salient to the speaker and the audience, there is exactly one object which is a table and it has a cup on it. And that is what (44) says. (For further discussion of incomplete definite descriptions, see Fitch 1985; Salmon 1991; Soames 2005.)

A variant of Strawson's criticism is available. Suppose that a speaker uttered (43) in a room in which there were many tables each with a cup on it. Moreover, suppose that there were no contextually salient tables and that the speaker had no one table in mind when he uttered (43). In that case, so the criticism goes, (43) is neither true nor false. No truth condition has been provided in these circumstances for (43). Uttering it is saying something unintelligible. (44), however, is false for the reason that Russell gave. So, (43) cannot be analysed in terms of (44) (Ramachandran 1993).

Russell might respond that this criticism is open to a dilemma. Suppose that we take it that, in those circumstances, the speaker's utterance of (43) lacks a truth condition and that the utterance is unintelligible. The speaker has failed to provide the contextual information needed to make his utterance intelligible. But then, to treat like with like, something similar should be the case with the Russellian analysis of (43). That analysis might be given by (45):

(45) Concerning . . . , there is exactly one object which is a table and whatever is a table has a cup on it.

With nothing filling in the gap in (45), (45) is not a genuine sentence. It is neither true nor false; indeed, it is unintelligible. But then the supposed discrepancy between the utterance of (43) and the Russellian analysis collapses (Morris 2007, p. 68).

Alternatively, suppose that by uttering (43) the speaker has produced a genuine sentence, something intelligible, but has not provided any contextual information to determine which table is in question. Then there is no restriction on the domain of quantification of the Russellian counterpart of (43), namely (44). In that case it is open to Russell to say that the speaker has said something intelligible but false.

The dilemma, then, is this. Either the speaker has said something unintelligible, in which case the Russellian counterpart to that utterance will be ill-formed and unintelligible. Or it is insisted that the Russellian counterpart to the utterence is intelligible and is false, in which case what the speaker said was itself intelligible and false. What Russell need not concede is that the speaker said something unintelligible and that the Russellian analysis of the utterance is a quantified sentence that is both intelligible and false. (For further discussion of Strawson's criticisms, see Nerlich 1965; Mates 1973. For further discussion of Ramachandran's criticism, see Bach 1994c; Ganeri 1995.)

To sum up, Strawson presented a theory of the use of definite descriptions which is intended to be a rival to Russell's theory of definite descriptions. According to Strawson's theory, definite descriptions can function as referring expressions, and when a speaker asserts a sentence of the form 'The F is G', the sentence that he or she asserts presupposes, but does not say that there is a unique F. Strawson makes three criticisms of Russell's theory. First, Strawson claims that Russell is mistaken in assuming that sentences can be true or false, that names refer, and that definite descriptions denote. In all these cases, it is uses of the linguistic items that can have the semantic properties in question. Second, Strawson claims that if you believe that no one is the King of France, then, contrary to Russell, you would not reply 'That's false' if someone said 'The King of France is wise'. The question of truth or falsehood does not arise because what the person has said mistakenly presupposes that there is a unique King of France. Third, Strawson claims that Russell's theory analyses a sentence such as 'The table is covered with papers' as the absurd claim that there exists exactly one table and it is covered with papers. The claim is absurd, according to the objection, because there plainly exist many tables.

7. Donnellan's criticisms of Russell and Strawson

We have seen that Russell thinks that definite descriptions are not referring expressions, but are quantifying phrases. We have also seen that Strawson thinks that some (though not all) uses of definite descriptions are ones in which those expressions are used to refer. Keith Donnellan criticizes both views. Donnellan emphasizes a distinction between two uses of definite descriptions: a distinction between what he calls 'attributive' and 'referential' uses of definite descriptions (Donnellan 1966, 1968).

Here is an example adapted from Donnellan to illustrate the distinction. Suppose that Smith, a well-loved member of the community, is found horribly torn apart. Sherlock Holmes inspects the remains and remarks to Watson:

(46) Smith's murderer is insane.

At this stage of the investigation, Holmes believes only that Smith was murdered. He does not have anyone in mind as the murderer. So there is no particular person that he is referring to or is intending to refer to. In this case, 'Smith's murderer' has an *attributive* use in Holmes' utterance of (46). As used in this way, (46) might be paraphrased as (47):

(47) Whoever murdered Smith is insane.

Suppose now that the police investigation proceeds and someone is charged with Smith's murder and put on trial. During the trial this person behaves bizarrely. Sitting in the public gallery, Holmes and Watson watch this behaviour, and again Holmes comments:

(46) Smith's murderer is insane.

Here Holmes is using the description 'Smith's murderer' as a convenient device for indicating who he is talking about. This is a *referential* use of the definite description. As used in this way, (46) might be paraphrased as (48):

(48) *That* man is insane.

In the case of the attributive use, the particular definite description that Holmes uses is essential to what he wants to say. Holmes wants to make a specific connection between someone's being Smith's murderer and that person's being insane. In the case of the referential use, the particular definite description that Holmes uses is inessential to what he wants to say. His intention is to say something about *that* man. Although he uses the description 'Smith's murderer', Holmes could as well have used any other definite description or expression provided only that it enabled him to say of *that* man that he is insane.

What determines whether a given use of a definite description is attributive or referential? There are two factors at play in Donnellan's account of what makes something a referential use of a definite description, but it is not clear how they are to be weighed against one another. One factor concerns the speaker's intentions: if the particular definite description used is inessential to

[margin note: could this be phrased in terms of utterances?]

who or what the speaker wishes to pick out, then the description is being used referentially. The other factor concerns the audience's uptake: if the particular description used is inessential to who or what the audience takes the speaker to be picking out, then the description is being used referentially.

With Donnellan's distinction in place, at least three consequences can be drawn. First, Holmes can use a definite description attributively regardless of whether he takes himself to know who Smith's murderer is. So he can still intend to say what (47) says when he utters (46), even if he has a particular person in mind as the suspect.

Second, Holmes can use a definite description referentially, succeed in referring to the person he has in mind, and say something true even if the person referred to does not satisfy the description. To see this, suppose that in fact no one murdered Smith – he was mauled by an escaped lion – and someone insane is falsely charged with Smith's murder. In the court room scene, Holmes refers to this person by using the description 'Smith's murderer' when he utters (46), and he says something true when he says that that person is insane. Holmes' utterance of (46) is true, then, given his use of the definite description to refer to someone who is in fact insane. If Watson were to reply 'He surely is insane, but perhaps he did not murder Smith', his reply would not mean that Smith's murderer might not have murdered Smith (Récanati 1981, p. 597). Holmes and Watson are referring to the same person, whether or not that person is in fact Smith's murderer. And Holmes could have used any other expression with the same reference to say of the same person that he is insane.

[margin note: even when the referent is not Smith's murderer?]

Third, the referential use of a definite description can be construed as a demonstrative use of descriptions. It is a use in which the descriptive component of a description is irrelevant to what is expressed by the sentence containing the description (Kaplan 1975). Drawing on terminology introduced by Kripke (Kripke 1972), a referential use of a description is the use of a rigid designator on a given occasion. As used on that occasion, the description designates the same object in every world in which it designates anything.

[margin note: and thus temporal]

What does this tell us about Russell's theory? Donnellan thinks that Russell's account of attributive uses of definite descriptions is mistaken. He also thinks that Russell overlooks referential uses of definite descriptions, and in addition that Strawson's own account of those uses is mistaken. Take these points in turn.

According to Donnellan, someone who utters (46) and uses the definite description attributively – that is to say, as uttering (47) – presupposes that there is exactly one person who murdered Smith. So, if that presupposition is

[margin note: attributive use requires presupposition]

false – if no person or if more than one person murdered Smith – then (46) has not been used to say something which is true or false. No statement is made if nothing satisfies the description.

Donnellan not only thinks that there are referential uses of definite descriptions, but also that Strawson's account of those uses is mistaken. Donnellan argues as follows. If Holmes utters (46) and uses the definite description referentially – that is to say, as uttering (48) – what Holmes is saying is that *that* man is insane. What Holmes says is true if and only if the man he picks out is insane. For this reason 'Smith's murderer' is a dispensable device in picking out the man in question, and it is irrelevant to what Holmes said whether the man is Smith's murderer or not.

up the predicate
takes on great
importance
w/ Donnellan's
ideas

For Strawson, a referential use of the expression 'Smith's murderer' would presuppose that there is exactly one person who murdered Smith. If that presupposition is false, then Holmes does not make a statement when he utters (46). According to Donnellan, however, it is irrelevant to the truth of (48) whether there is exactly one person who murdered Smith. Holmes' utterance does not make that presupposition. The description may be of instrumental value: it might help the speaker or the audience to believe that there is exactly one person who murdered Smith, but even that is not required. Suppose Holmes and Watson become convinced that the man in the dock is innocent. They might still use that description to say things about him. They might use it with black humour – to think that Scotland Yard could have thought that that man was a murderer! Since Holmes' referential use of 'Smith's murderer' does not presuppose that there is a unique murderer of Smith, Holmes' utterance of (46) makes a statement even though nothing satisfies the description. Moreover, the truth value of the statement he makes does not depend on whether anything satisfies the description.

How might Russell respond to Donnellan's criticisms? Saul Kripke has offered an influential reply defending Russell (Kripke 1977). Kripke begins by arguing that even if there are referential uses of definite descriptions in (say) English, it does not follow that Russell's theory of descriptions does not hold for English. Kripke invokes the following methodological principle (Kripke 1977, p. 16). Suppose that someone offers what they take to be counter-examples to an analysis of a certain class of sentences in English (say, description sentences). To evaluate whether those alleged counter-examples are genuine, we should construct a language for which the proposed analysis holds. We should then see whether the same cases can occur in it. Suppose we find that the cases in question can indeed occur in it. It then follows that they are not genuine counter-examples, since we have stipulated that the language is one in which the analysis holds. Yet if that is so, there is no case for thinking that the cases provide genuine counter-examples in the case of English either: if they can occur in a language where the analysis holds, then their occurrence in English is compatible with the analysis holding for English. Kripke follows this through by constructing some sample languages for which Russell's theory of descriptions holds and showing that cases such as Donnellan's case of Smith's murderer can arise in those languages too. Given the above methodological principle, those cases turn out not to have force against Russell's theory of descriptions as a theory of natural language.

Kripke further claims that the cases that Donnellan offers are counter-examples to Russell's theory only if they concern semantic facts. Kripke contends, however, that those cases concern pragmatic, not semantic, facts. When a speaker utters a sentence to refer to something, we should distinguish between what the speaker is referring to – what he had in mind and was alluding to – and what the speaker's utterance refers to. Take the case where Holmes is in the court room and says:

(46) Smith's murderer is insane.

What Holmes has asserted in asserting (46) is unaffected by pragmatic factors, such as what Holmes had in mind or what the reasons for Holmes' assertion were. According to Kripke, (46) is true if and only if Smith's murderer is insane. That is, (46) is true if and only if there is exactly one person who is a murderer of Smith and it is insane. To use Kripke's terminology, that person (if there is one) is the *semantic referent* of the definite description and the truth value of the sentence depends on whether that person exists and whether he or she has the property being attributed to it in (46). It is irrelevant to the truth value of (46) whether Holmes intends to refer to the man in the dock – the man widely thought to be Smith's murderer. Now Holmes may say something about the man that he intends to refer to. In Kripke's terminology, that man is the *speaker's referent* – the person who Holmes takes himself to be referring to. By uttering (46), Holmes may also be conveying that he takes himself to be referring to that man. This further information that he conveys is true if and only if the object that he takes himself to be referring to (i.e. *that* man) has the property Holmes is attributing to him (i.e. is insane).

The significance of Kripke's distinction is that, if Kripke is right, Russell's theory of descriptions is not undermined by referential uses of definite descriptions. (For discussion of Kripke's argument, see Devitt 1981;

Ramachandran 1996; Fitch 2004, chapter 3 §§1–3; Lumsden 2010. For further defences of Russell's theory against Donnellan's criticisms, see Searle 1979; Bach 1994b, chapter 5 §3 and chapter 6; Soames 1994; Predelli 2003. See Reimer 1998; Devitt 2004 for replies.)

8. Conclusion

Two key points emerge from Russell's theory of descriptions. First, definite descriptions do not always function as referring expressions. Second, they permit distinctions in scope to be drawn: they enable us to distinguish between 'The F is not G' and 'It is not the case that the F is G', or between 'Possibly, the F is G' and 'The F is possibly G'.

In the list of questions in the introduction to this book, (Q9) asked about the role of pragmatics in language. The distinction between semantics and pragmatics is vital for Russellians. They want to distinguish between the truth value of a sentence and its being appropriate or expedient or apposite to utter the sentence. The truth value of a sentence depends on what the sentence means and what the world is like. The appropriateness, expedience or appositeness of an utterance of a sentence depends on such contextual factors as what the course of the conversation has been, whom the audience is, what features of the context being described are important to the speaker or the audience, what language is being used, and the like. The same sentence can be uttered in different contexts for different reasons. To suppose that the truth value of the sentence shifts with such vagaries is to confuse matters. A question such as 'Did she say something false?' concerns semantics. Questions such as 'Whatever made her say that?' or 'Was that a peculiar thing to say?' concern pragmatics. Strawson may have pertinent things to say about the pragmatics of utterances of sentences containing definite descriptions, but his claims do not bear on the semantics of those claims. Or so Russellians will argue.

(Q10) asked whether there can be a systematic philosophical study of natural language. Some critics of Russell's theory of descriptions have regarded it as only a convenient device for use in connection with a formalized language. Strawson suggests that no theory of meaning for a natural language based on classical logic is tenable:

> Neither Aristotelian nor Russellian rules give the exact logic of any expression of ordinary language; for ordinary language has no exact logic. (Strawson 1950, p. 44. See also Searle 1969, p. 157)

Other philosophers see matters differently:

> [It] seems to me that one of the great merits of [Russell's] theory of descriptions is that it does throw light upon the use of a certain class of expressions in ordinary speech, and that this is a point of philosophic importance. (Ayer 1936, p. 23. See also Mates 1973, pp. 411, 417–18)

Applied to natural languages, Russell's theory attempts to offer, for any sentence of natural language containing a definite description, a logically equivalent sentence that contains no definite descriptions. Russellians might see the pessimism of philosophers such as Strawson or Searle as being due to a conflation of semantic with pragmatic issues. If we conflate those issues, and take Russell's theory to fail to heed (what are in fact) pragmatic considerations, we will be led mistakenly to think that his theory is ill-suited as a theory of description sentences in natural language.

Questions for discussion

Question 1
How might Russell argue that a sentence of the form 'The F is G' entails that there is at most one F? (See McCawley 1985 or Szabo 2005).

Question 2
It was suggested in §6 that, to solve the problem of incomplete definite descriptions, Russell could appeal to context in fixing the full content of the description. How significant was it that when we specify the context we tend to use indexical expressions ('the table in front of *me*') or demonstratives ('the table closest to *that* wall')? Do we have to use such expressions in specifying the context? (See Perry 1977 on the importance of the role of indexicals).

Question 3
Consider the following inference (Geach 1976b, p. 38):

(1) The youngest man who danced with his wife at the party was drunk, and his wife was Mary.
(2) So the youngest man who danced with Mary was drunk.

The puzzle is as follows. On the one hand, suppose we take 'his wife' to refer in both occurrences in (1) to the wife of the youngest man who danced with his wife. Since Mary is that wife, we should expect (2) to follow from (1). On the other hand, it is possible for (1) to be true and (2) false. 'The youngest man who danced with his wife at the party' might describe one man and 'The youngest man who danced with Mary' might describe another man. After all, the youngest man who danced with Mary might not be married to her or to anyone else. If the first man was drunk, (1) would be true. If the second man was not drunk, (2) would be false. So (2) does not follow from (1). We have mutually incompatible lines of thought. How should the puzzle be solved?

Question 4

How should Strawson account for a sentence such as 'Pegasus does not exist'? (Such a sentence makes a true negative existential statement).

Question 5

Strawson revised his earlier work by suggesting that, in a case of 'radical reference-failure', we should work out whether a sentence is true, false or truth valueless by considering both the sentence and its topic (Strawson 1971, p. 92ff). For example, saying 'The present King of France is wise' might be given in answer to various different questions, such as 'What is the present King of France like?', 'Which heads of state are wise?' or 'What is France's head of state like?' According to Strawson, if what we say is given in answer to the first question, what we say is neither true nor false, whereas if what we say is given in answer to either the second or third questions, what we say is false. We would be saying that one of the heads of state is the present King of France, or that France's present head of state is a king, respectively.

How plausible is Strawson's suggestion that whether what has been uttered has a truth value, or what its truth value is, depends on the topic – on what question it is an answer to?

Question 6

Some natural languages (such as Latin, Russian and Japanese) lack a definite article. Is this philosophically significant? Does it help vindicate Russell's claim that description sentences can be analysed away? Or does it indicate that his concern with the definite article was misguided?

Further reading

Davies, Martin (1981) *Meaning, Quantification, Necessity: Themes in Philosophical Logic* chapter VII.
Donnellan, Keith (1966) 'Reference and Definite Descriptions'.
Kaplan, David (1972) 'What is Russell's Theory of Descriptions?'

Larson, Richard and Gabriel Segal (1995) *Knowledge of Meaning: An Introduction to Semantic Theory* chapter 9.

Lycan, William G. (2008) *Philosophy of Language: A Contemporary Introduction* chapter 2.

Mendelsohn, Richard L. (2005) *The Philosophy of Gottlob Frege* chapter 6.

Morris, Michael (2007) *An Introduction to the Philosophy of Language* chapter 3.

Neale, Stephen (1990) *Descriptions* chapter 2.

Russell, Bertrand (1905) 'On Denoting'.

—(1918) 'The Philosophy of Logical Atomism' §VI.

—(1919) *Introduction to Mathematical Philosophy* chapter 16.

Sainsbury, Mark (1979) *Russell* chapter IV.

Strawson, P. F. (1950) 'On Referring'.

Taylor, Kenneth (1998) *Truth and Meaning: An Introduction to the Philosophy of Language* chapter II.

6

Grice on Meaning

---

1. Introduction

Paul Grice's theory of language has two chief components. First, and as we will see in this chapter, he seeks to show how meaning can be reduced to certain complex intentions on the part of speakers. Second, and as we will see in Chapter 7, he offers a theory of the rational conduct of conversation which systematically explains how people can communicate more than what they literally say.

In Chapter 3 §1, we introduced a distinction between foundational and structural theories of meaning. Grice presents a foundational theory of meaning, whereas Frege presents a structural one. A foundational theory of meaning primarily seeks to answer the question 'Why does a certain sentence have the meaning that it does (for a particular speaker or group of speakers)?' This kind of theory seeks to say what it is about the speaker or speakers that give the sentences they use the meanings that they have. By contrast, a structural theory of meaning primarily seeks to answer the question 'What is the meaning of a certain sentence (for a particular speaker or group of speakers)?' This kind of theory seeks to specify the meanings of the sentences of a language as used by some speaker or speakers, but without seeking to say why those sentences have those meanings.

As we have seen, the distinction between foundational and semantic theories can be illuminated by an analogy with two different kinds of theory in chemistry. One kind of theory might list the various chemical elements and their properties and specify which ones form which compounds. This kind of theory is analogous to a structural theory of meaning, a theory which lists what meanings different expressions in a given language have. A different kind of theory seeks to explain the properties of the chemical elements and thereby to explain why they form the compounds that they do. It seeks to explain why the chemical elements have the features they do and why they combine in the ways that they do. This kind of theory is analogous to a foundational theory of meaning, a theory which seeks to explain why our words and sentences mean one thing rather than another.

Having identified the kind of theory of meaning which Grice offers, in the next section we will explore his project about the nature of meaning.

2. Grice's project

What it is for linguistic expressions to have meaning? This general question generates various sub-questions. One sub-question concerns the relation between the meanings that sentences have in a given language and the meanings that sentences have in the mouths of particular speakers on particular occasions. Another sub-question concerns the relation between the meanings that sentences have in the mouths of particular speakers on particular occasions and the psychological states of those speakers. In this chapter, we will consider Grice's answers to all of these questions. Grice himself is concerned not only with linguistic meaning, but also with the still more general question of what it is for any sign, whether linguistic or non-linguistic, to have meaning and what gives it the particular meaning that it does on any particular occasion of use.

The first sub-question concerns the relation between the meanings that sentences have in a given language and the meanings that sentences have in the mouths of particular speakers on particular occasions. That sub-question marks an important distinction for Grice. It is the distinction between *sentence meaning* and *speaker meaning*. Let's explore this distinction further.

A cyclist's extending his arm to his left cannot make that a signal meaning that he is turning right just by his intending it to. Similarly, it is not up to any one single person what any given English sentence means. No one person can make a sentence of English mean one thing rather than another just by their intending to mean a particular thing by it. What such a sentence means is what the English language requires that it means. The kind of meaning that sentences are being taken to have here is called 'sentence meaning'.

In another respect, you can mean by a sentence something other than what the sentence means in the way just described. At the end of a meeting, a secret agent says to you, 'This conversation never happened'. The sentence meaning of what he has said is that *this conversation never happened*. So understood, what is meant is false since the conversation did happen. What the speaker meant, however, was to the effect that *I (the speaker) will deny that we had this conversation*. So understood, what he meant need not be false. (What he meant is true if and only if he denies that the two of you had that conversation.) This kind of meaning is called 'speaker meaning'.

Grice characterizes the distinction between sentence meaning and speaker meaning by saying that the meaning of a sentence is timeless, whereas a speaker means something by a sentence on a particular occasion. The distinction is then also known as the distinction between *timeless meaning* and *occasion meaning*.

However we choose to label this distinction, there is an issue about whether one kind of meaning is more fundamental than the other. Is sentence meaning more fundamental then speaker meaning, or *vice versa*? And, once we have identified what we take to be the more fundamental kind of meaning, there is a further question to be asked: is there anything more fundamental than that kind of meaning?

Grice's project consists in giving a series of answers to these questions. The first stage of his project is to argue that speaker meaning is more fundamental than sentence meaning. He argues for this by trying to reduce sentence meaning to conventional regularities among speaker meanings. That is to say, he offers necessary and sufficient conditions for sentence meaning in terms of conventional regularities among speaker meanings. The second stage of his project is to argue that speaker meaning is less fundamental than a speaker's propositional attitudes, and, in particular, the speaker's beliefs and intentions. Grice argues for this by trying to reduce speaker meaning to certain communicative intentions on the part of a speaker. This is to offer necessary and sufficient conditions for speaker meaning in terms of a speaker's communicative intentions.

If each of these reductions is successful, Grice would have reduced sentence meaning to the communicative intentions of speakers. Schematically, Grice's project, then, is as follows:

Grice's reductive project

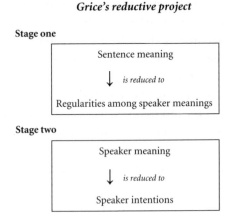

Stage one

Sentence meaning

↓ *is reduced to*

Regularities among speaker meanings

Stage two

Speaker meaning

↓ *is reduced to*

Speaker intentions

If both stages can be completed, the project succeeds in treating 'as basic the individual instance of meaning, by one speaker at one time, and gives a derivative status to every kind of general statement about meaning' (Bennett 1976, p. 9. See also Schiffer 1972, p. 13).

What would a reduction, whether of sentence meaning or of speaker meaning, involve? In the case of sentence meaning, the reduction provides an answer to the following question: For any indicative sentence *S*, what has to be the case for sentence (1) to be true?

(1) *S* means that *p*.

In the case of speaker meaning, the reduction provides an answer to the following question: For any indicative sentence *S* and utterer *U*, what has to be the case for sentence (2) to be true?

(2) *U* means that *p* by *S*.

Note that although Grice's reductive project did not extend beyond this second stage, it is possible to take the reduction still further. Grice's project is to reduce linguistic meaning (both sentence meaning and speaker meaning) to people's psychology. There is then the option of seeking to reduce people's psychology to something else in turn. For example, some philosophers have sought to reduce psychological states to functional states. A functional state is a state which is characterized by its having typical causes and typical effects when operating in a causal system of other such states. These functional states might then be found to be identical with certain physical states of people (Lewis 1972).

If this third stage in the reduction was successful, the overall reduction would have shown that both linguistic meaning and psychology can be understood in more fundamental terms. If what is fundamental are (say) functional states, and these functional states are physical states of people, then we would have shown how linguistic meaning and psychology can be naturalized. That is, we would have shown how there can be linguistic meaning and psychology in a world which can be completely characterized in terms of the natural sciences. Taking the world to be a natural world in this sense would have been shown to be compatible with taking the world to contain people who think and talk.

This third stage is mentioned here as an interesting possible development of Grice's project. Nevertheless, Grice's two-stage reduction might be successful even if the third stage were not. Alternatively, we might try to reduce linguistic meaning to something other than people's psychology as part of an overall programme to show that linguistic meaning can be naturalized (Laurence 1996).

We will now proceed to Grice's implementation of his two-stage project. (For other major contributions to the Gricean project, see Schiffer 1972; Bennett 1976; Loar 1981. Note that there is an issue about how to characterize Grice's project. In this section it has been interpreted as a reductive project, following e.g. Neale 1992, p. 543. This interpretation, however, has been challenged: see Grandy 1989, pp. 524–5; Avramides 1989.)

3. Grice's reductions

Grice pursues his reductive project in a series of papers (Grice 1957, 1968, 1969). The papers offer successive refinements of the reductions offered in earlier papers. These refinements are offered in order to meet weaknesses pointed out by Grice or by critics in his earlier attempted reductions. It will serve our purposes to start with Grice's original reductions. These involve relatively simple and tractable formulations, and so they are a good place to start. There is also a deeper reason why we are interested in relatively simple formulations. The more convoluted a formulation is, the less natural and plausible it seems. It is no accident that mathematicians, for example, seek relatively simple formulations and definitions in their work (Rota 1997). If a formulation already needed to be very complicated in order to avoid certain ingenious counter-examples, we could reasonably expect that the formulation remains vulnerable to still more inventive counter-examples.

Grice's reduction of sentence meaning to speaker meaning is given by (3):

> (3) Sentence S means that p if and only if people typically or standardly mean that p by S.

(3) claims that for a sentence S to mean what it does (for it to have a certain timeless meaning, as Grice puts it) is for a sufficiently large proportion of speakers to mean that p by that sentence on particular occasions. The combined result of these many individual speaker meanings is that there is a conventional regularity to the effect that these speakers mean that p by S.

The idea of a conventional regularity can be explained in the following way (Lewis 1975, pp. 5–6. Lewis's numbering has been changed):

> a regularity, R, in action or in action and belief, is a *convention* in a population P if and only if, within P, the following six conditions hold . . .
> (i)   Everyone conforms to R.
> (ii)   Everyone believes that the others conform to R.
> (iii) Each person's belief in (i) gives that person a good and decisive reason to conform to R himself . . .
> (iv) There is a general preference for general conformity . . .
> (v) R is not the only possible regularity meeting the last two conditions . . .
> (vi) Finally, the various facts listed in conditions (i) to (v) are matters of *common* (or *mutual*) *knowledge*: they are known to everyone, it is known to everyone that they are known to everyone, it is known to everyone that they are known to everyone, and so on.

The guiding idea here is that each speaker of a language conforms to certain regularities because of his or her expectations that others will do so. Lewis's account of convention was not specifically designed for the purposes of Grice's reduction of sentence meaning to speaker meaning, but there seems no reason why the Gricean cannot co-opt this, or an allied, account of the nature of convention in order to help bridge the gap between individual cases of speaker meaning and cases of sentence meaning. (Lewis 1969 is a book length treatment of this idea about convention. For objections to Lewis's account of convention, see Burge 1975; Grandy 1977, and for objections to Lewis's use of convention in explaining shared meanings, see Davidson 1984; Bennett 1985, pp. 602–3.)

Applying this idea of a convention, the reduction of sentence meaning to speaker meaning can be understood as follows. A sentence S in a community of speakers means that p if and only if there is a certain convention among those speakers. The convention is to the effect that, if any of those speakers utters S, then S means that p.

Grice's initial reduction of speaker meaning to speaker intentions is given by (4):

(4)   Utterer U means that p by sentence S if and only if U utters S with the intention of getting U's audience A to believe that p.

Sentence (4) is roughly the formulation offered in Grice 1957. It suits our present purposes initially to work with (4) rather than the more intricate reformulations that Grice and others later offer. (See Grice 1968, 1969; Schiffer 1972, pp. 63, 75–6; Bennett 1976, §53.) Sentence (4) offers a reduction of what it is for someone to mean that p when that person utters a particular sentence on a particular occasion. One of the assumptions motivating this reduction is that communication is a central function of language. Given this assumption, someone's meaning that p by uttering a sentence on a given occasion consists in that person assigning the sentence the role of communicating that p to the speaker's audience on that occasion. Now assigning a sentence such a role in a particular instance of communication is a matter of the speaker's having certain intentions about what role that sentence is to have in communication on that occasion. It is for this reason that a speaker's communicative intentions are the central component in Grice's reduction of speaker meaning.

Grice himself was dissatisfied with (4). There is a difference between telling someone something – communicating information – and simply letting the person know. For example, suppose a mob boss hires a private investigator to find out what Jake is up to. Consider two different cases. In the first, the investigator reports back to the boss and hands him a drawing of what Jake has been up to. In the second case, the investigator goes to the boss's office with the intention of reporting back. As he walks into the boss's office, however, he trips on the carpet and his folder full of photographs tips out onto the floor. The boss sees what Jake has been up to. In both outcomes the investigator had the intention of getting his boss to know what Jake has been up to. Only in the first case, however, does the investigator inform the boss. In the second case, the boss inadvertently finds out what Jake has been doing. Although the investigator has the intention, the boss does not form his beliefs because of that intention.

Grice takes the lesson to be that for communication to take place, the audience has both to come to believe the information the speaker is intending to convey and they have to form that belief by recognizing the speaker's intention to get them to form that belief. Grice offers the following reformulation of (4):

(5) Utterer U means that p by uttering sentence S if and only if U utters S with the intention of getting U's audience A to believe that p by means of A's recognition of that intention.

Communication between a speaker and his audience then depends on the audience knowing what the speaker intends to convey when he utters something.

In later work, Grice drops the appeal found in (4) and (5) to a self-referential intention (Grice 1968, 1969). Drawing on a suggestion found in Strawson 1964, Grice offers in its place the following account of speaker meaning:

(6) Speaker U means that p by uttering sentence S if and only if U utters S intending:
 (a) U's audience A to believe that p,
 (b) A to recognize that U intends (a), and
 (c) A's recognition that U intends (a) to function, in part, as a reason for (a).

(6) applies to the case of indicative utterances. In the case of non-indicative utterances, the speaker intends the audience to intend to perform some action (rather than to form some belief or to entertain some thought). For example, the speaker says 'Shut the window' meaning *shut the window* if and only if the speaker utters that sentence with the intention of getting the audience to intend to shut the window, and also intends the audience to form that intention by means of their recognition of the speaker's first intention. Likewise, the utterance of a sentence is a request for information if and only if the speaker intends the audience to intend to answer the question, and also intends the audience to form that intention by means of their recognition of the speaker's first intention.

What are these communicative intentions? Having such an intention does not seem to require any conscious mental process to produce it. Nor need we be consciously aware of them. Grice does not try to support his reduction by appealing to what introspection tells us about what, if any, intentions we characteristically have when we utter sentences. The reduction of a speaker meaning to a speaker's communicative intentions seeks to provide necessary and sufficient conditions for a speaker meaning that p by a given utterance. The test of Grice's theory is whether it specifies conditions that are necessary and sufficient. If we have reason to think it does, we will have some reason to think that speakers have the communicative intentions that the theory imputes to them. Speakers will have these intentions implicitly, if not consciously (Loar 1981, p. 252). (In §5, we will return to the issue of how plausible it is that speakers each have a certain complex of communicative intentions.)

What are the merits of Grice's project? First, the project would show how meaning can be explained in other terms, and the reduction would thereby enhance our understanding of what meaning is. Second, the reduction is not confined to linguistic meaning. It also applies to the meaning of such things as gestures or pictures. The reduction thereby locates linguistic meaning in the wider domain of all those phenomena which have meaning. Grice's reduction of meaning is then highly unifying. It provides a single reduction of the entire domain of meaning. Third, the project captures a widely shared intuition that what our words mean is a function of our use of those words. This intuition is captured in the following way. How we use our sentences on particular occasions depends on how we choose to use them, and that in turn is a matter of our intentions – what we choose to use those sentences to convey. Fourth, the project explains why speakers typically know what their words mean. If speaker meaning depends on speaker intentions, and we typically know what our own intentions are, we typically know the speaker meaning of our own words.

There is a further intuition which apparently supports the project. The intuition is that language originated in people's needs to communicate with one another. Grice even offers an account of how language came about and why. The account traces the development of language from its supposed origins in scattered instances of speaker meaning to the arrival of linguistic meaning, with words and sentences having stable shared meanings (Grice 1982. See also Suppes 1986, p. 113).

It is open for us to tell 'just so' stories about the origin of language, stories about how or why it might have come about. But philosophical offerings of this sort are armchair speculations and it is not clear why we should give more credence to one rather than another of them. It seems to be an empirical task for linguistic anthropology to say how language came about. Moreover, at least in the case of many phenomena, there is a distinction between an account of what the phenomenon is and an account of how it came about. Consider fencing, for example. One plausible origin of fencing is to be found in people trying to kill one another in battle with swords. Yet, fencing itself is a sport where the object is just to touch one's opponent with the blade. If you knew only what the origins of fencing were, you would not know what fencing is. Likewise, even if Grice's speculations about the origins of language were correct, it would be a further matter whether his theory about the nature of linguistic meaning – his reductive project – is correct.

Let's now turn to objections to each stage of Grice's project. In §4, we will consider some objections to Grice's reduction of sentence meaning to speaker meaning. In §5, we will consider objections to Grice's reduction of speaker meaning to speaker intentions. Critics of Grice concentrate on this second stage of his reductive project, so we will spend more time on their criticisms.

4. Objections: Sentence meaning

This stage of Grice's project faces several objections. One of them takes the form of a thought experiment. Others question the supposed role of rules or of intentions in accounting for sentence meaning.

Ziff's experimental subjects

Suppose that George's head is medically experimented on and that certain apparatus is inserted into his brain. When George is asked how he is feeling while the experiment is running, he responds with the following string of seemingly nonsense words 'Glyting elly beleg'. Later, after the experiment is over and the apparatus is removed, George says that, whenever he gave that response, he meant that he felt fine. He explains that, at the time, he thought that was what he meant and that everyone knew this. In this case, what George says has speaker meaning but it does not have sentence meaning (Ziff 1967, pp. 4–5). Now suppose that the experiment is carried out more widely, and specifically to all members of George's linguistic community, the community of English speakers. In this case, each speaker responds 'Glyting elly beleg' when asked how he or she feels, and each of their responses has speaker meaning because each of them means that he or she feels fine. On Grice's theory, 'Glyting elly beleg' means that *I feel fine* if only and if people typically or standardly mean that *I feel fine* by 'Glyting elly beleg'. Nevertheless, whatever Grice's theory says, 'Glyting elly beleg' does not mean anything at all. (For criticism, see Patton and Stampe 1969, pp. 10–11.)

The problem of novel utterances

A natural language, such as English or Swahili, can produce a denumerable infinity of sentences (i.e. a countable infinity of sentences). Very many of these sentences will never be uttered. Some of these sentences will never be uttered because they are too bizarre ('Norm chewed the piano while stamping his feet'). Other sentences will never be uttered because they are pointless (e.g. consider the sentence formed by the disjunction of the first sentence of *Pride and Prejudice* with the last sentence of the Boeing 747 flight maintenance manual). And still others are neither bizarre nor pointless but they will never be uttered because the human race will die out before they are uttered. Nevertheless, listeners or readers would immediately understand such 'novel' sentences of their language. This cannot be because there are pre-established conventions or expectations governing those individual sentences. Since those sentences have never been uttered, no such conventions or expectations govern them.

A connected objection concerns ambiguous sentences that have at least one meaning that has passed unnoticed (Ziff 1967, p. 7). For example, when someone says 'She's just driving me round the bend', we automatically take the speaker to be speaking idiomatically – to be saying, roughly, that she is causing the speaker great stress. The sentence also has a literal non-idiomatic meaning that typically never occurs to us. In this sense the sentence means that, at the moment of utterance, the speaker is in a vehicle which a female is driving and that she is taking the vehicle around a bend in the road.

A different kind of case again is given by the sentence 'No head injury is too trivial to ignore'. Most people would take that sentence to be unambiguous and to mean that *no head injury should be ignored, however trivial it may be*. The sentence in fact means something very different. It means that *every head injury should be ignored, no matter how trivial*. (Consider some syntactically similar sentences. 'No mistake is too trivial to correct' means that *every mistake should be corrected, no matter how trivial*. 'No child is too rude to look after' means that *every child should be looked after, no matter how rude*.) Either the sentence 'No head injury is too trivial to ignore' is unambiguous or it is not.

If it is unambiguous, most people do not understand the univocal meaning of the sentence. If it is ambiguous, most people do not even recognize one of its meanings and so have not used it with that meaning.

Lastly, some sentences are normally used with meanings other than their standard ones. For example, 'He is a rat' is predominantly used in its metaphorical sense (Coady 1976, p. 103).

Scepticism about rules of language

People often talk about the rules of language, but why should we suppose that there are such rules? Our linguistic behaviour has a motley character. Good reasons need to be given for thinking that there are systematic regularities to be found in it, or that it is regulated by rules. Consider the following sceptical case:

> . . . when we look at the acoustical complexity of real speech, when we think about the features we all recognize intuitively without being able to identify acoustically or by rule, varying features of prosody, rhythm, individual quirks of grammar, etc., it seems hopeless to think that this marvellous complexity can be caught in any set of rules. Moreover, the attempts that we now have are so pitiful in character, so totally unsatisfactory, and so crude in approximation, that scepticism at the very idea of being able to capture language in rules is easily supported. . . . We can and do speak and understand sentences that do not conform to any rules that we have in our heads. The grammatical rules of our speech are not at all like the rules of chess. They are like the rules of a children's game that are not codified and are continually changing. (Suppes 1986, pp. 115–16)

The objection from redundancy

Grice's project seeks to understand linguistic meaning in terms of speaker intention. We have seen that he seeks to reduce sentence meaning to regularities or conventions regarding what intentions speakers in a certain group share when they utter various sentences. But it is enough for those sentences to have the meanings that they do, that there are certain regularities or conventions regarding what the members of the group take the use of the sentences to be communicated. There is no need to suppose that Gricean intentions figure in the reduction of sentence meaning to regularities within a group:

> But once we have methods of communicating into which we have been trained, perhaps I need not care at all if you recognize my intention in uttering.

> It would be enough if you heard my words, because you will have been trained to take them in a certain way, and so taking them, you will understand me. (Blackburn 1984, p. 113)

According to this objection, then, whether or not Grice is correct to reduce speaker meaning to speaker intentions, there is no call to reduce sentence meaning to regularities *involving speaker intentions*.

5. Objections: Speaker meaning

In this section, we will consider some objections to Grice's reduction of speaker meaning to speaker intentions. To begin with, we will consider counter-examples to the claim that an utterance's being produced with the requisite intentions is sufficient for it to have speaker meaning. We will then consider counter-examples to the claim that an utterance's being produced with the requisite intentions is necessary for it to have speaker meaning. Following that, we will consider some further objections to Grice's reduction. These include epistemological objections, an objection from psychological implausibility, an additional objection from the possibility of novel utterances and an objection from the role of linguistic understanding.

Counter-examples to the sufficiency of Grice's theory

Recall Grice's reduction of speaker meaning:

> (6) Speaker U means that p by uttering sentence S if and only if U utters S intending:
> (a) U's audience A to believe that p,
> (b) A to recognize that U intends (a), and
> (c) A's recognition that U intends (a) to function, in part, as a reason for (a).

Grice's attempted reduction of speaker meaning to speaker intentions has provoked a number of counter-examples. Here are some counter-examples which seek to show that satisfying Grice's conditions for a case of speaker meaning is not sufficient for something's being a case of speaker meaning. In other words, these counter-examples seek to show that it is possible that Grice's conditions are met in a given case – someone has all of the intentions that Grice's theory requires – although it is not a case of someone's meaning something by a particular utterance on that occasion. (For the purposes of exposition, some incidental features of these counter-examples have been changed from the originals.)

Ziff's irritable academic

George is an irritable and recently sacked academic. He attends a job interview and is asked 'Why are you here?' George is incensed at being asked such an inane question and replies with a stream of apparent nonsense, 'Ugh ugh blugh blugh ugh blug blug'. He says this with the intention of offending the questioner. He intends the questioner to be offended by recognizing that first intention. Consequently, this case meets Grice's conditions for something to be an instance of speaker meaning. But, the counter-example concludes, George did not mean anything by what he uttered, and it is clear that that string of sounds does not mean anything (Ziff 1967, pp. 2–3. See Patton and Stampe 1969, p. 5 for criticism).

Black's gift

You give someone a gift out of gratitude. In doing so, you happen to have a number of intentions. You intend that the recipient thinks that you are grateful to them. You also intend that they recognize your first intention. Nevertheless, the counter-example continues, you are not communicating, or meaning that, you are grateful to them when you give them the gift (Black 1973, p. 263).

Black's furniture mover

I need your help to move the table. Without saying a word, I pick up my end of the table and pause. I intend you to pick up your end. I intend you to recognize that first intention. And I intend you to pick up your end of the table by your recognizing that I have that first intention. Nevertheless, according to the counter-example, my raising my end of the table is not a case of communication (Black 1973, p. 263).

Strawson's deceived eavesdropper

Ned is talking to Nate at a bar. Ned knows that another work mate, Frank, is nearby and can overhear them, but he can also tell that Frank does not realize that Ned knows this. Ned decides to hoodwink Frank. He says to Nate: 'Frank doesn't realise it but his boss thinks he's doing a bad job, so he's going to be sacked at the end of the week'. Ned intends each of the following: that Frank thinks that he's going to be sacked at the end of the week, and that Frank thinks that he is going to be sacked because he recognizes that Ned has that first intention. Yet, Ned is not talking to Frank; it is not a case of communication, in Grice's sense (Strawson 1964, p. 447).

Grice seeks to address this counter-example by requiring that, in a case of genuine communication, the audience should know *all* of the intentions the speaker had in making the utterance (Grice 1969, p. 159). A worry facing this, however, is that a range of progressively more complicated counter-examples can be devised, and that this requirement would involve the speaker having an indefinitely large number of further intentions (Black 1973, pp. 278–9).

Searle's masquerading soldier

Suppose that, during the part of World War II when Italy was on the side of Germany, an American soldier is captured by Italian troops. The soldier wants to convince these troops that he is a German officer in order to be released. Unfortunately, he does not know enough German or Italian to tell them that he is a German officer. So, what he does is to improvise: he uses what German he knows to dupe them into thinking that he is a German. As it happens, the American knows only one sentence of German, 'Kennst du das Land, wo die Zitronen blühen?', a line from Goethe that he memorized at school. He then utters this sentence. Grice's conditions are met: the American intends to produce a certain effect in them, namely, the effect of believing that he is a German officer, and he intends to produce this effect by means of their recognition of his intention. He intends that they should think that what he is trying to tell them is that he is a German officer. According to the counter-example, however, it does not follow that when the American utters the sentence he means that he is a German officer. In fact, the sentence means *Do you know the land where the lemon trees bloom?* (Searle 1969, p. 44. See Schiffer 1972, p. 28; Bennett 1976, p. 92 for criticism).

Ziff's madman

A madman says 'Gleeg gleeg gleeg' intending to make his audience believe that it is snowing in Tibet and intending that they recognize that he said what he did with that intention. Grice's conditions for the speaker's meaning that *it is snowing in Tibet* by 'Gleeg gleeg gleeg' are met. 'But the madman's cry did not mean anything at all; it certainly did not mean it was snowing in Tibet' (Ziff 1967, p. 5. But see Patton and Stampe 1969, pp. 11–12).

It might be tempting to address these and other counter-examples to Grice's reduction of sentence meaning to speaker intention by adding further conditions to the proposed reduction, just as Grice did in the transition from (4) to (5). But merely adding a new condition to the proposed reduction seems an *ad hoc* manoeuvre (MacKay 1972, p. 58). Suppose that there is no independent reason to think that a speaker has such a complicated array of communicative intentions when he or she utters a sentence. Then the claim that a speaker has such an array of communicative intentions in all and only cases of speaker meaning is made solely in order to save Grice's reduction from a counter-example. This is bad methodology because what is up for debate is the question whether the reduction is correct.

Why is Grice's account open to these and other counter-examples? Searle offers a two-part diagnosis of its weaknesses (Searle 1969, pp. 43–4). First, the account fails to explain the degree to which meaning is conventional or rule-governed. There is a connection between a speaker's meaning something by the sentence that he or she utters and what the sentence uttered means in the language to which it belongs. Yet, Grice's account fails to illuminate that connection.

The second weakness that Searle identifies is that Grice's account does not distinguish between the different kinds of effect that a speaker can intend to induce in an audience. Some of these effects require only that the audience recognizes the speaker's intentions. In the case of intentions to warn, to promise or to apologize, for example, the audience's recognizing the intention suffices for the audience to be warned, promised to or apologized to, respectively. The audience's recognizing the speaker's intention is sufficient for the intention's goal to be brought about. Other effects require more than that the audience recognizes the speaker's intentions. An audience's forming a belief or obeying a command or being intimidated require more than that it recognizes that the speaker intends any of these things. The audience's recognizing the speaker's intention is not sufficient for the intention's goal to be brought about. According to Searle, an account of speaker meaning should be concerned with the former class of effects but not with the latter. In addition, he claims that, in a case of speaker meaning, the speaker intends to follow the conventions governing the meanings of the sentences.

With these amendments to Grice's account in place, Searle thinks that he can address the above kinds of counter-examples. For instance, George, the irritable academic, is intending to offend his audience, but for an audience to be offended requires more on their part merely than that they recognize that George intends to offend them. Again, the masquerading soldier intends that the Italians believe that he is a German officer, but for the Italians to believe this requires more on their part merely than that they recognize that he intends to induce that belief in them. Furthermore, it is plainly not the case that, in German, the belief that the speaker is a German officer is standardly or conventionally induced in an audience by a speaker saying 'Kennst du das Land, wo die Zitronen blühen?' So, the soldier does not intend that his audience forms the belief that he is a German officer by their recognizing that the above is the case. For this reason what the soldier says does not mean that he is a German officer.

Searle's proposed amendments to Grice's theory face criticisms on points of detail and on a point of strategy. Regarding points of detail, if something is not the case, no one can recognize that it is the case. Since it is not the case that, in German, the belief that the speaker is a German officer is standardly or conventionally induced in an audience by his or her saying 'Kennst du das Land, wo die Zitronen blühen?', the Italians cannot be induced to recognize that it is the case. That is a fact, however, about the factive nature of the verb 'recognise': recognizing that p entails that p. It is enough for the counter-example's purposes that the American soldier intends his audience to *believe* that it is the case that the sentence he utters standardly means in German that he is a German officer. An audience can be induced to believe that something is the case, even if it is not the case. Next, let us grant that merely believing that someone intends you to believe that p does not entail that you believe that p. But it is enough for the counter-example's purposes that the American soldier intends to declare to the Italians that he is a German officer. An audience's recognizing a speaker's intention to declare that something is the case, and their thereby believing what he or she has declared is sufficient for the intention to be successful.

Let us turn to the point of strategy. Recall that Grice's overall reductive project consists in reducing sentence meaning (the meaning of a sentence type in a given language) to speaker meaning (the meaning of an utterance made by a speaker at a particular time and place), and in reducing speaker meaning in turn to speaker intentions. This requires that speaker intentions, and so speaker meaning, are each explanatorily more basic than sentence meaning. This, in turn, requires that the content of speaker intentions can be characterized without appeal to sentence meaning. Now one of Searle's amendments is that, in a case of speaker meaning, the speaker seeks to follow the conventions or rules governing expressions in the language being uttered. But these are conventions or rules governing expressions in sentence types. Hence, they are conventions or rules concerning sentence meaning. But then the proposed reduction of speaker meaning to speaker intentions will appeal to intentions whose content has to be explained in terms of sentence meaning. This runs contrary to the Grice's reductive project (Miller 2007, pp. 257–8).

Counter-examples to the necessity of Grice's theory

The following counter-examples claim that satisfying Grice's conditions for a case of speaker meaning are not necessary for something's being a case of speaker meaning. These counter-examples seek to show that it is possible that none of Grice's conditions are met in a given case – someone has none of the intentions that Grice's theory requires – although it is a case of someone's meaning something by a particular utterance on an occasion.

The problem of the informed audience

Here again is Grice's reduction of speaker meaning:

(7) Speaker U means that p by uttering sentence S if and only if U utters S intending:
  (a) U's audience A to believe that p,
  (b) A to recognize that U intends (a), and
  (c) A's recognition that U intends (a) to function, in part, as a reason for (a).

The current problem concerns clause (a) of (6). There are cases where someone means that p without intending to get their audience to believe that p. For example, when a schoolchild in an examination writes that Operation Barbarossa was launched in June 1941, the child is not intending to get the examiners to form a belief about when that event occurred. The child presumably believes that the examiners already have that belief.

In light of this kind of counter-example, Grice suggests replacing clause (a). The replacement clause says that U intends the following: A to believe that U believes that p. In terms of our example, the child intends the examiners to believe that the child believes that Operation Barbarossa was launched in June 1941 (Grice 1969).

One difficulty with this suggestion is that it seems to distort what people are doing when they communicate. In at least many cases, speakers seek to communicate information about how the world around them is, not information about the contents of their mental states. Of course, by saying (say) 'Grass is green', a speaker will also convey to you the information that the speaker believes that grass is green. But what the speaker means by 'Grass is green' was something about the world around him or her. What a speaker seeks to communicate is not confined to information about his or her mental states, and in this example what the speaker primarily sought to communicate was something to do with grass, not about his or her mental states (McDowell 1998, p. 38).

Another kind of counter-example concerns cases of reminding. You believe that dinner will be at seven. I know you believe this but say 'Dinner will be at seven' to remind you that dinner will be at seven. When I said 'Dinner will be at seven', I was not intending to induce the belief in you that dinner will be at seven. I knew you already had that belief. Moreover, I was not intending to induce the belief in you that I believed that dinner will be at seven. I may already know that you have that belief too. To address this problem, we might distinguish between a speaker's intending an audience to acquire a certain belief and the speaker's intending to *activate* that belief in them – to bring a belief, which they already have, to their conscious attention. But, this does not fully address the problem. There remains an issue about the content of what the speaker was trying to communicate in this case. I was not intending to get you to acquire or to activate any belief about what my mental states are. I was intending to get you to activate a belief about when dinner will be.

Besides, there are other difficulties. Here are two of them. First, need a speaker always be concerned about whether they are believed or not? Perhaps, a speaker might speak up out of a sense of urgency or because they like the sound of their own voice. Second, surely only a conceited speaker intends his audience to believe that p just because he has said so. To meet these difficulties, perhaps Grice should replace clause (a) with the clause that the speaker intends the audience actively to entertain p (or that the speaker intends the audience actively to entertain the thought that the speaker believes that p) (Neale 1992, p. 547).

The problem of the squeaky speaker

Grice thinks that, in cases of speaker meaning, the audience thinks that p because it recognizes the speaker's communicative intentions. He includes clause (c) as part of his reduction of speaker meaning because he wants to exclude cases in which some natural feature of the speaker's utterance makes it obvious that p. A problem facing Grice is that there seem to be possible cases of communication in which the audience forms the belief that p for precisely this reason. Consider a speaker who says in a squeaky voice 'I have a squeaky voice'. The audience may form the belief that the speaker has a squeaky voice because they have heard his voice. Nevertheless, it still seems that the speaker meant *I have a squeaky voice* by what he said (Neale 1992, p. 548). Clause (c) has to be abandoned.

The problem of soliloquy

Grice seeks to reduce speaker meaning to the speaker's having intentions to bring about certain changes in an audience. But, what about cases where a speaker utters sentences but where he believes that there is no audience? Call these cases of soliloquy (Ziff 1967, p. 4; Black 1973, p. 264; Yu 1979, p. 278). In such a case, the speaker does not intend to induce new beliefs or other changes in anyone. Consider, for example, a prisoner in solitary confinement formulating aloud his escape plans. He knows there is no audience – indeed, he desires that no one hears his escape plans – and yet the sentences he utters have speaker meaning. The speaker does not seem to be his own audience either, because he does not have any communicative intention to convey any of his beliefs to himself. No doubt, the speaker can have reasons for speaking to himself and so have intentions for doing so – it might be for company or to exercise his vocal cords. But, those considerations are irrelevant to the example because they are not intentions that belong to the set of communicative intentions specified by Grice's reduction.

One response which Griceans have offered is to claim that private non-communicative uses of language are parasitic on public communicative uses (Clark 1975, p. 108; Suppes 1986, pp. 119–20. See also Schiffer 1972, pp. 73–80). The claim here is that language was primarily devised for the purposes of communication, and that speaker meaning is then primarily to be understood in terms of a speaker's intentions to influence an audience. Nevertheless, even if that is the primary function of language, language can acquire other, subsidiary functions. One of these is the use of language in contexts lacking an audience. To take a parallel, the primary function of eating is sustenance, but it has a derivative function of providing enjoyment. The central cases are then ones where we eat for sustenance, and the cases where one eats for enjoyment, but not for sustenance, are subsidiary cases.

How persuasive is this analogy? Biological science offers a single account of the mechanism of eating – of what eating is – that applies to both kinds of cases. The difference in the two cases lies in the motivation for eating. The parallel should then be that we have a single account of speaker meaning that applies to both the so-called central and subsidiary cases. But, the original objection was just that Grice's account of speaker meaning does not apply to both kinds of cases. Let's grant that one kind of case involves a function that is more important or more frequently used than the function of the other kind of case. The issue was that both kinds of cases are instances of the same phenomenon, speaker meaning. An adequate account of that phenomenon should apply to every instance of it.

A different response is that, in cases of a private use of language, the speaker is intending to induce changes in a *hypothetical* audience, if not in an actual one (Grice 1969, pp. 174–7). The speaker intends that these changes would be brought about if an audience were present. The question then is how psychologically realistic this response is. The response is committed to claiming that in every case of the private use of language, the speaker is conceiving of himself or herself addressing an imaginary audience and seeking to induce changes in it. We will consider this type of objection further when we consider below how psychologically plausible Grice's theory is. (For further discussion, see Lycan 2008, p. 89.)

Ziff's fever victim

While delirious with fever, and unaware of any audience, someone says 'Claudius murdered my father'. What this person said has meaning. But since the speaker said it while he was delirious and was 'dead to the world', he was not intending to produce any effect in an audience. So, Grice's conditions for this to be a case of speaker meaning are not met (Ziff 1967, p. 4).

Ziff's irritable academic again

George, the irritable academic, goes for another interview. Again he is asked a question that he regards as demeaning. This time he utters something that sounds to his audience like gibberish but which is, as George knows, a sentence of Hopi that means *I don't know*. As before, George says something with the intention of offending the questioner, and he intends the questioner to be offended by recognizing that first intention. But, according to the counter-example, these intentions are irrelevant to what George's utterance means. What George meant, it is claimed, is that he didn't know (Ziff 1967, p. 3. See Patton and Stampe 1969, p. 6 for criticism).

Black's truthful liar

Lee is not a burglar but he is well known to be an incorrigible liar. The police question him about a spate of break-ins and ask him straight out whether he is a burglar. If he lies, he will say 'Yes'. But Lee also realizes that the police, knowing his reputation as a liar, will take his answer to be a reason to think that he is not a burglar. 'Knowing this, the only effect he can intend in the audience is the reverse of what he intends – and hence he will be telling the truth, willy-nilly' (Black 1973, p. 266).

Epistemological objections

The following epistemological objection has been levelled against Grice's theory of meaning (Biro 1979; Platts 1979, p. 91 makes a closely related objection). One key role that our utterances have is to tell other people what we intend to do. Grice seeks to explain the meaning of a speaker's utterances in terms of certain of his intentions, the speaker's communicative intentions. Now how can we know what communicative intentions a speaker has? If the speaker seeks to inform us by telling us, then the same problem arises. If the meaning of a speaker's utterances is to be explained in terms of his communicative intentions, how can we know what his communicative intentions are when he makes utterances seeking to inform us of his communicative intentions? To understand what he says, we would need to know what his communicative intentions are when making that utterance, and that is precisely the problem facing us. Suppose, then, that there is some independent means of knowing what a speaker's intentions are. (Perhaps, this is by means of observing the speaker's behaviour and the context in which he is talking.) But, if so, 'the intentions so discovered need not be construed as [communicative intentions]' (Biro 1979, pp. 247–8). Moreover, if there were such an independent source of knowledge, we could use it to find out what a speaker's communicative intentions were. A speaker's utterances would not be the only way in which a speaker conveyed to others what his communicative intentions were. 'Yet this is just what the theories we are considering [i.e. those such as Grice's] require' (Biro 1979, p. 248). The conclusion drawn is that, whatever enables people to understand what a speaker means, it need not be by means of knowing what communicative intentions the speaker has. But if this is so, then those intentions cannot be counted as themselves 'determinative or constitutive' of the meaning of his utterance. The meaning of what the speaker says 'must be specifiable without reference to' his communicative intentions (Biro 1979, p. 248).

The above argument faces a number of queries. Some of the premises are not evident. First, if there is an independent way of finding out a speaker's intentions, why is it that these intentions then 'need not' be construed as communicative intentions? Second, does Grice's theory require that a speaker's utterances would be the only way in which a speaker conveys his communicative intentions? How does that epistemological claim follow from anything Grice says about what speaker meaning is? The argument's conclusion faces a related query. Suppose that we do not need to know a speaker's communicative intentions in order to understand his utterances. It is not clear how it follows that what his utterances mean is not determined by his communicative intentions. By the same measure, we do not need to know a given sample of liquid's chemical structure in order to know that the liquid is water. It would be enough to know that it has been sold by a reputable shop as water. Nevertheless, it does not follow that whether the liquid is water is not determined by the liquid's chemical structure. A reduction of x (water, speaker meaning, . . .) to y (chemical structure, communicative intentions, . . .) says what x (more) fundamentally is. Given the reduction, knowledge of which things are y can provide one source of knowledge of which things are x, but the reduction does not entail that it is the only source.

Biro's response to this last query is that 'in the theory of meaning, there is, and can be, no distinction of the sort which underlies the [query]' (Biro 1979, p. 249). That is, there is no distinction between what an utterance's meaning reduces to and how we find out what that utterance means:

> One thing a theory of meaning for a language must make room for is an account of the knowledge a fully competent speaker of the language for which it is a theory possesses in virtue of being competent. Thus a theory of meaning must make possible a theory of how a hearer can come to know the meanings of the utterances he hears. The distinction between what constitutes the meaning of an utterance (or of a sentence or other favoured abstraction) and what conveys that meaning to a speaker of the language of which the utterance is a part is, from this point of view, a bogus one . . . . (Biro 1979, p. 249)

The relation between a theory of meaning and a theory of understanding is a vexed one, and Biro's claims are contentious. (For contrary claims, see Devitt 1983, pp. 89–90.) The distinction between what an utterance's meaning is and how we can tell what that meaning is seems to be a special case of the ubiquitous distinction between what something is and how we can tell whether that thing is present in a given case. It is one thing for something to be gold or a pancreas or a Stradivarius violin; it is quite another matter how to identify any of these things. Likewise, then, there would seem to be a distinction between what a given utterance means and how we can come to understand what it means.

In the above passage, Biro gives an argument against this presumption. As we will now see, his premises, however, are ambiguous. On one disambiguation, the premises do not entail the conclusion. On the other disambiguation, they beg the question.

Biro says that a theory of meaning for a language 'must make room' for a theory of what it is to understand that language, and that the former theory 'must make possible' the latter theory. Those claims are ambiguous. On one reading, they just mean that a theory of meaning for a language should be compatible with a theory of understanding of that language. But on that reading, the premises of Biro's argument are compatible with Grice's theory of meaning. Grice's theory does not exclude the possibility of there being a theory of what it is to understand a language. Since the conclusion of Biro's argument is incompatible with Grice's theory of meaning, it follows that, on the current reading, the premises of Biro's argument do not entail his conclusion. On another reading, the premises are claiming that a theory of meaning for a language is, or provides, a theory of understanding for that language. As Biro later puts it, 'a theory of meaning is a theory of the mastery of his language – giving a theory of meaning must involve giving an account of how a speaker can understand (come to know the meaning of) utterances in his language' (Biro 1979, p. 249). On this reading, however, the premises are only stating what the conclusion itself says, and so the premises beg the question. What was wanted was an argument for the conclusion, and yet, on this reading, the premises assume the very point at issue. For these reasons, Biro's argument against Grice fails: on neither reading do the premises lend support to the conclusion. (For further discussion of Biro's argument, see Suppes 1986, pp. 125–8.)

What kind of theory of understanding might supplement a theory of meaning such as Grice's? Here is one suggestion. A speaker's audience consists of people formulating and testing hypotheses about what the speaker means. These people have the creative capacity to generate hypotheses about what the sentences of the language the speaker is using mean. They test these hypotheses in their own speech. In particular, they utter sentences that they take to have a certain meaning in that language in order to try to achieve certain ends. The test is whether those ends are regularly achieved by those means. By observing speakers that they take to understand the language, they tell whether, and how far, those tests succeed. An audience member then acquires full linguistic competence when his or her hypotheses attain a suitably high level of predictive and explanatory power.

The account sketched here is in need of detailed development. Yet, there seems to be no reason why this cannot be done. Presumably, such work lies in the fields of cognitive science and psycholinguistics. The key point for our purposes is that understanding a speaker involves the same methodology of observation and trial-and-error theorizing familiar from the work of scientists and detectives. Such an account can readily complement Grice's theory of meaning – or, indeed, any other theory of meaning. As we will see in Chapter 7, Grice contributes to such an account with his theory of conversation. Grice's view is that an audience needs to tell what a speaker has said in order to tell what the speaker meant, and this transition is often made by appealing to the nature and purpose of rational conversation.

Lastly, Max Black raises concerns about how we can 'apply' Grice's theory to 'determine the content' of what people say to us (Black 1973, p. 275, his phrases). Black seems to be assuming that a theory of meaning should provide a criterion, a way of telling, what the speaker meaning of particular utterances is, and that Grice's theory takes this criterion to be given by speaker's intentions. The difficulties that arise when we try to deploy this criterion are then taken to impugn Grice's theory:

> . . . Grice's view puts the semantic cart in front of the horse: it is not perception of the speaker's intention to produce certain desired effects in the hearer that allows a hearer to determine the meaning of what is being said, but, vice versa, detection of the speaker's meaning enables a suitably competent hearer, assisted by previous experience, and by interpretation of the given sign produced in the course of this speech transaction, to infer the speaker's intention. (Black 1973, p. 276)

Grice's project was to reduce speaker meaning to speaker intentions. This concerns the metaphysical sense of 'determines'. This is the sense in which 'x determines y' means that y reduces to x. Black, however, seems to be concerned with a different sense of 'determines'. This is an epistemic sense of 'determines'. It is the sense in which 'x determines y' means that x enables us to tell whether y is the case. Not only are these different senses of the term 'determines', but they are compatible senses. It is compatible with x metaphysically determining y that y epistemically determines x. For example, H_2O metaphysically determines water. But we can tell whether some sample of liquid is a sample of H_2O rather than (say) H_2SO_4 by knowing that it is a sample of water. The same goes for meaning. According to Grice, speaker intention metaphysically determines speaker meaning. It is consistent with that thesis that *detection* of speaker meaning *enables* us to *infer* speaker intentions, to use Black's own epistemic terminology. (For further defences of Grice's theory against epistemological objections, see Neale 1992, pp. 551–3; Davies 2006, p. 97; Miller 2006, pp. 259–60.)

An objection from psychological implausibility

For the most part, understanding a speaker is nothing like as painstaking and deliberate a process as working out who killed Colonel Mustard or what black holes are. In fact, we very often understand speakers immediately and without any process of conscious inference. Does Grice over-intellectualize what it is to understand someone's utterances? Grice's reduction of speaker meaning to speaker intentions requires that a speaker has certain quite complex intentions when he or she utters a sentence with a certain speaker meaning. Some philosophers find this consequence implausible. They think that it is the exception rather than the rule that a speaker can detect communicative intentions whenever he or she says something with a given speaker meaning (Black 1973, pp. 272–4). It has also been alleged that, for Grice, even simple cases of communication 'require the postulation of far-fetched hidden intentions underlying automatic, unreflective actions' (Thomason 1990, p. 346).

Grice himself disclaimed 'any intention of peopling all our talking life with armies of complicated psychological occurrences' (Grice 1957, p. 386). But, need he have been so defensive? The objection assumes that it is implausible to claim that a speaker has communicative intentions unless the speaker can be consciously aware of having them. This assumption invites the response that

> . . . many of our expectations and intentions are such that we do not or cannot formulate them consciously to ourselves, not least the complex ones connected with linguistic rules and practices. That we have such intentions and such expectations is shown in what we do, not in what [we are conscious of]. (Walker 1975, p. 156. See also Grice 1957, p. 387)

In the case of a theory of how we come to understand the meaning of sentences of a language, the processes the theory describes are not supposed to be conscious either. In current terminology, the processes occur below the level of conscious awareness. It would not be special pleading for Grice to claim that intention formation as well as hypothesis formation and testing can occur at a non-conscious level. Consider vision. Some cognitive psychologists suggest that vision involves an information processing system in which the visual system formulates hypotheses about the array that the eye is presented with and, on this basis, forms hypotheses about how things are seen as. (Marr 1982 provides a seminal discussion.) The processing involved is not conscious. Likewise, sentences may have speaker meaning because of the intentions of the speakers, and those sentences are understood by an audience by means of hypotheses which it has devised. In these cases, certain crucial factors – the visual system's hypotheses or the speaker's intentions – need not be ones which anyone is consciously aware of. (See Chomsky 1965, p. 8; Loar 1981, pp. 247–53; McGinn 1981, pp. 293–8.) In fact, Richmond Thomason concedes that 'postulating such intentions is a fundamental tactic not only of Grice's methodology, but of much work in cognitive psychology', and he further admits that his own theory of communication adopts the same tactic (Thomason 1990, p. 346).

An objection from novel utterances

In §5, it was claimed that most sentences of a natural language never get to be uttered. Since those sentences are never uttered, they are never uttered with any speaker intentions. Nevertheless, the sentences have meaning. So, how can those sentences have the meanings that they do, according to Grice's theory? Some philosophers think that Grice's theory faces a serious difficulty here (notably, Platts 1979, pp. 89–90. See also Ziff 1967, pp. 6–7; Chomsky 1975, pp. 67–8; Yu 1979, p. 284).

Perhaps, the meaning of the sentences can be reduced to the hypothetical intentions of speakers: the intentions which speakers would have were they to utter those sentences. If so, either there is no constraint on what hypothetical intentions speakers would have or there is a constraint. Suppose that there is no constraint. Then speakers could associate any intentions with those sentences if they were to utter them. It then follows that, according to Grice's theory, those sentences could mean anything. They do not have determinate meanings. Yet, that consequence is false: even if they are never uttered, those sentences do have relatively determinate meanings.

Alternatively, there is a constraint on what intentions would be associated with each of these sentences. One constraint is what these sentences mean. Indeed, it has been claimed that this constraint is 'standard, and it is the only constraint' (Platts 1979, p. 90). The difficulty, then, is that the project to reduce speaker meaning to speaker intentions is compromised:

> . . . what members of a speech community *would* or *could* mean by x
> (a word or sentence) is dependent on (is equivalent to?) what x means in
> the language of the community, even if what they *do* (from time to time)

> mean, *simpliciter*, is not. But what a word or a sentence means in a language is a semantic fact, if anything is. Thus, once such qualifications are admitted, we have already moved to the level of linguistic meaning, and have thereby abandoned [Grice's reductive project]. (Biro 1979, p. 242)

The claim that there has to be a constraint or constraints on speaker meaning is supported by a widespread intuition. The intuition is that a given utterance of a sentence of (say) English cannot have the speaker meaning that it does unless the English language requires, or at least permits it to have, that meaning. After all, the intuition continues, no speaker could say 'Grass is green' and mean by that utterance that it is hot – or, at least, if the speaker does mean that, he or she will not convey the meaning successfully. It is concluded that speaker meaning is just as constrained by the requirements of natural language as sentence meaning is. (The intuition is contestable. A secret agent may use innocuous English sentences to convey vital secrets, and, if his contact knows the code, then the agent will have conveyed the meaning successfully.)

We will consider one line of reply to the objection from novel utterances. (For another reply, see Blackburn 1984, pp. 128–30. But see also Miller 2007, pp. 265–8. For a yet further reply, see Boër 1980, p. 145. Boër challenges Platt as to why Grice should have to assume that *sentence meaning* is one of the constraints on speakers' hypothetical intentions.)

It is natural to try to solve this problem of novel utterances by appealing to the compositionality of meaning. Although we can produce and understand countless sentences that we have never come across before, in these cases, we have already come across the component expressions and the sentence structures that they slot into. By understanding those words and those sentence structures, we can understand sentences composed of those expressions and which have those sentence structures, even if we have not previously encountered those sentences. For example, perhaps you have never before encountered the sentence 'The cat tickled the panda'. Nevertheless, you understand the component expressions and you understand how they are combined in that sentence. You then follow a procedure – a procedure running from sub-sentential components and sentence structures to sentence meanings – that delivers you an immediate understanding of the sentence.

Grice himself seems to have taken this approach to account for our understanding of novel sentences (Grice 1968, p. 235). But, what exactly are the procedures mentioned in the last sentence of the previous paragraph? Grice talks of our running 'resultant procedures' to calculate sentence meanings. Yet, a variant of the problem of novel sentences recurs. Just as there are potentially infinitely many sentences that we can understand but which we never utter, so too there are potentially infinitely many 'resultant procedures' that we can implement but which we have never implemented. Each novel sentence is yielded by one such procedure. Since we have never come across the sentence, we have never implemented the procedure. Are there any constraints on the procedures which we would run? If there are none, then we could go from any sub-sentential components and sentence structures to any sentence meaning. If there is a constraint, then it should be acknowledged by the theory of meaning. Now, first, Grice gives no indication of what this constraint is. Second, a promising suggestion about this constraint claims that the same account can be given of both (1) how the meaning of a sentence is composed out of the meanings of its components and (2) how the truth condition of a compound sentence is determined by the truth conditions of its component sentences. But, if this suggestion is taken up, Grice's project is displaced by another project: the project of reducing a sentence's meaning to a sentence's truth condition (Coady 1976, p. 109; Lycan 2008, pp. 94–6, 123–4). We will discuss the latter project at length in Chapter 8.

Here is another way to see the objection. Grice talks of our using 'resultant procedures' to calculate sentence meanings given certain information about names and predicates. This is information about reference – about which names refer to which objects – and about predicate satisfaction – about which objects satisfy which predicates. The notions of reference and satisfaction, however, are semantic notions. Grice's reductive project seeks to reduce semantic phenomena, such as meaning, to psychological phenomena. So, until reference and satisfaction are themselves reduced to psychological phenomena, they cannot be appealed to in order to help Grice's reduction of meaning.

What kind of account could Grice otherwise give of the compositional nature of language? The account would have to provide axioms specifying the reference of names as well as other axioms specifying the extensions of simple predicates. These axioms would be stated in terms of communicative intentions. For example, two such axioms might be the following:

(7) Speakers in a community C each intend that 'the Morning Star' is used to refer to the Morning Star.

(8) Speakers in a community C each intend that 'the Evening Star' is used to refer to the Evening Star.

The Morning Star is the brightest star visible in the morning sky, and the Evening Star is the brightest star visible in the evening sky. Notice, however, that sentences such as (7) and (8) involve what is known as an intensional or indirect context (see Chapter 3 §4). What this means is that even if expressions 'a' and 'b' refer to the same thing, and speakers in a certain community each intend that 'a' refers to a particular object o, it does not follow that those speakers each intend that 'b' also refers to o. For example, Babylonian astronomy failed to discover that the Morning Star is the same heavenly body as the Evening Star, and Babylonians believed that they were distinct heavenly bodies. So, if we take community C to be the Babylonians, they would have intended to use 'the Morning Star' to refer to the Morning Star, but they would not have intended to use 'the Morning Star' to refer to the Evening Star.

What substitutions are permissible in intensional contexts? What expressions can we substitute for 'the Morning Star' in (7) while preserving the truth value of (7)? As we saw in our discussion of Frege on indirect contexts in Chapter 3 §4, the only substitutions that are permissible within such contexts are those that preserve meaning. It is because 'the Morning Star' and 'the Evening Star' do not have the same meaning, and the latter cannot be substituted for the former in (7).

Here is the important point for our assessment of Grice. We have been considering what kind of compositional account of language Grice can provide. The account would offer various axioms expressed in terms of speakers' communicative intentions. But, which expressions can be substituted within these axioms, and so which theorems can be derived from the axioms, is determined by facts about what those expressions mean. The account would then presuppose facts about meaning, and so it could not provide a reduction of those facts. (See Taylor 1982 for this line of argument.)

To sum up, there is a general problem about how we can produce and understand novel sentences, sentences that we have not come across before. This problem provides an objection to Grice's reduction of speaker meaning to speaker intentions. It is natural to try to solve the problem by appealing to the compositionality of meaning. But, when we try to account for compositionality itself, either Grice's project has to appeal to meaning – the very thing it is trying to reduce – or it will appeal to considerations that lend themselves to a quite different account of meaning.

An objection from the role of understanding

If someone makes a request or issues an order, it seems to be one thing for you to understand what they have said and another for you to intend to comply with what they have said. In particular, you need not intend to comply with what they have said in order to understand what they have said (although the converse does not hold). This is most evident in a case where you hear the request or order being directed to someone else. Likewise, if someone states something, it seems to be one thing for you to understand what they have said and another for you to have any other propositional attitude to what they have said (cf. Wilson 1970, p. 296). In particular, you can believe or entertain the content of what someone has said only if you have understood it:

> Correct understanding . . . has logical priority: its absence prevents the generation of an appropriate propositional attitude "on the basis of the utterance." Only via understanding can the intended belief be appropriately generated. (Black 1973, p. 271)

In contrast, an audience can understand what has been said to it without its believing or being inclined to believe what it was told. Perhaps, the audience thinks that the speaker is an inveterate time-waster and liar: it hears him out but gives his words no further thought.

The significance of the above claims is that it seems that a speaker's primary intention should be to get his audience to understand him. But, what it is to understand a speaker's meaning is a semantic phenomenon, and so it is as much in need of reduction as speaker's meaning. 'This objection [if correct] discredits any intentionalist theory committed to explaining speaker's meaning in terms of some separable and independently identifiable hearer's response, or the intention to produce such a response' (Black 1973, p. 271).

The content of propositional attitudes

Grice seeks to reduce speaker meaning to speaker intentions. This involves reducing the meaning of what a speaker says on a given occasion to the speaker's having certain communicative intentions. Suppose that this reduction goes through. Those intentions have propositional content. When you have an intention, your intention is that such-and-such is the case. Suppose, a speaker has an intention that the audience forms the belief that (say) it is three o'clock. But, now the question arises: what accounts for the content of this propositional attitude? Why is the content of the speaker's intention *that the audience forms the belief that it is three o'clock* rather than *that the audience forms the belief that today is Friday*? In introducing Grice's reductive project in §3 of this chapter, we noted that Grice did not attempt to reduce speaker intentions to something more basic which does not have content. Grice's failure to attempt to address this issue has been thought by some philosophers to be a serious weakness of his project (e.g. Devitt and Sterelny 1999, p. 151. They seek to remove this weakness on pp. 151–4). Grice's project is not committed to any particular way of reducing the content of propositional attitudes. But it is committed to denying that their content is to be reduced to the content of sentences in public language. That is to say, to what Grice calls 'sentence meaning'. For otherwise Grice's reductive project would run in a circle and it would fail to explain any of the things which it seeks to explain. Sentence meaning would supposedly be explained in terms of regularities in speaker meaning. Speaker meaning would supposedly be explained in terms of speaker intention. And speaker intention would supposedly be explained back in terms of sentence meaning. To avoid the threat of this circle, and the ensuing explanatory vacuity, Grice's project requires a further stage in which the content of propositional attitudes is reduced to phenomena which themselves lack content.

6. Conclusion

There are three key ideas in Grice's theory of meaning. First, language is crucially a public means of communication. Second, all species of linguistic meaning can be reduced to speaker meaning: to the individual instances of meaning, to what one speaker at one time means. Third, meaning is a species of intending. The first idea might seem truistic, but it is not. For instance, it might be claimed that thinking is another essential function of language, or indeed that language has indefinitely many other functions besides communication. According to Chomsky, the function of language is the expression of thought, and linguistic competence is independent of the ability to communicate or of any other instrumental use of language, such as persuading or convincing (Chomsky 1964, pp. 9, 11–13, and 15, 1966, p. 60). Moreover, even if the first of Grice's ideas is granted, it does not entail the second idea. The idea that all species of linguistic meaning can be reduced to speaker meaning needs independent support (Yu 1979, pp. 280–1).

Grice's project addresses several of the questions that were raised in the introduction. (Q1) asked: What is the difference between marks and sounds that have meaning and those that do not? Grice takes this difference to lie in the difference between those marks and sounds that are produced by someone having a certain complex of intentions and those that are not. (Q2) asked: What gives words and sentences their particular meanings? Grice's answer is that someone means that p rather than that q because they intend to get their audience to believe that p (and do not intend their audience to believe that q) and that they intend their audience to form that belief by means of their recognizing the speaker's first intention. (Q3) asked: What is it to understand a word or sentence? Grice's answer is that an audience understands what a speaker has said if they have correctly identified the speaker's communicative intentions. (Q6) asked: What is the relation between the meaning of sentences and the content of thoughts? According to Grice, sentence meaning is ultimately reducible to speaker intentions. That is to say, the content of people's thoughts, *what* they are thinking, determines what the sentences they utter mean. (Q7) asked: How can a theory of the compositional nature of sentence meaning be given? In discussing the phenomenon of novel utterances, we saw that Grice's project struggles to give an account of the compositionality of meaning.

Questions for discussion

Question 1

Paul Yu argues that Griceans are unclear about whether their reductive project is supposed to *describe* how the expressions 'sentence meaning' and 'speaker meaning' are used, or whether it is supposed to *stipulate* a certain use for the expressions 'sentence meaning' and 'speaker meaning' (Yu 1979, §II). This distinction bears on how Griceans seek to address counter-examples to their reduction. If their project is a stipulative one, then the counter-examples can be rejected simply because the project is setting out how it is proposing to use 'sentence meaning' and 'speaker meaning', and there cannot be counter-examples to a proposal about how words should be used. Is Yu's accusation justified? If it is justified, has he identified a fault in Grice's project?

Question 2

In trying to defend Grice's theory against Biro's epistemological argument (§5), a distinction was drawn between giving an account of what meaning is and giving an account of how we know what the meaning of particular utterances are. It was suggested that Grice's theory is supposed to provides an account of the former kind only. As a consequence, it was further suggested, it is no criticism of Grice's theory that it does not also provide an account of the latter kind. But, what interest would a theory be if it provided an account of what meaning is without providing an account of how we could know what the meaning of any utterance is? Would there be any point in having such a theory? (Cf. Platts 1979, p. 92).

Question 3

Anita Avramides suggests that Grice's project faces various objections alleging that it is viciously circular. She thinks that these charges arise because Grice seeks to *reduce* linguistic meaning to psychology. She further thinks that these objections can be avoided if the reductive project is abandoned, and that in its place we seek only a 'reciprocal conceptual analysis' of the concept of meaning. Such an analysis seeks only to list various conceptual connections and to locate the target concept – here the concept of linguistic meaning – 'in a system of interrelated concepts' (Avramides 1989, p. 22). This kind of analysis does not require a non-circular definition of the target concept. It is enough to identify the conceptual connections between it and a family of other concepts. Which, if any, of the above objections facing Grice's project could be avoided if Griceans took this more accommodating approach?

Further reading

Blackburn, Simon (1984) *Spreading the Word* chapter 4.

Davis, Wayne A. (2003) *Meaning, Expression, and Thought* parts 1 and 2.

Grice, Herbert P. (1957) 'Meaning', (1968) 'Utterer's Meaning, Sentence Meaning and Word Meaning', and (1969) 'Utterer's Meaning and Intentions'.

Lycan, William G. (1998) *Philosophy of Language* chapter 7.

Miller, Alexander (2007) *Philosophy of Language* chapter 7.

Morris, Michael (2002) *An Introduction to the Philosophy of Language* chapter 13.

Récanati, François (1986) 'Defining Communicative Intentions'.

Taylor, Kenneth (1998) *Truth and Meaning: An Introduction to the Philosophy of Language* chapter VI §2.

Ziff, Paul (1967) 'On H. P. Grice's Account of Meaning'.

7

Grice on Conversation

1. Introduction

Semantics concerns those aspects of language to do with truth and reference. Pragmatics concerns those aspects of language to do with how it is used to achieve certain goals. In Chapter 4 §8, we noted one way in which the distinction between semantics and pragmatics is traditionally drawn. This said that semantics concerns all aspects of language which can be described by a truth conditional semantics for a language: a semantics which characterizes the meaning of sentences in terms of the conditions in which they are true. Pragmatics then concerns all other aspects of language. These include the types of speech act with which sentences are uttered and the use of non-literal language. In this chapter, we will consider another aspect of language which falls in the domain of pragmatics. This is the phenomenon of conversational implicature.

When we utter a sentence, we often say more than the sentence strictly and literally means. If you are asked where the nearest post office is and you say 'There's a post office around the corner', the sentence you uttered literally means that *there's a post office around the corner*. Strictly speaking, you did not say that the post office is open. Nevertheless, that is something that you meant. And there were various other things that you meant: that it is the nearest post office, that the way to get to the post office is by going around the corner and so on. But how do you manage to do this? How do you communicate more than the literal meaning of the sentence conveys? In this chapter, we will consider Grice's answers to these questions. His answers follow from his theory of how conversation is a rational activity governed by a certain overarching principle of cooperation.

2. The varieties of implicature

Grice distinguishes different aspects of the meaning of an utterance of a sentence. It will be useful to present these different aspects first in outline form. Grice distinguishes between:

(1) A sentence's *conventional meaning,*
(2) The *conversational implicatures* of utterances of that sentence and
(3) The *conventional implicatures* of those utterances.

Grice thinks that, for a large class of utterances, the total meaning of an utterance consists of what is said, what is conversationally implicated and what is conventionally implicated.

(1) The *conventional meaning* of a sentence concerns what is said when uttering the sentence on any occasion. Grice takes this aspect of the meaning of the sentence to be determined by the sentence's truth condition. When someone says something, the conventional meaning of the sentence uttered is part of the information the speaker conveys in the context.

(2) *Conversational implicature.* In many cases, the strict and literal meaning of a sentence – its conventional meaning – does not exhaust what a speaker means when he utters the sentence. The speaker is able to convey further information because of the interplay between three factors. These are the conventional meaning of the sentence uttered; the contextual information available to the speaker and the audience; and the assumption that the speaker is rationally engaging in

conversation. Sometimes the contribution of a speaker to a conversation seems to be less cooperative than it could be. To maintain the assumption that the speaker is rationally engaged in conversation, it is necessary to reconstrue what the speaker is saying – to take the speaker to be conveying more than the conventional meaning of the sentence he or she has uttered. This further information is a *conversational implicature* of what has been said in the context of utterance.

Grice also makes a distinction within the class of conversational implicatures between 'particularized' and 'generalized' conversational implicatures. If a conversational implicature is generated because of the particular context in which a certain sentence is uttered, a particularized conversational implicature has been generated. By contrast, if a conversational implicature is generated in cases where the context of the utterance is not as significant in generating it, a generalized conversational implicature has been brought about.

(3) *Conventional implicature.* Another aspect of the meaning of a sentence consists of what is conventionally associated with the words used although without being part of what is literally said. For example, the sentences 'He is a fireman; therefore, he is brave' and 'He is a fireman and he is brave' have the same truth conditions. In Grice's terminology, those sentences have the same conventional meaning. Nevertheless, the first sentence conveys more than the second one. What more is conveyed is that what is expressed by 'He is brave' is a consequence of what is expressed by 'He is a fireman'. This is conveyed by the use of the word 'therefore', but not by the use of the word 'and'.

Unlike a conversational implicature, a conventional implicature is generated irrespective of the context in which the sentence might be uttered and irrespective of considerations of how cooperative or rational the speaker might be.

We can represent the relations between these different aspects of meaning as follows (drawing on Neale 1992, p. 524):

Grice on conventional and conversational implicature

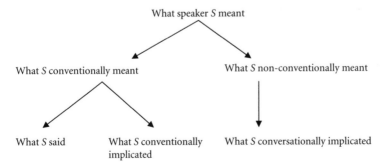

We will consider Grice's notion of conversational implicature in §§6 and 7, and his notion of conventional implicature in §8. To get to his notion of conversational implicature, however, we first need to consider his ideas about the principles and maxims governing the conduct of conversation. We will do this in §§3–5.

3. Conversation and rationality

Conversations are examples of collective behaviour. They are also examples of rational behaviour. Like many other human activities, language use is an activity which exploits certain means to achieve certain ends. Very often those ends could be achieved only through language use and only through cooperation with others. To achieve those ends, people use certain means and expect others to do the same if they share the same ends. This shared pursuit of ends engenders cooperation between speakers. Grice seeks to characterize the nature of that cooperation.

Conversations are not sequences of random, unrelated remarks. They serve purposes. If a conversation is being conducted, there has to be a degree of cooperation, and some convergence of purposes, between the participants to the conversation. If this were not the case, some of the speakers would have no reason to continue the conversation (Grice 1975, p. 26). Grice claims that there is a key principle that guides the efficient and rational exchange of information by cooperative speakers. We will consider this principle in §4 and various maxims that fall under it in §5.

4. The cooperative principle

Grice calls the principle of the rational and cooperative exchange of information 'the cooperative principle'. He formulates the principle as follows:

> Make your conversational contribution such as is required at the stage at which it occurs, by the accepted purpose or direction of the task exchange in which you are engaged.

Why think that speakers will in general act as the cooperative principle prescribes? Here are two considerations. First, according to Grice, the participants in a conversation have a common aim. Their contributions are also mutually dependent, and there is an understanding that the conversation should continue in a certain manner unless they agree otherwise. It is an empirical fact that speakers in general act as the principle prescribes. Second, the basis for that empirical fact is that anyone who wants to communicate must have an interest in conversations that will be useful only if they are conducted in accordance with the cooperative principle. So speakers follow the cooperative principle because they recognize that doing so has a pay-off that they would not otherwise enjoy.

5. The conversational maxims

Under the umbrella of the cooperative principle are four more specific maxims (or 'categories', as Grice calls them). Some of these maxims themselves have sub-maxims. The maxims and sub-maxims are as follows:

Category of Quantity

(1) Make your contribution as informative as is required (for the current purposes of the exchange).
(2) Do not make your contribution more informative than is required.

Category of Quality

(1) Do not say what you believe to be false.
(2) Do not say that for which you lack adequate evidence.

Category of Relation

(1) Be relevant.

Category of Manner

(1) Be perspicuous.

Here are some comments on these maxims. The maxim of quantity says that we should neither say too little nor say too much. Overinformativeness can be confusing because it raises side issues. Listeners may mistakenly think that there is some particular point to providing such extra information. Underinformativeness can mislead because the information given is too partial or meagre.

The relevance at issue in the maxim of relation is to be fixed contextually. That is, it is to be fixed by the subject matter of the conversation or by more general considerations. Grice admits that there are unexplored questions about what kinds of relevance there are, how they shift in a conversation, how conversations change topic and so on.

The maxim of manner involves such sub-maxims as: avoid obscurity of expression, avoid ambiguity, be brief and be orderly.

Grice thinks that it is reasonable to follow the cooperative principle and the maxims because conversations will be fruitful only if they are followed. Moreover, although the specific maxims and sub-maxims apply mostly to conversations, he thinks that suitable generalizations of them apply to any cooperative venture. Consider the maxim of relevance. There is some generalization of it that explains that if a chef wants to stir a pot, you are expected not to hand him a newspaper or a towel.

We will now turn to the different kinds of implicature that Grice discusses, starting with conversational implicature.

6. Conversational implicature

Suppose that a person asserts a sentence S in a certain context. What the person has stated is what S strictly and literally means. This is at least part of the information that the speaker conveys. In many cases, however, this kind of information does not exhaust the information that the speaker conveys in the context. In addition to what he says, the speaker may also implicate further information. There are three types of case to consider.

In the first type of case, the speaker exploits a conversational maxim. Here is an example.

Example A

Ned and Nate are in a car. Ned says that they are running out of petrol. Nate replies by saying:

(1) There's a station around the corner.

By saying (1), Nate does not state either (2) or (3):

(2) The petrol station is open.
(3) The petrol station is not out of petrol.

Sentence (1) does not entail (2) or (3). But, by saying (1), Nate conversationally implicates both (2) and (3). Otherwise what he says would be irrelevant to the conversation and would violate the maxim of relevance.

In the second type of case, a speaker violates a conversational maxim in order to convey more information than the sentence uttered strictly and literally expresses. Here are two examples:

Example B

Budgins is asked to provide a reference for someone seeking a job in finance. His reference contains no information about the applicant's financial ability and simply says the following:

(4) The applicant has good handwriting.

Budgins has provided precious little information and surely knows that he has. He seems to be violating the maxim of quantity by giving far less information than is appropriate in the circumstances. In particular, he has said nothing about the applicant's financial acumen. Why is this? The people requesting the reference can work all this out and will realize that Budgins is withholding information. In the circumstances that extra information would presumably be damaging for the applicant's chances of getting the job. So, Budgins is conversationally implicating that:

(5) The applicant is poor at finance.

Budgins is cooperative at one level – the level of what is conversationally implicated – even though he is not cooperative at the level of what is said. If he is following the cooperative principle, his violation of the maxim of quantity can be explained by taking his utterance to convey the additional information expressed by (5).

There are three other features of this example that are worth noting. First, in uttering (4), Budgins has not made the statement that the applicant is poor at finance. He has made the statement that the applicant has good handwriting. (5) is something that Budgins implicates by the statement he makes in uttering (4). So, there is a distinction between the statement Budgins makes in uttering (4) and what he meant by uttering (4). The statement he made expresses only the conventional meaning of (4).

Second, it might be that all that Budgins means when he utters (4) is what he implicates. That is, it might be that Budgins does *not* say that the applicant has good handwriting. Instead, Budgins only makes as if to say that because he has no intention of getting his audience to believe anything about the applicant's handwriting. The message that Budgins wants to send is at the level of what is conversationally implicated by his saying (4).

Third, a related point is that the truth values of (4) and (5) may differ. Perhaps, in fact, the applicant has terrible handwriting and is no good at finance. Then (4) is false and (5) is true. Budgins, however, may not care much about the truth value of what he has made as if to say. What he cares about is the truth value of what he is conversationally implicating. (For these last two points, see Neale 1992, p. 525.)

Here is another example of the same type:

Example C

Ned wants to get to the town of Amarillo and asks Tom how to get there. Tom replies:

(6) It's somewhere in Texas.

Tom's answer is, as he knows, less informative than Ned's question requires it to be. He is violating the maxim of quantity. But if he is following the cooperative principle, his violation of that maxim can be explained by taking his utterance to convey the additional information that:

(7) I (Tom) do not know exactly where Amarillo is in Texas.

The third type of case concerns a conflict between conversational maxims where the speaker follows one maxim at the expense of the other. Here is an example:

Example D

Ramona phones home to ask James where Choppy the cat is. James says:

(8) Choppy is either in the kitchen eating or asleep in the bedroom.

James has not been as informative as required. He has not said which room Choppy is in. So James is violating the maxim of quantity. Why is this? The second sub-maxim of the maxim of quality is: Do not say that for which you lack adequate evidence. If James is following the cooperative principle, his violation of the maxim of quantity can be explained by his following the maxim of quality and by taking his utterance to convey the additional information that:

(9) I (James) do not know which of the two rooms Choppy is in.

James does not want to mislead Ramona. By following the maxim of quality, James's uttering (8) conveys the implicature that he does not have enough evidence to say (and so does not know) which room Choppy is in.

Grice also applies his notion of conversational implicature to cases of irony and of metaphor. Here are examples of each.

Example E

Ben is a well-known peace campaigner. During a conversation he says 'The Central Intelligence Agency is a force for peace in today's world'. Given Ben's political outlook, he is violating the first sub-maxim of the maxim of quality: Do not say what you believe to be false. If Ben is following the cooperative principle, his violation of that maxim can be explained in the following way. Ben has not asserted that the C.I.A. is a force for peace in today's world. He has feigned asserting it. What he has in fact asserted is that the C.I.A. is not a force for peace in today's world. That is, the violation of the maxim can be explained by Ben's implicating that he means the negation of what he utters. He is speaking ironically.

Example F

Nana utters the sentence 'It's raining cats and dogs'. Given what it strictly and literally means, the sentence is obviously false, and surely Nana is not asserting it. Yet the negation of what the sentence strictly and literally means is so obviously true that surely Nana cannot be asserting it either. It would not be informative for her to assert something so plainly obvious. (This also distinguishes the example from a case of irony.) If Nana is following the cooperative principle, she can be construed as asserting that the rain is falling as heavily as if cats and dogs were falling from the sky. She is speaking metaphorically. (For an account of figurative speech along Gricean lines, see Martinich 1984.)

It was mentioned in §2 that Grice distinguishes between particularized and generalized conversational implicatures. Examples (A–C) are examples of particularized conversational implicatures. They are cases in which uttering a certain sentence carries a particular implicature because of special features of the context of utterance. In each case, the sentence might be uttered in other normal contexts without conveying the implicature. Nate can say 'There's a station around the corner' without implicating that there is a petrol station around the corner. For example, suppose that the context is one in which Ned and Nate do not need more petrol but in which they do need the police. Again, someone can say 'The C.I.A. is a force for peace in today's world' without implicating the opposite. Suppose, for example, that the sentence is uttered by a C.I.A. spokesperson at a press briefing.

A generalized conversational implicature is an implicature conveyed by a sentence in any context, provided that the speaker is taken to be following the cooperative principle. Example D is an example of this kind of conversational implicature. There is a general point behind that example. 'A or B' is logically weaker than 'A' and is logically weaker than 'B'. The disjunction does not entail either of those sentences, but each of them entails it. If someone asserts 'A or B' rather than asserting 'A' or asserting 'B', the speaker is being less informative than he or she could be. Given that the speaker is following the cooperative principle, the speaker is implicating that he or she has sufficient evidence to assert 'A or B' but not sufficient evidence to assert either of its disjuncts.

Grice's examples of generalized conversational implicatures include utterances of sentences containing 'and', 'if', 'every', 'a' or 'the'. In addition, they include intentional expressions such as 'look', 'feel' and 'try'. For example, uttering the sentence 'The bridge looks safe' has the generalized conversational implicature that the speaker does not know whether the bridge is safe. Given that the speaker is following the cooperative principle, the speaker is implicating that he or she lacks sufficient evidence to assert that he or she knows that the bridge is safe.

In sum, a conversational implicature is a generalized conversational implicature if the generation of the implicature is relatively independent of the context in which the conversation is occurring. The fact that the implicature is generated is itself to be explained by the cooperative nature of conversation. (For a book length treatment of generalized conversational implicature, see Levinson 2000.)

7. Features of conversational implicatures

How are conversational implicatures to be distinguished from entailments such as the following?

The lemon is yellow.
So the lemon has a colour.

Cliff is a bachelor.
So Cliff is unmarried.

The tomato is red and squashed.
So the tomato is squashed.

Grice suggests a number of features of conversational implicatures. The features of what he calls detachability and cancellability are particularly important. Grice does not take these features to be definitions of the expression 'conversational implicature' or as providing, either singularly or jointly, a decisive test for something's being a conversational implicature (Grice 1978, p. 114).

Detachability

This feature can be explained as follows. The implicature from p to q is detachable if and only if there is some other form of words which can be used to assert just what p 'might be used to assert' (as Grice puts it), but which does not have the implicature that q. In other words, the implicature is detachable if and only if we can paraphrase what p says in such a way that we can use the paraphrase to assert what we used p to assert, but, in addition, the paraphrase does not generate the implicature that q.

According to Grice, many conversational implicatures are non-detachable, whereas all conventional implicatures are detachable. (See §8 below for a discussion of conventional implicatures.) His thinking is that the conversational implicatures in question are attached to the content of what is being said, rather than to the particular words used to express that content. These implicatures cannot be 'detached' simply by changing the words in the utterance with synonyms. Take example B, the handwriting example. Suppose that, instead of saying:

(4)   The applicant has good handwriting,

Budgins had uttered a synonymous sentence such as:

(4*)   The applicant's handwriting is easily readable.

Given that the context is fixed, (4*), like (4), implicates that:

(5)   The applicant is poor at finance.

Notice, though, that entailments are also non-detachable. For example, 'Ena likes cats and Brian likes dogs' entails 'Ena likes cats'. Replacing 'cats' with 'felines' in the first sentence does not 'detach' the second sentence from the first. Again, it is very difficult to see how we could paraphrase sentences such as 'The lemon is yellow', 'Cliff is a bachelor' and 'The tomato is red and squashed' in such a way that they do not convey the information that the lemon has a colour, Cliff is a bachelor and the tomato is squashed, respectively. None of those cases appear to have the detachability feature. It follows that non-detachability is not a sufficient condition of an implicature being a conversational implicature.

Furthermore, some conversational implicatures are detachable. (Recall that Grice said only that many are non-detachable.) In particular, implicatures generated by violations of the maxim of manner ('Be perspicuous') are detachable. This is because these implicatures depend on how things are said and not simply on the content of what is said. It follows that non-detachability is not a necessary condition of an implicature being a conversational implicature.

Let's consider detachability further. Consider example G:

Example G

Would an utterance of (10) conversationally implicate (11) or would it entail it?

(10) Jeb sat down and took off his boots.
(11) Jeb sat down before he took off his boots.

Detachability shows that (10) conversationally implicates rather than entails (11). For there is another form of words which can be used to assert just what (10) might be used to assert, but which does not implicate (11). For instance, (10) might be paraphrased by (10*):

(10*) Jeb took off his boots and sat down.

(10*) can be used to make the same assertion as (10) – they have the same conventional meaning, in Grice's sense. But (10*) does not implicate (11).

The fact that (10) conversationally implicates (11) might be due to the fact that the maxim of manner tells speakers to be orderly. This might involve speakers reporting events in the order in which they happened, unless they have good reason to do otherwise. And sometimes a speaker might have reason to do otherwise. They might relate events starting with the most important ones, irrespective of when those events occurred in the full sequence that they are reporting.

Cancellability

This feature can be explained as follows. The implicature from p to q is cancellable if and only if we can consistently add a further clause to p

'withholding commitment to what would otherwise be implied'. In other words, the implicature is cancellable if and only if p can be supplemented with some further sentence that is consistent with p and which 'blocks' or 'cancels' the implicature.

To understand this feature further, consider example H:

Example H

Would an utterance of (12) conversationally implicate (13) or would it entail it?

(12) Hank tried to catch the train.
(13) Hank failed to catch the train.

Cancellability shows that (12) conversationally implicates rather than entails (13). For it is possible to add something consistent with (12) that cancels the implicature that Hank failed to catch the train. For example, the speaker might say:

(12*) Hank tried to catch the train but I (the speaker) do not know whether he failed to catch it.

Or he might say:

(12**) Hank tried to catch the train but I (the speaker) won't tell you whether he caught it.

In (12*), since the speaker denies that he knows that Hank failed to catch the train, he is adding something consistent with (12) that cancels the implicature that Hank failed to catch the train. The reason is as follows. Suppose that the speaker is following the maxim of quantity and trying to be as informative as the conversation requires. He says that he does not know whether Hank failed to catch the train. He does not say that he knows that Hank failed to catch the train. Presumably, the speaker is following the maxim of quality and not asserting what he does not have adequate evidence for, and asserting only what he has adequate evidence for. He would have asserted that Hank failed to catch the train if he had adequate evidence that Hank had done so. But he does not assert it. So, he does not have adequate evidence for the claim that Hank failed to catch the train. The speaker is then not committing himself to (13) when he utters (12*).

In (12**), the speaker indicates that he is opting out of normal conversational maxims. In particular, he is not trying to be as informative as possible. Grice thinks that when a speaker has evidently opted out of following the cooperative principle, his uttering a sentence which typically generates certain conversational implicatures would not generate those implicatures. It need not be irrational for a speaker to opt out of following the cooperative principle, and the speaker and his audience may have mutual knowledge that he has done so. A suspect undergoing police questioning might opt out of the cooperative principle so he cannot be led into compromising himself. Each party knows what the other is up to and may even know what the other knows. (For further discussion of Grice's tests for conversational implicature, see Blome-Tillmann 2008.)

8. Conventional implicature

According to Grice, connectives such as 'but', 'moreover' and 'so', and certain modifiers such as 'even' and 'still', have a conventional, non-truth conditional meaning. He calls this 'conventional implicature'. Unlike a conversational implicature, a conventional implicature is generated by the conventional meanings of the sentences used. That is, it is an implicature that is determined (at least in part) by the conventions governing the words used.

A conventional implicature is also unlike conventional meaning because, although a conventional implicature is conventionally associated with the words used in a sentence, it is not part of what is literally said by assertions of that sentence. Here are examples of some sentences and what they conventionally implicate:

Example I

(14) The house is clean but messy.
(15) There is some kind of contrast between a house being clean and its being messy: specifically, a house that is clean would not be expected to be messy.

(14) conventionally implicates (15) because of the conventional meaning of 'but'. 'p but q' conventionally implicates that q is contrary to expectation given p. A speaker who utters (14) implicates, without explicitly stating, (15).

Example J

(16) He is a fireman; therefore, he is brave.
(17) Being brave is an expected consequence of being a fireman.

(16) conventionally implicates (17) because of the conventional meaning of 'therefore'. Uttering (16) implies that someone's being brave is a consequence (i.e. can be inferred from) that person's being a fireman.

Example K

(18) She is not here yet.
(19) She is expected (at some point) to arrive here.

(18) conventionally implicates (19) because of the conventional meaning of 'yet'. Uttering (18) implicates without explicitly stating that she is expected (within some restricted time frame) to arrive here.

Example L

(20) Tim was not the winner of the race.
(21) Someone won the race.

(20) conventionally implicates (21) because of the conventional meaning of the sentence construction *It was not [noun phrase] who [verb phrase]*. Uttering (20) implicates without explicitly stating that there was a winner of the race.

In contrast to many conversational implicatures, Grice thinks that it is typically 'uncomfortable' (in his phrase) to negate a conventional implicature. For instance, negating (16) in example J yields the odd sentence 'It is not the case that he is a fireman; therefore, he is brave'.

In each example I–L, the conventional implicature is part of the information conveyed by the utterance of the sentence. The implicature is generated by some aspect of the meaning of the sentence. In examples I–K, the implicature is generated by the meaning of the words involved. In example L, the implicature is generated by the sentence's syntactic structure. Nevertheless, although the implicature is generated by a feature of the meaning of the sentence, what is implicated is not part of what is stated by an utterance of the sentence. The connectives or modifiers involved in the examples have a non-truth conditional meaning. Take example I. (14) would still be true even if the house were both clean and messy. In example J, (16) would be true even if someone's being brave was not a consequence of his being a fireman. In example K, (18) would be true even if she is not expected to arrive. And in example L, (20) would be true even if all the competitors were disqualified and no one won the race.

Grice's notion of conventional implicature is interesting and provides a valuable extension of his thinking about meaning. But what he says about it is sketchy: he tells us little about it beyond that it is determined (at least in part) by the conventions governing the words used. (For more on conventional implicature, see Sadock 1975; Potts 2005.)

9. Objections to Grice

Grice's account of conversation faces a number of objections. In this section, we will review some of them.

Do participants in a conversation have to have a mutual goal?

The cooperative principle assumes that, at every stage of a conversation, it is possible to tell its purpose or direction – to tell how the conversation proceeds from one stage to the next. This would be a joint purpose or a jointly agreed direction, one shared by all the contributors to the conversation. But is this assumption correct? Consider a police detective interviewing a crime suspect. Do the two of them need to share any mutual purpose at any given stage of the conversation? The suspect may seek to answer the detective's questions, but that is not the detective's general purpose in the interview. His general purpose is to convict those responsible for the crime. Such local cooperation, in the absence of global cooperation, depends on the conversation consisting of an interchange of questions and answers. Yet most conversations are not like that. For example, when two people are arguing about some issue, they may not have shared global purposes and, typically, they will not have shared local purposes. Trivial general purposes, such as to keep the conversation going or to establish the truth, are insufficiently specific, given what the cooperative principle requires of any conversation. And were the cooperative principle to require only such trivial general purposes, it would then be too weak to entail the various conversational maxims.

Furthermore, at any given stage in a conversation, a participant may take the conversation in a new direction, provided that there is some connection with the content of the preceding stage:

> In other words, at no stage in a conversation is there an accepted direction which determines the degree of appropriateness of the contributions by the conversants, and every participant has the right to change the direction as he sees fit, within certain limits. (Kasher 1976, p. 202. See also Searle 2002, pp. 187, 193–4)

It might be enough for Grice to emend his view as follows. He might drop the idea that participants in a conversation need to share some mutual goal. He might instead require that each participant reasonably expects that some of his or her goals will be advanced by the conversation (even if that would be at the cost of some of the other participants advancing their goals). A conversation might then be like a competitive game: each side goes into the game because they have a reasonable expectation of winning, although everyone knows that only one side can win (Grandy 1989, p. 521).

Can the conversational maxims be derived from the cooperative principle?

It seems that the maxims cannot be derived from the cooperative principle for the following reason. Even if conversations have shared aims, the cooperative principle places no constraint on the character of a contribution to any stage of a conversation beyond saying that it should contribute to those aims. The maxims, on the other hand, place quite specific constraints on the character of a contribution to any stage of a conversation. It is then difficult to see how the maxims, with their extra content, can be derived from the cooperative principle (Kasher 1976, pp. 202–5).

Note also that Grice seeks to derive the conversational maxims from a special assumption underlying the nature of language, namely the cooperative principle. But if the maxims can be derived from general principles of rationality that apply to any kind of action, linguistic or otherwise, then there would be no need to appeal to such a special assumption. (For efforts in this direction, see Kasher 1982.)

Why are only certain implicatures made in a given situation?

Suppose that Pop says to Ma 'I didn't tell you I'll need the car this afternoon'. Pop is implicating that he needs the car this afternoon. How would Grice's theory explain why this is what is implicated by Pop's remark? Perhaps Grice would seek to explain it in terms of the maxim of quantity. Ma reasons: Pop says that he did not tell me that he needed the car this afternoon. What was the point of his doing so? We both know that he has not previously told me that he would be needing the car this afternoon. But that is a trivial piece of information. So, the point of what he was saying lies elsewhere: it lies with the information that he needs the car.

That, however, is a poor explanation. It does not explain how Ma's interpretative reasoning begins. When someone says something trivial, we do not always seek a hidden meaning to what they say. That is what small talk is all about. So, it would be reasonable for Ma to interpret Pop's remark only as an innocent attempt at conversation. Furthermore, the suggested explanation also fails to show how the conclusion of the reasoning is reached. Grice's maxims do not provide guidance as to how Ma could arrive at the conclusion that Pop needs the car. There are many relevant informative things any one of which he could be saying, and Grice's maxims fail to restrict these to the claim that Pop needs the car (Thomason 1990, p. 353).

The problem of deriving conversational implicatures

Grice is clear that a speaker makes a conversational implicature only if that implicature can be derived by the audience, given what the speaker has said and given the assumption that he or she is following the cooperative principle:

> . . . the final test for the presence of a conversational implicature [has] to be, as far as I [can] see, a derivation of it. One has to produce an account of how it could have arisen and why it is there. And I am very much opposed to any kind of sloppy use of this philosophical tool, in which one does not fulfil this condition. (Grice 1981, p. 187)

The problem is that Grice does not offer any method or procedure for working out, for any given conversational implicature, what its content is (Harnish 1976; Hugly and Sayward 1979). It is then difficult to see how Grice can avoid his own charge of making 'sloppy use' of the device of conversational implicature.

The problem of differentiation

The problem here is that, given Grice's account, often an utterance made in a conversation would generate more conversational implicatures than is plausible. To help obviate this problem, Grice requires that conversational implicatures are non-trivial. For example, whenever a speaker asserts that p, although it does not follow that the speaker believes that p, all parties to the conversation can reasonably take it that the speaker believes that p. Yet the speaker's conveying that he or she believes that p is something obvious, something that can be elicited without any details of the context of the conversation. On these grounds, it is counted as a trivial case and excluded as an instance of a conversational implicature. Another class of cases that are excluded as trivial are cases involving mutual knowledge. For example, suppose we are having a conversation about our respective holiday plans. If you say 'I'm driving across France', you have conveyed that there are roads in France. What you have conveyed is mutual knowledge: you and I both know it, and each of us knows that the other knows it.

Grice does not offer a measure of triviality, but, in any case, the problem here runs deeper. Mutual knowledge plus a speaker's utterance may convey information that was not previously available to the audience, although the information conveyed does not seem to be a conversational implicature. For instance, suppose that, prior to the conversation, it was mutual knowledge that you would not take the car abroad until you had repaired the clutch. You are committed to the cooperative principle. Given what you have now said, that commitment plus the background information requires that the clutch has been repaired. You can reasonably expect me to realize this and so believe that the clutch has been repaired. You have done nothing to alter my belief. So you have conveyed the information that the clutch has been repaired. But this does not seem to be a conversational implicature of what you said; you were not trying to get this information across to me.

Still, this last comment might provide a guideline about how to emend Grice's theory. We might require that a speaker's conveying certain information counts as a conversational implicature only if the speaker intends that that information is conveyed (Grice 1961, p. 130; Neale 1992, p. 528). In our example, although you realize that I will believe that the clutch is repaired, and do nothing to make me think otherwise, you are not particularly concerned whether I believe it or not. If it were a case of conversational implicature, you would be concerned (Grandy 1989, pp. 522–3).

Dan Sperber and Deirdre Wilson offer a different response to the problem. They propose an alternative to the cooperative principle according to which there is a 'single principle governing every aspect of comprehension, the principle of relevance: The speaker tries to express the proposition which is the most relevant one possible to the hearer' (Sperber and Wilson 1982, p. 75). They characterize the notion of relevance in the following ways. First, 'other things being equal, the more contextual implications a proposition has, the more relevant it is' (Sperber and Wilson 1982, p. 103). Second, 'other things being equal, the smaller the amount of processing, the greater the relevance of the proposition' (Sperber and Wilson 1982, p. 105. See also Sperber and Wilson 1995 for a book length treatment of their account of the role of relevance in conversational implicature).

The problem of conflicting principles

When different maxims conflict, which one should a cooperative speaker follow? For example, suppose that you have an answer to a question, and that that answer is as informative as is required at that stage of the conversation, but your supporting evidence for the answer is partial. Then should you give that answer in the conversation? Yes, since one sub-maxim of quantity tells you to be informative. No, since one sub-maxim of quality tells you not to say things that you lack adequate evidence for. Recall example C. Ned wants to get to Amarillo and asks Tom how to get there. Tom replies:

(6) It's somewhere in Texas.

Tom's answer conversationally implicates:

(7) I (Tom) do not know exactly where Amarillo is in Texas.

Tom faces a conflict between the maxims of quantity and of quality for the above reasons. Quality wins out because, according to Grice, 'other maxims come into operation only on the assumption that this maxim of Quality is satisfied' (Grice 1975, p. 27). He develops this point elsewhere:

> The maxims do not seem to be coordinate. The maxim of Quality, enjoining the provision of contributions which are genuine rather than spurious (truthful rather than mendacious), does not seem to be just one among a number of recipes for producing contributions; it seems rather to spell out the difference between something's being, and (strictly speaking) failing to be, any kind of contribution at all. False information is not an inferior kind of information; it just is not information. (Grice 1987, p. 371)

The above may establish that the maxim of quality has primacy when compared with the other maxims, but it provides only a partial solution to the problem. What about conflicts between maxims other than the maxim of quality? For example, the maxim of relation tells speakers to be, among other things, brief. But that injunction can conflict with the sub-maxim of quantity that tells speakers to be as informative as possible. What then should speakers do?

Conversational implicatures within the scope of attitude verbs

Consider the following example:

Example M

 (22) Jeb ate some of the rations.
 (23) Jeb did not eat all of the rations.

Presumably uttering (22) in most contexts conversationally implicates (23). If the speaker believed that Jeb had eaten all of the rations, then to utter (22) would be to utter something true, but it would also be to violate the maxim of quantity. Given that the speaker is following the cooperative principle, the speaker uttered (22) because he did not believe that Jeb ate all the rations. Now consider example N:

Example N

 (24) Hank believes that Jeb ate some of the rations.
 (25) Hank believes that Jeb did not eat all of the rations.

It is tempting to think that a speaker's uttering (24) would, in most contexts, conversationally implicate (25). But notice that in this example the conversational implicature seems to occur within the scope of a propositional attitude verb, namely 'believes'. This fact means that we cannot reason in example N in the same way as we did in example M. We might reason as follows. If the speaker of (24) thinks that Hank believes that Jeb ate all of the rations, he would have said so. Since he did not, we conclude that it is not the case that Hank believes that Jeb ate all of the rations. The problem with this reasoning is that that conclusion is logically weaker than (25). That conclusion obtains if Hank is agnostic whether Jeb ate all of the rations. But (25) is incompatible with Hank being agnostic about that; (25) says that Hank believes that Jeb did not eat all of the rations.

 The lesson to be drawn is that the account Grice has offered cannot explain conversational implicatures occuring within the scope of propositional attitude verbs (Cohen 1971). (For further difficulties with Grice's account of conversational implicature, see Cohen 1977; Bach 1994a.)

10. Conclusion

It is useful to distinguish between the phenomenon of implicature and Grice's explanation of this phenomenon. The phenomenon is that speakers often mean more than what they explicitly say and that listeners readily recover information that is not given simply by the literal meaning of the sentences which they have heard. It is uncontroversial that there is such a phenomenon. What is controversial is how it should be explained. Grice's explanation is that we can expect people engaged in conversation to be engaged in a cooperative enterprize. We can thereby expect these people's conversational contributions to be truthful, relevant, informative and so on. Now, in some cases, taking at face value what a speaker has said would violate this expectation: the speaker would not be being as cooperative as the conversation required. The hearer takes this fact, and any other relevant information available, to work out what the speaker meant to convey on that occasion, in addition to what the sentence uttered literally means. In short, the speaker exploits the expectation of cooperation, the expectation is met, and the speaker's communicative intention is successful.

By seeking to explain the phenomenon of implicature by invoking pragmatics, Grice addresses (Q9), the question of the role of pragmatics in language. Pragmatics can be broadly defined as the study of purposive literal activity (Kasher 1982, p. 27). The ability to use language is a special case of a more general ability to use means to achieve ends. In the philosophy of language, the topic of pragmatics concerns our competence with using linguistic means for achieving linguistic purposes. Whereas semantics is concerned with the *interpretation* of sentences uttered in a given context, pragmatics is concerned with the *use* of interpreted sentences; with the speech acts that a speaker makes by using a sentence in a given context. These acts include not only such things as asserting and presupposing but also implicating (cf. Stalnaker 1972).

According to Grice, the differences between information provided by conventional meaning as opposed to information provided by conversational implicature are not random or haphazard. These differences can be fruitfully subjected to theoretical study because they are systematic and open to explanation. The explanation draws upon a general principle of human behaviour (the cooperative principle) and a series of maxims (the conversational maxims) that implement this principle in specific ways. There is a systematic correspondence between what a speaker means and what needs to be assumed to preserve the supposition that the speaker is following the cooperative principle and the various maxims. Roughly, implicature in general lies in the intersection between what is meant and what is not said explicitly (Thomason 1990, p. 352).

Grice's key views specifically about conversational implicature consist of four claims (following the introduction to Davis 1998). First, Grice seeks to define conversational implicature in terms of information conveyed by a speaker that is additional to the strict and literal meaning of what the speaker has said and that is conveyed because the speaker is following a certain principle of conversational cooperation. Second, he claims that conversational implicatures are generated by the cooperative principle and its associated maxims, given the strict and literal meaning of what a speaker has said in a certain context. Third, Grice thinks that an audience can work out what conversational implicatures a speaker is conveying by considering the strict and literal meaning of what the speaker said in a given context plus the assumption that the speaker is following the cooperative principle and its associated maxims. Fourth, Grice thinks it is more economical to postulate conversational implicatures rather than new word- and sentence-meanings. For example, Grice uses considerations of conversational implicature to explain why uttering 'Jeb sat down and took his boots off' conveys that the first event reported occurred before the second. He does not need to say that 'and' has one meaning in that sentence (a meaning involving temporal priority) and a different meaning in 'Jeb sat down and at the same time Ned walked in' (where the meaning of 'and' does not involve temporal priority). The conversational implicatures can be derived from principles that there is independent reason to believe, whereas postulating new word- or sentence-meanings would be *ad hoc*. That is, there is no independent reason to postulate them.

(Q10) asked whether there can be a systematic philosophical study of natural language. Some philosophers have thought that formal techniques in logic cannot shed light on the expressions of natural language. In particular, they have thought that natural language expressions, such as 'and', 'if-then', 'or', 'every' and 'some', differ in meaning from their formal language counterparts, '&', '⊃', '∧', '(∀x)' and '(∃x)' (see, e.g. Strawson 1952, chapter 2 part III and chapter 8). Grice thought these philosophers were mistaken and that the source of their mistake was to take certain implicatures (specifically, conventional implicatures or generalized conversational implicatures) to be part of the semantic content of sentences of natural language containing 'and', 'or' and the like.

What is the relation between Grice's theory of conversational implicature and his theory of meaning? There is a case for seeing the former theory as a component of the latter theory. On this view, conversational implicature is a form of speaker meaning and so is a matter of speaker intentions (Davis 2007). At the very least, the two theories are mutually illuminating and supporting, and it is more fruitful to consider them in tandem rather than in isolation (Neale 1992, p. 512).

Grice also saw a close connection between language and considerations of rationality. According to Grice, the principles used to interpret linguistic behaviour are (or, at any rate, are very closely related to) the principles used to interpret intentional non-linguistic behaviour. And he came to think of the philosophy of language itself as a branch of, what he called, 'rational psychology', or the study of rational human beings (Chapman 2005, p. 174. See also Searle 1999, p. 2075; Petrus 2010, pp. 2–4).

Questions for discussion

Question 1
Why do speakers make implicatures? What is the point of them? Why do not speakers convey all information directly, explicitly and semantically rather than indirectly and pragmatically? (For one possible answer, see Leech 1983, pp. 109ff).

Question 2
What is the connection (entailment, conventional implicature or conversational implicature) between the premise and conclusion in each of the following arguments? (You may have to assume for your answers that the arguments occur in normal contexts of utterance.)

(A) (1) Someone won the race.
    (2) I did not win the race.

(B) (1) The sheriff drew his gun and the cattle thief surrendered.
    (2) The sheriff's drawing his gun contributed to the cattle thief surrendering.

(C) (1) A white butterfly flew past the window.
    (2) It's not self-evident that all butterflies are white.

Examples (D) and (E) introduce scalar implicatures: implicatures involving the phrases 'at least *n* F's' or 'exactly *n* F's':

(D) (1) Jump doesn't own three cats.
    (2) Jump doesn't own at least three cats.

(E) (1) Jump doesn't own three cats; she owns four.
    (2) Jump does own at least three cats.

Note that the premises of (D) and (E) are compatible but that their conclusions are not.

Question 3

Does Grice's list of maxims cover all of the maxims that guide conversation? Are the following four examples already covered by the maxims? Can each of them be derived from the cooperative principle?

'Speak idiomatically'.
'Do not say what may harm you or your interests'.
'Be polite'.
'Make what you say conducive to the appropriate reply'.

Question 4

Why does 'It's beautiful but it's expensive' suggest that it should not be purchased, but 'It's expensive but it's beautiful' suggest that it should be purchased?

Question 5

In all the cases of conversational implicature discussed, the speaker utters a sentence with a certain literal meaning in order to implicate something else. But is there a class of cases in which a speaker utters a meaningless sentence in order to implicate something which may even be true? Sorensen 1996, pp. 205–6 offers this example: 'Gazillion' has no meaning and so 'There are a gazillion stars' has no meaning. But an astronomer could utter those words to implicate the truth that there is an enormous number of stars.

Is what the astronomer said meaningless, or is it a case of uttering something meaningful but slang (taking words like 'gazillion' or 'squillion' to mean something like *far more than a million*)? And if it is a case of conversational implicature, which conversational maxim or maxims are being exploited?

Question 6

Is it unreasonable for speakers not to follow the conversational maxims? Elinor Keenan has described a community of Malagasy speakers who make their conversational contributions deliberately uninformative, imprecise and obscure (Keenan 1976). This seems to be a counter-example to Grice's view. How might he address this case?

Question 7

Ordinary language philosophers have offered arguments of the following kind:
    Norman Malcolm: There is something odd about G. E. Moore's saying, in normal circumstances, 'I know that I have a hand'. So Moore was wrong to claim that he knew that he had a hand.

Gilbert Ryle: There would be something odd about your saying, in circumstances in which you have done something without being at fault, that you did it voluntarily. So it would be wrong to claim that you voluntarily performed an action when you were not at fault.

Ludwig Wittgenstein: There would be something odd about your saying, in normal circumstances in which you lifted a coffee cup, that you tried to lift the cup. So it would be wrong to claim that you tried to lift the coffee cup.

Given that an odd use of a term is a misuse of a term, these arguments claim that, because certain ways of using terms such as 'knows', 'voluntary' and 'tried to lift' are odd, those uses are misuses. The above philosophers further took the meaning of many terms to consist in how those terms are used. A misuse of a term is then taken to be something not in accord with that term's meaning. It was then inferred that odd uses of the terms would not be in accord with those terms' meanings, and so would not be used to say anything true. In that sense, those odd uses would yield only claims that were wrong.

Grice devises his theory of conversational implicatures with a view to criticizing such arguments. How do you think his theory might be used to criticize them? (See Adler 1994, but contrast Travis 1991, pp. 237–46). If we reject his theory, how else might those arguments be criticized?

Further reading

Davis, Wayne A. *Implicature: Intention, Convention, and Principle in the Failure of Gricean Theory*.

Grandy, Richard E. (1989) 'On Grice on Language'.

Grice, Herbert P. (1975) 'Conversational Implicature', (1978) 'Further Notes on Logic and Conversation', and (1981) 'Presupposition and Conversational Implicature'.

Lycan, William G. (2008) *Philosophy of Language* chapter 13.

Récanati, François (2012) 'Pragmatics' in Manuel Garciá-Carpintero and Max Kölbel (eds.) *The Continuum Companion to the Philosophy of Language*.

Searle, John R. (1975b) 'Indirect Speech Acts'.

Soames, Scott (2003b) *Philosophical Analysis volume 2: The Age of Meaning* chapter 9.

Taylor, Kenneth (1998) *Truth and Meaning: An Introduction to the Philosophy of Language* chapter VI §4.

8

Quine on Meaning

1. Introduction

W. V. O. Quine subjects the notion of meaning to trenchant criticism. In this chapter, we will consider the criticisms he makes in his paper 'Two Dogmas of Empiricism' and in his book *Word and Object* (Quine 1951, 1960 respectively). Quine's scepticism about meaning does not take the (epistemic) form of doubting whether we can know truths about what words and sentences mean. It takes the (metaphysical) form of scepticism about whether words and sentences mean anything. In Quine's terminology, he doubts whether there is a 'fact of the matter' (in his phrase) about what our words and sentences mean. Quine not only thinks that talk of the meaning of a sentence is not talk of any kind of entity. He thinks that 'there is no fact of the matter' whether any sentence has one meaning rather than another. Quine's paper 'Two Dogmas of Empiricism' contains two key lines of argument of particular interest to our purposes. The first concerns the circularity of attempts to define 'synonymy' and related terms. The other concerns the nature of confirmation and the so-called Quine-Duhem thesis. We will consider these lines of argument in turn in §§2 and 3, respectively. In chapter 2 of his book *Word and Object*, Quine argues that since all the empirical data fail to settle how sentences of any given language should be translated, then there is no such thing as a uniquely correct translation of a language. We will examine this thesis, the thesis of the indeterminacy of translation, and its supporting lines of argument in §§4–6.

2. Quine on defining 'synonymy'

If people have height, they can be classified according to their height. Any pair of people (at a given time) will have the same height, or similar heights or dissimilar heights. By knowing what the basis of this classification is, we are able to make informed judgements about people's heights, including people's comparative heights. Now, if sentences have meanings, then presumably they can be classified according to their meaning. Any pair of sentences will have the same meaning, or similar meanings or dissimilar meanings. By knowing what underlies this classification, we will be able to make informed judgements about the meanings of sentences, including how similar in meaning they are. (Similar considerations hold with respect to words and their meanings.)

Talk of sameness of height is well defined, but what about talk of sameness of meaning (i.e. of synonymy)? How is it to be defined? In his 1951 paper 'Two Dogmas of Empiricism', Quine argues that various proposed definitions of 'synonymy' are circular. One proposal is that sentences S and S^* are synonymous if and only if the sentence 'S if and only if S^*' is analytic. The question which then arises is: what does 'analytic' mean? If we are told that an analytic sentence is a sentence which is true in virtue of its meaning, we are talking about meaning again – the very talk that we wanted clarified in the first place. It might then be proposed that an analytic sentence is a sentence whose negation is self-contradictory. Yet that raises the question: what does 'self-contradictory' mean? It stands in exactly the same need of clarification as 'analytic' does.

In this fashion, Quine identifies a collection of terms – 'synonymy', 'analytic', 'self-contradiction', 'necessary truth' and 'semantic rule' – which can be defined only in terms of other members of the collection but each member of which remains as obscure as the others (Quine 1951, §§1–4, 1960, p. 159). But, if 'synonymy' is an obscure term, then so is the claim that some pairs of sentences are synonymous. And if talk of sentences being synonymous (having the same

[handwritten margin note: if there is such a thing as meaning it follows that there must be synonymous meaning]

meaning) is unintelligible, then so too is even talk of sentences have meaning (cf. Grice and Strawson 1956, p. 146).

What does Quine's argument achieve? Some philosophers are untroubled by the circularity that Quine uncovers. The term 'synonymy' is not alone in being part of a tightly interconnected collection of terms, none of which is definable in terms outside of the collection. To take a humdrum example, the names of days of the week form another such closed network. Moreover, provided that the number of terms in a given network is sufficiently large, those same philosophers take the circularity involved in the network to be benign:

> . . . a circle of explication need not be a vicious one, provided it is wide enough to enable a logician to uncover nontrivial aspects of the structure of the concepts involved. (Hintikka 1975, p. 135, footnote 31)

Quine seems to assume that a given term is intelligible only if an explicit non-circular definition of it is available. (A definition is non-circular if and only if each of the terms in the definition can be understood without having to understand the term being defined.) It is because this assumption is not met in the case of 'synonymy' that Quine rejects the term as unintelligible. Quine's assumption, however, is suspect. On pain of there being an infinite regress of terms being non-circularly defined by other terms, at least some terms are not non-circularly definable. (See also Miller 2007, pp. 133–6.)

Perhaps, the deeper concern that Quine raises is about the lack of explanatory power of the notions of meaning and analyticity (Rey 1994, pp. 82–95). What are these notions supposed to explain? People are disposed to apply certain words to some things and not others. Given the presence of certain things, they are prepared to assent to certain sentences but not others. More generally still, people's judgements about which words apply to which things and which words would apply to which things display certain patterns and projections. These are data that require explanation. The notions of meaning and analyticity purport to be part of the explanation of these data. It is because of people's alleged access to shared word- and sentence-meanings that they agree in which words they apply to which things. Quine finds this purported explanation empty. Part of his reason is that, as we have just seen, there is no way to define 'synonymy' which does not appeal to other terms drawn from the theory of meaning – 'analyticity', 'necessity' and the rest. Another reason is that Quine thinks that a better explanation of the data is given by his behaviouristic theory of how language is learnt. That theory dispenses with the theory of meaning's catalogue of terms and uses only the austere notion of stimulus meaning: of what people are disposed to assent to (or dissent from) given certain stimuli. It remains highly debatable, though, whether Quine's rival theory is satisfactory (Rey 1994, pp. 86–92).

3. Verificationism and the Quine-Duhem thesis

The logical positivists' principle of verification claims that the meaning of a sentence is determined by the method for empirically confirming or disconfirming it (see, e.g. Ayer 1936, chapter 1). Verificationism about meaning thereby identifies the meaning of a sentence with the set of possible observations that would confirm the sentence or disconfirm it, respectively. It follows from this doctrine that two sentences are synonymous if and only if they are confirmed (disconfirmed) by the same observations.

Quine objects to this account of sentence meaning on the grounds that confirmation (and disconfirmation) has a holistic character. This is known as the doctrine of confirmational holism and also as the Quine-Duhem thesis. Drawing on earlier work by Pierre Duhem, Quine contends that a theoretical sentence in isolation does not imply any observation sentences. Such a sentence needs to be supplemented by a battery of auxiliary statements, including statements describing the experimental apparatus, the theory taken to govern that apparatus, statements reporting the presence or absence of other observationally relevant factors and the like. When a scientist looks down a microscope to test some claim in virology, he or she needs to assume a great deal about the operation of microscopes, about how bright illumination does not affect the virus, that the sample on the slide is representative and so on. Therefore, it is only a large set of theoretical sentences, only 'a corporate body' in Quine's phrase, which implies observation sentences. Consequently, although a set of theoretical sentences can be associated with a set of possible observations, no individual theoretical sentence is so associated (Duhem 1906, Chapter 4; Quine 1951, §5).

We might take Quine's argument to be a *reductio* of verificationism (following Lycan 2008, p. 107). In fact, though, the non-holistic version of verificationism which Quine criticizes has resources with which to address his criticism. Work in proof theoretic semantics has explored the idea that different theoretical sentences have different deductive roles. That is, they occupy

[handwritten margin note: So we're drawing on a body of fact + sentences we make any true we every observation.]

different positions in derivations in which they are used to infer the same consequences. It is open to verificationists to concede that sentences in a theory are not distinguishable with respect of the observational consequences of that theory. But verificationists can further maintain that those sentences are distinguishable by the different positions they occupy in the derivations which produce those observational consequences (Prawitz 1994, §II). (For further discussion of Quine's confirmational holism and its bearing on meaning, see Rey 1994, pp. 78–81; Miller 2007, pp. 139–40.)

Quine draws an important corollary from his conformational holism. Observation confirms or disconfirms only an entire body of theoretical sentences. Observation does not single out any one of those sentences for confirmation or disconfirmation. Consequently, if that body of sentences receives disconfirmation from experience, we have latitude in which sentence or sentences to revise our belief in. Whatever revision we make is guided by considerations of simplicity, conservativism (minimizing the number of sentences revised) and coherence (maximizing the explanatory power of the resulting body of sentences). Nevertheless, these considerations do not privilege any sentences. So no sentence is immune from revision: there is no sentence which we are obliged to retain whatever observations we make. Now, an analytic sentence would be a sentence true in virtue of meaning and not because of how the world is. So an analytic sentence would be immune from revision on the basis of observation. Quine concludes that there are no analytic sentences. Consider a sentence of the form 'Sentence S is synonymous with sentence S^*'. If such a sentence were true, it would be true in virtue of what the sentence means. That is to say, it would be analytic. Given that there are no analytic sentences, no sentence of the form 'S is synonymous with S^*' is true. And that is to say that no sentences are synonymous.

4. The thesis of the indeterminacy of translation

The force of Quine's arguments in 'Two Dogmas of Empiricism' is that there are no analytic sentences and that no pairs of sentences are synonymous. The force of Quine's argument in chapter 2 of *Word and Object* is that there are no truths about what words or sentences mean. This is the implication of his thesis of the indeterminacy of translation (Quine 1960, chapter 2). A correct translation of one language into another is one which pairs the sentences of the one language with the sentences of the other which have the same meaning. Quine's thesis is that, for any language, there is more than one translation which fits all of the possible data, but where these translations are mutually incompatible. Given this thesis, Quine says that there is no correct translation of the sentences of the language. It follows that the sentences of the language do not have the same meaning as the sentences of any other language. Given the link we have seen between sentences having the same meaning and sentences having meaning, Quine concludes that no sentence has meaning.

Quine offers two arguments for his indeterminacy thesis: the 'argument from below' (Quine 1960, chapter 2) and 'the argument from above' (Quine 1970). We will consider them in turn in §§5 and 6.

5. The argument from below

This argument draws on issues concerning the availability of competing translations of sub-sentential expressions (such as predicates) and thereby the availability of competing translations of entire sentences.

If people's sentences have meaning, presumably what those sentences mean is determined by how people use sentences. How people use sentences is a matter of how people behave and are disposed to behave, and consequently

> there are no meanings, nor likenesses nor distinctions of meaning, beyond what are implicit in people's dispositions to overt behaviour. (Quine 1969, p. 29)

It follows that, if people's sentences have meaning, knowledge of how people behave and are disposed to behave would provide knowledge of what people mean. Quine then subjects this supposed source of knowledge to scrutiny. He does so by considering the predicament of a radical translator: someone who has access to the behavioural facts of an alien race and who, on that basis alone, has to work out what the aliens mean. To set about this project, the radical translator seeks to compile a translation manual. This manual purports to correlate each sentence of the alien language with a sentence of the translator's own language which has the same meaning. Quine calls each entry in a translation manual correlating an alien word with some familiar word an 'analytical hypothesis'.

Quine offers the following thought experiment (Quine 1960, pp. 51–2). Suppose that you are a radical translator seeking to translate some alien language from scratch. The only data available to you concerns how the aliens behave and are disposed to behave, including the sounds and marks which they make (though *not* the meanings of those sounds and marks):

> All the objective data he (the linguist) has to go on are the forces that he sees impinging on the native's surfaces and the observable behavior, vocal and otherwise, of the native. (Quine 1960, p. 28)

Your task is then to construct a translation manual correlating sentences of the alien language with those of your own language. Suppose that, by guesswork, you have identified the aliens' indicators for assent and dissent. You now try to work out what the aliens mean by their word 'Gavagai'. You notice that they use the word in the presence of rabbits. Whenever a rabbit is present, you ask 'Gavagai?' and the aliens give their assent. Whenever no rabbit is present, you ask 'Gavagai?' and the aliens give their dissent. Is this evidence that 'Gavagai?' means *there is a rabbit*? Quine points out that there are rival hypotheses about what it means which are also compatible with the behavioural evidence and so have not been ruled out. Perhaps 'Gavagai' means *there is an undetached rabbit part*, that is, *there is a part of a rabbit which is not detached from every rabbit*. (Or perhaps it means *there is an instance of the property being a rabbit*. Or perhaps it means *there is a time-slice of a four-dimensional rabbit-whole*.) Whenever a rabbit is present, so is an undetached rabbit part, and vice versa. So evidence for the presence of the one entity is evidence for the presence of the other. Since behavioural evidence is the only evidence relevant to translation, the evidence does not decide between the competing translations. Quine concludes that no translation is correct. He summarizes matters as follows:

> Manuals for translating one language into another can be set up in divergent ways, all compatible with the totality of speech dispositions, yet incompatible with one another. In countless places they will diverge in giving, as their respective translations of the sentences of the one language, sentences of the other language which stand in some sort of equivalence however loose. (Quine 1960, p. 20. See also pp. 27 and 73–4)

It does not help you to ask the aliens follow-up questions. The questions will have to be posed in the aliens' language – a language which you have yet to understand. You may say something in the alien language and take yourself to be asking *Is this rabbit the same as that rabbit?* In doing so you assume that a certain alien phrase which you have uttered means *the same as*. In making that assumption, however, you overlook other hypotheses about what it might mean. Perhaps it means *is part of the same rabbit as*, and that the question in alien that you asked means *Is this undetached rabbit part a part of the same rabbit as that rabbit part?* Again, behavioural evidence fails to identify which of these questions was the one you asked, and so it fails to identify the meaning of the answer the aliens give in reply. (See Quine 1960, p. 72. For a discussion of this Quinean manoeuvre, see Rosenberg 1967, pp. 414–15; Evans 1974; Hookway 1988, pp. 150–9.)

The 'argument from below' might equally be called the 'too many manuals' argument. According to the argument, the evidence does not single out any one manual as correct. In particular, there are at least two translation manuals which are consistent with the data but which give incompatible translations for some sentence of the alien language. In this sense, there are 'too many' equally eligible manuals specifying the meanings of the words and sentences of the alien language. Since the manuals are incompatible, they cannot all be correct interpretations of the language. Yet, since the manuals are equally eligible, none of them is the correct manual. So, *nothing* provides the correct translation of the language: translation is indeterminate. Given that the sentences of a language have a meaning only if something provides the correct translation of the language, the sentences of the alien language lack meaning. The alien language in question, however, was an arbitrarily selected language. The above line of argument can be run for any language. A correct translation manual is one which pairs the sentences of one language with the sentences of another language which have the same meaning. So if no translation manual is correct, there is nothing which the sentences of any language mean.

6. The argument from above

Of his two principal arguments, Quine sees the argument from above as the more important. This argument draws on issues concerning the under-determination of theory by evidence.

The evidence for a theory does not entail that theory. No number of actual or possible black ravens entails that all ravens are black. For, however extensive the evidence is, it is consistent with some raven being non-black. This point is often put by saying that evidence underdetermines theory. As for science, so for translation: no number of actual or possible observations of the aliens' behaviour entails any theory of the meaning of their sentences. Although in this respect the theory of meaning is no different from (say) physical theory, Quine claims that 'the indeterminacy of translation is something additional'

(Quine 1970, p. 180). By the underdetermination of theory by data, which physical theory is correct is not settled by all actual and possible evidence. Nevertheless, there are a vast number of physical truths about the world. Take the totality of these physical truths. According to Quine, physical theory contrasts with the theory of meaning in the following way. The totality of physical truths determines which physical theories are true and which are false. That same totality fails to determine, however, which theories about the meaning of the aliens' sentences are true and which are false:

> Where indeterminacy of translation applies, there is no real question of right choice; there is no fact of the matter even to *within* the acknowledged under-determination of a theory of nature. (Quine 1968, p. 275)

> Theories of translation are not only underdetermined *as* physics is under-determined, but underdetermined even by the totality of truths expressible in terms of physics. (Kirk 1986, p. 136)

In short, theories of the meaning of the aliens' sentences are underdetermined not only by all actual and possible evidence, but also by all physical truths. Yet, if putative truths about meaning are determined by anything, they are determined by physical truths. Quine concludes that there are no truths about meaning.

How do the arguments from above and from below stand to each other? The premise set of the argument from above is logically stronger than the premise set of the argument from below – the former entails the latter but not vice versa – because truths about people's behaviour and dispositions to behave form a proper sub-set of the totality of physical truths. So, if Quine sees a dialectical need to offer the argument from above, then it seems that he has to admit that there is a failing in the argument from below. Otherwise, the argument from below would suffice to establish the indeterminacy thesis. Quine says that critics have been misled in taking the gavagai example to state 'the ground' of the indeterminacy thesis and that, in seeking to counter the example, they took themselves to cast doubt on the thesis (Quine 1970, p. 178). Perhaps so, but then all that would be called for on Quine's part would be this point of clarification, not a new argument altogether.

We saw that the argument from below begins as follows. If sentences have meaning, what those sentences mean is determined by how people use sentences. How people use sentences is a matter of how people behave and are disposed to behave. It was then inferred that, if people's sentences have meaning, knowledge of how people behave and are disposed to behave would provide knowledge of what people mean.

Three comments on the above line of thought are available. First, if use is construed in a narrowly behavioural way, it does not determine meaning. We learn languages by observing others' behaviour. Given this construal of what it is to use words, people's use of words provides the evidential basis on which we induce what they mean. It does not follow that people's use of words, so understood, determines what people's words mean. (See also Currie 1993, pp. 479–81.)

Second, in the sense in which use does determine meaning, use should not be construed in some narrowly behavioural way. There are other factors which plausibly have a role in determining what people mean besides how they behave and are disposed to behave. These include, for example, factors relating people's use of words to their environment or to their internal physiological states (Landesman 1970, p. 333; Friedman 1975, p. 365).

Hilary Putnam presents an important thought experiment to show the role of a speaker's environment in determining the meaning of many of a speaker's words (Putnam 1975 especially pp. 223–9). A competent English speaker will use the word 'water' to pick out a certain transparent, odourless liquid which is found in lakes and rivers and which flows from taps. Perhaps that description captures most, if not all, of what the speaker knows about what 'water' refers to. In particular, the speaker might not know the chemical composition of the stuff which 'water' refers to. Nevertheless, Putnam maintains, such a speaker does not use 'water' to refer to *any* transparent, odourless liquid found in lakes and rivers and which flows from taps. A version of Putnam's thought experiment goes as follows. Suppose that Oscar is one such English speaker. He travels by rocket to another planet, call it 'Twin-Earth', which is much like Earth except that the transparent, odourless liquid which fills rivers and lakes and which flows from taps on Twin-Earth does not have the same chemical composition as the stuff on Earth which is called 'water'. Is the liquid on Twin-Earth water? Putnam thinks that it is not because it lacks the same chemical composition of the stuff which fills the rivers and lakes on Earth. Given that that liquid is not water, it follows that the word 'water' does not refer to it. What Putnam takes this to show is that at least one of the factors which determines the reference of 'water' is a feature of the environment (viz. the chemical composition of the stuff referred to by the word) which a competent user of that word need not be aware of. After all, prior to the chemical revolution of 1750, no English speaker knew what the chemical composition of water is.

While Putnam's thought experiment seeks to bring out the role of a speaker's natural environment in at least partly determining the references of many of the speaker's words, further thought experiments are offered by Tyler Burge to show the role of a speaker's *social* environment in at least partly determining the references of all of the speaker's words (Burge 1979a).

Turning to our third criticism of Quine's argument from below, the inference involved in the argument is questionable. Even if As determine Bs, it does not follow that any amount of knowledge about As provides knowledge about Bs. Perhaps the As are very numerous and their way of determining the Bs very complicated. Indeed, perhaps their way of determining the Bs is in an unsurveyably chaotic pattern. Perhaps too what we would have to know about the As to get knowledge of Bs would be humanly impossible as our senses are too crude and undiscriminating and our powers of reasoning, attention and memory too limited (cf. Williamson 1994, pp. 205–9).

The argument from below itself seems to be a species of underdetermination argument in which the information which underdetermines claims about what the aliens mean is restricted to information about alien behaviour and dispositions to behave. Given this, we can proceed to the argument from above. Since its premise set entails the premise set of the argument from below, if the argument from above fails, so too does the argument from below (cf. Friedman 1975, p. 360).

The argument from above is essentially as follows. If our sentences have meaning, their meaning is determined by the totality of physical truths. The meaning of our sentences is not determined by the totality of physical truths. Therefore, our sentences lack meaning. The argument is valid but is it sound? In particular, how can Quine justify the second premise? In offering this argument, Quine has deliberately set aside the gavagai thought experiment, and so no support is to be sought from that quarter. Quine admits truths about (say) chemistry because he supposes that the totality of physical truths determines all chemical truths. But what is the reason for thinking that that totality determines truths about chemistry but not about meaning? Justification for the crucial premise is required but not provided (Friedman 1975, §III; Chomsky 1975, pp. 179–204).

Dagfinn Føllesdal takes Quine's argument from below to be as follows:

> . . . the only entities we are justified in assuming are those that are appealed to in the simplest theory that accounts for all the evidence, These entities and their properties and inter-relations are all there is to the world, and all

> there is to be right or wrong about. All truths about these are included in
> our theory of nature. In translation we are not describing a further realm of
> reality, we are just correlating two comprehensive languages/theories
> concerning all there is. (Føllesdal 1975, p. 32)

Stephen Neale offers the following account of the above passage from
Føllesdal:

> The point here is that there can be more than one translation manual
> compatible with everything there is to know about the states and
> distributions of all elementary particles, and hence no basis on which to
> select between such manuals. This interpretation of Quine's thesis is
> illuminating in that it avoids construing indeterminacy as the statement of
> any ontological dogma attributable to Quine's adherence to physicalism. If
> the theory of nature accounts for the totality of possible evidence, then
> there is no good reason to postulate entities purported to play explanatory
> roles in some other theory – for instance, a theory of understanding
> behaviour – when such entities are not seen doing any work within the
> overall theory of nature. Take intensional entities [such as propositions].
> Many philosophers feel quite comfortable with such entities; to borrow Paul
> Grice's newfangled ontological Marxism "They work therefore they exist".
> On Quine's account we should subscribe to the free-market counter: "They
> are not cost-effective therefore they do not exist." If the theory of nature
> makes no appeal to intensional entities then no sense can be made of their
> existence, we have no identity criteria for them. (Neale 1987, p. 306)

It is difficult to see how these passages progress matters. Take them in turn.
The argument offered by Føllesdal has as its premise the claim that all truths
about the entities we are justified in believing in are stated in the simplest
theory that accounts for all the evidence ('our theory of nature'). It concludes
that 'In translation we are not describing a further realm of reality, we are
just correlating two comprehensive languages/theories concerning all there is'.
That inference seems to be a *non sequitur*. Nothing in the argument tells us
why truths about translation do not figure in the simplest theory that accounts
for all the evidence. The issue is not whether in translation we describe a
further realm of reality – a realm in addition to the one described by our theory
of nature. The issue is more basic than that: it is whether in translation we
describe reality.

Neale attempts to fill this gap in Føllesdal's argument. Since he tells us that
the indeterminacy thesis does not depend on physicalism, it is curious that he
should characterize the thesis as the claim 'that there can be more than one

translation manual compatible with everything there is to know about the states and distributions of all elementary particles'. For physicalism says that all truths are determined by the states and distributions of all elementary particles, and Neale's characterization of the indeterminacy thesis is that translation is not determined by those states and distributions. But let's set this aside. Neale's argument can be summarized as follows. The overall theory of nature accounts for the totality of possible evidence. So there is no good reason to postulate entities purported to play explanatory roles in some other theory. The theory of meaning posits entities (such as meanings) which the overall theory of nature does not. So there is no good reason to postulate those entities. That argument is valid, but to tell whether it is sound, we need to understand what the phrase 'the overall theory of nature' amounts to. What exactly counts as belonging to this theory? Neale faces a dilemma. If 'the overall theory of nature' is another name for particle physics – the study of the states and distributions of all elementary particles – then the argument proves too much. Chemistry, for instance, postulates entities (such as chemical compounds) which particle physics does not. By Neale's pattern of argument, it follows that there is no good reason to posit such chemical entities. (This does not seem to be a route that Neale wants to go down: see Neale 1987, p. 316.) However, if 'the overall theory of nature' is taken in a more inclusive sense, so that it is not confined to particle physics and includes sciences such as chemistry as well, then it needs to be explained why the theory of meaning should not also be included in the overall theory of nature. Otherwise, it would be arbitrary to claim that chemical elements and compounds do work within the overall theory of nature but that meanings do not. But, of course, if the theory of meaning is included within the overall theory of nature, then Neale's premise that the theory of meaning posits entities (such as meanings) which the overall theory of nature does not is false.

The other argument that Neale offers concerns a case in which a population *P* uniformly asserts a certain expression ø given a certain pattern of stimuli (and does not assert it in its absence). Different speakers in this language formulate different theories about what ø means. But, Neale continues:

> The native speakers' respective theories are empirically indistinguishable and hence it makes no sense to say that there is such a thing as the correct usage of ø beyond correlation with the same stimuli across *P,* hence it makes no sense to say that there is a fact of the matter as to the meaning of ø. (Neale 1987, p. 307)

Neale's argument does not refurbish Quine's case for the indeterminacy thesis. It seems to be a more abstract statement of the gavagai thought experiment. In that thought experiment, a population uses the expression 'Gavagai' when and only when they make certain observations. What does 'Gavagai' mean? One hypothesis says that it means *rabbit*; another that it means *undetached rabbit part*. Those hypotheses are empirically indistinguishable. The argument from below concludes that there is no fact of the matter as to what 'Gavagai' means.

Moreover, even if we grant the lemma that there is no such thing as the correct usage of ø beyond correlation with the same stimuli across *P*, it is not clear how Neale infers from there being empirically indistinguishable theories about what ø means to the conclusion that there is no fact of the matter as to the meaning of ø. Here is a counter-example to that pattern of reasoning. There are empirically indistinguishable theories about the structure of space and time (Sklar 1985, pp. 6, 56). One theory takes space and time to be absolute, so that things in space and time are like things in a container. Another takes space and time to be relative, so that things in space and time stand in spatial and temporal relations to each other but are not contained in absolute space and time. Nevertheless, this need not be taken (and most of today's physicists do not take it) as showing that there is no fact of the matter about the structure of space and time. More generally, for any unobservable entities (such as space-time structure, sub-atomic particles, and classes), there will be empirically indistinguishable theories which make incompatible claims about those entities. It does not obviously follow that there is no fact of the matter about which of those theories is correct (cf. Lycan 1984, p. 224).

In sum, Quine's indeterminacy thesis is a radical and thought-provoking thesis, but we have found it difficult to find a good non-question-begging argument in support of it.

7. Conclusion

Some philosophers regard semantics as a form of scientific inquiry. (As we will see in Chapter 9, Donald Davidson takes just such a view.) Semantic theories seek to uncover and describe semantic truths. These theories are tested by empirical data concerning speakers' intuitions about valid inferences, grammatical strings of words, and synonymous expressions. Theories are then selected on the basis of how well they express these and allied phenomena. Quine, however, thinks that semantics is not a science. According to him, it does not follow scientific methods of inquiry and there are no semantic truths for it to uncover. (It is very curious that Davidson endorses Quine's arguments for his view: see, e.g. Davidson 1973.)

Quine can be identified as making three sceptical claims about language. We have concentrated on the first. This is the claim that translation is indeterminate: it is neither true nor false whether any sentence is the correct translation of another. The most that can be said is that one sentence is the translation of another according to some translation manual. No translation manual, however, is itself correct.

Second, Quine claims that syntax is indeterminate: given any two extensionally equivalent grammars, it is neither true nor false that one of them is the correct grammar of a language. Quine writes:

> If . . . we held every grammar to be as authentic as every extensionally equivalent grammar, and to be preferred only for its simplicity and convenience, then deep structure loses its objectivity but need not lose its place. (Quine 1972, p. 395)

Presumably, Quine's thinking is that, in interpreting an alien speaker, there is no evidence which could distinguish between the native having one grammar as opposed to another if the grammars are extensionally equivalent. Given that evidence cannot settle between the grammars, it is neither true nor false that the alien has the one grammar rather than the other (Quine 1972; Neale 1987).

Third, Quine claims that logical form is indeterminate: a sentence does not have a uniquely correct logical form. A logical form is assigned to a sentence by a paraphrase, but which paraphrase to adopt is a context-dependent matter, and so, this will vary according to the purposes of the semanticist. These include clarifying which deductive inferences the sentence figures in, what its ontological commitments are, disambiguation and so on. Accordingly, there is no such thing as *the* logical form of a sentence, something which is the task of semantics to discover (Quine 1960, pp. 260–2).

Quine's scepticism about the existence of meaning is a remarkable thesis. If it is correct, there is no difference between those marks and sounds that we suppose have meaning and those that we suppose do not. Many of the questions which were posed in the introduction to this book assumed that there is such a difference. If that distinction is illusory, many of those questions lapse. There is no more a question about what it is for words or sentences to have meaning or about what it is to understand words or sentences than there is a question about what holds the Earth up. Those questions are misguided because of the mistaken assumptions that they make about the world. Moreover, Quine does not present the only case for scepticism about the existence of meaning (see also Goodman 1949, 1953; Kripke 1982). Simply meeting his arguments, then, does not dispel the sceptical threat.

It is an interesting issue as to how much of Quine's overall philosophy would need to be rejected in order to block his arguments for scepticism about meaning. For example, Quine argues that the analytic-synthetic distinction lacks epistemological or explanatory significance; that the notions of meaning and of necessity can be dispensed with in our overall account of the world; that it is only our total system of beliefs (and not any part of it) which receives empirical confirmation (or disconfirmation); and that the world consists solely of physical events and classes of these. Unless these claims can be shown to be independent of Quine's scepticism about meaning, any considerations in support of these claims will also support his scepticism, and any objections to his scepticism will also be objections to these claims. There is then an issue about whether these claims can be disentangled from Quine's scepticism. Which of these striking claims can be retained even if Quine's scepticism about meaning is rejected? Which ones would need to be abandoned? (Surprisingly, perhaps all of them can be retained: Kirk 1986, chapter 12.)

Questions for discussion

Question 1
To what extent does Quine's argument from below depend on behaviourism: the doctrine that people's mental life consists in how those people behave and are disposed to behave? (Chomsky 1968; Quine 1968).

Question 2
The argument from below claims that when an alien says 'Gavagai', one hypothesis says that 'Gavagai' means *rabbit*, whereas a rival hypothesis says that it means *undetached rabbit-part*. Those hypotheses have different meanings. So, does Quine's argument itself have to assume that sentences do have meaning? If so, does that reveal an absurdity in the indeterminacy thesis? (Rosenberg 1967, pp. 415–18; Katz 1998, chapter 4 §4.2)

Question 3
Quine claims that if there is no fact of the matter about what other people's sentences mean, there is no fact of the matter about what the contents of other

people's psychological attitudes are (Quine 1960, p. 221). It follows that there is no fact of the matter about what they believe or desire. Quine further claims that his arguments apply to one's own case: 'on deeper reflection, radical translation begins at home' (Quine 1969, p. 46). It follows that there is no fact of the matter about what you believe or what you desire. Is there something paradoxical about that conclusion? Is it a conclusion which could be rationally acceptable to you? (Bradley 1969; Searle 1984).

Question 4

Quine's indeterminacy of translation thesis says that there is no fact of the matter about what the meaning of our words and sentences are. Could the same arguments that he offers in support of it also be used to argue that there is no fact of the matter about what our words refer to? (cf. Quine 1969, p. 35).

Further reading

Chomsky, Noam (1969) 'Quine's Empirical Assumptions'.

Hookway, Christopher (1988) *Quine* chapter 9.

Kemp, Gary (2006) *Quine: A Guide for the Perplexed* chapter 3.

Kirk, Robert (1986) *Translation Determined*.

Lycan, William G. (1984) *Logical Form in Natural Language* chapter 9.

Miller, Alexander (2007) *Philosophy of Language* chapter 4.

Morris, Michael (2007) *An Introduction to the Philosophy of Language* chapter 11.

Quine, Willard V. O. (1960) *Word and Object* chapter 2.

—(1970) 'On the Reasons for the Indeterminacy of Translation'.

Weiss, Bernard (2010) *How To Understand Language: A Philosophical Inquiry* chapter 10.

Zabludowski, Andrzej (1989) 'On Quine's Indeterminacy Doctrine'.

9

Davidson on Extensional Theories of Meaning

1. Introduction

In Chapter 3 §1, we introduced a distinction between foundational and structural theories of meaning. Grice presents a foundational theory of meaning, whereas Frege and (as we will see) Davidson present structural theories of meaning. A foundational theory of meaning seeks to answer the question 'Why does a certain sentence have the meaning that it does (for a particular speaker or group of speakers)?'. This kind of theory seeks to say what it is about the speaker or speakers that give the sentences they use the meanings which they have. A structural theory of meaning primarily seeks to answer the question 'What is the meaning of a certain sentence (for a particular speaker or group of speakers)?'. This kind of theory seeks to specify the meanings of the sentences of a language as used by some speaker or speakers, but without seeking to say why those sentences have those meanings.

Although Frege and Davidson both offer structural theories of meaning, their theories have some important differences. Unlike Frege, Davidson dispenses with the distinction between sense and reference. Davidson repudiates the suggestion that talk of meaning is to be construed as talk of certain entities, meanings. (Here, Davidson was influenced by reasons given by Quine: see Chapter 8.) Consequently, he repudiates Frege's postulation of senses. Whereas Frege seeks to explain how names and predicates have meaning by claiming that they express senses, Davidson suggests that a term's meaning can be construed in terms of its contribution to the meaning of sentences in which it figures, and without appeal to any entity associated with the term. Moreover, Davidson construes the meaning of a sentence in terms of that sentence's truth condition, and his construal does not appeal to any entity associated with the sentence (such as a proposition or Fregean thought).

Davidson takes the chief goal of the philosophy of language to be to understand natural language. He pursues this goal by seeking to say what it is that people know that enables them to understand a given language. Whatever this knowledge is, it enables someone to acquire justified beliefs about the world by hearing or reading sentences. For example, by hearing someone utter 'There is a squirrel in the grass', we can acquire the justified belief that there is a squirrel in the grass. Davidson argues that our knowing the condition under which the speaker's utterance is true is all we need to know for us to acquire that justified belief. His reasoning is as follows. 'There is a squirrel in the grass' is true if and only if there is a squirrel in the grass. Suppose a certain speaker says 'There is a squirrel in the grass', and suppose too that what this speaker asserts is known usually to be true, then we can conclude that there is a squirrel in the grass.

Davidson initiates a programme which develops this line of reasoning. The programme seeks to show that there is a systematic link between the truth condition of each sentence of a language and what we need to know in order to understand those sentences. The link in question is provided by a certain kind of truth theory for that language: a theory of what it is for sentences in that language to be true.

In this section, we have seen that Davidson seeks a structural theory of the meaning of sentences of a language as opposed to a foundational theory. In §2, we will see another feature of the kind of theory of meaning that Davidson seeks, namely that it is an extensional theory of meaning.

2. Extensional contexts

The kind of theory of meaning that Davidson offers is often described as an extensional theory of meaning. What does this mean? To answer this question, we need to see what extensional contexts are.

The extension of a term is the thing to which it applies. Here is how this claim is to be understood in the case of names, predicates and sentences:

The extensions of names, predicates and sentences

Names: The extension of a name is the reference of the name.

Predicates: The extension of a predicate is the set of things to which that predicate applies.

Sentences: The extension of a sentence is its truth value.

So, for example, the extension of 'the Eiffel Tower' is the Eiffel Tower, the extension of the predicate 'is a tower' is the set of towers and the extension of the sentence 'The Eiffel Tower is in Paris' is the truth value true. To take another example, the extension of 'Joseph Stalin' is Joseph Stalin, the extension of the predicate 'is a dictator' is the set of dictators and the extension of the sentence 'Joseph Stalin is in Paris' is the truth value false.

A language can be thought of as a way of putting names, predicates and sentences into linguistic contexts (Blackburn 1984, p. 286). For example, the context provided by 'the capital of' takes names of countries to generate complex expressions referring to capital cities. Names, predicates and sentences can be embedded in still more complex contexts. To take another example, the name 'Hungary' occurs in both 'Hungary was a democratic country' and in 'Following the 1989 revolution, Hungary was a democratic country'. The predicate 'was a democratic country' occurs in both sentences. The first sentence is also embedded in the second.

A linguistic context is extensional if and only if the extension of the context is a function of the extensions of its components. So, for instance, the context formed by 'the capital of ' is extensional because its extension (viz., a capital city) is a function of the name of any country. Again, the context 'Every . . . is a . . .' is extensional because when it is completed by a pair of predicates to form a sentence (such as 'Every sailor is a drinker'), the extension of the sentence (viz., a truth value) is a function of the extensions of the predicates. Suppose that all and only drinkers are gamblers. Then 'drinker' and 'gambler' have the same extension. It further follows that 'Every sailor is a drinker' and 'Every sailor is a gambler' have the same extension. Lastly, a language is extensional if and only if all of its contexts are extensional.

We can summarize these points as follows:

Extensional contexts

Where 'C( )' is a context,

1. **Names.** $C(a)$ is extensional if and only if

$$C(a)$$
$$a = b$$
$$\therefore C(b)$$

2. **Predicates.** $C(F)$ is extensional if and only if

$$C(F)$$
$$(\forall x)\,(Fx \equiv Gx)$$
$$\therefore C(G)$$

3. **Sentences.** $C(s_1)$ is extensional if and only if

$$C(s_1)$$
$$s_1 \equiv s_2$$
$$\therefore C(s_2)$$

Mathematical language and the best understood logics are extensional. Natural languages, however, apparently are not: they are apparently non-extensional. Given that 'Jeb sat down' and 'Jeb took his boots off' are both true, it does not follow that 'Jeb sat down before Jeb took off his boots' is true. Nor does it follow that it is false. Again, although 'John F. Kennedy was assassinated' and 'The Earth moves' are both true, and although 'Galileo believed that the Earth moves' is also true, 'Galileo believed that John F. Kennedy was assassinated' is false (cf. Chapter 3 §4).

Understanding natural languages solely in terms of extensional constructions would enable us to apply our best understood logical systems to those languages. The above observations, however, show that such an approach faces substantive challenges.

3. Davidson's programme

Davidson's programme has an agenda which consists of the following series of questions:

Qu1   What is a theory of meaning to do?
Qu2   What does it take for such a theory to be adequate?
Qu3   Which theory of meaning is adequate?

The remainder of Davidson's programme consists of his answers to those questions. Let's consider each of the questions in turn.

Qu1 asks 'What is a theory of meaning to do?' Davidson sometimes calls the kind of theories he devises as providing 'a theory of meaning' and sometimes as providing 'a theory of logical form'. It also supposedly provides an empirical theory about natural languages:

> . . . the task of a theory of meaning as I conceive it is not to change, improve or reform a language, but to describe and understand it. (Davidson 1967a, p. 34)

Davidson spells out this task in more detail in terms of four specific requirements (Davidson 1970, p. 56).

The first is that a theory of meaning for a language should give the meaning of every sentence in the language. 'The theory [should] provide a method for deciding, given an arbitrary sentence, what its meaning is' (Davidson 1970, p. 56).

The second requirement is that the theory should provide an account of the meaning of the sentences by taking each sentence to be constructed from sub-sentential expressions drawn from a finite list. The sentence should be able to be built up from these expressions using a finite number of constructions. In addition, this process of construction should show how the meaning of each sentence is determined by the meanings of the component expressions plus the constructions used. '[A theory of meaning] must lead us to see the semantic character of the sentence – its truth or falsity – as owed to how it is composed, by a finite number of applications of some of a finite number of devices that suffice for the language as a whole, out of elements drawn from a finite stock (the vocabulary) that suffices for the language as a whole' (Davidson 1968, p. 95).

The third requirement is that, in specifying the meanings of individual sentences, the theory should use the same concepts as the sentences whose meanings are being specified (Davidson 1970, p. 56).

The fourth requirement is that the theory is empirically testable (Davidson 1967a, p. 24 and 1970, p. 60).

Qu2 asks 'What does it take for such a theory to be adequate?' Davidson claims that a theory of truth for a natural language is a theory of meaning which meets the above four requirements. In addition, a theory of truth will provide a description of the logical form of the sentences of the language. By revealing the logical form of those sentences, the theory can reveal their ontological commitments. The ontological commitments of a sentence consist in what has to exist in order for that sentence to be true (Quine 1960 pp. 238-42). For example, Davidson elsewhere argues that the logical form of a sentence such as

(1)   Brutus brutally stabbed Caesar on the Ides of March

involves ontological commitment not only to individuals (Brutus and Caesar) but also to events (an event of stabbing), where an event is a particular that occurs at a specific place and time (Davidson 1967b). (1) is to be understood as saying that there exists an event such that it is a stabbing of Caesar by Brutus and it is brutal and it occurred on the Ides of March:

(2) $(\exists x)$ Stabbing(Brutus, Caesar, x) & Brutal(x) & Occurred (x, Ides of March)

(1) entails that Brutus stabbed Caesar in the Ides of March, and it also entails that Brutus stabbed Caesar. A merit of Davidson's construal is that it shows why this is so. Each of the entailed sentences follows from (2) by conjunction elimination.

In Quine's terminology, (2) is a 'regimentation' of (1) (Quine 1960, chapter 5). (2) is a regimentation of (1) if (2) can play the same theoretical role that (1) has, it is formulated in logical notation (specifically, that of first-order logic), and it is more clear and simple than (1) in the sense that it conveys what (1) does more explicitly and without ambiguity.

It is not obvious that the truth of any action sentence requires not only that objects exist but also that events exist. Davidson is claiming that the grammatical form of an action sentence need not fully reveal its logical form. (For this terminology, see Chapter 5 §2.) This is what is revealed by regimenting these sentences. This aspect of Davidson's programme also shows how considerations in the philosophy of language can give us reason to revise our views about what exists. Perhaps pre-philosophically, many of us have not believed that events exist – or, at any rate, we have not realized that many of the sentences we utter are true only if events exist. Perhaps also, when we have started doing philosophy, some of us take the view that events do not exist (e.g. Horgan 1978). If Davidson's account of the logical form of action sentences is correct, then we have not realized that the action sentences we utter are ontologically committed to events. We have also failed to realize that, by believing any of these sentences, we are thereby ontologically committed to events. (For a further discussion of this topic, see Fodor 1970; Harman 1972, pp. 44–6.)

Davidson's full answer to Qu2 is given by his answers to the following sub-questions:

Qu2a What is a theory of truth?
Qu2b Why would a theory of truth for a natural language satisfy Davidson's four requirements for a theory of meaning?
Qu2c Why would a theory of truth for a natural language be a theory of the logical form of sentences of that language?

Qu2a asks 'What is a theory of truth?' In answering this question, Davidson turns to Alfred Tarski's work on defining a truth predicate for formal languages (Tarski 1944, 1956). Tarski provides a way of defining a truth predicate 'true-in-L' for a formal language L. The definition takes the form of a certain kind of theory of truth for L. In particular, the theory is based on L's syntactic structure and consists of a finite number of axioms. The theory is called a 'Tarskian truth theory, or T-theory, for L'. A T-theory for L enables us to derive, for every sentence s of L, a theorem (or 'T-sentence', as it is also called) which specifies s's truth condition.

Each such theorem has the following basic form:

(SCHEMA) 's' is true if and only if p

where 's' is replaced by a sentence of L, and 'p' is replaced by a sentence of the language in which the T-theory is formulated. Tarski calls L, the language being studied, an 'object-language'. He calls the language in which the T-theory is formulated a 'meta-language'.

Tarski proves that a truth definition for a language L is materially adequate. This means that the predicate 'is true-in-L' which the truth definition provides is co-extensive with the pre-theoretical predicate 'is true' if and only if the following condition is met. For every sentence s of L, the truth definition implies a T-sentence such that what replaces p is a translation of s. There is also a requirement that the object-language and the meta-language must meet certain formal conditions. (For a recent and very accessible discussion of Tarski's theory of truth, see Burgess and Burgess 2011, chapter 2.)

Let's confine our attention to a class of languages which contain only indicative sentences and which do not contain ambiguous sentences ('She poured champagne into the flute') or tensed sentences ('I am going to the gym') or sentences containing demonstratives or indexicals ('The treasure is buried here'). Making these restrictions makes it easier to present this key element of Davidson's programme. After that is done, we will relax the restrictions and add the needed complications.

Suppose that our meta-language contains English as its object language. Then consider the English sentence 'Mount Vesuvius is a volcano'. SCHEMA specifies the truth condition of that sentence as follows:

> 'Mount Vesuvius is a volcano' is true if and only if Mount Vesuvius is a volcano.

On the left-hand side of the above biconditional, we have a name of the sentence in question. We have formed a name of it by writing down the sentence and enclosing it in quote marks. On the right-hand side of the biconditional, we have a specification of the truth condition of the sentence named on the left-hand side. We use the meta-language to specify that truth condition. Since we are working with an example in which the meta-language contains the object language, we can use the same object language sentence to specify its own truth condition. And this is why the right-hand side of the biconditional is filled in the way which it is.

There are infinitely many instances of SCHEMA. These instances will be generated from the non-logical axioms of the theory. Davidson further requires that the theory has only finitely many such axioms. He makes this requirement in order to prevent the theory being trivialized by taking each instance of SCHEMA to be a non-logical axiom of the theory.

Qu2b asked 'Why would a theory of truth for a natural language satisfy Davidson's four requirements for a theory of meaning?' The first requirement was that a theory of meaning for a language should give the meaning of every sentence in the language. Davidson takes a Tarskian truth theory to meet this requirement because it entails the T-sentence of each sentence of the language. We have just seen that, when the object-language is contained in the meta-language, the description that replaces 's' on the left-hand side of SCHEMA is given by the sentence that replaces 'p'. In that case, Davidson proposes reading 'if and only if' in SCHEMA as *means that*. Since the truth theory entails the T-sentence corresponding to every sentence of the language, that theory can be taken as giving the meaning of every sentence of the language. Davidson puts the point as follows:

> I suggest that a theory of truth for a language does, in a minimal but important respect, do what we want, that is, give the meanings of all independently meaningful expressions on the basis of an analysis of their structure (Davidson 1970, p. 55).

> There is a sense, then, in which a theory of truth accounts for the role each sentence plays in the language insofar as that role depends on the sentence's being a potential bearer of truth or falsity; and the account is given in terms of structure. . . My purpose in putting the matter this way is to justify the claim that a theory of truth shows how "the meaning of each sentence depends on the meanings of the words" (Davidson 1970, p. 61).

> [A Tarskian truth theory gives] necessary and sufficient conditions for the truth of every sentence, and to give truth conditions is a way of giving the meaning of a sentence. To know the semantic concept of truth for a language is to know what it is for a sentence – any sentence – to be true, and this amounts, in one good sense we can give to the phrase, to understanding the language. (Davidson 1967, p. 24)

Davidson's proposal is that, by constructing Tarskian truth theories for natural language, we can understand sentences in terms of their truth conditions, and we can understand the meanings of sub-sentential expressions (i.e. expressions which compose those sentences) in terms of their systematic contribution to the truth conditions of sentences.

This proposal can be understood as advocating the replacement of 'means that' with 'if and only if'. This would be to take the proposal as a case of what Carnap and Quine call 'explication' (Carnap 1950, chapter 1; Quine 1960, §53). An explication of a given term does not provide a synonym of it; instead, it replaces it with more precise and informative terms. This is what occurs, for example, in science's replacement of the imprecise qualitative terms 'hot' and 'cold' with a more precise quantitative talk of 'degrees of temperature'. Taking Davidson's proposal to be an explication of our talk of meaning, his proposal is then that:

> . . . what is worth saving in our informal (or pre-theoretic) views and questions about meaning can be captured well enough in a theory that does not talk of meaning at all, but only of truth, truth conditions and related notions. In

swapping old questions and claims about meaning for new ones about truth, the trade is not intended to be even. The new claims are not expected to be equivalent with the old, but better. What is lost in the transition are all the obscurities and confusions to which the notion of meaning is heir. What is gained is the extensional clarity of the notion of truth, and the potential of producing a fruitful empirical theory invoking the notion. (Stich 1976, p. 206. See also Reeves 1974, p. 345; Lepore 1982, p. 282)

In place of specifying the meaning of a given sentence in a language, then, the truth theory specifies the truth condition of the sentence. So, for example, instead of saying that 'Planets move in ellipses' means that *planets move in ellipses*, the truth theory entails that 'Planets move in ellipses' is true if and only if planets move ellipses. Davidson wrote that:

The theory of meaning will have done its work if it provides, for every sentence *s* in the language under study, a matching sentence (to replace '*p*' [in SCHEMA]) that, in some way yet to be made clear, 'gives the meaning' of *s*. One obvious candidate for the matching sentence is just *s* itself, if the object language is contained in the meta-language: otherwise a translation of *s* in the meta-language. As a final bold step, let us try treating the position occupied by '*p*' extensionally; to implement this, sweep away the obscure 'means that', provide the sentence that replaces '*p*' with a proper sentential connective, and supply the description that replaces '*s*' with its own predicate. The plausible result is [that *s* is true] if and only if *p*. What we require of a theory of meaning for a language L is that without appeal to any (further) semantic notions it places enough restrictions on the predicate ['is true'] to entail all sentences got from schema T when '*s*' is replaced by a structural description of a sentence of L and '*p*' by that sentence. (Davidson 1967a, p. 23)

Davidson's second requirement is that a theory of meaning should provide an account of the meaning of sentences by taking each sentence to be constructed from components drawn from a finite list. In the case of a Tarskian truth theory, this requirement is addressed by explaining how, in an extensional language, the truth conditions of complex sentences are a function of the truth conditions of their component sentences, and of how the truth conditions of atomic sentences are a function of the satisfaction conditions of their component expressions. Take a complex sentence such as 'Mount Vesuvius is a volcano and Rome is in Italy.' The truth condition of that conjunction is a function of the truth conditions of its conjuncts. Take an atomic sentence such as 'Mount Vesuvius is a volcano'. The truth condition of that sentence is a function of the satisfaction conditions of its component expressions, the name 'Mount Vesuvius' and the predicate 'is a volcano'. The satisfaction condition of

'Mount Vesuvius' is: for any x, 'Mount Vesuvius' names x if and only if Mount Vesuvius $= x$. The satisfaction condition of 'is a volcano' is: for any x, x satisfies 'is a volcano' if and only if x is a member of the set of volcanos.

Davidson's third requirement is that, in specifying the meanings of individual sentences, the theory should use the same concepts as the sentences whose meanings are being specified. Given that sentences featuring ambiguity, demonstratives, indexicals and the like have been set aside, this requirement is also met. Recall SCHEMA:

SCHEMA   's' is true if and only if p

If the object language is contained in the meta-language, 'p' can be replaced by the sentence whose description replaces 's'. So the right-hand side of instances of SCHEMA will use only those concepts used by the left-hand side of instances of SCHEMA:

> The striking thing about T-sentences is that whatever machinery must operate to produce them, and whatever ontological wheels must turn, in the end a T-sentence states the truth conditions of a sentence using resources no richer than, because the same as, those of the sentence itself. Unless the original sentence mentions possible worlds, intensional entities, properties, or propositions, the statement of its truth conditions does not. (Davidson 1973, p. 132)

Davidson's fourth requirement is that a theory of meaning is empirically testable. Davidson argues that this requirement is met by a truth theory. A truth theory is a formalized theory that entails an infinite number of T-sentences. Since those T-sentences are testable, the theory is testable. As Davidson puts it:

> . . . we need only ask, in selected cases, whether what the theory avers to be the truth conditions for a sentence really are. A typical case might involve deciding whether the sentence 'Snow is white' is true if and only if snow is white. (Davidson 1967a, p. 311)

This form of testing may appear trivial, but that is because the meta-language contains the object language and so it is easy to see whether the consequences of the theory are true. At any rate, what is not trivial is devising a theory that has only true consequences. Furthermore, when a meta-language does not contain an object language, testing a truth theory is a decidedly non-trivial task. Then the sentence that replaces 's' in SCHEMA is not identical to the sentence that replaces '*p*' in SCHEMA, but the theorist still has to establish that the two replacing sentences have the same truth value.

If we are to test empirically whether a truth theory for a given language is a theory of meaning for that language, we need to be able to tell whether a given T-sentence that the theory entails is true without having to know what the sentence named on its left-hand side means. Davidson thought that we can be in that epistemic situation if we take two factors into account. First, 'the fact that speakers of a language hold a sentence to be true (under observed circumstances) [is] prima facie evidence that it is true under those circumstances' (Davidson 1974, p. 152). Second, 'we can know that a speaker holds a sentence to be true without knowing what he means by it or what belief it expresses for him' (Davidson 1975, p. 162). To test which sentences a speaker holds true, Davidson recommended that the theorist follows a procedure that Quine called 'radical interpretation' (Quine 1960, p. 28):

> We will try to notice under what conditions the alien speaker assents to or dissents from a variety of his sentences. The relevant conditions will, of course, be what we take to be the truth conditions of his sentences. We will have to assume that most of his assents are to true, and his dissents from false, sentences - an inevitable assumption since the alternative is unintelligible. (Davidson 1970, p. 62)

We can now turn to Qu2c: 'Why would a theory of truth for a natural language be a theory of the logical form of sentences of that language?' We have seen that a Tarskian theory of truth explains how the truth conditions of sentences depend on the satisfaction conditions of their components. Such a theory also entails that all sentences with a certain logical form are true. These sentences can be taken to form the class of logical truths for that language. Furthermore, by taking certain sentences to be logical truths, the truth theory is testable in a further respect. It can be tested by comparing its claims about which sentences of the object language are logically true with our independent views on the matter. Where the theory agrees with such an independent view, the theory receives a degree of empirical confirmation:

> . . . the theory entails not only that these sentences are true but that they will remain true under all significant rewritings of their non-logical parts. It is hard to imagine how a theory of meaning could fail to read a logic into its object language to this degree; and to the extent that it does, our intuitions of logical truth, equivalence and entailment may be called upon in constructing and testing the theory. (Davidson 1967a, p. 318)

The final question remaining is Qu3, 'Which theory of meaning is adequate?' We are now in a position to see why Davidson thinks that a Tarskian truth theory for a language is a theory of meaning for that language.

To summarize, Davidson makes the following four key claims:

Davidson's key claims about meaning

(A) A truth theory for a language L should entail all sentences of L obtainable from the following schema:

  SCHEMA   's' is true if and only if p

by replacing 's' with a structural description of a sentence of L, and 'p' with that sentence.

(B) The truth theory thereby gives the truth condition for each sentence of L.

(C) In doing so, the truth theory thereby gives the meaning of each sentence of L.

(D) To have that truth theory is to know what it is for any sentence of L to be true, 'and this amounts, in one good sense, we can give to the phrase, to understanding the language' (Davidson 1967a, p. 24).

---

4. Problems facing Davidson's programme

In this section, we will consider a series of problems facing Davidson's programme. We will also assess to what extent his programme can meet them.

The extensionality objection

If the following sentence is true:

  (3)   Sentence S (as used by some speaker) means that p

then a sentence of the following form is true:

  (4) S is true if and only if p.

But is the converse true? Suppose that our truth theory for English entails the following sentence:

(5) 'Snow is white' is true if and only if snow is white.

Now 'Grass is green' and 'Snow is white' are materially equivalent: either both are true or both are false. So, we can substitute the former for the latter on the right-hand side of (5). This results in

(6) 'Snow is white' is true if and only if grass is green.

Yet, whereas (5) correctly specifies the meaning of 'snow is white', (6) does not. The problem generalizes: Davidson's programme seems committed to saying that all materially equivalent sentences have the same meaning. All true sentences will have the same meaning as one another, and all false sentences will have the same meaning as one another. (See Reeves 1974, p. 356 and Chihara 1975, pp. 12–14 for developments of this problem.)

Davidson took the lesson of this objection to be that it is only the members of a privileged subset of T-sentences that generate corresponding sentences about meaning:

> A theory of truth will yield interpretations only if its T-sentences state truth conditions in terms that may be treated as 'giving the meaning' of object language sentences. Our problem is to find constraints on a theory strong enough to guarantee that it can be used for interpretation. (Davidson 1974, p. 150)

But how is Davidson to single out the desired subset? He makes a number of attempts at this. We will consider them next.

The appeal to laws

One response that Davidson makes is to say that what marks out biconditionals such as (5) is that they are derived from empirical theories of English speakers' linguistic behaviour and that they are law-like sentences. That is, these sentences are statements of laws of nature. Davidson puts the point as follows:

> Sentences of the theory are empirical generalizations about speakers, and so must be not only true but lawlike. "'Snow is white' is true if and only if grass is green" presumably is not a law, since it does not support appropriate counterfactuals. (Davidson 1967a, p. 26, note added in 1982. See also Davidson 1976)

The idea is that a sentence such as (5) is not only true, but is a statement of a law of nature. There is a law-like connection between snow's being white and the truth of the sentence 'Snow is white'. By contrast, a sentence such as (6) may be true, but it is not a statement of a law of nature. There is no law-like connection between grass's being green and the truth of the sentence 'Snow is white'.

This response faces a number of difficulties. First, given the conventional aspect of language, T-sentences are not statements of laws of nature. It seems to be a convention that, in English, 'snow' means *snow*. It is not a law of nature that, in English. 'snow' means *snow*. A *fortiori*, it is not a law of nature that 'Snow is white' is true in English if and only if snow is white.

Some philosophers think that it is not a convention but a conceptual truth that 'Grass is green' is true *in English* if and only if grass is green. Whether or not they are correct, their view does not entail that T-sentences are statements of laws of nature (Fodor and Lepore 1992, pp. 85–6).

Second, even if we assume that T-sentences are statements of laws of nature, this will not distinguish between those truth theories that are meaning theories and those that are not. Consider a truth theory that entails (7):

(7) 'Snow is white' is true if and only if snow is white and $7 + 5 = 12$.

The right-hand side of (7) is materially equivalent to the right-hand side of (5). But, the right-hand side of (7) does not give the meaning of 'Snow is white'. Nevertheless, the right-hand side of (7) is also law-like. It is a law of nature that snow is white and $7 + 5 = 12$, given that it is a law of nature that snow is white.

Here is another example. Suppose that truth theory T_1 entails (8):

(8) 'The gas is ammonia' is true in English if and only if the gas is ammonia.

and that truth theory T_2 entails (9):

(9) 'The gas is ammonia' is true in English if and only if the gas is $NH3$.

Either both (8) and (9) are statements of laws of nature or neither are. Suppose that they both are. Nevertheless, the right-hand side of (9) does not specify the meaning of the sentence named on its left-hand side.

The appeal to canonical proofs

A second response that Davidson makes to the problem of extensionality is that we should consider not just which T-sentences a truth theory entails, but also how the theory entails them. According to this response, a truth theory that is a theory of meaning should entail T-sentences by means of the linguistic structure of the sentences named on the left-hand side of the T-sentences. The truth theory should show that the semantic properties of the sentence are determined by the semantic properties of its component expressions plus the sentence's syntactic structure. By giving the truth conditions of the sentences named on the left-hand side of T-sentence in this way, the sentences on the right-hand side give the meaning of those sentences named on the left-hand side.

What is then wrong with sentences such as (6)? Davidson's response is that any truth theory which entails (6), but which takes sentences to have a compositional semantics, will assign the wrong truth conditions to other sentences in which 'snow' and 'white' occur. For instance, it will assign the wrong truth conditions to sentences such as 'That is snow' and 'That is white'. It will claim that 'That is white' is true if and only if that is green. More generally:

> The fact that each axiom of a truth theory has its impact upon an infinite number of T-sentences does indeed have the consequence that it is difficult for counterfeit theories to pass the test. (Evans and McDowell 1976, p. xv)

This response, however, has a dubious consequence. It has the consequence that there could not be a language that lacked a compositional structure. According to the response, it is partly because of similarities between the structures of 'Snow is white' and 'That is snow' that the former means that snow is white. More generally, unless each sentence of a language has such structural similarities to other sentences of the language, then none of them would have determinate truth conditions. But that consequence is dubious because it does seem possible for a language to lack a compositional structure. Consider a linguistic community whose members would say 'Alpha' whenever we would say 'Snow is white', who would say 'Beta' whenever we would say 'Grass is green', who would say 'Gamma' whenever we would say 'That is snow' and so on. 'Alpha', 'Beta', 'Gamma' and the rest are unstructured expressions. If such a language is possible, compositionality is not necessary for solving the extensionality problem (Fodor and Lepore 1992, pp. 65–6).

Nor is compositionality sufficient. First, it can rule out 'Grass is green' as providing the truth condition of 'Snow is white' only because 'snow' and 'grass' are not co-extensive: they do not apply to exactly the same things. The appeal to compositionality does not help in cases where expressions are co-extensive but differ in meaning, such as with the expressions 'triangular' (i.e. having exactly three internal angles) and 'trilateral' (i.e. having exactly three sides). Consider a truth theory which entailed the following T-sentence:

(10) 'Each face of a pyramid is triangular' is true in English if and only if each face of a pyramid is trilateral.

Sentence (10) is true. It also meets the compositionality requirement because, even if 'triangular' and 'trilateral' occur in demonstrative sentences, 'This is triangular' is true if and only if this (same object) is trilateral. Nevertheless, (10) does not give the meaning of 'Each face of a pyramid is triangular'.

Second, suppose that (11) is a T-sentence of a certain truth theory:

(11) 'Snow is white' is true in English if and only if snow is white.

Now (11) entails (12):

(12) 'Snow is white' is true in English if and only if snow is white and all mice are mice.

Sentence (12) is also a T-sentence entailed by the truth theory. Where (12) differs from (11) is that it includes a logical truth as one of the conjuncts on its right-hand side. Both (11) and (12) are true, yet only (11) correctly states the meaning of 'Snow is white'. Moreover, citing the truth conditions of demonstrative sentences does not help because, although 'This is snow' is true if and only if this is snow, it is also true if and only if this is snow and all mice are mice.

Davidson thinks that such cases can be excluded by requiring that the T-sentences of a truth theory follow from its axioms by 'canonical proofs' (Davidson 1970, 1974). These canonical proofs would be from biconditional to biconditional via (and only via) the base clauses of a Tarskian truth definition. (12), however, is derivable only by additional logical machinery such as the logical truth that all cats are cats.

A difficulty with this rejoinder is that the original problem as much affects the axioms of a truth theory as its theorems. For instance, a truth theory could take as an axiom:

$(\forall x)$ (x satisfies 'is white') if and only if (x is white and all mice are mice).

Sentence (12) is derivable from that axiom by a canonical proof, and so the problem re-emerges (Quine 1977, p. 226).

The appeal to radical interpretation

A third response that Davidson makes is to place constraints on which truth theories are theories of meaning that are drawn from considerations to do with radical interpretation. These are considerations concerning our understanding the language of newly encountered ('alien') speakers. According to Davidson, the meaning of a sentence that replaces *s* in SCHEMA is not given by a single biconditional – by the appropriate substitution instance of SCHEMA – but is given by the truth theory as a whole. We can specify the meaning of a sentence in a language only by specifying the meaning of all the sentences in that language:

> If sentences depend for their meaning on their structure, and we understand the meaning of each item in the structure only as an abstraction from the totality of sentences in which it features, then we can give the meaning of any sentence (or word) only by giving the meaning of every sentence (and word) in the language. Frege said that only in the context of a sentence does a word have meaning; in the same vein he might have added that only in the context of the language does a sentence (and therefore a word) have meaning. (Davidson 1967a, p. 22)

The first claim made in the above quote, however, is dubious. It entails that a novice could not learn the meaning of a sentence in a language without learning the meaning of every sentence in the language. That consequence is false. Someone learning English might learn the meaning of (say) 'Elephants have trunks' without learning (say) 'Petrology is the study of rocks'. (For further criticism, see Vermazen 1971, pp. 542–3 and Reeves 1974, pp. 348–9.) The topic of radical translation is an important one in Davidson's philosophy of language, and we will return to it in §5 below.

The appeal to the indeterminacy of translation

A further response of Davidson's draws upon Quine's claim that there is no fact of the matter about how a sentence should be translated. (This is Quine's thesis of the indeterminacy of translation: Quine 1960, chapter 2. The thesis was discussed in Chapter 8 §§4–6.) Suppose we want to translate the speech of aliens. Quine claims that all of the evidence about how those aliens behave or are disposed to behave does not single out any one potential translation as uniquely correct. Suppose that we think of a truth theory for a language as a manual for translating from the object language to the meta-language. In parallel fashion, Davidson claims that all the evidence that we could gather on those aliens' behaviour and behavioural dispositions does not single out any one potential translation as uniquely correct. To take sentences (5) and (6) again, all of the evidence we could gather is compatible with a truth theory that translates 'Snow is white' as meaning that *snow is white*, but also with a truth theory that translates 'snow is white' as meaning that *grass is green*. Neither truth theory is singled out by the evidence as uniquely correct.

What should we make of this response? To defend a philosophical theory from an objection, we should appeal only to claims that are less controversial than the theory we are seeking to defend. To appeal to Quine's indeterminacy thesis, however, is to appeal to something even more controversial than Davidson's theory of meaning. Moreover, Quine does distinguish between standard and anomalous translations: he recommends that we work with our current translation manual because it is instrumentally useful (rather than correct). Accordingly, he would accept a translation of 'Snow is white' as meaning that *snow is white* and would reject one that translated it as meaning that *grass is green*. So, the lessons that Quine draws from his thesis conflict with those that Davidson wants from it. (For further discussion, see Reeves 1974, pp. 350–1.)

An objection from the nature of meaning

Davidson's programme requires that, for each language, there is a truth theory that shows how the meaning of each sentence of that language is determined by the meaning of its sub-sentential expressions and by the sentence's syntactic structure. It has been questioned, however, whether 'linguistic meaning is something which can be captured in an explicit statement' (Morris 2007, p. 192). A parallel is drawn with the case of works of art. Works of art are meaningful. The meaning of an art work is determined by the meaning of its parts. But 'we do not in general think that the significance of a work of art can be captured in an explicit statement' (Morris 2007, p. 192).

This objection assumes that works of art have meaning in the same sense in which words or sentences do. That assumption is mistaken. A sentence's meaning determines what the truth condition of that sentence is. An art work, however, does not have a truth condition. A painting or a film or a sculpture is not true or false. It does not bear inferential relations to anything: it does not entail and it is not entailed by anything. Similarly, a video installation or a textile art work cannot be a premise or a conclusion of an argument. None of these things has propositional content. The sense in which an art work has meaning is the sense in which it can be aesthetically significant or valuable, or it is the sense in which the work resonates with a viewer. It may be that this kind of meaning cannot be captured in an explicit statement. But, since it is not the same kind of meaning as words and sentences have, no case has been made here against Davidson's programme.

The problem of testability

Since T-sentences are theorems of a Tarskian truth theory, their right-hand sides are expressed in a regimented language. Moreover, as we saw with Davidson's explication of action sentences in §3, the right-hand sides of T-sentences may involve surprising formulations. It is then difficult to see how T-sentences can be empirically testable consequences of a truth theory of a natural language, since it is difficult to judge the truth values of such sentences (Stich 1976, pp. 216–18; Blackburn 1984, p. 289). Yet, even if these features of T-sentences diminish their testability, they do not eradicate it (Lycan 1984, chapter 2 §1). T-sentences can still be tested against our pre-theoretical beliefs about what entails what, about what has to exist for the left-hand side of T-sentences to be true and so forth, even if we need philosophical training to understand their right-hand sides.

The problem of demonstratives

How should we give the truth conditions for sentences such as 'I am hungry' or 'That is red'? What is special about these sentences is that they include indexical or demonstrative expressions such as 'I' or 'that'. A token of such a sentence has a truth value only if certain contextual factors are specified, such as who the utterer of the sentence is, what time it was uttered at and so on. In response, Davidson treats the truth of a sentence containing a demonstrative as involving a relation between a sentence, a speaker and a time. The truth conditions of our examples would then be given as follows:

(13) 'I am hungry' is true as (potentially) spoken by person p at time t if and only if p is hungry at t.

(14) 'That is red' is true as (potentially) spoken by p at t if and only if the object demonstrated by p at t is red at t.

Notice, however, how the specification of the truth conditions of these sentences differs from the simple form presented by SCHEMA, namely:

(SCHEMA) 's' is true if and only if p

Evidently, SCHEMA needs to be revised to accommodate cases involving those sentences containing demonstratives (Chihara 1975, p. 7).

Moreover, we should not take the examples of (13) and (14) to license such things as (15):

(15) 'It is raining here now' is true as spoken by Jack at noon if and only if it is raining where Jack spoke at noon.

The problem with (15) is that Jack may not know that he is Jack (since he may be suffering from amnesia) or he may not know that it is noon when he is speaking (Perry 1979). So, in the case of T-sentences about demonstrative sentences, 'the right side of the biconditional never translates the sentence for which it is giving the truth conditions' (Davidson 1976, p. 175). Nevertheless, those T-sentences can be informative about the corresponding demonstrative sentences, and their right-hand side will be 'systematically related' to the meaning of the sentence named on their left-hand side (Davidson 1969, p. 46). (For other concerns facing Davidson's account of demonstrative sentences, see Blackburn 1984, pp. 298–9.)

The problem of ambiguous sentences

How should we give the truth conditions for sentences such as 'Jack is sitting by a bat' or 'Jo is holding a flute'? What is special about these sentences is that they are examples of lexical ambiguity. Since the sentences contain an ambiguous word, the sentences themselves are ambiguous. Giving the truth condition of the first example as:

(16) 'Jack is sitting by a bat' is true if and only if Jack is sitting by an artefact designed for striking balls

would be mistaken. Someone might utter 'Jack is sitting by a bat' when Jack was sitting by a member of a species of small, winged mammals, and what that person said would not be false if Jack was not sitting by an artefact designed for striking balls. Davidson says this about the problem of ambiguity:

> As long as ambiguity does not affect grammatical form, and can be translated, ambiguity for ambiguity, into the meta-language, a truth definition will not tell us any lies (Davidson 1967a, p. 30).

The idea here seems to be that the truth condition of a sentence containing an ambiguous term is given by a sentence in the meta-language that contains a corresponding ambiguous term. To take our earlier example, we would then specify the truth condition of an ambiguous sentence in the following way:

(17) 'Jack is sitting by a bat' is true if and only if Jack is sitting by a bat.

But, consider the following problem case (Chihara 1975, p. 8):

(18) 'Few if any bats can be dropped from a ten-storey building without being damaged' is true as spoken by x at time y if and only if few if any bats can be dropped from a ten-storey building without being damaged.

There are circumstances in which we know that someone speaking at a certain time who uttered the sentence 'Few if any bats can be dropped from a ten-storey building without being damaged' is saying something true. Perhaps we know the speaker is someone who is a very reliable informant on the topics that he or she speaks on. So in those circumstances, we know that the left-hand side of (18) is true as spoken by some person at a certain time. Nevertheless, we would not know that the right-hand side of (18) is true unless we know what 'bat' means on that occasion of utterance. Now, if the right-hand side of (18) is disambiguated, the result will be a false biconditional. The reason for this was given in connection with (16) above. Alternatively, if the right-hand side of (18) is not disambiguated, we will be unable to test the truth of (18). (For further discussion of the problem of ambiguous sentences as it faces Davidson's programme, see Parsons 1973; Lycan 1984, chapter 2 §2; Cohen 1985.)

The problem of sentences which are not truth apt

Davidson takes a Tarskian truth theory for a language to provide a theory of meaning for that language. Whatever the prospects of his programme for sentences which can be true or false (i.e. that are truth apt), there are two problem cases. One concerns sentences that are not declarative in form: questions, commands, requests and the like. The other concerns sentences that are declarative in form but that (allegedly) are not truth apt. Ethical sentences are often taken to be examples of such sentences. On this view, such sentences express speakers' attitudes and are not used to make assertions (Ayer 1946, chapter 6).

Davidson's response to the first problem is similar to Frege's (see Chapter 4 §3). Frege distinguishes between the *sense* of a sentence – the aspect of the meaning of a sentence relevant to determining its truth conditions – and the *force* with which the sentence is uttered in a particular context – whether to make an assertion, or to put something up for consideration or to ask a question. Davidson also distinguishes between two features of sentences. There is the declarative component, which is truth apt. There is also a component which determines how the declarative component is to be taken. Davidson called this second component 'the mood-setter'. A further aspect of the truth theory specifies truth conditions for the mood-setters. In the case of a sentence such as 'Close the door!', the mood-setter is true if and only if the utterance has imperatival force. The content of the imperative is given by an indicative sentence for which there is a corresponding T-sentence. Davidson denies that there is a convention that a speaker's uttering a sentence in a certain mood (such as the imperatival mood) is what classifies a sentence as being of a certain kind (such as issuing an order). Instead, he claims that a mood-setter labels what kind of utterance a given utterance belongs to. For example, the sentence 'Mind your head' has the structure: 'My next utterance has imperatival force: you will mind your head'. (For further discussion of this topic, see Davidson 1979; Segal 1990; Lepore and Ludwig 2007, chapter 12.)

The second problem case concerns sentences which are declarative in form but which (allegedly) are not truth apt. A robust response to this problem case is to deny that there are any sentences having both features. In particular, the response maintains that if a sentence is declarative in form, it is truth apt. The argument for this claim is as follows. It is sufficient for a sentence to have a truth condition that there is a way of saying what the sentence says. Now we can use a declarative sentence to say what the sentence says. For example, we can say: 'Grass is green' is true if and only if grass is green. On the right-hand side of the biconditional, we use a sentence to say what the sentence named on the left-hand side says. We thereby use a declarative sentence to state its own truth condition. If a sentence has a truth condition, there is a condition under which the sentence is true. And that is to say that the sentence is truth apt.

This response has currency in some quarters (see, e.g. Morris 2007, p. 191; Lycan 2008, p. 119), but it remains controversial (see Jackson et al. 1994). It should also be noted that some philosophers have thought that noncognitivism about ethical sentences is compatible with the above response (see, e.g. Blackburn 1984, p. 196; Smith 1994). That too, however, is a controversial view (see Divers and Miller 1994).

To sum up, in this section we have seen a series of objections to Davidson's programme. Some of those objections, such as the testability objection and the objection from the nature of meaning, seem to have good answers. But others remain, notably the extensionality objection, even though Davidson deploys a wealth of ingenious attempts to solve them. The persistence of this objection, in particular, indicates its seriousness for Davidson's programme. In the case of still other objections, such as the problem of ambiguous sentences and the problem of demonstratives, any complications which Davidson's programme has to undergo in order to meet them diminishes the appeal of the programme.

5. Radical interpretation

Davidson's central claim about language is that it is publicly available:

> Language is in its nature . . . intersubjective; what someone else's words mean on a given occasion is always something that we can in principle learn from public clues (Davidson 1982, p. 174).
>
> The theory of truth we must presume lies in available facts about how speakers use the language. When I say available, I mean publicly available – available not only in principle, but available in fact to anyone who is capable of understanding the speaker or speakers of the language. (Davidson 1982, p. 182. See also Davidson 1974, p. 128; Quine 1992, p. 38)

Just as the meanings of sentences are publicly available, so too, Davidson says, are the contents of propositional attitudes (Davidson 1982, p. 200). The view that emerges is that someone is saying something only if other people can understand what is being said and that someone is thinking something only if other people can tell what is being thought.

The above view needs clarifying. One issue to be addressed concerns how stringent or otherwise the sense of 'can' is. The less stringent its sense is, the less significant the view is. Suppose you devise a code. However intricate the code is and however circumspect you are in not revealing it, the code can be broken. You can choose, by whim or by a change of policy, to divulge it and explain it to other people by using a language that they already understand. Alternatively, a Rosetta stone can fall out of the sky with the code revealed on it. Again, even if you keep your thoughts to yourself, you can choose to divulge them to others using a language that they already understand. If Davidson's view is to be noteworthy, it needs to involve a notion of public availability more demanding than the one which these examples are working with. The question then is how it is to be spelt out and how it is to be defended as appropriate.

Another issue to be addressed concerns the connection between language use and communication. We can agree that if the sentences of a language are used to communicate, other people can come to understand what those sentences mean. That, however, is an uncontentious fact about what it is to communicate. Communication is always communication with someone, and to communicate with someone is to get them to understand what you mean. Moreover, there is a question about whether a language might be used to serve some purpose other than communication. For example, it seems possible that a language might be devised for the purpose of formulating the inferences that its users make. (This issue was canvassed when we discussed Grice's theory of meaning in Chapter 6 §6.) Inference is a ubiquitous feature of our lives. To express a chain of reasoning and to keep track of the steps and principles involved, someone might want to formulate it in words. Yet, if the language is not used for communication (and perhaps that person has another language for the purposes of communication), it need not be the case that other people can come to understand what the sentences of that language mean.

Davidson utilizes his view about the publicity of language in two ways. First, he thinks that it constrains the kind of evidence that a theory of the meaning of a language should account for. Just by observing the behaviour of speakers, and, in particular, by establishing which sentences they hold true, an observer should be able to work out what the best truth theory (and so what the meaning theory) of that language is. Davidson called this procedure 'radical interpretation'. It is a constraint invoked to single out those truth theories of languages that are meaning theories of those languages.

Second, Davidson takes his view about the publicity of language to have a striking anti-sceptical consequence. One form of scepticism is found in Descartes' writings. It claims that few of our beliefs are justified. Perhaps our beliefs about the contents of our present conscious experiences are true, and perhaps also our beliefs about certain rudimentary claims in logic and mathematics are true. Aside from them, however, all of our other beliefs are open to doubt. We could be deceived by an evil demon into thinking that there is an external world populated by other human beings, squirrels, trees and the like. The sceptic claims that although we may have a wealth of beliefs about the external world, since we cannot rule out his evil demon possibility, none of those beliefs are justified.

According to Davidson, the sceptic is mistaken (Davidson 1977, p. 201). Davidson's route to this conclusion concerns what is involved in interpreting speakers. In order to interpret the sentences of someone, we need to make various assumptions about that person. We need to assume that they are coherent, and this involves an assumption that they follow some laws of logic. We also need to assume that what they are saying is true, at least by our own lights:

> We will have to assume that in simple or obvious cases most of [a speaker's] assents are to true, and his dissents from false, sentences – an inevitable assumption since the alternative is unintelligible (Davidson 1970, p. 62).
>
> Widespread agreement is the only possible background against which disputes and mistakes can be interpreted. Making sense of the utterances and behaviour of others, even their most aberrant behaviour, requires us to find a great deal of reason and truth in them. To see too much unreason on the part of others is simply to undermine our ability to understand what it is they are so unreasonable about. (Davidson 1974, p. 153)

Davidson takes it to be a principle about how to interpret the speech of others that we should maximize the degree of agreement between what we believe and what they believe. We should interpret other speakers as charitably as possible. Neil Wilson called this 'the principle of charity' (Wilson 1959). Maximizing the area of agreement between them and us in turn involves interpreting as many of their beliefs as possible as being true. It follows that their beliefs (and so ours) do not involve massive error, contrary to the sceptic.

In §5, we saw that Davidson thinks that we can be in a position to know that a given T-sentence is true without knowing whether the sentence named on its left-hand side is true. Part of the reason which Davidson offers is that 'the fact that speakers of a language hold a sentence to be true (under observed circumstances) [is] prima facie evidence that it is true under those circumstances' (Davidson 1974, p. 152). The argument from charity explains why Davidson thinks that there is such a fact. Truth conditions should be assigned to sentences of a language L under the constraint that most of the sentences held by speakers of L are true.

Nevertheless, Davidson's argument faces a series of queries. People's beliefs about things that are not directly connected to observable events are beliefs which we do not assume are mostly likely to be true. We do not assume that the ancient Greeks' beliefs about the structure of matter or the origin of stars are mostly true. Davidson himself admits that 'it makes sense to accept intelligible error and to make allowance for the relative likelihood of various kinds of mistake' (Davidson 1974, p. 136). The ancient Greeks' erroneous beliefs about stars and matter are explicable: even though their theories were false, the false consequences of those theories were not obvious and many of their observable consequences were obviously true. Little wonder, then, why they continued to believe false theories about unobserved things (Grandy 1973, p. 443; Fodor and Lepore 1992, p. 101).

Furthermore, even if we should interpret a speaker in such a way as to maximize agreement between his or her beliefs and ours, how does it follow that the beliefs we share are true? Granted that if we believe that p, we believe that p is true, but it does not follow that p is true. So, the fact that we share the belief that p with a speaker does not entail that p is true.

Davidson has a response to this query:

> For imagine . . . an interpreter who is omniscient about the world . . . The omniscient interpreter, using the same method as the fallible interpreter, finds the fallible speaker largely consistent and correct. By his own standards, of course, but since these are objectively correct, the fallible speaker is seen to be largely correct and consistent by objective standards. (Davidson 1989, p. 151. See also Davidson 1977, p. 201)

Davidson's response begs the question. It assumes an interpreter who is omniscient, and hence has no false beliefs. It further assumes that this interpreter will find 'the fallible speaker' (i.e. any speaker) 'largely consistent and correct'. Those assumptions indeed jointly entail that the speaker is largely consistent and correct. The problem is that both assumptions will obtain only in a case in which the speaker is not largely mistaken. In any other case if the interpreter is omniscient, he or she will not find the speaker 'largely consistent and correct'. Or, if the interpreter finds the speaker 'largely consistent and correct', then he or she is not omniscient and shares many false beliefs with the speaker. The sceptical challenge is how we can rule out the possibility that the speaker is largely mistaken, and so that we are in a situation in which the assumptions do not both obtain. (For further criticisms of Davidson's argument, see McGinn 1977b; Vermazen 1983; Bennett 1985, p. 610; Craig 1990.)

Davidson also appeals to Wittgenstein's private language argument:

> The central argument against private languages is that, unless a language is shared, there is no way to distinguish between using the language correctly and using it incorrectly; only communication with another can supply an objective check. If only communication can provide a check on the correct use of words, only communication can supply a standard of objectivity in other domains. (Davidson 1991, p. 210)

The argument that Davidson sketches here seems to run as follows. Using a language requires that there is a distinction between correct and incorrect uses of it. That, in turn, requires that there is an objective check between the two kinds of uses. The only thing that can provide that check is communication. Hence, using a language requires that the language can be communicated.

A questionable step in that argument is the move from there being a distinction between correct and incorrect uses of a language to requiring that there is a way of checking these uses. It is open for us to reply that not every distinction needs to be accompanied by a way of checking that distinction. One way of seeing this is to suppose that, for every distinction, there is some way of checking that distinction. Now, what about the first such check? There is a distinction between correct and incorrect uses of running the check. So, there has to be a second kind of check (a check on checks) that distinguishes between the two uses. But now consider this second kind of check. There is a distinction between correct and incorrect uses of running *it*. So there has to be a third kind of check (a check on checks on checks). And we are launched on an infinite regress of kinds of checks. Now it may strike you as absurd that there has to be such an infinite series. It may seem to you that it can be a fact that there is a distinction between correct and incorrect uses of a check without there having to be a further check, let alone an infinite hierarchy of checks. But if you were to accept that view, you would be conceding that there can be a distinction without there having to be a way of checking that distinction. Yet, if that is so, there seems no reason why there cannot be a distinction between correct and incorrect uses of language, even if there is no way of checking these uses. It seems that Davidson would have to assume a verificationist principle to the effect that there is a distinction between As and Bs only if there is a way of checking which things are As and which Bs (see Ayer 1946, chapter 1).

But such a verificationist principle would itself need justification. (For an assessment of the principle, see Lycan 2008, chapter 8.)

A further line of argument that Davidson appeals to turns on considerations of how he thinks that a first language is learnt:

> What we learn first is to associate what in the end turn out to be one-word sentences ('Mama', 'No', 'Dog', 'Blue') with situations, events, objects and their features. Soon the child learns the magical power of making sounds adults find appropriate and hence reward. These are only preliminaries to fully fledged talk and thought . . . [but] these primitive relations between two people in the presence of stimuli from a shared world contain the kernel of ostensive learning. (Davidson 1998, p. 86)

The picture which Davidson sketches here takes language acquisition to originate with the association of rudimentary sentences with things in the speaker's environment. Since different speakers have access to the same environment, they can make the same associations between words and things. For this reason, their languages are publicly accessible. Whether this picture is correct, however, is contentious. An alternative account sees language learning as a matter of hypothesis formation and confirmation. When a language learner hears sentences, she forms hypotheses about what those sentences mean. When those hypotheses receive some confirmation (by positive reinforcement by speakers or by the environment), the learner's beliefs acquire a corresponding degree of support about what those sentences mean. (We addressed this issue in Chapter 6 §5 when we discussed whether Grice's theory of meaning is psychologically plausible. In addition to the references given there, see also Fodor 1975, pp. 34–42, 58–9 for a discussion of some of the relevant psycholinguistic literature.)

To sum up this section, according to Davidson, nothing can be a language unless it can be radically interpreted. That is, something is a language only if the truth theory for that language can be identified by publicly available evidence. Now it may be that, given observations plus relevant background assumptions, linguists can reliably infer to the best truth theory of a language. It does not follow, however, that from observations alone – by means of radical interpretation – linguists can reliably infer to the best truth theory of a language. So it does not follow that radical interpretation is possible. (See Blackburn 1984, chapter 2 §4 and chapter 8 §4; Weiss 2010, chapter 7 for further discussion.)

6. Conclusion

Let us turn to the questions raised in the book's introduction. First and foremost, Davidson's programme addresses (Q5): What is the relation between meaning and truth? According to Davidson, as a first approximation, a Tarskian theory of truth for a language provides a theory of meaning for that language. (We have seen that Davidson subsequently adds various constraints to that initial proposal.) Given his answer to that question, his answers to various other questions automatically follow.

(Q2) asked: What gives words and sentences their particular meanings? Davidson's answer is that the meaning of a particular sentence consists in its truth condition, and the meaning of a particular word consists in the contribution it makes to determining the truth conditions of the sentences that it occurs in.

(Q3) asked; What is it to understand a sentence or word? Davidson's answer is that a Tarskian truth theory of a language gives the meaning of every sentence of that language by entailing the T-sentence of each sentence. By knowing those T-sentences, and thereby knowing the truth conditions of sentences and the contributions component expressions make to the truth conditions of sentences in which they figure, a speaker understands his or her language.

Davidson also thinks that his theory of meaning answers (Q7): How can a theory of the compositional nature of sentence meaning be given? Davidson's answer is that a Tarskian truth theory shows how, in an extensional language, the truth conditions of complex sentences are a function of the truth conditions of their component sentences, and it also shows how the truth conditions of atomic sentences are a function of the satisfaction conditions of their components.

With all of the above answers in place, Davidson is well advanced in addressing the very general question posed by (Q10): How can there be a systematic philosophical study of natural language? His programme is supposed to provide a detailed answer to that question. Interestingly, Davidson takes the execution of that programme – the formulation and testing of semantic theories – to be an empirical matter. Semanticists are taken to be scientists who seek to discover truths about particular natural languages. Their theories are tested against empirical data, such as speakers' unreflective word usage, the intuitions they unreflectively accept as valid, their intuitions about grammaticality and synonymy and so on. Theories are then selected according to whether they provide the best potential explanation of the phenomena, in the same fashion as any scientific theory is selected for its providing the best explanation of certain phenomena.

It is important to be clear about what Davidson's programme sets out to do and what it does not set out to do, otherwise we are in danger of making misguided criticisms of it. Take (Q3): What is it to understand a language? Davidson's programme seeks to describe something (sentences' truth conditions) which, if known, would produce such understanding. There are, however, other important general questions about language, such as: How does a speaker acquire a language? How does a speaker store or represent it? How does a speaker put his or her linguistic knowledge to use? Those are good questions, but Davidson's programme does not seek to answer them (Lepore 1982, p. 290). Hence, his programme is not committed to saying that speakers store linguistic information in the form of T-sentences or that they construct proofs of T-sentences when they understand sentences.

Davidson's programme revitalized the philosophy of language. It connects issues to do with meaning with issues to do with truth in a fashion which had not been done since Frege. It also connects issues about the nature of language with other traditional philosophical issues to do with logic, epistemology, mind and action. In his efforts to show that a truth theory for a language is a theory of meaning for that language, Davidson is led to consider how truth theories can be empirically supported. This, in turn, raises issues in the philosophies of mind and action, and that broadens the scope of Davidson's programme. On a more negative note, however, it is not clear whether the epistemological considerations concerning radical interpretation have an important role to play in the philosophy of language.

Questions for discussion

Question 1

Davidson says that T-sentences (such as: 'Snow is white' is true if and only if snow is white) state empirical claims and can be used to test truth theories. Yet those sentences seem to be true because of their form, and, if that is so, how can they be used to provide empirical tests of truth theories? (Cf. Lepore 1982, pp. 287–8).

Question 2

Davidson's programme relies on the idea that sentences have truth conditions. Does this require that a philosophically informative or 'substantive' theory, such as the correspondence theory of truth, can be given for truth? Would failure to provide such a theory undermine Davidson's programme? (Cf. Dummett 1959; Bar-on et al. 2000).

Question 3

Davidson's programme emphasizes the claim that sentence meaning is compositional: that the meaning of a sentence is determined by the meanings of its component expressions together with the syntactic structure of the sentence. Yet not all sentence meanings seem to be formed compositionally. Consider the sentences 'He squeezed her hand' and 'He squeezed a lemon'. Here the meaning of the complement ('her hand', 'a lemon') seems to affect the meaning of the verb in each sentence. Consider also the expressions 'red wine', 'red hair' and 'red face'. Here the meaning of the noun seems to affect the meaning of the adjective in each case. The lesson seems to be that when words are combined, they affect one another's meaning. Is this reason to abandon the claim that language is compositional?

Question 4

What does knowledge of a sentence's truth condition consist in? If this knowledge were explicit, it would seem to consist just in knowledge of the corresponding T-sentence. But could not someone do that even if he or she did not understand the sentence? If the knowledge were implicit (knowledge that a person need not be able to formulate), it would have to consist in an ability to decide, in principle, whether or not the sentence's truth condition is satisfied. But is it plausible to think that you have such an ability in the case of every sentence you understand? (Dummett 1991, chapters 4 and 14).

Further reading

Davidson, Donald (1967a) 'Truth and Meaning', (1969) 'True to the Facts', (1970) 'Semantics for Natural Languages', and (1973) 'Radical Interpretation' in his *Inquiries into Truth and Interpretation*.

Glüer, Kathrin (2012) 'Theories of Meaning and Truth Conditions' in Manuel Garciá-Carpintero and Max Kölbel (eds.) *The Continuum Companion to the Philosophy of Language*.

Lepore, Ernest and Kirk Ludwig (2007) *Donald Davidson's Truth Theoretic Semantics* especially chapter 1.

Lycan, William G. (2008) *Philosophy of Language* chapter 9.

—(2010) 'Direct Arguments for the Truth Conditions Theory of Meaning'.

Miller, Alexander *Philosophy of Language* chapter 8.

Morris, Michael (2007) *An Introduction to the Philosophy of Language* chapters 6 and 7.

Platts, Mark de Bretton (1979) *Ways of Meaning* chapters II and V §2.

Soames, Scott (2009) *Philosophical Essays volume I* essays 7 and 8.

Taylor, Kenneth (1998) *Truth and Meaning: An Introduction to the Philosophy of Language* chapter III.

10

Lewis on Intensional Theories of Meaning

1. Introduction

In Chapter 9, we considered Donald Davidson's programme in semantics. Davidson seeks to explicate sentence meaning in terms of the truth conditions of those sentences, where the truth conditions of the sentences of a language are assigned by a Tarskian truth theory for that language. We saw something of the promise that Davidson's programme enjoys but also various difficulties facing it. Some philosophers think that these difficulties can be avoided by basing semantic theory not on Tarskian truth theory but on modal logic: the logic of what is necessary and of what is possible. Necessary truth and possible truth (modal truth) is often construed in terms of truth at possible worlds. Accordingly, a programme known as 'possible worlds semantics' has been developed.

In Chapter 3 §1, a distinction was introduced between foundational and structural theories of meaning. Grice presents a foundational theory of meaning, whereas Frege and Davidson present structural theories of meaning. Possible worlds semantics is also a structural theory of meaning. A structural theory of meaning primarily seeks to answer the question 'What is the meaning of a certain sentence (for a particular speaker or group of speakers)'? It seeks to specify the meanings of the sentences of a language as used by some speaker or speakers, but without seeking to say why those sentences have those meanings.

Possible worlds semantics was originally formulated by a number of philosophers and logicians, notably Carnap (1956), Hintikka (1961, 1969), Kripke (1963), Lewis (1969, chapter 5, 1970) and Montague (1974). David Lewis is singled out here just because his work provides an accessible introduction to what soon became an increasingly sophisticated and technical research programme. (Anderson 1984 provides a valuable introduction to some of these technical developments.)

2. Intensional logic

To begin with, we should distinguish between extensional and non-extensional (or intensional) contexts. These are contexts in which expressions or sentences can occur. We investigated extensional contexts in Chapter 8 §2. Let us now turn to intensional contexts. Traditionally, two features have characterized intensional contexts. The first is failure of substitutivity of expressions with the same extension. Consider Eubulides' paradox of the Hooded Man. This paradox proceeds in the following way. Consider sentence (1):

(1) Ned does not know who the man under the hood is.

Suppose that (1) is true. Suppose that the man under the hood is in fact Ned's father. Then 'the man under the hood' and 'Ned's father' apply to the same person: they have the same extension. Substituting 'Ned's father' for 'the man under the hood' yields:

(2) Ned does not know who Ned's father is.

Although (1) is true, nevertheless (2) may be false. This tells us that (1) and (2) each involve intensional contexts. An expression of the form '*x* knows (or: does not know) ...' generates an intensional (or indirect) context. The substitution of expressions that occur within such a context with other co-referring expressions is not guaranteed to preserve the truth value of the sentence in question. (We first encountered this phenomenon in Chapter 3 §4 when we considered Frege's theory of indirect sense and reference.)

The other feature which is characteristic of intensional contexts is failure of existential generalization. (3) entails both (4) and (5):

(3) Jack rang the bell on Bagel's door.
(4) Someone rang the bell on Bagel's door.
(5) Jack rang the bell on someone's door.

If we regiment (4) and (5) using predicate logic, we obtain the following existential generalizations:

(4*) $(\exists x)$ (x rang the bell on Bagel's door).
   That is, there exists someone who rang the bell on Bagel's door.

(5*) $(\exists x)$ (Jack rang the bell on x's door).
   That is, there exists someone x such that Jack rang the bell on x's door.

(3), then, entails existential generalizations formed from (3) by replacing a singular term with an existential quantifier.

By contrast, consider the relation between (6) and (7):

(6) Zeus was worshipped by the Greeks as the father of the gods.
(7) Someone was worshipped by the Greeks as the father of the gods.

Regimenting (7) using predicate logic yields:

(7*) $(\exists x)$ (x was worshipped by the Greeks as the father of the gods).
   That is, there exists someone who was worshipped by the Greeks as the father of the gods.

On the face of it, (6) is an apparently true sentence describing something that the Greeks did, namely, worshipping Zeus as the father of the gods. (6), however, apparently entails (7). But regimenting (7) as (7*) shows that (7) is false. Zeus does not exist. So there exists no one who was worshipped by the Greeks as the father of the gods. So whereas we can existentially generalize on (3) to derive both (4) and (5), we cannot existentially generalize on (6) to derive (7). This failure of existential generalization tells us that (6) involves an intensional context. Specifically, it tells us that the expression 'was worshipped by' generates an intensional context. Forming an existential generalization by replacing the first term in a sentence of the form '. . . was worshipped by . . .' with a variable bound by an existential quantifier is not guaranteed to preserve the truth value of the sentence.

Other expressions which generate intensional contexts are propositional attitude verbs such as 'believes', 'imagines' or 'fears'. 'Knows' is a propositional attitude verb which, as we have seen, has the first characteristic of intensionality: failure of substitutivity of co-extensive terms. Notice, however, that it does not have the second characteristic of intensionality: failure of existential generalization. If Ned knows that Nate is around the corner, it follows that there exists something such that Ned knows that it is round the corner. Having the first characteristic of intensionality is taken to be a necessary and sufficient condition for a context to be an intensional context. It follows from the above that having the second characteristic is not a necessary condition for a context to be an intensional context. It is, however, sufficient for it to be an intensional context.

3. Possible worlds semantics

Modal logic extends the semantics for classical first-order predicate calculus. To begin with, let's look at classical first-order predicate calculus. The semantics for a first-order language assigns an interpretation to that language. This interpretation associates the language with a domain of individuals. The universal and existential quantifiers are taken to range over this domain. Each predicate in the language is associated with a certain set: each one-place predicate is associated with a set of individuals in the domain, each two-place predicate is associated with a set of ordered pairs of individuals in the domain and so on. We can then define, relative to such an interpretation, what it is for a sentence of the language to be true, what it is for a singular term to refer and what it is for an open formula to be satisfied by a sequence of individuals. The truth of a sentence is the truth of that sentence relative to the actual interpretation of the language. The interpretation will specify, for each singular term, the individual that it refers to. It will also specify, for each predicate letter, the set of ordered n-tuples of individuals in the domain which satisfy it.

Modal logic extends this type of truth definition to a richer language. It introduces the idea of a sentence being true in a possible world. An interpretation for such an enriched language is to be understood as follows. Each possible world is assigned a domain of individuals and an extension for each predicate. The interpretation will specify, for each singular term, the individual that it refers to each possible world. It will also specify, for each predicate, the set of ordered n-tuples of individuals in the domain which satisfy it in each possible world. Lastly, we specify which of the possible worlds in the interpretation represents the actual world. In this way, then, singular terms, predicates and sentences have an extension relative to a possible world. An assignment of an extension relative to a possible world can be thought of as a function from a world to an extension. Such an assignment or function is known as an *intension*. (For more on modal language and modal logic, see Melia 2003, chapter 2.)

Possible worlds semantics has much in common with Davidson's theory of meaning. Both take truth conditions to be central to the nature of meaning. Where they differ is that possible worlds semantics has a different view from Davidson of what truth conditions are. Here are its key claims.

A possible world is a condition in which a sentence is true. A sentence which is possibly true is true in some condition. It is a sentence which is true in some possible world. A sentence which is not possibly true (i.e. which is impossible) is true in no condition; it is true in no possible world. A sentence which is necessary is true in all conditions; it is true in all possible worlds. A sentence which is contingent is true in some condition and is not true in some other condition. It is a sentence which is true in some possible world but not true in some other possible world.

A sentence's truth condition is the set of possible worlds in which it is true. On the assumption that a sentence's meaning is its truth condition, this meaning – or *intension*, as it is known – is then the set of worlds in which it is true. For example, the meaning of the English sentence 'A cat is purring' is the set of worlds in which some cat is purring. The proposition which 'A cat is purring' expresses is identified with that set.

Sentence meaning

The meaning of a sentence = the set of possible worlds in which that sentence is true = the proposition which the sentence expresses.

The members of any pair of synonymous sentences are true in the same set of worlds. The members of any pair of non-synonymous sentences differ in truth value at some world. One sentence entails another if and only if there is no world in which the first sentence is true and the second sentence is false.

A sentence is ambiguous if and only if there is a world in which the sentence is both true and false, without contradiction. (This arises because the sentence expresses more than one proposition, and one of those propositions is false, whereas the other is true at that world.)

If the meaning of a sentence is identical to the actual and possible conditions in which it is true, what is it to understand a sentence? Consider two worlds. In world A, the door is open. In world B, the door is closed. Suppose the sentence 'The door is closed' is true at world A but false at world B. Knowing that the sentence is true at A but false at B is what distinguishes someone who understands the meaning of the sentence from someone who does not (Cresswell 1985 introduction and chapter 5). Consider the following sentence:

(8) The U.S. President is a Democrat.

Sentence (8) is true in any given world if and only if whoever is the US President at that world is a member of the set of Democrats at that world. To understand the meaning of 'the U.S. President' is to know who would be the US President under various possible conditions. Likewise, to understand the predicate 'is a Democrat' is to know who would be a Democrat under various possible conditions. So, if we understand those meanings, we know whether (8) is true in any given world. That is, we know the set of worlds in which (8) is true. And that, according to possible worlds semantics, is to know what (8) means – to know which proposition (8) expresses. To know whether (8) is true – that is, to know whether (8) is true in the actual world – involves something additional. It would require knowing whether the actual world is a member of the set of worlds in which (8) is true.

As we have just seen, possible worlds semantics assigns meanings to the component expressions of sentences and not just to complete sentences. These expressions combine compositionally to determine a sentence's truth condition. Let's see what account possible worlds semantics provides for the meaning of names, predicates and predicate adverbs, respectively.

The meaning of a singular term (such as a name or definite description) is given by what the term refers to under various conditions. The meaning of a singular term is a function which specifies, for each possible world, what the term refers to in that world. For example, the meaning of the name 'Barack Obama' is a function from (e.g.) the actual world to a certain person at the actual world, namely, Barack Obama.

A distinction can be drawn between different kinds of singular terms. In Kripke's terminology, the name 'Barack Obama' is a rigid designator: it picks out the same person at every world in which it refers (Kripke 1972, pp. 74ff). This means that the term, which we use to refer to some object in the actual world, refers to the same object in every world in which that object exists. By contrast, a definite description such as 'the 44th U.S. President' is not a rigid designator. It is a function from the actual world to Barack Obama. But, in a possible world which is very similar to the actual world except that John McCain won the 2008 presidential election, the description is a function from that world to McCain, not Obama.

These matters can be summarized as follows:

Singular term meaning		
Function	*Argument*	*Value*
The meaning of a singular term	Possible world w	What the term refers to at w

The meaning of a predicate is given by what the predicate applies to under various conditions. The meaning of a predicate is a function which specifies, for each possible world, what set of things at that world the predicate applies to. For example, the meaning of the predicate 'is asleep' is a function from each world to the set of things which are asleep at that world. So 'is asleep' applies, at the actual world, to the things that are actually asleep, whereas at another world it applies to those things that are asleep at that world – a set of things which may or may not differ from the set of things that are actually asleep. In summary form:

Predicate meaning I		
Function	*Argument*	*Value*
The meaning of a predicate	Possible world w	The set of things at w which the predicate applies to

Possible worlds semantics provides another, but equivalent, way of thinking about the meaning of predicates. It runs as follows. A one-place predicate, such as 'is asleep', combines with a singular term to form a sentence. More generally, an n-place predicate combines with n singular terms to form a sentence.

The meaning of a predicate can also be understood as a function from the meaning of each singular term to the meaning of a sentence formed out of that singular term and that predicate. For example, the meaning of 'is asleep' is a function from the meaning of (e.g.) the name 'Ned' to the meaning of the sentence 'Ned is asleep'. In summary form:

Predicate meaning II		
Function	*Argument*	*Value*
The meaning of a predicate	The meaning of a singular term	The meaning of a sentence

Our two tables, predicate meaning I and II, are compatible. They concern the same function, the meaning of a predicate. They differ in what they take as the argument for that function. The table for predicate meaning I takes as its arguments possible worlds. The table for predicate meaning II takes as its arguments the meanings of singular terms. The same function maps these different arguments to different values. In the first table, the values are sets of things at possible worlds. In the second table, the values are the meanings of sentences.

Lastly, a predicate adverb (such as 'slow') is a function from a predicate ('is a runner') to a different predicate ('is a slow runner'). In summary form:

Predicate adverb meaning		
Function	*Argument*	*Value*
The meaning of a predicate adverb	The meaning of a predicate	The meaning of a predicate

In general, then, possible worlds semantics seeks to account for meanings in terms of functions taking individuals or functions to further functions. These functions are set-theoretic constructions out of possible worlds and possible individuals. These constructions form an extensive domain as they include sets of possible individuals, sets of those sets and so on. Richard Montague developed a very sophisticated hierarchy of higher-order intensions as part of his project to translate sentences of natural language into a system of intensional logic in which logical properties and relations are defined over formulas. These formulas are construed as unambiguous translations of English sentences. (See Montague's papers 'Universal Grammar' and 'The Proper Treatment of Quantification in English' in his 1974 collection.)

4. Advantages of possible worlds semantics

Possible worlds semantics provides an elegant and economical semantic theory. The only notions it needs are those provided by modal logic. Moreover, Jaakko Hintikka suggests that

> the only entities needed in the so-called theory of meaning are, in many interesting cases, and perhaps even in all cases, merely what is required in order for the expressions of our language to be able to refer. (Hintikka 1969, p. 87)

Hintikka's point can be understood as follows. Following Quine, a distinction can be drawn between the theory of meaning and the theory of reference (Quine 1961). The theory of meaning concerns such notions as meaning, proposition, synonymy, analyticity and entailment. The theory of reference concerns such notions as reference, naming, truth and extension. How are we to understand the notions in the theory of meaning? As we saw in Chapter 8, Quine was pessimistic about whether those notions are so much as intelligible. If, however, we introduce possible worlds semantics, we can understand at least many of the notions of the theory of meaning, such as meaning, proposition and entailment, in terms of notions drawn from the theory of reference. By doing so, we do not need to posit *sui generis* entities for the purposes of the theory of meaning: we do not need to suppose that, in addition to what we need to posit for the theory of reference, there are additional entities which need to be posited for the purposes of the theory of meaning, such as *sui generis* meanings or propositions.

Possible worlds semantics has a number of other striking advantages. It promises to solve some long-standing philosophical problems while avoiding some of the problems that face Davidson's programme. We will next consider a selection of these advantages.

The problem of intensional contexts

Some sentences do not occur in extensional contexts. For example, although 'The 44th U.S. President is a Democrat' is true, 'It is necessary that the 44th

U.S. President is a Democrat' is false. The 44th US President is a Democrat, but he or she might not have been. Possible worlds semantics has a straightforward account of such sentences. 'The 44th U.S. President is a Democrat' is true if and only if in the actual world the 44th US President is a Democrat. 'It is necessary that the 44th U.S. President is a Democrat' is true if and only if in all worlds the 44th US President is a Democrat. The meanings (or intensions) of the expressions 'It is necessary that' and 'It is possible that' are functions from sentences meanings to sentence meanings. The meaning of 'It is necessary that' is a function which, given the meaning of (say) 'The 44th U.S. President is a Democrat' as an argument, has, as its value, the meaning of 'It is necessary that the 44th U.S. President is a Democrat'.

The problem of informative identity sentences

Possible worlds semantics offers a solution to Frege's problem of informative identity sentences (Chapter 1 §3). Frege introduces pairs of sentences such as

(9)   The Morning Star is the Morning Star.
(10) The Morning Star is the Evening Star.

where the Morning Star is the brightest star visible in the morning sky and the Evening Star is the brightest star visible in the evening sky. (9) and (10) differ in what Frege calls 'cognitive value'. (9) is obviously true and uninformative, whereas (10) is informative and not obviously true. Frege explains this difference in cognitive value by saying that 'the Morning Star' and 'the Evening Star' differ in sense, and so that (9) and (10) differ in sense.

Possible worlds semantics explains the difference in cognitive value between (9) and (10) without positing senses. Its alternative explanation is that, although 'the Morning Star' and 'the Evening Star' refer to the same object in the actual world, they refer to different objects at some possible worlds. At every world, what is referred to by 'the Morning Star' is identical to what is referred to by 'the Morning Star'. For this reason, (9) is uninformative. At only some worlds, however, what is referred to by 'the Morning Star' is identical to what is referred to by 'the Evening Star'. Since (10) says that the object referred to by the one expression is identical to the object referred to by the other expression, (10) is informative. At no world is what (9) says false, but at some worlds, what (10) says is false. So, (10) is informative: it says, of the actual world, that it is one of the worlds in which (10) is true.

The problem of propositional attitude reports

Similar considerations to the above can be applied to propositional attitude reports such as (11) and (12):

(11) Angela knows that the Morning Star is the Morning Star.
(12) Angela knows that the Morning Star is the Evening Star.

Given that the references of 'the Morning Star' and 'the Evening Star' differ at some worlds, there are worlds at which (11) is true but (12) is not. Consider a world at which Angela knows that the Morning Star is the Morning Star, but also at which the Morning Star is not the Evening Star. At such a world, (11) is true but (12) is false (Hintikka 1969, p. 90). Since the references of 'the Morning Star' and 'the Evening Star' differ at some worlds, their meanings differ. Consequently, the meanings of (11) and (12) differ. If knowledge reports describe a relation between a person and a proposition, (11) and (12) describe relations between the same person and different propositions. (11) reports that the knowledge relation holds between Angela and the proposition that the Morning Star is the Morning Star, whereas (12) reports that the knowledge relation holds between Angela and the different proposition that the Morning Star is the Evening Star.

The problem of non-synonymous but co-extensive terms

Possible worlds semantics avoids the problem posed by terms which differ in meaning but which (contingently) apply to the same things. For example, the term 'renate' means *creature with a kidney*, whereas 'cordate' means *creature with a heart*. All and only things that are renates are cordates. So, despite the fact that the terms differ in meaning, they apply to the same things.

Possible worlds semantics accommodates this case because, although the terms in fact apply to the same things, it is possible that they apply to different things. It is possible, for instance, for a creature with a heart to lack kidneys. In the idiom of possible worlds, the extensions of the two terms differ across worlds: there is some world in which something is a creature with kidneys but is not a creature with a heart. For that reason, the terms 'renate' and 'cordate' differ in meaning.

Contexts of utterance and circumstances of evaluation

Possible worlds semantics has the resources to draw a distinction between the context in which an utterance is made (the context of utterance) and the circumstances in which that utterance is evaluated as true or false (its circumstances of evaluation). The context of utterance is the situation in which a certain sentence is uttered by a certain speaker at a certain place and time. The circumstances of evaluation are the possible worlds relevant to determining the truth value of the sentence. As David Kaplan puts it, those circumstances are 'the actual and counterfactual situations with respect to which it is appropriate to ask for the extensions of a given well-formed expression' (Kaplan 1989, p. 502). Let's consider an example:

(13) I am here now.

(13) generates a puzzle. Whenever a speaker utters (13), he or she utters something true. In fact, there is no possible world in which a speaker utters (13) but fails to say something true. Nevertheless, (13) is not a necessary truth. It is not a necessary truth that the speaker is located at that place at that time.

The solution to the puzzle lies in seeing that the reference of an expression, such as 'I', 'here' or 'now', has to be relativized to both a context of utterance and to a circumstance of evaluation. In the case of many sentences, context and circumstance coincide. They consist in the state of the actual world, given a certain speaker at a certain time and place. In the case of sentences such as (13), however, context and circumstance come apart. To evaluate whether (13) is necessarily true, we need to shift the circumstance of evaluation – the possible worlds relevant to the evaluation of whether (13) is a necessary truth – but keep fixed the context of utterance. As uttered in a certain context of utterance, a speaker uses (13) to pick out a certain person (the speaker), place, and time, and says that he or she is at that place and at that time. Nevertheless, there are worlds at which the speaker is not at that place at that time. Those worlds are relevant to the evaluation of whether (13) expresses a necessary truth. Given those worlds, what (13) says is not a necessary truth.

An argument for possible worlds semantics

Finally, here is a direct argument by David Lewis for possible worlds semantics:

> In order to say what a meaning is, we may first ask what a meaning does, and then find something that does that.
> A meaning for a sentence is something that determines the conditions under which the sentence is true or false. It determines the truth value of the sentence in various possible states of affairs, at various times, at various places, for various speakers, and so on. (Lewis 1970, p. 191)

The point of Lewis's argument seems to be as follows (Lycan 2008, p. 129). Suppose that you understand a certain sentence. Then, given complete knowledge of what a given possible world is like, you would know whether that sentence is true or false. One implication of this is that, given each world, the meaning of a sentence determines the sentence's truth value at that world. Accordingly, the meaning of a sentence is at least a truth condition: a set of worlds in which that sentence is true.

5. Problems for possible worlds semantics

Possible worlds semantics is not free of problems. In this section, we will consider some major problems which it faces, as well as some lines of reply which are open to it. Some of the problems facing Davidson's programme recur: What account can be given of non-declarative sentences? What account can be given of context-dependent sentences such as demonstrative sentences? Is the semantics empirically testable? The solutions canvassed for those particular problems by Davidson's programme can be carried over here, and so, we will not go over this ground again.

The problem of logically equivalent sentences

Logically equivalent sentences (such as pairs of sentences of the form '¬p ∧ ¬q' and '¬(p ∨ q)') are true in the same possible worlds. It follows that, according to possible worlds semantics, those sentences have the same meaning. Yet that consequence seems mistaken.

One response to this problem was made by Carnap (Carnap 1956, §14). He took meanings or intensions to have structure. He then explains what it is for two sentences to have what he calls the same intensional structure:

> If two sentences are built in the same way out of corresponding designators with the same intensions, then we shall say that they have the same intensional structure. (Carnap 1956, p. 56)

The guiding idea here is that to introduce intensional structure is to introduce a more 'fine-grained' notion of meaning, so that logically equivalent sentences that do not have the same intensional structure do not have the same meaning. Expressions have the same intensional structure if and only if their logical forms are constructed in the same way and that they have components with the same intensions. To take one of Carnap's examples, consider '2 + 5' and 'II sum V'. ' + ' and 'sum' are functors for the addition function. Given what the expressions '2' and 'II' mean, those terms have the same meaning. Likewise with respect to the expressions '5' and 'V'. Carnap concludes that the original sentences have the same intensional structure and so have the same fine-grained meaning. For a similar reason, so too do '2 + 5' and 'sum(II, V)'. By contrast, '2 + 5' and '(I sum I) sum III' do not have the same intensional structure and so do not have the same fine-grained meaning. Again, sentences of the form '¬p ∧ ¬q' and '¬(p ∨ q)' are logically equivalent, but their logical forms are not constructed in the same way out of expressions with the same intensions. (For a further discussion of the problem of logical equivalence, see Stalnaker 1984, pp. 24–5, 72.)

The problem of necessarily co-extensive singular terms

Possible worlds semantics takes the meaning of a referring expression to be a function from each world to the reference of the expression at that world. This approach explains why expressions such as 'Hillary Clinton' and 'the wife of Bill Clinton' have different meanings. Even though they have the same reference at the actual world, they differ in reference at some other worlds, since at some worlds, Hillary Clinton is not the wife of Bill Clinton. Nevertheless, this approach runs into apparent difficulties with singular terms which are necessarily co-extensive. Consider the following pairs of examples:

(14) The integer that is the immediate successor of 1; the only even prime number.

(15) The first drawing of a triangle; the first drawing of a trilateral.

Necessarily, the integer that is the immediate successor of 1 (i.e. the number 2) is the only even prime number. So, the two complex expressions in (14) pick out the same number at every world. The meaning of 'the integer that is the immediate successor of 1' and the meaning of 'the only even prime number' are functions from each world to the same number. It follows that those functions are identical, and so that the meanings of those expressions are identical. Similar reasoning applies to the complex expressions in (15). Nevertheless, neither the complex expressions in (14) nor those in (15) have the same meaning (Katz and Katz 1977, p. 88).

Note that we have singled out the *complex* expressions in (14) and (15) for discussion. Perhaps Carnap's ideas about intensional isomorphism can be carried over from the case of sentences to that of singular terms to show that the complex expressions in (14) are not intensionally isomorphic and so differ in fine-grained meaning. But how can his ideas be used to show that the complex expressions in (15) differ in meaning? It might be suggested that, for example, 'triangle' and 'trilateral' can each be defined and that their definitions reveal that these expressions are not intensionally isomorphic. It would then follow that the complex expressions in (15) are themselves not intensionally isomorphic.

The problem of necessary truth

There is a related problem to the problem of logical equivalence. According to possible worlds semantics, the meaning of a sentence is the set of possible worlds in which that sentence is true. Now a sentence that is necessarily true is true at all worlds. It follows that every necessarily true sentence is true at all worlds, and so that every such sentence has the same meaning. Every such sentence expresses the necessarily true proposition. (Similar reasoning shows that every necessarily false sentence has the same meaning, and that it expresses the necessarily false proposition.) The problem of necessary truth is that it seems that someone may believe one necessarily true sentence without believing another, even though possible worlds semantics says that those sentences express the same proposition. For example, the sentences '3 + 5 = 8' and 'There are infinitely many primes' both express the necessarily true proposition. Yet Ned may understand both sentences, believe what is expressed by the first and yet not believe what is expressed by the second (Katz and Katz 1977, p. 88).

Robert Stalnaker offers an ingenious response to this problem (Stalnaker 1984, pp. 73–7 and 1999, pp. 12–16). It involves distinguishing between different propositions that are easily run together. The proposition that $3 + 5 = 8$ is identical to the proposition that there are infinitely many prime numbers. So believing that $3 + 5 = 8$ is identical to believing that there are infinitely many prime numbers. It is a matter of believing the same proposition. Given that Ned believes that $3 + 5 = 8$, he does believe that there are infinitely many primes. But this does not exhaust what Ned believes and what he does not believe. Consider the sentences '3 + 5 = 8' and 'There are infinitely many prime numbers'. Ned believes that '3 + 5 = 8' expresses a truth, but he does not believe that 'There are infinitely many prime numbers' expresses a truth. So Ned believes a further proposition, namely, the proposition that '3 + 5 = 8' expresses a truth. (That proposition is contingently true because, although the sentence '3 + 5 = 8' expresses a truth, it could have meant something else which is not true.) A yet further proposition is the proposition that 'There are infinitely many prime numbers' expresses a truth. Ned does not believe that proposition.

In our example, then, there are three relevant propositions:

(16) The proposition that $3 + 5 = 8$ ($=$ the proposition that there are infinitely many prime numbers).

(17) The proposition that '$3 + 5 = 8$' expresses is true.

(18) The proposition that 'There are infinitely many prime numbers' expresses is true.

Ned believes the propositions reported by (16) and (17), but does not believe the proposition reported by (18). According to Stalnaker, it is only by confusing (18) with (16) that we should think that Ned does not believe that there are infinitely many prime numbers.

Stalnaker's account can be extended to informative mathematical identity sentences. Take an example. 'The second largest prime number less than 100 is the second largest prime number less than 100' and 'The second largest prime number less than 100 is 89' are both true identity sentences. Since the sentences express necessary truths, then, according to possible worlds semantics, they express the same proposition. Yet the first sentence is uninformative, whereas the second is informative. So it might seem that someone, Nate, could understand both sentences but believe what is expressed by the first sentence without believing what is expressed by the second. But that would be impossible if those sentences express the same proposition.

Stalnaker's account would give the following construal of this example. There are three propositions to distinguish:

(19) The proposition that the second largest prime number less than 100 is the second largest prime number less than 100 ($=$ the proposition that the second largest prime number less than 100 is 89).

(20) The proposition that 'The second largest prime number less than 100 is the second largest prime number less than 100' expresses is true.

(21) The proposition that 'The second largest prime number less than 100 is 89' expresses is true.

Nate believes both (19) and (20) but fails to believe (21). Let us see why. First, Nate believes the proposition that the second largest prime number less than 100 is the second largest prime number less than 100. That is the same proposition as the proposition that the second largest prime number less than 100 is 89. So

Nate believes the proposition that the second largest prime number less than 100 is 89. So Nate believes (19). Second, Nate believes the sentence 'The second largest prime number less than 100 is the second largest prime number less than 100' expresses something true. Ask him whether he believes what that sentence says, and he would tell you that he does. So Nate believes (20). Third, Nate does not believe the sentence 'The second largest prime number less than 100 is 89' expresses something true. Ask him whether he believes what that sentence says and he would tell you that he does not. He is unsure whether that sentence says something true. So Nate does not believe (21).

What this account seeks to show in this case is that it is consistent with there being just one true mathematical proposition that there are informative mathematical identity sentences. The distinction between sentences and propositions is crucial to this account. A declarative sentence is a piece of language. A proposition is a set of worlds. Different sentences can express the same proposition. In particular, all true mathematical sentences express the same mathematical proposition. In the case of some mathematical sentences, it may be obvious that each of those sentences expresses a true proposition. In the case of other mathematical sentences, it may be far from obvious that each of those sentences expresses a true proposition. So someone may believe the proposition that mathematical sentence S expresses a true proposition, and that same person may not believe the proposition that some other mathematical sentence S^* expresses a true proposition, when in fact S and S^* both express the same true mathematical proposition.

(For criticism of Stalnaker's account, see Katz and Katz 1977, p. 90; Baldwin 1985, p. 629; Field 1986, pp. 428, 446; Cresswell 1988, pp. 516–18; Nuffer 2009.)

It is worth assessing the overall significance of the last three problems that we have considered. Those problems might be taken to show that possible worlds semantics 'leaves something out' in its account of the semantics of expressions. On this view, what possible worlds semantics offers is a surrogate for meaning, not an accurate account of what meaning itself is. Let's pursue this issue further by seeing what David Lewis has to say about the matter.

Lewis's possible worlds semantics involves two key devices. First, there are functions from worlds to extensions at those worlds. We are already familiar with this idea; Lewis calls such functions 'intensions'. Second, there are, what he calls, 'semantically interpreted phrase markers'. A phrase marker is something which represents the syntax of a phrase or sentence, perhaps in a series of stages. This can be represented as a downwards branching tree as more and more of the syntactic structure of the phrase is revealed. By being semantically interpreted, each stage (or 'node' of the tree) is also assigned an intension. In this way, a semantically interpreted phrase marker will assign an intension and a syntactic category (such as verb or noun phrase) at each 'node' of its representation of some phrase.

Lewis notes that intensions differ from meanings because differences in meaning 'may not carry with them any difference in intension' (Lewis 1970, p. 196). He also notes that semantically interpreted phrase markers 'cut meanings too finely' (Lewis 1970, p. 201). Classifying in terms of intensions is too coarse-grained because pairs of expressions such as 'trilateral' and 'triangular' have the same intension and so will be classified as having the same meanings. Classifying in terms of semantically interpreted phrase markers is too fine-grained because any expressions or sentences with different syntactic structures will be classified as differing in meaning (Katz and Katz 1977, p. 89, note 37).

What, then, should a possible worlds semanticist make of meanings? Lewis comments that:

> Perhaps some entities of intermediate fineness can also be found, but I doubt that there is any uniquely natural way to do so. (Lewis 1970, p. 201)

Lewis does not elaborate on this claim further and what he says is open to interpretation. One interpretation that can be made is that Lewis is suggesting that it is unlikely that there are any 'entities of intermediate fineness', or, at any rate, that there are no such entities which form a suitably natural or non-gerrymandered class. So although there are intensions and there are semantically interpreted phrase markers, there is unlikely to be anything else besides so far as semantics is concerned. If 'meanings' is taken to be a name for those putative intermediate entities, then there are no meanings.

Fred Katz and Jerry Katz claim that if there are no meanings (as so construed), then the distinction between intensions and semantically interpreted phrase markers is, in their words, 'a nonsense'. Their argument for this claim is that saying that intensions are too coarse-grained and that semantically interpreted phrase markers are too fine-grained requires that there are 'entities of intermediate fineness'. Otherwise, it would be 'like saying that one microscope adjustment is too coarse and another too fine but there is nothing to be seen on either a finer adjustment than the first or a coarser adjustment than the second' (Katz and Katz 1977, p. 89).

That objection, however, rests heavily on the metaphor of coarse- and fine-grainedness and exploits the fact that these terms mark a difference of degree.

The metaphor is itself dispensable and, in its absence, the objection lacks force. What the metaphor was used to help express were the following facts: assuming that there are meanings, (a) some expressions can differ in meaning without differing in intension and (b) some expressions can differ in their semantically interpreted phrase markers without differing in meaning. Putting matters in those more neutral terms leaves it open whether there is a class of entities in addition to intensions and semantically interpreted phrase markers which deserve to be called meanings. The suggestion that there is no such class of additional entities is then not obviously 'nonsense'. For that reason, the Katz's objection seems too swift: they fail to show that, on the suggested interpretation of Lewis's remark, what he is saying is absurd.

The problem of the missing constraint

We want a theory of the logical form of sentences to be testable. One way in which such a theory might be tested would be partly due to any constraints it places on the syntax of sentences. If linguists independently discover that the syntax of those sentences do (or that they do not) meet those constraints, then there is some confirmation (or some disconfirmation) of the theory. But does possible worlds semantics impose such a constraint? Gilbert Harman is sceptical:

> The main difficulty with the alternative approach via possible worlds lies in its very generality and adaptability to whatever a linguist might say about syntax. One cannot use the possible worlds approach to help with grammar since it puts no constraint on grammar. (Harman 1972, p. 65)

Let's suppose that the objection is correct in claiming that possible worlds semantics puts no constraint on the syntax of sentences. The semantics was not designed to 'help with grammar,' however, so it is not as though it fails to achieve a goal which it was set. Moreover, it is not clear that possible worlds semantics is unique among philosophical semantic theories in this regard. Take Russell's theory of descriptions (see Chapter 5). Russell recognizes that expressions of the form 'the F' have to have sufficient syntactic complexity to account for scope distinctions. This means that they have to have parts which are like variables at some level of grammar. Beyond this, however, Russell's theory does not require any particular account of syntax (Stevens 2011). Lastly, it is not clear why Harman's objection should constitute 'the main difficulty' with possible worlds semantics. It does not lack other constraints. Proponents of possible worlds semantics take its main constraint to be that it should correctly state the truth conditions of modal sentences. In addition, the other problems posed in this section are precisely objections that it does not meet various plausible constraints. To the extent that these constraints have been met, there is reason to think that possible worlds semantics does have supporting evidence.

The problem of possible worlds

Up until now, we have taken the notion of a possible world for granted. But many philosophers will not go along with such talk. There are various reservations that they might have. Here are three of them. First, some of them say that possible worlds do not exist:

> There *are* no possible worlds except the actual one: so what are we up to when we talk about them? (Mackie 1973, p. 90. See also Lycan 2008, p. 131)

Second, some philosophers claim that when people talk about what is possible or what is necessary, they do not take themselves to be talking about possible worlds. Consider, for example, what possible worlds semantics says about counterfactual conditionals: conditionals of the form 'if it were the case that p, it would be the case that q'. Lewis supposes that worlds are arranged 'spheres' according to how similar they are to the actual world in various respects. A counterfactual of the form 'If it were the case that p, it would be the case that q' is true if and only if at the most similar world to the actual world in which p is true, q is also true (Lewis 1973, chapter 1). Lewis's account has prompted the following complaint:

> This elaborate account, presupposing a system of possible worlds and nested spheres containing them, surely does not describe what the user of a counterfactual ordinarily means or intends to convey. It must be taken as a proposed linguistic reform, as a description of something that counterfactual conditional sentences *could* mean without diverging too far from their present use . . . . (Mackie 1973, p. 88)

Third, some philosophers claim that modal talk and possible worlds talk alike is obscure. To talk of merely possible objects requires that we have some way of saying when such objects are identical and when they are non-identical. Yet, there is no non-arbitrary way of doing this:

> Take, for instance, the possible fat man in that doorway; and, again, the possible bald man in that doorway. Are they the same possible man, or two

possible men? How do we decide? How many possible men are there in
that doorway? Are there more possible thin ones than fat ones? How many
of them are alike? Or would their being alike make them one? Are no *two*
possible things alike? Is this the same as saying that it is impossible for two
things to be alike? Or, finally, is the concept of identity simply inapplicable
to unactualized possibles? But what sense can be found in talking of
entities which cannot meaningfully be said to be identical with themselves
and distinct from one another? These elements are well-nigh incorrigible.
(Quine 1948, p. 4)

We do not have space here to address fully all of these worries about
possible worlds talk. (For a discussion of Quine's worries about modality,
see Plantinga 1974 appendix and Melia 2003, chapter 3 and the references
for that chapter on p. 185 of Melia's book.) We will take up just the first and
second challenges. Possible worlds semanticists use the notion of a possible
world, but that leaves open what they take a possible world to be. When
Mackie denies that there are other possible worlds, he is thinking of possible
worlds as things of the same kind as our physical universe: worlds as things
composed of objects in space-time relations to each other. Notoriously, some
possible worlds semanticists do think of possible worlds in this way (Lewis
1986a, chapter 1). There are, however, other ways of thinking of possible
worlds. In fact, immediately after making the above claims, Mackie goes
on to state and accept a construal of what possible worlds are in terms of
'what people do in the way of considering, supposing, inserting or excluding
elements in a picture, and so on' (Mackie 1973, p. 90). At least one possible
worlds semanticist has endorsed and developed just such a view (Stalnaker
1984, pp. 50–1). Again, Kripke warns against thinking of other possible
worlds as 'something like distant planets' (Kripke 1972, p. 15. See also
pp. 43–4). As a philosophical prophylactic, he suggests that it is more fruitful
to think of a possible world as a 'possible state (or history) of the world' or
as a 'counterfactual situation' (Kripke 1972, p. 15). So understood, talk of
possible worlds seems benign rather than bizarre. (For further discussion,
see Davies 1981, pp. 198–201; Lycan 1984, pp. 286–94; Fitch 2004, pp. 14–16,
21; Soames 2002, p. 23.)

Let us turn to the second challenge. The challenge was that when people
talk about what is possible or necessary, they do not take themselves to be
talking about possible worlds and relations between them. One reply open to
the possible worlds semanticist is to concede the point but to attach no
significance to it. It need not be part of possible worlds semantics to suppose

that there is a suppressed parameter concerning possible worlds in ordinary sentences. Instead, possible worlds semantics is adopted because of its technical and conceptual resources. In this respect, construing sentences in terms of possible worlds semantics is no different from construing sentences in terms of the first-order predicate calculus. Here is what Quine says about construing some of the expressions of natural language sentences as quantifiers and truth functions:

> When we move from verbal sentence to logical formulas we are merely retreating to a notation that has certain technical advantages, algorithmic and conceptual . . . No one wants to say that the binominals of Linnaeus or the fourth dimension of Einstein or the binary code of the computer were somehow implicit in ordinary language; and I have seen no more reason to so regard the quantifiers and truth functions. (Quine 1972, p. 395)

Possible worlds semanticists can follow the same line when they construe natural language sentences as involving quantifiers that range over possible worlds.

6. Hyperintensional semantics

We have seen that there is a distinction between two kinds of contexts, extensional and intensional contexts. (The notion of an extensional context was explained in Chapter 8 §2. The notion of an intensional context was explained in §2 of this chapter.) A context C is *extensional* if and only if the following condition is satisfied:

> If p is materially equivalent to q, then $C(p)$ is materially equivalent to $C(q)$.

For example, take the negation operator. Suppose that p and q are materially equivalent. Suppose, in particular, that they are both true. Then 'It is not the case that p' and 'It is not the case that q' are materially equivalent: they are both false. Having explained what an extensional context is, we can explain what an intensional context is in terms of it. A context is *intensional* if and only if it is not extensional.

There are two further contexts to consider: hyperintensional contexts and non-hyperintensional contexts. A hyperintensional context is a special case of an intensional context. We can explain the notion of a hyperintensional context by first introducing the notion of a non-hyperintensional context.

A context is *non-hyperintensional* if and only if the following condition is satisfied:

If p is logically equivalent to q, then C(p) is logically equivalent to C(q).

A context is *hyperintensional* if it is not non-hyperintensional.

Let's see some examples of these new contexts. It was noted above that a hyperintensional context is a special case of an intensional context. An example of a context that is both intensional and hyperintensional is the context '... believes that ...'. All truths are materially equivalent. Suppose Ned believes some truths. Call one of them p. There are some other truths that he does not believe. He is ignorant of them. Call one of them q. 'Ned believes that p' is true. 'Ned believes that q' is false. So the context '... believes that ...' is intensional. Logical truths are logically equivalent. Ned believes some logical truths. Call one of them r. There are some logical truths that he does not believe. He is ignorant of them. Call one of them s. 'Ned believes that r' is true. 'Ned believes that s' is false. So the context '... believes that ...' is hyperintensional.

An example of a context that is intensional and non-hyperintensional is the context 'It is logically necessary that ...'. All truths are materially equivalent. Let t and u be two such truths. Suppose further that t is a logical truth and that u is not. A given proposition is a logical truth if and only if it is logically necessary that the proposition is true. Then 'It is logically necessary that t' is true, whereas 'It is logically necessary that u' is false. So the context 'It is logically necessary that ...' is intensional. As noted, logical truths are logically equivalent. A logical truth is true in all logically possible situations. In other words, it is logically necessary that it is true. To take our earlier examples, r and s are logical truths. Then 'It is logically necessary that r' is true, and 'It is logically necessary that s' is also true. Both of the sentences 'It is logically necessary that r' and 'It is logically necessary that s' are themselves logical truths. It follows that they are logically equivalent. So the context 'It is logically necessary that ...' is non-hyperintensional.

By the late 1960s, a number of philosophers and logicians saw the need to investigate and develop hyperintensional logics. (Pioneering publications include Cresswell 1973, 1975; Tichý 1971, 1975, 1986, 1988.) Part of the reason for this was the realization that hyperintensional notions are key to many ideas and discussions in the philosophies of logic, language, mind and science, as well as various other branches of philosophy. Here are four examples.

We have already considered belief. Consider knowledge. Take an example used above. Suppose that (22) is true:

(22) Ned knows that $3 + 5 = 8$.

The following sentences are logically equivalent:

(23) $3 + 5 = 8$.
(24) There are infinitely many prime numbers.

Substituting (23) with (24) in (22) yields:

(25) Ned knows that there are infinitely many prime numbers.

But (25) may be false even if (22) is true, since Ned may not know what prime numbers are. What this example tells us is that, like belief contexts, knowledge contexts, contexts of the form '. . . knows that . . .', are hyperintensional contexts. Similar reasoning can be used to show that propositional attitude verbs, such as '. . . desires . . .', '. . . hopes . . .', '. . . expects . . .' and so on, generate hyperintensional contexts.

Consider explanation. An engineer might ask: Why did the metal expand? This might be answered by (26):

(26) The metal expanded because the metal was heated.

Now, the following sentences, (27–29), are logically equivalent:

(27) The metal was heated.
(28) The metal was heated and $7 + 5 = 12$.
(29) The metal was heated and if all cats are cats, then all cats are cats.

(28) and (29) are each formed by conjoining (27) with different necessary truths. Despite their logical equivalence with (27), neither (28) nor (29) explain why the metal expanded. The extra information they contain is explanatorily irrelevant, and substituting (27) as it occurs in (26) with (28) or with (29) does not provide a satisfactory explanation. This tells us that explanatory contexts, contexts of the form '. . . because . . .', are hyperintensional contexts.

Consider meaning. The meaning of the English sentence 'The metal was heated' is given by (27). (27) and (28) are logically equivalent. Yet, (28) does not give the meaning of the sentence 'The metal was heated'. This tells us that contexts of the form 's' means that 'p' are hyperintensional contexts.

Consider logical consequence. (30) is a contingent truth. (31–3) are each necessary truths. Yet, only (33) logically follows from (30):

(30) Barack Obama is a Democrat.
(31) All eye doctors are oculists.
(32) Hesperus is Phosphorus.
(33) Either Barack Obama is a Democrat or Barack Obama is not a Democrat.

This tells us that contexts of the form 'q logically follows from p' are hyperintensional contexts. (This is not the only notion of validity we have. There is also a notion according to which every necessary truth validly follows from any arbitrary claim.)

In addition, there is a current trend in metaphysics to use certain concepts which introduce hyperintensional contexts, such as the concepts of ontological dependence, ground, real definition, reduction and fundamentality (e.g. Schaffer 2009, p. 364).

There are various ways of developing a hyperintensional semantics (Nolan 2009). Here are some sketches of approaches which might be taken. One approach closely follows possible worlds semantics. It takes the meaning (or hyperintension) of a sentence or sub-sentential expression to be a triple consisting of (A) a possible world, (B) an associated intension, plus (C) something which indicates the logical form of the expression or which carries information about the syntax of the expression. Another approach uses both possible worlds and impossible worlds. What does not vary across possible worlds varies across impossible worlds. Across all possible worlds, something is trilateral if and only if it is triangular. But, at some impossible world, something is trilateral but not triangular. In this way, using both possible and impossible worlds enables us to draw more fine-grained distinctions than using possible worlds alone (Nolan 1997). A third approach takes the meaning (the hyperintension) of a sentence or sub-sentential expression to be a 'tree' whose nodes are themselves possible worlds intensions (cf. Lewis 1986a, pp. 49–50). Still further approaches are available, such as proof theoretic semantics, in which the meaning of a sentence is explained in terms of a canonical proof (or canonical verification) of that sentence (Prawitz 1971), and procedural semantics for hyperintensional semantics, in which the meaning of an expression is taken to be a procedure specifying what operations are to apply to which of the procedure's components in order to arrive at the procedure's product (Duží et al. 2010). Proponents of this last approach take themselves to be presenting a rigorous development of Frege's notion of sense.

What are the strengths of hyperintensional semantics? It captures various intuitions about (e.g.) synonymy which many people may have but which possible worlds semantics fails to capture. We saw this in the case of the Katzs' objection to Lewis's semantics. To take another example, although 'If something is an emerald, it is green' and its contrapositive 'If something is not green, it is not an emerald' are logically equivalent, some people intuit that they differ in meaning. Moreover, this difference in meaning may have important implications for confirmation theory (Schlesinger 1974, chapter 1).

Hyperintensional semantics also seems well placed to account for propositional attitude contexts. Sentences such as (27–29) are logically equivalent but have different meanings (hyperintensions). If belief contexts, for example, are hyperintensional contexts, there is then no puzzle about how someone may believe one such sentence but fail to believe another sentence, even though those sentences are logically equivalent and the person understands both sentences.

Nevertheless, propositional attitude contexts continue to raise difficulties. Hyperintensional semantics faces the problem of so-called Mates sentences (Mates 1952; Burge 1978). Hyperintensional semantics says that the truth value of a sentence is necessarily unchanged if component expressions of that sentence are replaced by hyperintensionally equivalent expressions. 'Violin' and 'fiddle' have the same hyperintension. Hyperintensional semantics says that the truth value of a sentence containing one of these expressions, even a propositional attitude report, is necessarily unchanged if the other expression is substituted for it. Thus, since (34) and (35) have the same hyperintension, necessarily they have the same truth value:

(34) Ned plays the violin.
(35) Ned plays the fiddle.

The above principle of substitution plausibly licenses substitution in simple belief reports such as (36) and (37):

(36) Whoever believes that Ned plays the violin believes that Ned plays the violin.
(37) Whoever believes that Ned plays the violin believes that Ned plays the fiddle.

Iterating propositional attitudes, however, provides an apparent counter-example to the substitution principle:

(38) Nobody doubts that whoever believes that Ned plays the violin believes that Ned plays the violin.

(39) Nobody doubts that whoever believes that Ned plays the violin believes that Ned plays the fiddle.

Consider Angela: she accepts (38) but doubts (39). She thinks that there is someone who believes that Ned plays the violin yet who does not believe that Ned plays the fiddle. Notice that even if Angela is mistaken in what she thinks, although (38) is true, what she thinks is sufficient to make (39) false.

If it succeeds, this kind of case is a counter-example to the principle that the truth value of a sentence is necessarily unchanged if expressions with the same hyperintension are substituted for one another within it. It would follow that propositional attitude contexts, such as (38) and (39), are more fine-grained than even hyperintensional contexts. Whether the counter-example succeeds is, however, a controversial matter (Prior 1971, pp. 51–6; Yagisawa 1984; Owens 1986).

We have considered a series of theories of meaning in Chapter 9 and in this chapter. Those theories present increasingly fine-grained views of meaning. Davidson's truth theoretic programme is a programme belonging to extensional semantics. It offers an account of the meaning of sentences in terms of the conditions in which, as a matter of fact, those sentences are true. Possible worlds semantics is a theory belonging to intensional semantics. It offers an account of the meaning of sentences in terms of the conditions across possible worlds in which those sentences are true. Hyperintensional semantics offers, in turn, a still more fine-grained account of the meaning of sentences. Different sentences may differ in meaning in the sense of expressing different hyperintensions, even if the conditions in which they are true match across possible worlds.

7. Conclusion

There is no consensus in philosophy about the standing of possible worlds semantics. Its proponents take it to be invaluable in clarifying, and perhaps solving, various philosophical problems such as problems concerning modality, propositional attitudes and the objects of propositional attitudes.

In terms of the questions set out in the introduction to this book, possible worlds semantics also inherits all of the answers that Davidson's truth theoretic programme provides. Critics of possible worlds semantics doubt whether it has any philosophical value because they query the notions of possible world, proposition and identity across worlds. According to these critics, the introduction of possible worlds semantics does nothing to solve the philosophical problems we already have, and it serves only to add to our stock of problems (Quine 1972, pp. 492–3). Hyperintensional semantics marks a further development in the field of semantics. It shows great promise in addressing some problems facing both truth conditional semantics and possible worlds semantics. The problem we saw near the end of §6, the problem of Mates sentences, recalls the problem we canvassed in Chapter 1 §6 and again in Chapter 8 §2 of establishing when sentences express the same sense. We have already seen that people's propositional attitudes seem able to make more fine-grained distinctions than distinctions between different senses. (See, e.g. the wager/bet example in Chapter 1 §6.) The problem of Mates sentences is that people's propositional attitudes seem to make more fine-grained distinctions than distinctions between different hyperintensions. Our discussion has turned full circle.

Questions for discussion

Question 1
Solve the following paradox:

(1) If it is a necessary truth that p, then p could not have been false.
(2) If it is a necessary truth that p, then p is true.
(3) If p is true, it is a possible truth that p.
(4) If it is a possible truth that p, then p could have been false.
(5) So if it is a necessary truth that p, then p could have been false. [By (2–4)]
(6) So if it is a necessary truth that p, then p could have been false and p could not have been false. [By (1) and (5)]

Question 2
The following three claims each seem plausible. (1) Something is informative only if it rules out possibilities. (2) A necessary truth does not rule out possibilities. (3) Some necessary truths are informative. The problem is that (1)–(3) are jointly inconsistent. How should this problem be solved?

Question 3

Possible worlds semantics says that a sentence is ambiguous if and only if there is a world in which the sentence is both true and false, without contradiction. But could there be a sentence which expresses two propositions both of which are true in all possible worlds? What would be an example? Would it be correct to call such a sentence ambiguous?

Question 4

Assess the following objection: 'Possible worlds semantics says that sentences are true at worlds. So it says that sentences involve a hidden parameter: truth at a world. But most people understand sentences without even having heard of possible worlds or knowing what truth at a world is. So possible worlds semantics has to be mistaken'.

Further reading

Carnap, Rudolf (1956) *Meaning and Necessity: A Study in Semantics and Modal Logic* chapter 1.

Fox, Chris and Shalom Lappin (2005) *Foundations of Intensional Semantics*.

Katz, Fred and Jerrold J. Katz (1977) 'Is Necessity the Mother of Intension?' §III.

Lewis, David (1970) 'General Semantics'.

Lycan, William G. (2008) *Philosophy of Language* chapter 10.

Nelson, Michael (2012) 'Intensional Contexts' in Manuel Garciá-Carpintero and Max Kölbel (eds.) *The Continuum Companion to the Philosophy of Language*.

Stalnaker, Robert C. (1984) *Inquiry* chapters 1, 3, 4 and 5.

Stalnaker, Robert (2011) 'Possible Worlds Semantics: Philosophical Foundations'.

Taylor, Kenneth (1998) *Truth and Meaning: An Introduction to the Philosophy of Language* chapter IV.

Tichý, Pavel (1971) 'An Approach to Intensional Analysis', (1975) 'What Do We Talk About?', (1986) 'Constructions'.

Conclusion

We will close by considering two broad questions: What should be the relation of the philosophy of language to linguistics? And what should be the relation of the philosophy of language to the other branches of philosophy?

What should be the relation of the philosophy of language to linguistics? Linguistics is the scientific study of language. But there are rival views about what else should be said about what linguistics is. For example, one view takes linguistics to be a branch of cognitive psychology which is concerned with mental representations. Linguistics then seeks to provide a theory of certain of the capacities and behaviours of speakers and hearers by properties of their internalized grammars (and perhaps other aspects of the speakers' or hearers' psychology) (Chomsky 1972, p. 1; Fodor 1985; George 1989; Laurence 2003; Cain 2010). A rival view takes linguistics to be concerned with a distinct domain from psychology (namely, a domain consisting of public language sentence-types) to make distinct claims, and to use distinct methods (Katz 1998). It might seem that we need to resolve this taxonomic debate in order to answer our original question. In fact, we are better placed to tackle that question after we address the following methodological issue. This is an issue about what kind of evidence is relevant to establishing a theory in linguistics. A range of views is possible here, but let us consider two polar opposites. One is a 'purist' view. This says that the evidence is confined to people's intuitions about grammaticality, synonymy, ambiguity and the like. Jerrold J. Katz takes this view and combines it with the view that linguistics is concerned with the study of languages, where a language is a structured abstract object (Katz 1998). A rival view favours a more 'eclectic' approach. This allows that evidence can be drawn from considerations about how language is used, how it is learnt, about the neurology of speaker and hearers, and, more generally, from any considerations that bear on the psychology of speakers and hearers (Fodor 1985, p. 150). The view that linguistics is a branch of psychology would provide a clear rationale for the latter methodological approach.

Interestingly, the above two taxonomic views of the nature of linguistics and the above two views about the proper methodology of linguistics need not coincide. Even if linguistics is thought of as being concerned with languages understood as abstract objects – as Katz claims – linguistics can still be an empirical science (Soames 1991, p. 580).

We can also understand better the relation between the philosophy of language and linguistics by considering what we already think about the more general relation between philosophy and psychology. And, in so far as philosophical considerations bear on claims made in psychology, if any of those psychological claims bear on linguistics, then so too will those philosophical considerations. Lastly, given such an account, there would seem to be no reason why the direction of evidence would be only one way – from philosophy to psychology and then linguistics. For example, many linguists think that the central task of linguistics is to answer the following question. What is the range of languages that are learnable by human beings? A language might be abstractly possible and yet be impossible for us to learn. So there is then a pressing issue about which languages are humanly possible. In addition to work in linguistics on syntax and phonology, some work on truth conditional semantics has suggested a constraint on humanly learnable languages (see Barwise and Cooper 1981; Soames 1985, pp. 221–3).

The approach outlined here is of a piece with the method of reflective equilibrium. That method addresses the questions: Which theories should we believe? What data should we take to be reliable? In its most general form, the method of reflective equilibrium answers these questions by reflecting on *all* of our current theories and *all* of our current data (Goodman 1955, pp. 61–6). We should believe those theories that are the most likely, given which data is reliable. We should believe the data that is the most reliable, given which theories are most likely. Each consideration informs the other and we seek the best balance between them. That is, we seek the most systematic and simple selection of theories and data. This is a 'global' account of inquiry. Inquiry involves forming an overall system or network of claims which we seek to make as coherent and simple as possible. The same method can be adopted at the more 'local' level of the philosophy of language. We seek coherence between our views in the philosophy of language and our other views in philosophy, with no view having a special standing over the others. We also seek a wider coherence between our views in philosophy and our other views about the world. Even on this broader canvass, none of these views have a special standing over the others.

What should be the relation of the philosophy of language to the other branches of philosophy? To see what is at issue here, it helps to consider two sharply opposing answers. It should be stressed that these answers are not the only, or perhaps the most promising, answers to the question. In intellectual life, examining polarized views is often a good heuristic for getting to understand the nature of a given debate and in forming our own views.

One answer promotes the priority of the philosophy of language in philosophy. This 'priority' view is championed by Dummett and various other philosophers influenced by Frege (Dummett 1981, chapter 12; Wright 1983, chapter 1). As Dummett sees the history of modern philosophy, Descartes established epistemology as the foundation of philosophy. This meant that, for any claim of philosophical interest, the key question concerns what epistemic justification we have for that claim. Questions about what that claim meant or how it might be perspicuously represented are, at best, subsidiary. Dummett further sees Frege as replacing epistemology with the philosophy of language as the foundation of philosophy. Given this replacement, Dummett thinks that 'philosophy has, as its first if not its only task, the analysis of meanings' (Dummett 1981, p. 669). Dummett and like-minded philosophers draw the following consequences for other disciplines in philosophy, such as epistemology and ontology:

> . . . until we have first achieved a satisfactory analysis of the meanings of the relevant expressions, we cannot so much as raise questions of justification and truth, since we remain unclear about what we are attempting to justify or what it is about whose truth we are enquiring. (Dummett 1981, p. 667. See also pp. 494–8)

> there can be no philosophical science of ontology, no well-founded attempt to see past our categories of expression and glimpse the way in which the world is truly furnished. (Wright 1983, p. 52. See also pp. 7–8, 13–14)

> . . . the proper formulation and treatment of ontological questions must rest upon a prior analysis of the logical structure of language. (Hale 1991, p. 146. See also Hale 1987, pp. 3–4, 10–14)

The priority view, then, claims that the philosophy of language has a foundational role in philosophy, and it takes philosophy's chief role to be the analysis of the meaning of sentences. In slogan form: 'language-games first; ontology second' (Wright 2002, p. 156).

In fact, in later work, Dummett is less insistent that the philosophy of language provides the foundation of philosophy. He explains that he regards the question of whether language precedes thought as something open to argument (Dummett 1991, p. 3). What he remains committed to, however, is the view that the philosophy of mental and linguistic representation provides the foundation of philosophy.

Whether Frege himself subscribes to the priority view is a matter of debate. For instance, one interpretation of Frege's work takes his chief task to be epistemological and, specifically, to be that of showing how our knowledge of mathematics can be *a priori* and certain. Frege's interest in language is then derivative and selective: he is interested in certain aspects of language (such as the semantics of identity sentences and the semantics of arithmetical sentences) just because an account of them is needed in the interest of his overall epistemological project (Currie 1976, 1982 introduction).

We will not pursue the exegetical issue of whether or not Frege subscribes to the priority view. Our question is: should we subscribe to it? Dummett does not offer explicit arguments for the view; he appears to take it as a given. What might be influencing Dummett is a commitment to linguistic philosophy: an approach to philosophy that characteristically uses the methods of linguistic analysis to solve philosophical problems. The history of philosophy in the later half of the twentieth century, however, has not borne out this approach's ambitions (Searle 1999, p. 2072).

There might still seem something plausible about the priority view. After all, it might be claimed, we cannot sensibly argue for or against a claim unless we already understand it. But that claim is truistic, and it would be surprising if a thesis as striking as the priority view rests upon a truism. Moreover, it is one thing to understand a claim (something that we do all the time) and another thing to have a philosophical analysis of the claim (something exceedingly difficult and rarely, if ever, achieved). The priority view does not merely require us to understand claims prior to debating them but to have an analysis of those claims prior to the debate.

Furthermore, for any philosophically interesting claim, there are typically rival analyses of it. For example, sentences about physical objects have been given a realist analysis in terms of sentences about mind-independent matter but also a phenomenalist analysis in terms of sentences about experiences and possible experiences. These analyses are in conflict. How should we settle between them? What data can we use? The priority view involves a self-imposed restriction to semantic data alone. But there seems no call for this restriction. We might draw on a wider source of data by considering, for example, the metaphysical and epistemological consequences of these analyses. Does one of these analyses involve more ontological commitments than the other analysis? If so, how well do we understand these extra kinds of entity? And do we have a plausible epistemology of them? If an analysis involves commitment to new entities, or to obscure entities, or to epistemologically inaccessible entities, whereas a rival analysis involves none of these commitments, then there is some (defeasible) reason for taking the second analysis to be the correct analysis. This is precisely one of the lines of argument that Berkeley uses against Locke's realist analysis of physical object sentences and in favour of his own idealist analysis of them (Berkeley 1710, §§16–17). But, if we accept that we can draw upon such a wide source of data in assessing analyses, then the priority view goes by the board. We should not seek to provide an analysis of the meaning of a claim prior to settling any epistemological or metaphysical issues involving the claim. (For further critical discussion of the priority view, see MacBride 2003, pp. 126–8.)

In rejecting the priority view, we need not accept any other branch of philosophy as foundational. The reason for this is that we need not accept a model of philosophy which sees it in terms of a foundation and a supported structure. Each of the various sub-disciplines of philosophy makes claims and seeks to support those claims by drawing on relevant data. These sub-disciplines are not isolated from one another. Nor is any sub-discipline privileged over the others.

David Lewis's methodology echoes these views in two respects. First, he states a 'refusal to take language as a starting point in the analysis of thought and of modality' (Lewis 1986b, p. *xi*). Second, he advocates the method of reflective equilibrium in philosophical inquiry. As he puts it, 'a reasonable goal of a philosopher is to bring [our opinions] into equilibrium' (Lewis 1986b, p. *x*).

We saw above some reasons why the philosophy of language does not have a foundational role. The same reasons show that no sub-discipline of philosophy has a foundational role. Consider epistemology, for example. Taking epistemology to have a foundational role concerning any claim of philosophical interest would be to take the question 'How could we justify that claim?' to be the question that we need to answer before all others. But we cannot answer it before all others. In addressing that question, we need at the same time to consider such questions as 'What is the claim about?' and 'What important implications does the claim have?' None of these questions can be satisfactorily addressed in isolation from the others.

At best, some claims made by one sub-discipline may be better supported, or have wider implications or be better understood than some claims made by another sub-discipline. In the case of other claims made by these two sub-disciplines, however, the situation may be reversed. We should seek simplicity and systematicity in the conjunction of all our philosophical claims without favouring any sub-discipline's claims.

Whereas the priority view takes the analysis of linguistic meaning to be prior to other philosophical tasks, there is also a view whose proponents regard as the polar opposite to the priority view. This is the view that says that it is a serious mistake to reason from considerations about linguistic meaning to conclusions about the non-linguistic world. The view has been held by a number of philosophers but receives a book length treatment in Dyke 2007. Dyke takes proponents of the priority view to be committing a fallacy, 'the representational fallacy' as she calls it. This fallacy is said to involve 'a general strategy of reading metaphysics off language' (Dyke 2007, p. 7) or, more specifically, of 'a general philosophical tendency to place too much emphasis on the significance of language when doing ontology' (Dyke 2007, p. 14). Now to have a misplaced tendency is not to commit a fallacy. And exactly what is fallacious about 'reading off' metaphysics from language?

A claim that might seem similar to Dyke's has been made elsewhere. This is the complaint that some philosophers have sought to draw important metaphysical conclusions on the alleged basis of considerations solely about the philosophy of language. Here are two examples. First, Putnam argues from considerations about our referential practices to the conclusion that the identity of species and of substance kinds depend on their instances sharing certain unobserved essential properties (Putnam 1975). Second, Dummett argues from considerations about the communicability of meaning to the conclusion that the meaning of a sentence has to be completely manifested in the sentence's use and cannot involve any private mental content (Dummett 1975). Putnam's argument has been criticized on the grounds that it makes various non-trivial essentialist assumptions that are not themselves part of the philosophy of language (Salmon 1981, p. 5). Dummett's argument has been criticized on the grounds that its radical conclusions about sentence meaning follow only given certain contentious philosophical assumptions, not all of which are about the nature of meaning (Craig 1982, p. 564). Let's grant that these criticisms are good ones. Nevertheless, they do not expose the target arguments as committing the so-called representational fallacy. That was supposed to be the fallacy of 'reading metaphysics off language' or of placing 'too much emphasis on the significance of language when doing ontology'. But the critics are making a different charge. Their charge is that, although the arguments purport to draw conclusions solely on the basis of considerations in the philosophy of language, in fact, the arguments also make assumptions that are not drawn from the philosophy of language.

What exactly is the representational fallacy? If the priority view commits this fallacy, then so does even the more moderate approach of reflective equilibrium outlined above. That view allowed that data and claims drawn from the philosophy of language can have an evidential bearing on claims made by other sub-disciplines in philosophy. Yet, according to the representational fallacy, that would be a mistake. So what is the supposed error in arguing from claims about language to claims about non-linguistic reality? The issue involves two sub-tasks: identifying a genuine error and then identifying arguments which have actually been offered which commit the error.

Dyke thinks that a sentence of the form '*a* is F' can be true without entailing 'the existence of the entities apparently referred to by terms in the sentence' (Dyke 2007, p. 4), even where the reference to those entities cannot be paraphrased away. That is to say, she thinks that '*a* is F' can be true although *a* does not exist and even if the sentence cannot be paraphrased in such a way as to omit any term with the same meaning as '*a*'. She also thinks that the sentence can be true although nothing is F and even if the sentence cannot be paraphrased in such a way as to omit any term with the same meaning as 'F'.

One way of bringing out this view is to consider the following metaphysical picture. On this picture, only the fundamental elements of physics exist. The distribution of these fundamental physical elements through space and time makes true many sentences. These include sentences about the distribution of these elements, but they also include sentences about humdrum things. Shadows do not exist: they are not fundamental physical elements. But the distribution of the fundamental physical elements through space and time makes true many sentences about shadows. It is because the fundamental physical elements are arranged just so that (say) 'The tree in the quad casts a long shadow in the afternoon' is true. Similarly, there are no holes: holes are not fundamental physical elements. But the distribution of the fundamental physical elements through space and time make true many sentences about holes. It is because the fundamental physical elements are arranged just so that (say) 'There are many holes in this piece of cheese' is true. Perhaps at our world there exist more than the fundamental physical entities. All that matters for our purposes here is that we see how, even in our world, there could be many truths but comparatively few kinds of entities; there could be many truths but comparatively few truthmakers.

Let's grant this line of thought, at least for the sake of argument. How does it substantiate the charge that there is such a thing as the representational fallacy and that anyone has committed it? Given that it is widely acknowledged that there are empty names (names that do not refer to anything), few philosophers are going to argue from there being a sentence 'a is F' to the conclusion that something is F. Perhaps the fallacy is in inferring from the premise that 'a is F' is a true sentence to the conclusion that something is F. Yet there seems to be no fallacy in inferring from the premise that 'There exists an F' is a true sentence to the conclusion that at least one F exists. Yet both inferences 'read off' metaphysics (i.e. something about non-linguistic reality) from language. Why is the first inference fallacious if the second one is not? Remember that the representational fallacy is supposed to involve inferring *any* metaphysical conclusions from premises about language.

Moreover, philosophers of language have long been circumspect about what existential consequences they draw from true sentences. For example, the apt use of metaphors ('He put his life on the line') or of idioms ('Variety is the spice of life') have typically not been taken to license a commitment to referents for 'the line' or 'the spice of life'. Nor have these philosophers supposed that metaphorical or idiomatic claims can be paraphrased by non-metaphorical or non-idiomatic claims without loss of content. (See Black 1954–55, §§3–4 for a classic discussion of this last issue.)

Here, then, is an important point of agreement with Dyke. There *is* a danger of reading metaphysics off too simplistically from language. The above examples show that a given piece of language might suggest a piece of metaphysics, although it does not give us reason to believe in that metaphysics. But, as noted, philosophers of language have been attentive to this issue, and have sought to distinguish the various functions of language, such as the literally descriptive and the idiomatic.

Language is a representational system. Dyke claims that language can provide correct representations of the world – correct representations in which shadows are long and holes are many – even if there are no such things as shadows and holes. But, by the same reckoning, perception and thought are representational systems. Perception and thought can each provide correct representations of the world – correct representations in which shadows are long and holes are many – even if there are no shadows or holes. Do philosophers or scientists or the man in the Clapham BMW also stand guilty of 'reading metaphysics off perception and experiment' or of placing 'too much emphasis on the significance of perception or thought when doing ontology'? Are these things which anyone is guilty of? In fact, any cognitive system we use for drawing conclusions about the world is going to be a representational system and so is apparently open to some generalized version of the representational fallacy. This makes it both harder to see what special fallacy philosophers of language have committed and whether there is a fallacy there at all.

Dyke admits that her description of the fallacy is vague. The difficulty we have faced here is that the descriptions offered have *either* been too vague for the charge of fallacy to be substantiated *or* so encompassing that the charge faces every means we have of representing reality. In the absence of further clarification of Dyke's charge, considerations in the philosophy of language retain their relevance for informing claims outside of the philosophy of language. (For further critical discussion of the representational fallacy, see Eklund 2008.)

To conclude, we can expect to understand better both the world and the ways in which we represent the world by thinking about how language works and what our words mean. At the same time, however, our thinking about language and linguistic meaning should be responsive to issues in metaphysics, epistemology, the philosophy of mind and linguistics. Considerations in the philosophy of language can inform other philosophical claims, without priority being given to it or to any other part of philosophy.

Further reading

Chomsky, Noam (2000) 'Linguistics and Philosophy'.
Dummett, Michael (1981) *Frege: Philosophy of Language* chapter 12.
Dyke, Heather (2007) *Metaphysics and the Representational Fallacy*.
Fodor, Jerry A. (1985) 'Some Notes on What Linguistics is About'.
Laurence, Stephen (2003) 'Is Linguistics a Branch of Psychology?'.

Glossary

Anaphora

In anaphora, the interpretation of a given expression depends on the interpretation of another expression. A case of anaphora can also be a case where what a given expression refers to depends on what another given expression refers to. For example, in 'Rummy has a snout but he has no tail', the reference of 'he' depends on who or what 'Rummy' refers to.

Bivalence

The principle of bivalence says that every sentence is either true or false.

Compositionality

Compositionality says that the meaning of a sentence is determined by the meanings of its components and on how those components are arranged together (their syntactic relations to one another). Compositionality explains how we can devise and understand novel sentences: sentences that we have not encountered before.

Constative

This was J. L. Austin's term for the utterance of a sentence that has a truth value.

Context

The context of an utterance is any background knowledge assumed to be shared by the speaker and the audience that contributes to the audience's interpretation of what the utterance means and what the speaker means by the utterance.

Context principle

This is Frege's principle that words have meaning only in the context of a sentence (Frege 1884, p. x). The principle has been taken to support the idea that sentences are the primary vehicle of meaning and that words have meaning derivatively.

Convention

Some regularities in the behaviour of a group of people involve the (tacit or explicit) agreement of its members to behave in those ways. The people agree to behave in those ways because doing so serves various goals which they have, even though those same goals could have been served by adopting some other regularities of behaviour. The regularities in question are conventions.

Conventional implicature

A speaker can implicate something rather than say it. Unlike a **conversational implicature**, an audience does *not* work out what is being implicated by reflecting on what was said in the light of Grice's conversational maxims. Instead, the audience immediately understands what is being implicated because of the particular words that the speaker used.

Conversational implicature

This is an implicature of what a speaker says that an audience can work out by applying Grice's **conversational maxims** on what the speaker said.

Conversational maxim

Conversations are rational activities. These activities are governed by rules or norms which determine when they are rationally conducted. Grice formulated a supermaxim – the cooperative principle – which requires a speaker to *make your conversational contribution such as is required, at the stage in which it occurs, by the accepted purpose or direction of the talk exchange in which you are engaged.* Grice offers various conversational maxims which are supposed to follow from the cooperative principle. These are supposed to spell out in more detailed and specific ways how the cooperative principle guides the rational conduct of conversation.

Criterion of identity

A way of telling whether entities of the same kind are identical. For example, when is the direction taken by one line identical to the direction taken by another line? Frege suggested that they are identical if and only if those lines are parallel (Frege 1884, p.77).

Declarative sentence

This is a sentence whose form enables it to be asserted and also for it to be true or false.

Definite description

This is a description of the form 'the F'. Note that possessives, such as 'John's dog', are also to be construed as definite descriptions: 'John's dog' is to be construed as 'the dog that belongs to John'.

Domain

The domain of a quantifier is the class of things over which that quantifier ranges.

Empty name

An empty name is a name which fails to refer to anything. Standard examples include 'Excalibur', 'Sherlock Holmes' and 'Vulcan'.

Extension

A term's extension is what the term applies to. The extension of a name is the object which that name picks out. The extension of a predicate is the set of things to which that predicate applies. For example, the extension of 'solid' is the class of solid things. The extension of a sentence is a truth value.

Extensional

A context C is extensional if and only if the following condition is satisfied:

If p is materially equivalent to q, then $C(p)$ is materially equivalent to $C(q)$

For example, negation introduces an extensional context. If p and q are materially equivalent, then not-p and not-q are materially equivalent.

First-order logic

This is also known as predicate logic. It is the logic governing the logical constants. These include the quantifiers ('for all' and 'for some'), the sentential connectives ('and', 'or', 'not' and 'if then') and identity.

Force

The force of an uttered sentence is the speech act which it makes. This speech act may be an assertion, or a command, or a question and so on.

Formal language

A formal language is a language whose syntax and semantics are explicitly specified by means of the apparatus of a metatheory such as set theory.

Foundational theory of meaning

This kind of theory seeks to say what it is about the speaker or speakers that give the sentences they use the meanings that they have.

Function

A pattern of correlation between an input (or argument) and an output (or value). For example, given the numbers 6 and 8 as arguments, the addition function yields the number 14 as value.

Functor

A term which specifies a **function**. For example, '$x + y$' is a functor which specifies the addition function.

Hyperintensional context

This is a type of **intensional context**. Substituting logically equivalent sentences in a hyperintensional context need not preserve truth value. For example, Euclid proved that there are infinitely many prime numbers. Now, '$3 + 5 = 8$' and 'there are infinitely prime numbers' are logically equivalent. But, it is false that Euclid proved that $3 + 5 = 8$.

Illocutionary force

This is the **force** (as opposed to the meaning) of an utterance. Austin describes it as an aspect abstracted away from the total speech act. Sentence contents can be uttered for different purposes or forces. You can utter a sentence to state something, or to issue an order, or to pose a question. (See also **locutionary act** and **perlocutionary act**.)

Implicature

In saying something, a speaker may convey more information than he or she is given by the meaning of what he or she says. This additional information is an implicature of the utterance. Implicatures are generated by conversational features peculiar to the context of utterance or by conventional features of the sentence uttered. See **conventional implicature**, **conversational implicature** and **conversational maxim**.

Indirect context

This is a context in which someone is reported as saying something (an indirect speech context) or in which someone is reported as having a certain propositional attitude (a propositional attitude context). An indirect context is an example of an **intensional context**.

Intension

An intension is a function from a possible world to an extension at that world.

Intensional context

A context is intensional if and only if it is not **extensional**. For example, the contexts introduced by '. . . hopes that . . .' and '. . . sees that . . .' are intensional contexts. (These examples are also **hyperintensional contexts**.)

Literal meaning

What an expression or sentence literally means on a given occasion of utterance is to be contrasted with what is communicated indirectly, or metaphorically or ironically. Each of the latter is an example of non-literal meaning. For example, someone who says 'The name is on the tip of my tongue' is not usually claiming that a name is to be found on the tip of his or her tongue. Instead, the speaker is conveying something non-literally: they are conveying that they cannot yet think of the name which they want to utter.

Locutionary act

This is the meaning (as opposed to the **force**) of an utterance. Austin describes it as an aspect abstracted away from the total speech act. (See also **illocutionary act** and **perlocutionary act**.)

Logical equivalence

Sentences (or propositions) are logically equivalent if and only if they have the same truth value in every logically possible situation.

Material equivalence

Two sentences are materially equivalent if and only if both are true or both are false.

Modal context

A context concerning what is necessary or what is possible (the modalities). Necessity concerns what is necessarily the case. Possibility concerns what is possibly the case.

Natural language

A natural language, such as Swedish, Russian or Mandarin, is a language which infants acquire through the usual process of education. A natural language is to be contrasted with a **formal language**.

Negative existential statement

An existential statement is of the form 'the F exists' or of the form '*a* exists'. A negative existential statement is either of the form 'the F does not exist' or of the form '*a* does not exist'.

Non-hyperintensional context

A context is non-hyperintensional if and only if the following condition is satisfied:

If p is logically equivalent to q, then C(p) is logically equivalent to C(q)

The contexts 'it is logically possible that . . .' and 'it is logically necessary that . . .' are non-hyperintensional.

n-place predicate

Predicates have different numbers of free places in them. A one-place predicate has one free place, a two-place predicate has two free places and so on. Completing all of the places in a predicate yields a sentence. That is, an *n*-place predicate combines with *n* singular terms to form a sentence.

n-tuple

An n-tuple of individuals is a set of individuals. If there is just one individual in the set, *n* takes value 1; if there is a pair of individuals in the set, *n* takes value 2; if there is a triple of individuals in the set, *n* takes value 3 and so on.

Performative

A performative is a verb phrase 'ø' which has the following property. By uttering 'I (hereby) ø' in the appropriate circumstances and with the appropriate intention, a speaker thereby brings it about that he or she øs. For example, by uttering 'I promise to pay you back' in the appropriate circumstances, the speaker has thereby promised that he or she will pay you back. Again, by uttering 'I sentence the accused to five years in prison' in the appropriate circumstances, the speaker thereby sentences the accused to five years in prison.

Perlocutionary act

This concerns the intended consequences of a speech act. For example, when you state something (an illocutionary act), the perlocutionary act is to convince your audience; when you apologize for something (a different illocutionary act), the perlocutionary act is for your audience to forgive you; and when you request something (a yet further illocutionary act), the perlocutionary act is for your audience to accede something. (See also **locutionary act** and **illocutionary act**.)

Pragmatics

Pragmatics concerns features of the utterance of sentences to do with the effects of those utterances. These effects include the **force** of utterances and also the **implicatures** of utterances. More fully, the study of pragmatics is the study of the ability of competent speakers to use language to achieve certain ends.

Predicate

A one-place predicate, such as '. . . is asleep', contains one place for a singular term. If a singular term is inserted into that place, the result is a sentence. A two-place predicate, such as '. . . is to the left of . . .', contains two places for singular terms. If a singular term is inserted into each place, the result is a sentence. Traditional grammar distinguishes between the subject and the predicate as the main parts of a sentence. More recently, linguists distinguish different syntactic categories such as noun phrases and verb phrases.

Presupposition

This is a relation between sentences. Sentence S presupposes sentence S^* only if the following condition is met: S is true or false only if S^* is true. For example, 'He is married to his second wife' presupposes 'He has been married before'.

Proposition

The content of a sentence as uttered in a given context. Propositions are also often taken to be the objects of propositional attitudes. A belief is always a belief that some proposition or other is true, a desire is always a desire that some proposition or other is true and so on. Propositions are then entities posited to serve the above theoretical roles.

Propositional attitude reports

Many of the psychological states of people are reported as states of someone bearing a certain psychological state to a certain **proposition**. We might report someone as believing (psychological attitude) *that there's whiskey in the jar* (a proposition), or as hoping (psychological attitude) *that there's a doctor in the house* (a different proposition) and so on.

Propositional knowledge

This is knowledge *that* something is the case; knowledge that a certain proposition is true. It is often contrasted with knowledge *how* (e.g. knowledge of how to tie a shoelace), although there is a dispute whether this contrast is a fundamental one and whether knowing how can be understood in terms of knowing that.

Quantifier

An expression that quantifies general terms. For example, 'every', 'all', 'each', 'some' and 'at least one' are quantifiers.

Semantic innocence

Expressions are semantically innocent if they do not undergo any change in their reference when embedded in indirect contexts.

Semantics

Semantics concerns the truth conditions of sentences.

Sense

For Frege, the sense of an expression is an aspect of its meaning in addition to what the expression refers to.

Sentence meaning

This is what a sentence can be used to say.

Speech act

To utter a sentence or series of sentences is to perform a linguistic action. Like actions in general, such a speech act is performed to serve some purpose of the agent and so it can be assessed in terms of its rationality – how well its performance serves that purpose.

Structural theory of meaning

This kind of theory seeks to specify the meanings of the sentences of a language as used by some speaker or speakers but without seeking to say why those sentences have those meanings.

Sub-sentential expression

A component expression of a sentence which is not itself a sentence.

Syntax

Syntax concerns the rules governing well-formed sentences.

Truth condition

This is the condition under which a sentence would be true.

Truth conditional theory of meaning

This theory says that a sentence's meaning is at least its truth conditions.

Truth function

A truth function takes as an argument a sentence(s) S_1 with a certain truth value, and has, as its value, a sentence S_2 whose truth value is a function of the truth value of S_1. For example, negation is a truth function. Given a true sentence S as an argument, its value is the false sentence *not-S*. Given a false sentence not-S as an argument, its value is the true sentence *not-not-S*.

Use theory of meaning

This theory says that a sentence's meaning is how the sentence is used, where a sentence's use consists in the conditions in which the sentence is accepted.

References

Note: In referring to Frege's works, this book uses the page numbers of the original publications since these appear in many translations of his works, usually in the margins or in brackets.

Adler, Jonathan E. Adler. (1994), 'Testimony, Trust, Knowing', *The Journal of Philosophy*, 91: 264–75.

Ahmed, Arif. (2007), *Saul Kripke*, (London: Continuum).

Alston, William. (1963), 'Meaning and Use', *The Philosophical Quarterly*, 51: 107–24.

—(2000), *Illocutionary Acts and Sentence Meaning*, (Ithaca, NY: Cornell University Press).

Anderson, C. Anthony. (1984), 'General Intensional Logic', in Dov M. Gabbay and Franz Guenther (eds), *Handbook of Philosophical Logic* volume II, (Dordrecht, Holland: D. Reidel Publishing Company), 355–85.

—(1987), 'Review of Leonard Linsky, *Oblique Contexts*' *Philosophy and Phenomenological Research*, 48: 153–9.

Austin, John L. (1946), 'Other Minds', *Proceedings of the Aristotelian Society*, supplementary volume 20: 148–87.

—(1962), *How To Do Things With Words*, (Oxford: Oxford University Press).

Ayer, Alfred J. (1936), *Language, Truth and Logic* (second edition), (London: Gollancz Press).

Bach, Emmon. (1974), *Syntactic Theory*, (New York: Holt, Rinehart and Winston).

Bach, Kent. (1975), 'Performatives are Statements Too', *Philosophical Studies*, 28: 229–36.

—(1994a), 'Conversational Implicature', *Mind and Language*, 9: 124–62.

—(1994b), *Thought and Reference*, (Oxford: Oxford University Press).

—(1994c), 'Ramachandran *vs*. Russell', *Analysis*, 54: 183–6.

Bach, Kent and Robert Harnish. (1979), *Linguistic Communication and Speech Acts*, (Cambridge, MA: MIT Press).

Baldwin, Thomas. (1975), 'Indirect Reference', *Analysis*, 35: 79–83.

—(1985), 'Review of Robert C. Stalnaker, *Inquiry*', *Mind*, 94: 627–30.

Barker, Stephen J. (2007), 'Semantics without the Distinction between Sense and Force', in Savas L. Tsohatzidis (ed.), *John Searle's Philosophy of Language: Force, Meaning and Mind*, (Cambridge: Cambridge University Press), 190–210.

Bar-On, Dorit, Claire Horisk and William G. Lycan. (2000), 'Deflationism, Meaning and Truth Conditions', *Philosophical Studies*, 101: 1–28.

Barwise, John and Robin Cooper. (1981), 'Generalized Quantifiers and Natural Language', *Linguistics and Philosophy*, 4: 159–219.

Beaney, Michael. (1996), *Frege: Making Sense*, (London: Duckworth Press).

Bell, David. (1979), *Frege's Theory of Judgement*, (Oxford: Oxford University Press).

—— (1990), 'How 'Russellian' was Frege?', *Mind*, 99: 267–77.

Bennett, Jonathan. (1976), *Linguistic Behaviour*, (Cambridge: Cambridge University Press).

—— (1985), 'Critical Notice of Donald Davidson, *Inquiries into Truth and Interpretation*', *Mind*, 94: 601–26.

Berkeley, George. (1710), *A Treatise Concerning the Principles of Human Knowledge*, edited by Kenneth P. Winkler, (Indianapolis: Hackett Publishing Company, Inc).

Beth, Evert W. (1963), 'Carnap's Views on the Advantages of Constructed Systems Over Natural Languages in the Philosophy of Science', in Paul Arthur Schilpp (eds), *The Philosophy of Rudolf Carnap*, (La Salle, IL: Open Court Press), 469–502.

Bird, Graham. (1981), 'Austin's Theory of Illocutionary Force', *Midwest Studies in Philosophy*, 6: 345–70.

Biro, John. (1979), 'Intentionalism in The Theory of Meaning', *The Monist*, 62: 238–58.

Black, Max. (1954), 'Frege on Functions', in his *Problems of Analysis: Philosophical Essays*, (London: Routledge and Kegan Paul), 229–54.

—— (1954–55), 'Metaphor', *Proceedings of the Aristotelian Society*, 55: 273–94.

—— (1963), 'Austin on Performatives', *Philosophy*, 38: 217–26.

—— (1973), 'Meaning and Intention: An Examination of Grice's Views', *New Literary History*, 4: 257–79.

Blackburn, Simon. (1984), *Spreading the Word: Groundings in the Philosophy of Language*, (Oxford: Oxford University Press).

—— (1988), 'Attitudes and Contents', *Ethics*, 98: 501–17.

Blackburn, Simon and Alan Code. (1978), 'The Power of Russell's Criticism of Frege: "On Denoting"', *Analysis*, 38: 65–77.

Block, Ned. (1986), 'Advertisement for a Semantics for Psychology', in Peter A. French, Theodore E. Uehling Jr and Howard K. Wettstein (eds), *Midwest Studies in Philosophy X*, (Minnesota: University of Minnesota Press), 615–78.

Blome-Tillmann, Michael. (2008), 'Conversational Implicature and the Cancellability Test', *Analysis*, 68: 156–60.

Boër, Stephen E. (1979), 'Meaning and Contrastive Stress', *The Journal of Philosophy*, 88: 263–98.

—— (1980), 'Review of Mark Platts, *Ways of Meaning*' *Linguistics and Philosophy*, 4: 141–56.

Boisvert, Daniel R. and Christopher M. Lubbers. (2003), 'Frege's Commitment to an Infinite Hierarchy of Senses', *Philosophical Papers*, 32: 31–64.

Bradley, Francis H. (1897), *Appearance and Reality*, (Oxford: Oxford University Press).

Bradley, M. C. (1969), 'How Never to Know What You Mean', *The Journal of Philosophy*, 66: 119–24.

Broackes, Justin. (1987), 'Thoughts and Definitions', *Analysis*, 47: 95–100.

Brock, Stuart. (2002), 'Fictionalism About Fictional Characters', *Noûs*, 36: 1–21.

Burge, Tyler. (1975), 'On Knowledge and Convention', *The Philosophical Review*, 84: 249–55.

— (1978), 'Belief and Synonymy', *The Journal of Philosophy*, 75: 119–38.

— (1979a), 'Individualism and the Mental', *Midwest Studies in Philosophy* IV, 73–122.

— (1979b), 'Sinning Against Frege', *The Philosophical Review*, 88: 398–432.

— (1979c), 'Frege and the Hierarchy', *Synthese*, 40: 265–81.

— (1990), 'Frege on Sense and Linguistic Meaning', in David Bell and Neil Cooper (eds), *The Analytic Tradition*, (Oxford: Basil Blackwell), 30–60.

Burgess, Alexis G. and John P. Burgess. (2011), *Truth*, (Princeton, NJ: Princeton University Press).

Cain, Mallahan J. (2010), 'Linguistics, Psychology, and the Scientific Study of Language', *Dialectica*, 64: 385–404.

Cargile, James. (1979), *Paradoxes: A Study in Form and Predication*, (Cambridge: Cambridge University Press).

Carnap, Rudolf. (1937), *The Logical Syntax of Language*, (London: Routledge and Kegan Paul).

— (1947), *Meaning and Necessity*, (Chicago, IL: University of Chicago Press).

— (1950), *Logical Foundations of Probability*, (Chicago, IL: University of Chicago Press).

— (1956), *Meaning and Necessity: A Study of Semantics and Modal Logic*, (Chicago, IL: University of Chicago Press).

Carney, James D. and G. W. Fitch. (1979), 'Can Russell Avoid Frege's Sense?', *Mind*, 88: 384–93.

Carruthers, Peter. (1983), 'On Concept and Object', *Theoria*, 49: 49–86.

Chapman, Siobhan. (2005), *Paul Grice, Philosopher and Linguist*, (Basingstoke: Palgrave Macmillan).

Chihara, Charles S. (1975), 'Davidson's Extensional Theory of Meaning', *Philosophical Studies*, 28: 1–15.

Chisholm, Roderick M. (1964), 'J. L. Austin's *Philosophical Papers*', *Mind*, 73: 1–26.

Chomsky, Noam. (1957), *Syntactic Structures*, (Berlin: Mouton de Gruyter).

— (1964), *Cartesian Linguistics*, (New York: Harper and Row).

— (1965), *Aspects of the Theory of Syntax*, (Cambridge, MA: MIT Press).

— (1968), 'Quine's Empirical Assumptions', *Synthese*, 19: 53–68.

— (1972), *Language and Mind*, (New York: Harcourt Brace Jovanovich).

— (1975), *Reflections on Language*, (New York: Random House).

— (2000), 'Linguistics and Philosophy', in Robert Cummins and Denise Dellarosa Cummins (eds), *Minds, Brains, and Computers: The Foundations of Cognitive Science*, (Oxford: Blackwell), 464–83.

Church, Alonzo. (1956), *Introduction to Mathematical Logic* volume I, (Princeton, NJ: Princeton University Press).

Clark, Michael. (1975), 'Utterer's Meaning and Implications about Belief', *Analysis*, 35: 105–8.

Coady, C. A. J. (1976), 'Review of Stephen R. Schiffer, *Meaning*' *Philosophy*, 51: 102–9.

— (1981), 'Review of David Holdcroft, *Words and Deeds: Problems in the Theory of Speech Acts*' *Philosophy*, 56: 580–2.

Cohen, L. Jonathan. (1964), 'Do Illocutionary Forces Exist?', *The Philosophical Quarterly*, 14: 118–37.

— (1971), 'The Logical Particles of Natural Language', in Yehoshua Bar-Hillel (ed.), *Pragmatics of Natural Language*, (Dordrecht, Holland: D. Reidel Publishing Company), 50–68.

— (1973), 'The Non-Existence of Illocutionary Forces: A Reply to Mr Burch' *Ratio*, 15: 125–31.

— (1974), 'Speech Acts', in Thomas A. Sebok (ed.), *Current Trends in Linguistics volume 12: Linguistics and Adjacent Arts and Sciences*, (The Hague and Paris: Mouton), 173–209.

— (1977), 'Can The Conversationalist Hypothesis Be Defended?', *Philosophical Studies*, 31: 81–90.

— (1985), 'A Problem about Ambiguity in Truth Theoretical Semantics', *Analysis*, 45: 129–34.

Craig, Edward. (1982), 'Meaning, Use and Privacy', *Mind*, 91: 541–64.

— (1990), 'Davidson and the Sceptic: The Thumbnail Version', *Analysis*, 54: 213–14.

Cresswell, Maxwell J. (1973), *Logics and Languages*, (London: Methuen Press).

— (1975), 'Hyperintensional Logic', *Studia Logica*, 34: 25–38.

— (1985), *Structured Meanings: The Semantics of Propositional Attitudes*, (Cambridge, MA: MIT Press).

— (1988), 'Review of Robert C. Stalnaker, *Inquiry*' *Linguistics and Philosophy*, 11: 515–19.

Cummins, Robert. (1979), 'Intention, Meaning and Truth Conditions', *Philosophical Studies*, 35: 345–60.

Currie, Gregory. (1976), 'Was Frege a Linguistic Philosopher?', *The British Journal for the Philosophy of Science*, 27: 79–92.

— (1982), *Frege: An Introduction to His Philosophy*, (Sussex: Harvester Press).

— (1984), 'Frege's Metaphysical Argument', *The Philosophical Quarterly*, 34: 329–42.

— (1993), 'On The Road to Antirealism', *Inquiry*, 36: 465–83.

Davidson, Donald. (1965), 'Theories of Meaning and Learnable Languages', in Yehoshua Bar-Hillel (ed.), *Proceedings of the 1964 International Congress for Logic, Methodology, and Philosophy of Science* volume 2, (Amsterdam: North-Holland Publishing Company), 383–94. Reprinted in Donald Davidson. (2001a), *Inquiries into Truth and Interpretation* (second edition), (Oxford: Oxford University Press), 3–17. (Page references are to the reprint).

— (1967a), 'Truth and Meaning', *Synthese*, 17: 304–23. Reprinted in his (2001), *Inquiries into Truth and Interpretation* (second edition), (Oxford: Oxford University Press), 17–37. (Page references are to the reprint).

— (1967b), 'The Logical Form of Action Sentences', in Nicholas Rescher (ed.), *The Logic of Decision and Action*, (Pittsburgh: University of Pittsburgh Press), 81–95. Reprinted in his (2001b), *Essays on Actions and Events*, (Oxford: Oxford University Press), 105–49. (Page references are to the reprint).

— (1968), 'On Saying That', *Synthese*, 19: 130–46. Reprinted in his (2001a), *Inquiries into Truth and Interpretation* (second edition), (Oxford: Oxford University Press), 93–108. (Page references are to the reprint).

— (1969), 'True to the Facts', *The Journal of Philosophy*, 66: 748–64. Reprinted in his (2001a), *Inquiries into Truth and Interpretation* (second edition), (Oxford: Oxford University Press), 43–54.

— (1970), 'Semantics for Natural Languages', in Visentini Bruno et al. (eds), *Linguaggi nella Società e nella Tecnica*, (Milan: Edizoni do Communità), 177–88. Reprinted in his (2001b), *Essays on Actions and Events*, (Oxford: Oxford University Press), 55–64. (Page references are to the reprint).

— (1973), 'Radical Interpretation', *Dialectica*, 27: 314–28. Reprinted in his (2001a), *Inquiries into Truth and Interpretation* (second edition), (Oxford: Oxford University Press), 125–40. (Page references are to the reprint).

— (1974), 'Belief and the Basis of Meaning', *Synthese*, 27: 309–23. Reprinted in his (2001a), *Inquiries into Truth and Interpretation* (second edition), (Oxford: Oxford University Press), 141–54. (Page references are to the reprint).

— (1975), 'Thought and Talk', in Samuel Guttenplan (ed.), *Mind and Language*, (Oxford: Oxford University Press), 7–23. Reprinted in Donald Davidson. (2001a), *Inquiries into Truth and Interpretation* (second edition), (Oxford: Oxford University Press), 155–71. (Page references are to the reprint).

— (1976), 'Reply to Foster' in Gareth Evans and John McDowell (eds), *Truth and Meaning*, (Oxford: Oxford University Press), 33–41. Reprinted in his (2001a), *Inquiries into Truth and Interpretation* (second edition), (Oxford: Oxford University Press), 171–80. (Page references are to the reprint).

— (1977), 'The Method of Truth in Metaphysics', in Peter A. French, Terence E. Uehling Jr and Howard K. Wettstein (eds), *Midwest Studies in Philosophy 2: Studies in the Philosophy of Language*, (Minneapolis: University of Minnesota Press). Reprinted in his (2001a), *Inquiries into Truth and Interpretation* (second edition), (Oxford: Oxford University Press), 199–214. (Page references are to the reprint).

— (1979), 'Moods and Performances', in Avishai Margalit (ed.), *Meaning and Use*, (Dordrecht: Kluwer Academic Press), 9–20. Reprinted in his (2001a), *Inquiries into Truth and Interpretation* (second edition), (Oxford: Oxford University Press), 109–22. (Page references are to the reprint).

—(1982), 'Empirical Content', *Grazer Philosophische Studien*, 16–17: 271–89. Reprinted in Donald Davidson. (2001b), *Subjective, Intersubjective, Objective: Philosophical Essays volume 3*, (Oxford: Oxford University Press): 159–76. (Page references are to the reprint).

—(1984), 'Communication and Convention', *Synthese*, 59: 3–17. Reprinted in his (2001a), *Inquiries into Truth and Interpretation* (second edition), (Oxford: Oxford University Press), 265–80. (Page references are to the reprint).

—(1989), 'A Coherence Theory of Truth and Knowledge', in Ernest Lepore (ed.), *Truth and Interpretations: Perspectives on the Philosophy of Donald Davidson*, (Oxford: Blackwell), 307–19. Reprinted in his (2001b), *Subjective, Intersubjective, Objective: Philosophical Essays volume 3* (second edition), (Oxford: Oxford University Press), 137–58. (Page references are to the reprint).

—(1991), 'Three Varieties of Knowledge', in A. Philip Griffiths (ed.), *A. J. Ayer: Memorial Essays*, (Cambridge: Cambridge University Press), 153–66. Reprinted in his (2001b), *Subjective, Intersubjective, Objective: Philosophical Essays volume 3* (second edition), (Oxford: Oxford University Press), 205–20. (Page references are to the reprint).

—(1998), 'The Irreducibility of the Concept of the Self', in Marcelo Stamm (ed.), *Philosophie in synthetischer Absicht*, (Stuttgart: Klett-Cotta). Reprinted in his (2001b), *Subjective, Intersubjective, Objective: Philosophical Essays volume 3* (second edition), (Oxford: Oxford University Press), 85–93. (Page references are to the reprint).

Davies, Martin. (1981), *Meaning, Quantification, Necessity: Themes in Philosophical Logic*, (London: Routledge and Kegan Paul).

—(2006), 'Foundational Issues in the Philosophy of Language', in Michael Devitt and Richard Hanley (eds), *Blackwell Guide to Philosophy of Language*, (Oxford: Blackwell), 19–40.

Davis, Wayne A. (1998), *Implicature: Intention, Convention, and Principle in the Failure of Gricean Theory*, (Cambridge: Cambridge University Press).

—(2003), *Meaning, Expression, and Thought*, (Cambridge: Cambridge University Press).

—(2007), 'How Normative is Implicature?', *Journal of Pragmatics*, 39: 1655–72.

Devitt, Michael. (1981), 'Donnellan's Distinction', in Peter A. French, Theodore E. Uehling Jr and Howard K. Wettstein (eds), *Midwest Studies in Philosophy* VI, (Minnesota: University of Minnesota Press), 511–24.

—(1983), 'Dummett's Anti-Realism', *The Journal of Philosophy*, 80: 73–99.

—(2004), 'The Case for Referential Descriptions', in Anne Bezuidenhout and Marga Reimer (eds), *Descriptions and Beyond*, (Oxford: Oxford University Press), 280–306.

Devitt, Michael and Kim Sterelny. (1999), *Language and Reality: An Introduction to the Philosophy of Language* (second edition), (Cambridge, MA: MIT Press).

Diller, Antoni. (1993a), 'Is the Concept *Horse* an Object?', *Modern Logic*, 4: 345–66.

—(1993b), 'On the Sense of Unsaturated Expressions', *Philosophical Papers*, 22: 71–9.

Divers, John and Alexander Miller. (1994), 'Why Expressivists about Value Should Not Love Minimalism about Truth', *Analysis*, 54: 12–19.

Dolby, David. (2009), 'The Reference Principle – a defence', *Analysis*, 69: 286–96.

Donnellan, Keith. (1966), 'Reference and Definite *Descriptions*', *The Philosophical Review*, 77: 281–304.

—(1968), 'Putting Humpty Dumpty Together Again', *The Philosophical Review*, 77: 203–15.

Dretske, Fred I. (1972), 'Contrastive Statements', *The Philosophical Review*, 81: 411–37.

Dudman, Victor H. (1970), 'Frege's Judgement Stroke', *The Philosophical Quarterly*, 20: 159–61.

—(1972), 'The Concept Horse', *Australasian Journal of Philosophy*, 50: 67–75.

—(1976), '*Bedeutung* for Predicates', in Matthis Schirn (ed.), *Studien zu Frege, volume III*, (Stuttgart-Bad Cannstatt: Frommann-Holzboog), 71–84.

Duhem, Pierre. (1906), *The Aim and Structure of Physical Theory*, translated by Philip P. Wiener, (Princeton, NJ: Princeton University Press, 1954).

Dummett, Michael. (1959), 'Truth', *Proceedings of the Aristotelian Society*, 59: 141–62.

—(1975), 'The Philosophical Basis of Intuitionistic Logic', in H. E. Rose and J. C. Shepherdson (eds), *Logic Colloquium '73*, (Amsterdam: North Holland), 5–40.

—(1981a), *Frege: Philosophy of Language* (second edition), (London: Duckworth Press).

—(1981b), *The Interpretation of Frege's Philosophy*, (London: Duckworth Press).

—(1991), *The Logical Basis of Metaphysics*, (London: Duckworth Press).

—(2010), *The Nature and Future of Philosophy*, (Columbia: University of Columbia Press).

Duží, Marie, Bjørn Jespersen, and Pavel Materna. (2010), *Procedural Semantics for Hyperintensional Logic: Foundations and Applications of Transparent Intensional Logic*, (Berlin: Springer).

Dyke, Heather. (2007), *Metaphysics and the Representational Fallacy*, (London: Routledge).

Eklund, Matti. (2008), 'Review of Heather Dyke *Metaphysics and the Representational Fallacy*', *Notre Dame Philosophical Reviews*, 2008.11.03. Online at: http://ndpr.nd.edu/review.cfm?id=14565.

Evans, Gareth. (1974), 'Identity and Predication', *The Journal of Philosophy*, 72: 343–63.

—(1982), *The Varieties of Reference*, (Oxford: Oxford University Press).

—(1985), 'Understanding Demonstratives', in his *Collected Papers*, (Oxford: Oxford University Press), 291–321.

Evans, Gareth and John McDowell. (1976) (eds), *Truth and Meaning: Essays in Semantics*, (Oxford: Clarendon Press).

Feldman, Richard. (1986), 'Davidson's Theory of Propositional Attitudes', *Canadian Journal of Philosophy*, 16: 693–712.

Field, Hartry. (1986), 'Review of Robert C. Stalnaker, *Inquiry*' *Philosophy of Science*, 53: 425–48.

Fitch, Gregory W. (1985), 'Indeterminate Descriptions', *Canadian Journal of Philosophy*, 14: 257–76.

— (2004), *Saul Kripke*, (Chesham, Buckinghamshire: Acumen Publishing Limited).

Fodor, Jerry A. (1970), 'Troubles with Actions', *Synthese*, 21: 298–312.

— (1975), *The Language of Thought*, (Cambridge, MA: Harvard University Press).

— (1985), 'Some Notes On What Linguistics is About', in Jerrold Katz (ed.), *The Philosophy of Linguistics*, (Oxford: Oxford University Press), 146–60.

— (1990), *A Theory of Content and Other Essays*, (Cambridge, MA: MIT Press).

Fodor, Jerry A. and Ernest LePore. (1991), 'Why Meaning (Probably) Isn't Conceptual Role', *Mind and Language*, 6: 328–43.

— (1992), *Holism: A Shopper's Guide*, (Oxford: Blackwell).

Føllesdal, Dagfinn. (1975), 'Meaning and Experience', in Samuel Guttenplan (ed.), *Mind and Language*, (Oxford: Oxford University Press), 25–44.

Fox, Chris and Shalom Lappin. (2005), *Foundations of Intensional Semantics*, (Oxford: Blackwell).

Frege, Gottlob. (1879), *Begriffsschrift*, edited and translated by T. W. Bynum as *Conceptual Notation*, (Oxford: Oxford University Press, 1972).

— (1884), *Grundlagen der Aritmetik*, translated by J. L. Austin as *Foundations of Arithmetic: A Logic-Mathematical Enquiry into the Concept of Number*, (Oxford: Basil Blackwell, 1950).

— (1891), 'Function and Object', in Peter Geach and Max Black (eds and trans.), *Translations from the Philosophical Writings of Gottlob Frege*, (Oxford: Blackwell, 1952), 21–41.

— (1892a), 'On Sense and Reference', in Peter Geach and Max Black (eds and trans.), *Translations from the Philosophical Writings of Gottlob Frege*, (Oxford: Blackwell, 1952), 56–78.

— (1892b), 'On Concept and Object', in Peter Geach and Max Black (eds and trans.), *Translations from the Philosophical Writings of Gottlob Frege*, (Oxford: Blackwell, 1952), 42–55.

— (1892–1895), 'Comments on Sense and Meaning', in Hans Hermes, Friedrich Kambartel, and Friedrich Kaulbach (eds), *Posthumous Writings*, Peter Long and Roger White (trans.), (Oxford: Basil Blackwell, 1979), 118–25.

— (1893), *Grundgesetze der Arithmetik*, (Jena: Verlag Hermann Pohle, Band I). Partial translation by Montgomery Furth as *The Basic Laws of Arithmetic*, (Berkeley, CA: University of California Press, 1964).

— (1894), 'Review of Edmund Husserl, *Philosophie der Arithmetik* I', extract in Michael Beaney (ed.), *The Frege Reader*, (Oxford: Basil Blackwell, 1997), 224–6.

— (1903), 'Frege on Definitions', in Peter Geach and Max Black (eds and trans.), *Translations from the Philosophical Writings of Gottlob Frege*, (Oxford: Blackwell, 1952), 159–72.

—(1904), 'What is a Function?', in Peter Geach and Max Black (eds and trans.), *Translations from the Philosophical Writings of Gottlob Frege*, (Oxford: Blackwell, 1952), 107–16.

—(1918), 'The Thought: A Logical Inquiry', in Peter Geach (ed. and trans.), *Logical Investigations*, (Oxford: Blackwell, 1977), 1–30.

—(1919), 'Negation', in Peter Geach and Max Black (eds and trans.), *Translations from the Philosophical Writings of Gottlob Frege*, (Oxford: Blackwell, 1952), 117–35.

—(1979), 'Comments on Sense and Reference', *Posthumous Writings*, translated by Peter Long and Roger White, (Oxford: Blackwell), 118–25.

—(1980), *Philosophical and Mathematical Correspondence of Gottlob Frege*, Gottfried Gabriel, Han Hermes, Friedrich Kambartel, Christian Thiel and Albert Veraart (eds and trans.), (Chicago, IL: University of Chicago Press).

Friedman, Michael. (1975), 'Physicalism and the Indeterminacy of Translation', *Noûs*, 9: 353–74.

Fromkin, Victoria, Robert Rodman, and Nina Hyams. (1978), *An Introduction to Language*, (New York: Holt, Rinehart and Winston).

Furth, Montgomery. (1968), 'Two Types of Denotation', in Nicholas Rescher (ed.), *Studies in Logical Theory, APQ Monograph Series ii*, (Oxford: Blackwell), 9–45.

Ganeri, Jonardon. (1995), 'Contextually Incomplete Descriptions – A New Reply to Ramachandran', *Analysis*, 55: 287–90.

Geach, Peter T. (1950), 'Russell's Theory of Descriptions', *Analysis*, 10: 84–8.

—(1963), 'Frege', in P. T. Geach and G. E. M. Anscombe, *Three Philosophers*, (Oxford: Basil Blackwell), 127–62.

—(1965), 'Assertion', *The Philosophical Review*, 74: 449–65.

—(1972), 'Saying and Showing in Frege and Wittgenstein', in K. J. Jaakko Hintikka (ed.), *Essays on Wittgenstein in Honour of G. H. von Wright, Acta Philosophica Fennica* 28, (Amsterdam: North Holland), 54–70. Reprinted in John V. Canfield (ed.), *The Philosophy of Wittgenstein* volume 3, (New York: Garland Publishing), 30–47.

—(1976a), 'Critical Notice of Michael Dummett, *Frege: Philosophy of Language*', *Mind*, 48: 436–49.

—(1976b), 'Back-Reference', in Asa Kasher (ed.), *Language in Focus: Foundations, Methods and Systems. Essays in Memory of Yehoshua Bar-Hillel*, (Dordrecht, Holland: D. Reidel Publishing Company), 25–39.

—(1980), 'Some Problems about the Sense and Reference of Proper Names', *Canadian Journal of Philosophy*, supplementary volume VI: 83–96.

George, Alexander. (1989), 'How Not to Become Confused About Linguistics', in Alexander George (ed.), *Reflections on Chomsky*, (Oxford: Basil Blackwell), 90–110.

Gibbard, Allan. (1990), *Wise Choices, Apt Feelings: A Theory of Normative Judgement*, (Cambridge, MA: Harvard University Press).

318 References

Ginet, Carl. (1979), 'Performativity', *Linguistics and Philosophy*, 3: 245–65.

Glüer, Kathrin. (2012), 'Theories of Meaning and Truth Conditions', in Manuel Garciá-Carpintero and Max Kölbel (eds), *The Continuum Companion to the Philosophy of Language*, (London: Continuum), 84–105.

Goodman, Nelson. (1949), 'On Likeness of Meaning', *Analysis*, 10: 1–7.

— (1953), 'On Some Differences About Meaning', *Analysis*, 13: 90–6.

— (1955), *Fact, Fiction and Forecast*, (Cambridge, MA: Harvard University Press).

Grandy, Richard E. (1973), 'Reference, Meaning and Belief', *The Journal of Philosophy*, 70: 439–52.

— (1977), 'Review of David Lewis, *Convention: A Philosophical Study*', *The Journal of Philosophy*, 74: 129–39.

— (1989), 'On Grice on Language', *The Journal of Philosophy*, 86: 514–25.

Green, Karen. (2006), 'A Pinch of Salt for Frege', *Synthese*, 150: 209–28.

Grice, Herbert P. (1957), 'Meaning', *The Philosophical Review*, 66: 377–88. Reprinted in his (1989), *Studies in the Way of Words*, (Harvard, MA: Harvard University Press), 213–23.

— (1961), 'The Causal Theory of Perception', *Proceedings of the Aristotelian Society*, supplementary volume 35: 121–52. Reprinted (with omissions) in his (1989), *Studies in the Way of Words*, (Harvard, MA: Harvard University Press), 224–47.

— (1968), 'Utterer's Meaning, Sentence Meaning and Word Meaning', *Foundations of Language*, 4: 225–42. Reprinted in his (1989), *Studies in the Way of Words*, (Harvard, MA: Harvard University Press), 117–37.

— (1969), 'Utterer's Meaning and Intentions', *The Philosophical Review*, 68: 147–77. Reprinted in his (1989), *Studies in the Way of Words*, (Harvard, MA: Harvard University Press), 86–116.

— (1975), 'Logic and Conversation', in Peter Cole, John P. Kimball and Jerry L. Morgan (eds), *Syntax and Semantics volume 3: Speech Acts*, (New York: Academic Press), 41–58. Reprinted in his (1989), *Studies in the Way of Words*, (Harvard, MA: Harvard University Press), 22–40.

— (1978), 'Further Notes on Logic and Conversation', in Peter Cole (ed.), *Syntax and Semantics volume 9: Pragmatics*, (New York: Academic Press, New York), 113–28. Reprinted in his (1989), *Studies in the Way of Words*, (Harvard, MA: Harvard University Press), 41–57.

— (1981), 'Presupposition and Conversational Implicature', in Peter Cole (ed.), *Radical Pragmatics*, (New York: Academic Press), 183–98.

— (1982), 'Meaning Revisited', in N. V. Smith (ed.), *Mutual Knowledge*, (New York: Academic Press), 223–43. Reprinted in his (1989), *Studies in the Way of Words*, (Harvard, MA: Harvard University Press), 283–303.

— (1987), 'Retrospective Epilogue', in his (1989), *Studies in the Way of Words*, (Harvard, MA: Harvard University Press), 339–85.

Grice, Herbert P. and P. F. Strawson. (1956), 'In Defense of a Dogma', *The Philosophical Review*, 65: 141–58.

Haack, R. J. (1978), 'Davidson on Learnable Languages', *Mind*, 87: 230–49.

Hale, Bob. (1986), 'The Compleat Projectivist: Critical Notice of Simon Blackburn, *Spreading the Word*', *The Philosophical Quarterly*, 36: 65–84.

— (1987), *Abstract Objects*, (Oxford: Basil Blackwell).

— (1991), 'Review of Keith Campbell, *Abstract Particulars*' *Mind*, 100: 142–6.

— (1993), 'Can There Be A Logic of Attitudes?', in John Haldane and Crispin Wright (eds), *Reality, Representation and Projection*, (Oxford: Oxford University Press), 337–63.

— (2002), 'Can Arboreal Knotwork Help Blackburn out of Frege's Abyss?', *Philosophy and Phenomenological Research*, 65: 144–9.

Hare, Richard M. (1952), *The Language of Morals*, (Oxford: Oxford University Press).

— (1970), 'Meaning and Speech Acts', *The Philosophical Review*, 79: 3–24.

Harman, Gilbert. (1967), 'Quine on Existence and Meaning, I. The Death of Meaning', *The Review of Metaphysics*, 21: 124–51.

— (1972), 'Logical Form', *Foundations of Language*, 9: 38–65.

Harnish, Robert M. (1976), 'Logical Form and Implicature', in Thomas G. Bever, Jerrold J. Katz, and D. Terence Langendoen (eds), *An Integrated Theory of Linguistic Ability*, (New York: Crowell), 313–91.

Harrison, Jonathan. (1962), 'Knowing and Promising', *Mind*, 71: 443–57.

Heal, Jane. (1978), 'On The Phrase 'Theory of Meaning'', *Mind*, 87: 359–75.

Heck, Richard G. (2002), 'Do Demonstratives have Senses?', *Philosophers' Imprint*, 2/2: 1–33.

Heidelberger, Herbert. (1975), 'Dummett on Frege's Philosophy of Language', *Metaphilosophy*, 6: 35–43.

Hintikka, Jaakko. (1961), 'Modality and Quantification', *Theoria*, 27: 119–28.

— (1969), 'Semantics for Propositional Attitudes', in his *Models for Modalities*, (Dordrecht, Holland: D. Reidel Publishing Company), 87–111.

— (1975), 'Quine on Quantifying In – A Dialogue', in his *The Intentions of Intentionality and Other New Models for Modalities*, (Dordrecht, Holland: D. Reidel Publishing Company), 102–36.

Holdcroft, David. (1978), *Words and Deeds: Problems in the Theory of Speech Acts*, (Oxford: Oxford University Press).

Holland, Alan. (1978), 'Carnap on Frege on Indirect Sense', *Analysis*, 38: 24–32.

Hom, Christopher. (2008), 'Perjoratives', *Philosophy Compass*, 5: 164–85.

— (2010), 'The Semantics of Racial Epithets', *The Journal of Philosophy*, 105: 416–40.

Hookway, Christopher. (1988), *Quine*, (Cambridge: Polity Press).

Horgan, Terence. (1978), 'The Case Against Events', *The Philosophical Review*, 87: 28–42.

Hornsby, Jennifer. (2001), 'Meaning and Uselessness: How to Think about Derogatory Words', in Peter A. French and Howard K. Wettstein (eds), *Midwest Studies in Philosophy* XXV, (Minnesota: University of Minnesota Press), 128–41.

— (2006), 'Speech Acts and Performatives', in Ernest Lepore and Barry C. Smith (eds), *The Oxford Handbook of Philosophy of Language*, (Oxford: Oxford University Press), 893–909.

Horsten, Leon. (2008), 'Impredicative Identity Criteria', *Philosophy and Phenomenological Research*, 80: 411–39.

Houston, John. (1970), 'Truth Valuation of Explicit Performatives', *The Philosophical Quarterly*, 20: 139–49.

Hugly, Philip and Charles Sayward. (1979), 'A Problem About Conversational Implicature', *Linguistics and Philosophy*, 3: 19–25.

Jackson, Frank. (1998), *From Metaphysics to Ethics: A Defence of Conceptual Analysis*, (Oxford: Clarendon Press).

Jackson, Frank, Graham Oppy and Michael Smith. (1994), 'Minimalism and Truth Aptness' *Mind*, 103: 287–302.

Jubien, Michael. (1996), 'The Myth of Identity Conditions', *Philosophical Perspectives*, 10, Metaphysics: 343–56.

Kaplan, David. (1972), 'What is Russell's Theory of Descriptions?', in David Pears (ed.), *Bertrand Russell*, (Garden City, NY: Anchor Books), 227–44.

— (1975), 'How to Russell a Frege-Church', *The Journal of Philosophy*, 72: 716–29.

— (1989), 'Demonstratives', in Joseph Almog, John Perry and Howard Wettstein (eds), *Themes from Kaplan*, (Oxford: Oxford University Press), 481–563.

Kasher, Asa. (1976), 'Conversational Maxims and Rationality', in Asa Kasher (ed.), *Language in Focus: Foundations, Methods and Systems. Essays in Memory of Yehoshua Bar-Hillel*, (Dordrecht, Holland: D. Reidel Publishing Company), 197–216.

— (1982), 'Gricean Implicature Revisited', *Philosophica*, 29: 25–44.

Katz, Fred M. and Jerrold J. Katz. (1977), 'Is Necessity the Mother of Intension?', *The Philosophical Review*, 86: 70–96.

Katz, Jerrold J. (1998), *Realistic Rationalism*, (Cambridge, MA: MIT Press).

Keenan, Elinor. (1976), 'On the Universality of Conversational Implicatures', *Language in Society*, 5: 67–80.

Kemp, Gary. (2006), *Quine: A Guide for the Perplexed*, (London: Continuum).

Kirk, Robert. (1986), *Translation Determined*, (Oxford: Oxford University Press).

Klement, Kevin C. (2003), 'The Number of Senses', *Erkenntnis*, 58: 302–23.

Kneale, William and Martha Kneale. (1962), *The Development of Logic*, (Oxford: Oxford University Press).

Kripke, Saul. (1963), 'Semantic Considerations on Modal Logic' *Acta Philosophica Fennica* 16: 83–94.

— (1972), 'Naming and Necessity', in Donald Davidson and Gilbert Harman (eds), *Semantics of Natural Language*, (Dordrecht, Holland: D. Reidel Publishing Company), 253–355, 763–9. Reprinted as (1980), *Naming and Necessity*, (Oxford: Blackwell). (Page references are to the reprint).

— (1977), 'Speaker's Reference and Semantic Reference', in Peter A. French, Theodore E. Uehling Jr and Howard K. Wettstein (eds), *Midwest Studies in Philosophy II*, (Minnesota: University of Minnesota Press), 255–76.

— (1979), 'A Puzzle about Belief', in Avishai Margalit (ed.), *Meaning and Use*, (Dordrecht and Boston: Reidel), 239–83.

— (1982), *Wittgenstein on Rules and Private Language*, (Oxford: Blackwell).

Künne, Wolfgang. (1989), 'Review of Bob Hale, *Abstract Objects*' *Ratio* (New Series), 11: 89–100.

Landesman, Charles. (1970), 'Scepticism about Meaning: Quine's Thesis of Indeterminacy', *Australasian Journal of Philosophy*, 48: 320–37.

Larson, Richard and Gabriel Segal. (1995), *Knowledge of Meaning: An Introduction to Semantic Theory*, (Cambridge, MA: MIT Press).

Laurence, Stephen. (1996), 'A Chomskian Alternative to Convention-Based Semantics', *Mind*, 105: 269–301.

— (2003), 'Is Linguistics a Branch of Psychology?', in Alex Barber (ed.), *Epistemology of Language*, (Oxford: Oxford University Press), 69–106.

Leech, Geoffrey. (1983), *Principles of Pragmatics*, (New York: Longman).

Leeds, Stephen. (1979), 'Semantic Primitives and Learnability', *Logique et Analyse*, 85–86: 99–108.

Lemmon, Edward J. (1962), 'Sentences Verifiable By Their Use', *Analysis*, 22: 86–9.

Lepore, Ernest. (1982), 'In Defense of Davidson', *Linguistics and Philosophy*, 5: 277–94.

Lepore, Ernest and Kirk Ludwig. (2007), *Donald Davidson's Truth Theoretic Semantics*, (Oxford: Oxford University Press).

Levinson, Stephen C. (1983), *Pragmatics*, (Cambridge: Cambridge University Press).

— (2000), *Presumptive Meanings: The Theory of Generalized Conversational Implicature*, (Cambridge, MA: MIT Press).

Lewis, David. (1969), *Convention*, (Oxford: Blackwell).

— (1970), 'General Semantics', *Synthese*, 22: 18–67. Reprinted with postscript in his *Philosophical Papers* volume I, (Oxford: Oxford University Press): 189–232.

— (1972), 'Psychophysical and Theoretical Identifications', *Australasian Journal of Philosophy*, 50: 249–58.

— (1975), 'Languages and Language', in Keith Gunderson (ed.), *Minnesota Studies in the Philosophy of Language* volume VII, (Minneapolis: University of Minnesota Press): 3–35.

— (1978), 'Truth in Fiction', *American Philosophical Quarterly*, 15: 37–46.

—(1981), 'What puzzling Pierre does not believe', *Australasian Journal of Philosophy*, 59: 283–9. Reprinted in his (1999), *Papers in Metaphysics and Epistemology*, (Cambridge: Cambridge University Press), 408–17.

—(1986a), *On The Plurality of Worlds*, (Oxford: Blackwell).

—(1986b) *Philosophical Papers* volume 1, (Oxford: Oxford University Press).

Linsky, Leonard. (1983), *Oblique Contexts*, (Chicago, IL: University of Chicago Press).

Loar, Brian. (1981), *Mind and Meaning*, (Cambridge: Cambridge University Press).

Lumsden, David. (2010), 'The Relationship Between Speaker's Reference and Semantic Reference', *Language and Linguistics Compass*, 4: 296–306.

Lycan, William G. (1974), 'Could Propositions Explain Anything?', *Canadian Journal of Philosophy*, 3: 427–34.

—(1984), *Logical Form in Natural Language*, (Cambridge, MA: MIT Press).

—(2008), *Philosophy of Language: A Contemporary Introduction* (second edition), (London: Routledge).

MacBride, Fraser. (2003), 'Speaking with Shadows: A Study of Neo-Logicism', *The British Journal for the Philosophy of Science*, 54: 103–63.

—(2006), 'Predicate Reference', in Ernest Lepore and Barry C. Smith (eds), *The Oxford Handbook of Philosophy of Language*, (Oxford: Oxford University Press), 422–75.

—(2011), 'Impure Reference: A Way Around the Concept *Horse* Paradox', *Philosophical Perspectives*, 25: 297–312.

MacKay, Alfred F. (1972), 'Professor Grice's Theory of Meaning', *Mind*, 81: 57–66.

Mackie, Jhon L. (1973), *Truth, Probability, and Paradox: Studies in Philosophical Logic*, (Oxford: Clarendon Press).

Makin, Gideon. (2000), *Metaphysics of Meaning: Frege and Russell on Sense and Denotation*, (London: Routledge).

Margalit, Avishai. (1978), 'The "Platitude" Principle of Semantics', *Erkenntnis*, 13: 377–95.

Marr, David. (1982), *Vision: A Computational Investigation Into the Human Representation and Processing of Visual Information*, (Cambridge, MA: MIT Press).

Marshall, William. (1953), 'Frege's Theory of Functions and Objects', *The Philosophical Review*, 62: 374–90.

—(1955), 'Sense and Reference: A Reply', *The Philosophical Review*, 65: 342–61.

Martin, Robert M. (1987), *The Meaning of Language*, (Cambridge, MA: MIT Press).

Martinich, Aloysius P. (1984), 'A Theory for Metaphor', *Journal of Literary Semantics*, 12: 35–6.

Mates, Benson. (1952), 'Synonymity', in Leonard Linsky (ed.), *Semantics and the Philosophy of Language*, (Illinois: The University of Illinois Press at Urbana), 111–36.

—(1973), 'Descriptions and Reference', *Foundations of Language*, 10: 409–18.

Matthews, Robert. (1986), 'Learnability and Semantic Theory', in Ernest Lepore (ed.), *Truth and Interpretation: Perspectives on the Philosophy of Donald Davidson*, (Oxford: Blackwell), 49–58.

McCawley, James D. (1985), 'Actions and Events despite Bertrand Russell', in Ernest Lepore and Brian McLaughlin (eds), *Actions and Events: Perspectives on the Philosophy of Donald Davidson*, (Oxford: Basil Blackwell), 177–92.

McDowell, John. (1977), 'On The Sense and Reference of A Proper Name', *Mind*, 86: 159–85.

— (1984), '*De Re* Senses', *The Philosophical Quarterly*, 34: 283–94.

— (1998), 'Meaning, Communication, and Knowledge', in his *Meaning, Knowledge and Reality*, (Harvard, MA: Harvard University Press), 29–50.

McGinn, Colin. (1977a), 'Semantics for Nonindicative Sentences', *Philosophical Studies*, 32: 301–11.

— (1977b), 'Charity, Interpretation, and Belief', *The Journal of Philosophy*, 74: 521–35.

— (1981), 'Review of Noam Chomsky, *Rules and Representations*', *The Journal of Philosophy*, 78: 288–98.

— (2000), *Logical Properties: Identity, Existence, Predication, Necessity, Truth*, (Oxford: Oxford University Press).

Mendelsohn, Richard L. (2005), *The Philosophy of Gottlob Frege*, (Cambridge: Cambridge University Press).

Mill, John S. (1843), *A System of Logic, Ratiocinative and Inductive*, (New York: Harper and Brothers).

Miller, Alexander. (2003), *An Introduction to Contemporary Metaethics*, (Oxford: Polity Press).

— (2007), *Philosophy of Language* (second edition), (London: Routledge).

Milne, Peter. (1986), 'Frege's Context Principle', *Mind*, 95: 491–5.

Montague, Richard. (1974), *Formal Philosophy*, Richmond H. Thomason (ed.), (New Haven, CT: Yale University Press).

Moravcsik, Julius M. E. (1974), 'Linguistics and Philosophy', in Thomas A. Sebok (ed.), *Current Trends in Linguistics volume 12: Linguistics and Adjacent Arts and Sciences*, (The Hague and Paris: Mouton), 3–35.

Morris, Michael. (2007), *An Introduction to the Philosophy of Language*, (Cambridge: Cambridge University Press).

Neale, Stephen. (1987), 'Meaning, Grammar, and Indeterminacy', *Dialectica*, 41: 301–19.

— (1990), *Descriptions*, (Cambridge, MA: MIT Press).

— (1992), 'Paul Grice and the Philosophy of Language', *Linguistics and Philosophy*, 15: 509–59.

Nelson, Michael. (2012), 'Intensional Contexts', in Manuel Garciá-Carpintero and Max Kölbel (eds), *The Continuum Companion to the Philosophy of Language*, (London: Continuum): 125–52.

Nerlich, Graham. (1965), 'Presuppositions and Entailment', *American Philosophical Quarterly*, 2: 33–42.

Nolan, Daniel. (1997), 'Impossible Worlds: A Modest Approach', *Notre Dame Journal of Formal Logic*, 38: 535–72.

—(2009), 'The Age of Hyperintensionality' online at: http://substantialmatters. blogspot.com/2009/03/age-of-hyperintensionality.html.

Noonan, Harold. (1996), 'The 'Gray's Elegy' Argument – and Others', in Ray Monk and Anthony Palmer (eds), *Bertrand Russell and the Origins of Analytical Philosophy*, (Bristol: Thoemmes Press), 65–102.

Noonan, Harold W. (2001), *Frege: A Critical Introduction*, (Cambridge: Polity Press).

—(2006), 'The Concept Horse', in P. F. Strawson and Arinndam Chakrabarti (eds), *Universals, Concepts and Qualities: New Essays on the Meaning of Predicates*, (Aldershot: Ashgate Publishing Limited): 155–76.

Nuffer, Gerhard. (2009), 'Stalnaker on Mathematical Information', *The Southern Journal of Philosophy*, 47: 187–204.

Oliver, Alex. (1999), 'A Few More Remarks on Logical Form', *Proceedings of the Aristotelian Society*, 99: 247–72.

—(2005), 'The Reference Principle', *Analysis*, 65: 177–87.

—(2010), 'What Is A Predicate?', in Michael Potter and Thomas Ricketts (eds), *The Cambridge Companion to Frege*, (Cambridge: Cambridge University Press), 118–48.

Oliver, Alex and Timothy Smiley. (2005), 'Plural Descriptions and Many-Valued Functions', *Mind*, 114: 1039–68.

Oppy, Graham. (1992), 'Why Semantic Innocence?', *Australasian Journal of Philosophy*, 70: 445–54.

Owens, Joseph. (1986), 'Synonymy and The Nonindividualistic Model of the Mental', *Synthese*, 66: 361–82.

—(1995), 'Pierre and the Fundamental Assumption', *Mind and Language*, 10: 250–73.

Parsons, Kathryn P. (1973), 'Ambiguity and the Truth Definition', *Noûs*, 7: 379–93.

Parsons, Terence. (1981), 'Frege's Hierarchy of Indirect Sense and the Paradox of Analysis', *Midwest Studies in Philosophy*, VI: 37–57.

—(1986), 'Why Frege Should Not Have Said 'The Concept Horse is Not a Concept'', *History of Philosophy Quarterly*, 3: 449–65.

Patton, T. E. and D. W. Stampe. (1969), 'The Rudiments of Meaning: On Ziff on Grice', *Foundations of Language*, 5: 2–16.

Pelletier, Francis J. (1994), 'The Principle of Semantic Compositionality', *Topoi*, 13: 11–24.

Perry, John. (1977), 'Frege on Demonstratives', *The Philosophical Review*, 86: 474–97.

—(1979), 'The Problem of the Essential Indexical', *Noûs*, 13: 3–21.

Petrus, Klaus. (2010), 'Introduction: Paul Grice, Philosopher of Language, But More Than That', in Klaus Petrus (ed.), *Meaning and Analysis: New Essays on Grice*, (Basingstoke, Hampshire: Palgrave), 1–30.

Plantinga, Alvin. (1974), *The Nature of Necessity*, (Oxford: Oxford University Press).

Platts, Mark de Bretton. (1979), *Ways of Meaning: An Introduction to a Philosophy of Language*, (London: Routledge and Kegan Paul).

Potts, Chris. (2005), *The Logic of Conventional Implicatures*, (Oxford: Oxford University Press).

Prawitz, Dag. (1971), 'Ideas and Results in Proof Theory', in Jens Erik Fenstad (ed.), *Proceedings of the Second Scandinavian Logic Symposium (Oslo 1970)*, (Amsterdam: North Holland), 235–308.

— (1994), 'Quine and Verificationism', *Inquiry*, 37: 487–94.

Predelli, Stefano. (2003), 'Russellian Description and Smith's Suicide', *Acta Analytica*, 18: 125–41.

Priest, Graham. (1995), *Beyond the Limits of Thought*, (Cambridge: Cambridge University Press).

— (2005), *Towards Non-Being: The Logic and Metaphysics of Intentionality*, (Oxford: Oxford University Press).

Prior, Arthur N. (1971), *Objects of Thought*, (Oxford: Oxford University Press).

Putnam, Hilary. (1975), 'The Meaning of 'Meaning'', in his *Mind, Language and Reality: Philosophical Papers* volume 2, (Cambridge: Cambridge Philosophical Press), 215–71.

— (1981), *Reason, Truth and History*, (Cambridge: Cambridge University Press).

Quine, Willard Van O. (1948), 'On What There Is', *The Review of Metaphysics*, 48: 21–38. Reprinted in his *From A Logical Point of View* (second edition), (New York: Harper and Row, 1961), 1–19.

— (1950), *Methods of Logic*, (New York: Holt Books).

— (1951), 'Two Dogmas of Empiricism', *The Philosophical Review*, 60: 20–46. Reprinted in his *From A Logical Point of View* (second edition), (New York: Harper and Row, 1961): 20–46.

— (1960), *Word and Object*, (Cambridge, MA: MIT Press).

— (1968), 'Reply to Chomsky', *Synthese*, 19: 274–83.

— (1969), *Ontological Relativity and Other Essays*, (New York: Columbia University Press).

— (1970), 'On The Reasons for the Indeterminacy of Translation', *The Journal of Philosophy*, 67: 178–83.

— (1972), 'Methodological Reflections on Current Linguistic Theory', in Donald Davidson and Gilbert Harman (eds), *Semantics of Natural Language*, (Dordrecht, Holland: D. Reidel Publishing Company), 442–54.

— (1977), 'Review of Gareth Evans and John McDowell, *Truth and Meaning: Essays in Semantics*', *The Journal of Philosophy*, 74: 225–41.

— (1992), *Pursuit of Truth*, (Cambridge, MA: Harvard University Press).

Ramachandran, Murali. (1993), 'A Strawsonian Objection to Russell's Theory of Descriptions', *Analysis*, 53: 209–12.

— (1996), 'The Ambiguity Thesis versus Kripke's Defence of Russell', *Mind and Language*, 11: 371–87.

Ramsey, Frank P. (1925), 'Universals', *Mind*, 34: 401–17.

Récanati, François. (1981), 'On Kripke on Donnellan', in Herman Parret, Marina Sbisà, and Jef Verschueren (eds), *Possibilities and Limitations of Pragmatics*, (Amsterdam: John Benjamin), 593–630.

— (1986), 'Defining Communicative Intentions', *Mind and Language*, 1: 213–42.

— (1987), *Meaning and Force*, (Cambridge: Cambridge University Press).

— (2012), 'Pragmatics', in Manuel Garciá-Carpintero and Max Kölbel (eds), *The Continuum Companion to the Philosophy of Language*, (London: Continuum), 185–202.

Reck, Erich. (1987), 'Frege's Influence on Wittgenstein: Reversing Metaphysics via the Context Principle', in William W. Tait (eds), *Early Analytic Philosophy: Frege, Russell, Wittgenstein*, (Chicago, IL: Open Court), 123–85.

Reeves, Alan. (1974), 'On Truth and Meaning', *Noûs*, 8: 343–59.

Reimer, Marga. (1998), 'Donnellan's Distinction/Kripke's Test' *Analysis*, 58: 89–100.

Rein, Andrew. (1985), 'Frege and Natural Language', *Philosophy*, 60: 513–24.

Rey, Georges. (1994), 'The Unavailability of What We Mean: A Reply to Quine, Fodor and Lepore', *Grazer Philosophische Studien*, 46: 61–101.

Rieber, Steven. (1992), 'Understanding Synonyms without Knowing That They Are Synonymous', *Analysis*, 52: 224–8.

Rosenberg, Jay F. (1967), 'Synonymy and the Epistemology of Linguistics', *Inquiry*, 10: 405–20.

Rota, Gian-carlo. (1997), 'The Phenomenology of Mathematical Beauty', *Synthese*, 111: 171–82.

Routley, Richard. (1982), 'On What There Isn't', *Philosophy and Phenomenological Research*, 43: 151–78.

Russell, Bertrand. (1903), *Principles of Mathematics*, (Cambridge: Cambridge University Press).

— (1905), 'On Denoting', *Mind*, 14: 479–93.

— (1912), *The Problems of Philosophy*, (Oxford: Oxford University Press).

— (1918), 'The Philosophy of Logical Atomism', in his (1956), *Logic and Knowledge*, Robert Charles Marsh (ed.), (London: Allen and Unwin), 177–281.

— (1919), *Introduction to Mathematical Philosophy*, (London: George Allen and Unwin).

— (1944), 'Reply to Criticisms', in Paul Arthur Schilpp (ed.), *The Philosophy of Bertrand Russell*, (Chicago, IL: Northwestern University), 681–741.

Sadock, Jerrold M. (1975), 'The Soft, Interpretative Underbelly of Generative Semantics', in Peter Cole, John P. Kimball and Jerry L. Morgan (eds), *Syntax and Semantics volume 3: Speech Acts*, (New York: Academic Press), 383–96.

Sainsbury, Mark. (1979), *Russell*, (London: Routledge).

Salmon, Nathan. (1981), *Reference and Essence*, (Princeton, NJ: Princeton University Press).

——(1989), 'Illogical Belief', *Philosophical Perspectives* 3, *1989, Action Theory and Philosophy of Mind*, 243–85.

——(1990), 'A Millian Heir Rejects the Wages of *Sinn*', in C. A. Anderson and Joseph Owens (eds), *Propositional Attitudes: The Role of Context in Logic, Language and Mind*, (Stanford, CA: Center for the Study of Language and Information, Stanford University), 215–47.

——(1991), 'The Pragmatic Fallacy', *Philosophical Studies*, 63: 83–97.

Schaffer, Jonathan. (2009), 'On What Grounds What', in David J. Chalmers, David Manley and Ryan Wasserman (eds), *Metametaphysics: New Essays on the Foundations of Ontology*, (Oxford: Oxford University Press), 347–83.

Schiffer, Stephen. (1972), *Meaning*, (Oxford: Oxford University Press).

——(1987), *Remnants of Meaning*, (Cambridge, MA: MIT Press).

Schlesinger, George. (1974), *Confirmation and Confirmability*, (Oxford: Clarendon Press).

Schroeder, Mark. (2008), 'What is the Frege-Geach Problem?', *Philosophical Compass*, 3/4: 703–20.

——(2010), *Noncognitivism in Ethics*, (London: Routledge).

Searle, John R. (1958), 'Russell's Objections to Frege's Theory of Sense and Reference', *Analysis*, 18: 137–43.

——(1968), 'Austin on Locutionary and Illocutionary Acts', *The Philosophical Review*, 77: 405–24.

——(1969), *Speech Acts: An Essay in the Philosophy of Language*, (Cambridge: Cambridge University Press).

——(1975a), 'The Logical Status of Fictional Discourse', *New Literary History*, 6: 319–32.

——(1975b), 'Indirect Speech Acts', in Peter Cole, John P. Kimball, and Jerry L. Morgan (eds), *Syntax and Semantics, 3: Speech Acts*, (New York: Academic Press), 59–82.

——(1979), 'Referential and Attributive', *The Monist*, 62: 190–208.

——(1980), 'Minds, Brains and Programs', *Behavioural and Brain Sciences*, 3: 417–24.

——(1983), *Intentionality: An Essay in the Philosophy of Mind*, (Cambridge: Cambridge University Press).

——(1984), 'Indeterminacy, Empiricism and the First Person', *The Journal of Philosophy*, 81: 123–46.

——(1989), 'How Performatives Perform', *Linguistics and Philosophy*, 12: 535–58.

——(1999), 'The Future of Philosophy', *Philosophical Transactions: Biological Sciences*, 354: 2069–80.

——(2002), 'Conversation', in his *Consciousness and Language*, (Cambridge: Cambridge University Press), 180–202.

Segal, Gabriel. (1990), 'In the Mood for a Semantic Theory', *Proceedings of the Aristotelian Society*, 91: 103–18.

Sklar, Lawrence. (1985), *Philosophy and Spacetime Physics*, (Berkeley, CA: University of California Press).

Smith, Michael. (1994), 'Why Expressivists about Value Should Love Minimalism about Truth', *Analysis*, 54: 1–12.

Soames, Scott. (1985), 'Semantics and Psychology', in Jerrold J. Katz (ed.), *Philosophy of Linguistics*, (Oxford: Oxford University Press), 204–26.

— (1991), 'The Necessity Argument', *Linguistics and Philosophy*, 14: 575–80.

— (1994), 'Donnellan's Referential/Attributive Distinction', *Philosophical Studies*, 73: 149–68.

— (2002), *Beyond Rigidity: The Unfinished Semantic Agenda of Naming and Necessity*, (Oxford: Oxford University Press).

— (2003a), *Philosophical Analysis in the Twentieth Century, volume 1: The Dawn of Analysis*, (Princeton, NJ: Princeton University Press).

— (2003b), *Philosophical Analysis in the Twentieth Century, volume 2: The Age of Meaning*, (Princeton, NJ: Princeton University Press).

— (2005), 'Why Incomplete Definite Descriptions do not Defeat Russell's Theory of Descriptions', *Teorema*, 24: 7–30.

— (2009), *Philosophical Essays volume I. Natural Language: What It Means and How We Use It*, (Princeton, NJ: Princeton University Press).

Sorensen, Roy. (1985), 'An Argument for the Vagueness of "Vague"', *Analysis*, 45: 134–7.

— (1996), 'The Metaphysics of Words', *Philosophical Studies*, 81: 193–214.

Sosa, David. (1996), 'The Import of the Puzzle About Belief', *The Philosophical Review*, 105: 373–402.

Sperber, Dan and Deidre Wilson. (1982), 'Mutual Knowledge and Relevance in Theories of Comprehension', in N. V. Smith (ed.), *Mutual Knowledge*, (New York: Academic Press), 61–85.

— (1995), *Relevance: Communication and Cognition* (second edition), (Oxford: Blackwell).

Stalnaker, Robert. (1999), *Context and Content*, (Oxford: Oxford University Press).

— (2011), 'Possible Worlds Semantics: Philosophical Foundations', in Alan Berger (ed.), *Saul Kripke*, (Cambridge: Cambridge University Press), 100–15.

Stalnaker, Robert C. (1972), 'Pragmatics', in Donald Davidson and Gilbert Harman (eds), *Semantics of Natural Language*, (Dordrecht, Holland: D. Reidel Publishing Company), 380–97.

— (1984), *Inquiry*, (Cambridge, MA: MIT Press).

Stampe, Dennis W. (1975), 'Meaning and Truth in the Theory of Speech Acts', in Peter Cole, John P. Kimball, and Jerry L. Morgan (eds), *Syntax and Semantics volume 3: Speech Acts*, (New York: Academic Press), 1–39.

Stevens, Graham P. (2005), *The Russellian Origins of Analytic Philosophy*, (London: Routledge).

— (2011), 'Logical Form in *Principia Mathematica* and English', *Russell*, 31: 9–28.

Stich, Stephen P. (1976), 'Davidson's Semantic Program', *Canadian Journal of Philosophy*, 6: 201–27.

Strawson, Peter F. (1949), 'Truth', *Analysis*, 9: 83–97.

— (1950) 'On Referring', *Mind*, 59: 320–44.

— (1952), *Introduction to Logical Theory*, (London: Methuen Press).

— (1954), 'Reply to Mr. Sellars', *The Philosophical Review*, 63: 216–31.

— (1964), 'Intention and Communication in Speech Acts', *The Philosophical Review*, 73: 439–60.

— (1971), 'Identifying Reference and Truth Values', in his *Logico-Linguistic Papers*, (London: Methuen Press), 75–95.

Sullivan, Peter. (1994), 'The Sense of "A Name of a Truth Value"', *The Philosophical Quarterly*, 44: 476–81.

Suppes, Patrick. (1986), 'The Primacy of Utterer's Meaning', in Richard E. Grandy and Richard Warner (eds), *Philosophical Grounds of Rationality: Intentions, Categories, Ends*, (Oxford: Oxford University Press), 109–29.

Swoyer, Chris. (1998), 'Complex Properties and Logics for Properties and Relations', *Journal of Philosophical Logic*, 27: 295–325.

Szabó, Zoltán Gendler. (2000), 'Compositionality as Supervenience', *Linguistics and Philosophy*, 23: 475–505.

Tarski, Alfred. (1944), 'The Semantic Conception of Truth and the Foundations of Semantics', *Philosophy and Phenomenological Research*, 4: 342–60.

— (1956), 'The Concept of Truth in Formalised Languages', in his *Logic, Semantics, Metamathematics: Papers from 1923 to 1938*, edited and translated by John Corcoran (second edition), (Indianapolis: Hackett Publishing Company, 1983), 152–278.

Taylor, Barry. (1982), 'On The Need For A Theory of Meaning in A Theory of Meaning', *Mind*, 91: 183–200.

Taylor, Kenneth. (1998), *Truth and Meaning: An Introduction to the Philosophy of Language*, (Oxford: Blackwell).

Thomason, Richmond M. (1990), 'Accommodation. Meaning, and Implicature: Interdisciplinary Foundations for Pragmatics', in Philip R. Cohen, Jerry Morgan and Martha E. Pollock (eds), *Intentions in Communication*, (Cambridge, MA: MIT Press), 325–63.

Tichý, Pavel. (1971), 'An Approach to Intensional Analysis', *Noûs*, 5: 273–97.

— (1975), 'What Do We Talk About?', *Philosophy of Science*, 42: 80–93.

— (1986), 'Constructions' *Philosophy of Science*, 53: 514–34.

— (1988), *The Foundations of Frege's Logic*, (Berlin: Walter de Gruyter).

Travis, Charles. (1991), 'Annals of Analysis: Critical Notice of Paul Grice, *Studies in the Way of Words' Mind*, 100: 237–64.

Van Heijenoort, J. (1977), 'Frege on Sense Identity', *Journal of Philosophical Logic*, 6: 103–8.

— (1986), 'Frege on Vagueness', in Leila Haaparanta and Jaakko Hintikka (eds), *Frege Synthesised: Essays on the Philosophical and Foundational Work of Gottlob Frege*, (Dordrecht, Holland: D. Reidel Publishing Company), 31–45.

Vermazen, Bruce. (1971), 'Semantics and Semantics', *Foundations of Language*, 7: 539–55.

— (1983), 'The Intelligibility of Massive Error', *The Philosophical Quarterly*, 33: 69–74.

Walker, Ralph C. S. (1975), 'Conversational Implicatures', in Simon Blackburn (ed.), *Meaning, Reference and Necessity: New Studies in Semantics*, (Cambridge: Cambridge University Press), 133–81.

Walton, Kendall. (1990), *Mimesis as Make-Believe: On the Foundations of the Representational Arts*, (Cambridge, MA: MIT Press).

Weiner, Joan. (2004), *Frege Explained: From Arithmetic to Analytic Philosophy*, (Chicago and La Salle, IL: Open Court).

Weiss, Bernhard. (2010), *How To Understand Language: A Philosophical Inquiry*, (Durham, NC: Acumen Publishing Limited).

Weitzman, Laura. (1997), 'Frege on the Individuation of Thoughts', *Dialogue*, 36: 563–74.

Wetzel, Linda. (1990), 'Dummett's Criteria for Singular Terms', *Mind*, 99: 239–54.

Wiggins, David. (1976), 'Frege's Problem of the Morning Star and the Evening Star', in Matthias Schirn (ed.), *Studien zu Frege, volume III*, (Stuttgart-Bad Cannstatt: Frommann-Holzboog), 221–55.

— (1984), 'The Sense and Reference of Predicates: A Running Repair to Frege's Doctrine and a Plea for the Copula', *The Philosophical Quarterly*, 34: 311–28.

Williams, B. A. O. and P. T. Geach. (1963), 'Imperative Inference', *Analysis*, 23: 30–42.

Williamson, Timothy. (1988), 'Review of Bob Hale, *Abstract Objects*', *Mind*, 97: 487–90.

— (1994), *Vagueness*, (London: Routledge).

Wilson, N. L. (1959), 'Substances without Substrata', *The Review of Metaphysics*, 12: 521–39.

— (1970), 'Grice on Meaning: The Ultimate Counter-example', *Noûs*, 4: 295–302.

Wolterstorff, Nicholas. (1970), *On Universals: An Essay in Ontology*, (Chicago, IL: University of Chicago Press).

Wright, Crispin. (1983), *Frege's Conception of Numbers as Objects*, (Aberdeen: Aberdeen University Press).

— (2001), 'Why Frege Does Not Deserve His Grain of Salt: A Note on the Paradox of 'The Concept Horse' and the Ascription of *Bedeutungen* to Predicates', in Bob Hale and Crispin Wright, *The Reason's Proper Study: Essays Towards A Neo-Fregean Philosophy of Mathematics*, (Oxford: Oxford University Press), 72–90.

— (2002), 'Human Nature?', in Nicholas Smith (ed.), *Reading McDowell: On Mind and World*, (London: Routledge), 140–59.

Yagisawa, Takashi. (1984), 'The Pseudo-Mates Argument', *The Philosophical Review*, 93: 407–18.

Yu, Paul. (1979), 'On the Gricean Program about Meaning', *Linguistics and Philosophy*, 3: 273–88.

Zabludowski, Andrzej. (1989), 'On Quine's Indeterminacy Doctrine', *The Philosophical Review*, 98: 35–63.

Ziff, Paul. (1967), 'On H. P. Grice's Account of Meaning', *Analysis*, 28: 1–8.

Index